FICTION AND THE NORTHERN IRELAND

⌐L CHƆNT
ГH D'

Fiction and the Northern Ireland Troubles since 1969: (de-)constructing the north

Elmer Kennedy-Andrews

FOUR COURTS PRESS

Published by
FOUR COURTS PRESS LTD
7 Malpas Street, Dublin 8, Ireland
email: info@four-courts-press.ie
http://www.four-courts-press.ie
and in North America by
FOUR COURTS PRESS
c/o ISBS, 5824 N.E. Hassalo Street, Portland, OR 97213.

ISBN Paperback 1-85182-713-7
ISBN Hardback 1-85182-714-5

A catalogue record for this title
is available from the British Library.

ACKNOWLEDGEMENTS

The author would like to thank the University of Ulster for research and
publishing grants, and for granting him study leave to complete the
writing of this book. Special thanks go to the Dean of Arts at Coleraine,
Professor Robert Welsh, for his encouragement and support throughout.

Printed in Great Britain
by MPG Books, Bodmin, Cornwall

Contents

CHAPTER ONE

Reading positions: the (Northern) Irish cultural debate

Since 1969 and the most recent outbreak of the Northern Irish Troubles (as the polit-ical violence has euphemistically come to be called) there has been a remarkable lit-erary production emanating from the North about the Northern 'situation'. Such has been the impact of the political violence on society, culture and the imagination that it would be hard to think of another regional literature with such a widely shared focus of thematic interest, though, of course, there is great diversity in standpoint and attitude – so great, that it isn't possible to speak of a distinctive 'school' or 'tradition' of Northern writing. This resurgence of Northern writing at the same time as the re-irruption of the Troubles in 1969 was surely no coincidence. The Troubles gave a spe-cial urgency to the literary impulse, and opened up new themes and emotional pos-sibilities for the prospective artist. The writers, we might say, were hurt into writing by the need to explore and to understand the specific tensions, divisions and ambi-guities inherent in Northern society. Yet politics and society did not take over the cre-ative imagination completely: the most significant feature of the literature has been its resistance to, and liberation from, orthodoxy and ideology, its commitment to the 'world elsewhere' made possible by language.

Popular fiction writers cashed in early (and continue to do so), exploiting the Troubles to cater for a mass market which feeds voraciously on thrillers and romances. For serious literary engagement with the Troubles we tend to think of poetry and even drama rather than fiction. Poets such as Heaney, Longley, Mahon, Muldoon, McGuckian and Carson, and playwrights such as Friel, Parker and McGuinness, who have all written out of the Troubles have, since the 1960s, built international rep-utations for themselves, and it is their work which we usually think of in connection with the so-called 'Northern (Re)naissance'. The fiction of the Troubles has been rather slower coming into the limelight, despite the long and venerable tradition of Ulster fiction writing which John Wilson Foster has identified in his magisterial *Forces and Themes in Ulster Fiction* (1974), and the international success of older contem-porary fiction writers such as Michael McLaverty, Sam Hanna Bell, Brian Moore and Maurice Leitch. The fiction writers at first seemed ill-at-ease with the social and polit-ical issues of the conflict, and never ventured far beyond a conservative Realism. Eve Patten, in an essay 'Fiction in conflict: Northern Ireland's prodigal novelists' (1995) identifies 'two limiting trends in Northern Irish fiction'.[1] The first is the writers' con-

---

1 In I.A. Bell (ed.), *Peripheral Visions: Images of Nationhood in Contemporary British Fiction* (Cardiff: University

tinued adherence to a Realist aesthetic, which she views as both a deliberate strategy on the part of serious writers to distinguish themselves from the popular sentiment and sensationalism of pulp fiction, and as symptomatic of a general tendency in Irish fiction towards journalism and sociology. The second debilitating factor is 'a novelistic obligation to offer a consensual (and usually apolitical) liberal humanist comment on the predicament'.[2] However, recent fiction from Northern Ireland, she believes, shows signs of reinvigoration. A new generation of writers who have come of age since the beginning of the Troubles have challenged the 'ingrained sterility' and overcome 'the multiple straitjacket of literary insularity, narrative realism and ideological responsibility'.[3] Like the poets, these novelists, Patten argues, have been able to free themselves from obligation to a national literary tradition and have begun to experiment with techniques which destabilise both received conceptions of Northern Ireland and conventional notions of the Northern Irish novel. Patten characterises the new writing as follows:

> It marks the overdue exploitation of literary strategies such as perspectivism, ambiguity and displacement which, although categorically post-modern, may also be perceived as attributes of a sustained constitutional and psychological identity crisis germane to any representations of a contemporary Northern Irish self-image.[4]

Gerry Smyth, in his chapter on the Northern Irish novel in *The Novel and the Nation* (1997) endorses Patton's view of a revitalised Northern Irish fiction thanks to postmodernist transformations of traditional form:

> Many writers have sensed a need to challenge the received forms of 'Troubles' narrative, and to develop new languages and new perspectives as a contribution to the imagination of change.[5]

Drawing on Joe Cleary's essay, '"Fork-tongued on the border bit": partition and the politics of form in contemporary narratives of the Northern Irish conflict' (199),[6] Smyth identifies three received forms of Troubles narrative: the Realist thriller, the 'national romance' (where the union of the lovers from opposing communities – 'love-across-the-barricades' – stands as metaphor for a larger social and political reconciliation), and 'domestic fiction' ('in which the private, feminised realm of love and desire offers an escape from the public, masculine realm of political abstraction').[7] The 'new languages and new perspectives', according to Smyth,

---

of Wales Press, 1995), pp 128–48, p. 131.   2 Ibid., p. 131.   3 Ibid., p. 133.   4 Ibid., pp 129–30.   5 London: Pluto Press, 1997), p.116.   6 In *South Atlantic Quarterly*, 95, 1 (Winter 1996), pp 227–76.   7 Smyth, pp 114–16.

have been brought about through an imaginative re-working of these traditional forms, and 'the introduction of a degree of distance into the novelistic vision',[8] whether physical (the adoption of perspectives from outside Ulster) or discursive (for example, the use of irony, parody and other alienating devices).

This recent efflorescence of Northern Irish Troubles fiction in the late '80s and '90s should not be allowed to occlude the achievement of older writers such as Benedict Kiely, Jennifer Johnston, Eugene McCabe, Terence de Vere White, Francis Stuart, Brian Moore, Maurice Leitch and Bernard MacLaverty, who made important contributions in the '70s and early '80s. Nor should we overestimate the transformative effect of postmodernism since most Troubles fiction, even that written in the '80s and '90s (with certain notable exceptions), continues to adhere to a basically Realistic aesthetic, though often incorporating elements of postmodern style. Nevertheless, it is true that, as Neil Corcoran says, 'the novel rather than the poem or the play appears to have become the most significant and energizing form'.[9] Where the poetry of Northern Ireland since 1969 has been a 'poetry of obliquity', says Corcoran, the novel of the period has been 'much more straightforwardly addressed to the situation itself and the issues it raises'.[10] Corcoran's distinction is broadly true: the poets' 'obliquity' declares itself in their penchant for transcultural analogising, and their commitment to the pressing claims of the lyric self, while, on the other hand, the 'straightforwardness' of the novel's engagement with current social realities is discernible in its preoccupation with such themes as the psyche of the terrorist killer, the experience of the victims of terrorism, the socio-political context of the Troubles, the conflict between claims of personal freedom and those of communal responsibility, the legacy of traditional (Nationalist or Loyalist) mythologies, women and the Troubles, and the family in the Troubles. In Corcoran's view, 'it is the exceptional combination of this intensity of preoccupation with an adventurous variety of means that gives the novel of Northern Ireland a large part of its claim on our attention'.[11] In suggesting that only relatively few Troubles fictions may be considered truly 'adventurous' in their means, and that a serviceable and adaptable Realism has formed the basis of much of this fiction, I do not mean to take away from the importance which Corcoran attaches to the novel of Northern Ireland. Indeed, the critical industry which it has generated in the last few years is graphic testimony to its importance. As well as the essays by Patten and Cleary, and the book by Gerry Smyth, mention may also be made of: Laura Pelaschiar's *Writing the North: The Contemporary Novel in Northern Ireland* (1998); *Northern Narratives*, a collection of ten essays edited by Bill Lazenbatt (1999); *Contemporary Irish Fiction: Themes, Tropes, Theories* (2000), edited by Liam Harte and Michael Parker, containing half a dozen essays relating to Northern fiction; a special Contemporary

---

8 Ibid., p. 116.   9 Neil Corcoran, *After Yeats and Joyce: Reading Modern Irish Literature* (Oxford: Oxford University Press, 1997), p. 154.   10 Ibid., p. 154.   11 Ibid., p. 164.

Irish Fiction issue of the *Irish University Review* (Spring-Summer 2000) which also includes half a dozen essays on Northern fiction; and Christine St Peter's *Changing Ireland: Strategies in Contemporary Women's Fiction* (2000), which contains a chapter on 'Troubles Novels from the North'. These critical works service a total of almost 400 novels relating to the Troubles since 1969 and written since that date.[12]

The present study, as its title would indicate, is based on the notion, propounded by the French philosopher Jacques Derrida, of the world as text: writers and readers understand and make sense of the Northern Troubles through the various prior texts and discourses in which the conflict has been represented. Each of the many ways of writing and reading the Troubles is, to some degree, ideologically conditioned. The reader takes up one or more of a variety of reading positions, each premised on a distinctive paradigm of the relationship between literature and politics, each harbouring a distinctive theory of historical narrative, each tied to a particular interpretation of the violence. The Troubles give a special piquancy to Seamus Deane's Marxian assertion of the socio-historical grounds of textual production:

> There is no such thing as an innocent text, even if it was only published yesterday. Reading is never innocent: it belongs to culturally specific situations and moments ... There is no such thing as an objective factual history which has somehow been distorted by a series of mythologies invented by various bigoted groups. There is no such thing as objective history, and there is no innocent history. All history and literature, as far as I understand them, are forms of mythology. This is not to take away other functions from literature and not to deny it its specific features, but to make the point that all literature is linked to various forms of historical mythology.[13]

Deane here reminds us that as readers we are not free interpretative agents, but all the time our responses are controlled by the codes and strategies of the text and our own socially constructed subjectivity. Since there is no such thing as objectivity in history, and no transcendent category of the aesthetic, interpretation must always take place within a theoretical framework or enabling narrative. To deny such a framework or narrative is itself an ideologically conditioned position.

In this view of language as a form of political and social control, and of 'truth' as relative and pragmatic rather than absolute, functioning only in a specific social and historical context, the idea of 'Northern Ireland Troubles' is clearly going to be intensely

---

12 'Literature of the Troubles by Bill Rolston', Cain Web Service, http://cain.ulst.ac.uk/bibdbs/ chrnovel.htm
13 Seamus Deane, 'Canon fodder: literary mythologies in Ireland', in Jean Lundy and Aodán MacPóilin (eds.), *Styles of Belonging: The Cultural Identities of Ulster* (Belfast, Lagan Press, 1992), pp 22–33, pp 25–6.

problematic. For a start, the term 'Northern Ireland' is contestable because it carries with it some recognition of constitutionalised partition and is thus an unacceptable designation to Nationalists. Republicans and Nationalists prefer the clumsy 'Six Counties'. Protestants favour 'Ulster', though the Irish province of Ulster also included Co. Donegal, Co. Monaghan and Co. Cavan. The most neutral appellation is perhaps 'The North', though, since it is a geographical rather than political signifier, it doesn't entirely satisfy Unionists. 'The North of Ireland' almost – but not quite – recognises political realities. The situation of a people so deeply divided that they cannot agree who they are or what to call themselves clearly offers rich comic potential which writers such as Lionel Shriver, Robert MacLiam Wilson and Colin Bateman have readily exploited. Thus, we have Bateman's hero in *Divorcing Jack* advising an American visitor:

> 'Stick to calling it Northern Ireland, although you'll hear variations. If you're a Loyalist you'll call it Ulster, if you're a Nationalist you call it the North of Ireland or the Six Counties, if you're the British Government you call it the Province'.
> 'And what do you call it, Mr Starkey?'
> 'Home'.[14]

The other term, 'Troubles', a euphemism for political violence carried over from the political upheavals in Ireland of the 1920s, is equally fraught with difficulty. The cultural historian and theorist, David Lloyd, traces 'two distinct understandings of violence' (125) – nationalist and imperialist – within Irish historiography:

> For nationalist historiography, the violence of Irish history is symptomatic of the unrelenting struggle of an Irish people forming itself in sporadic but connected risings against British domination. The end of this history of violence lies in the independent nation state.[15]

The other kind of violence is what he calls 'subaltern' violence which, viewed from the standpoint of 'imperialist'/'revisionist'/'hegemonic' history

> is understood as an atavistic and disruptive principle counter to the rationality of legal constitution as barbarity is to an emerging civility, anarchy to culture … From such a perspective, violence is radically counter-historical, even against narrative, always represented as an outburst, an 'outrage', spasmodic and without a legitimating teleology.[16]

14 London: HarperCollins, 1995, p. 46.   15 David Lloyd, *Anomalous States: Irish Writing and the Post-Colonial Moment* (Dublin: Lilliput Press, 1993), p. 125.   16 Ibid., pp 125–6.

For the humanistic, bourgeois narrative to maintain its hegemonic control, political violence can be understood only as outside the law, disruptive, discontinuous, unavailable for narration. By representing violence as irrational outrage, anarchy unleashed, the history of domination is made to appear as a legitimate process of civilisation. For what both the 'nationalist' and 'imperialist'/'revisionist' perspectives have in common is their recognition that the end of violence is the formation of a new social and political order. Within Nationalist history, violence is sanctioned, resistance is self-legitimating, to the extent that it is successful in contributing to the founding of the state. Thus, one man's 'terrorist' is another man's 'freedom-fighter'; 'criminal murder' in one context is 'the armed struggle' in another; an 'outrage' at one historical moment is 'heroic action' at another. There is state terrorism as well as paramilitary terrorism. Political violence, it would seem, always needs to be theorised or narrativised in order to make sense of it. With reference to the contemporary IRA, Clair Wills insists on the need to acknowledge the political context of the violence. To dismiss IRA terrorism as 'violent, postmodern *bricolage*',[17] she says, is to connive in the terrorists' enemies' denial of the roots and causes of violence. In considering the theory of narrative suggested by IRA acts of violence, she infers a hybrid narrative composed of anti-modernist mythic or symbolic elements (the enabling myth of a return to a pre-colonial Gaelic past) and more obviously political modes of representation (the IRA's symbolic, and Sinn Féin's political, representativeness) deriving from progressive Enlightenment values of the European nation-state. Reacting against Wills' critical effort to re-order violence into a totalising narrative, Peter McDonald affirms the possibilities of absorbing violence 'by destabilizing narrative, making it harder to "make sense" of the shower of particulars'.[18] McDonald distrusts tendencies towards coherence and completion, advocating instead narrative modes which distort, hybridise and problematise narrative, and resist 'any sense of coherence which might provide a larger placing or direction within other available narratives'.[19] For McDonald, in the painfully divided circumstances of Northern Ireland the successful narrative knows it is not innocent, is always shadowed by doubt.

In a Northern Irish culture marked by crisis and discontinuity, there is inevitably a variety of critical paradigms for understanding the relationship between violence and narrative. The range of positions from which to write or to read the North and its Troubles may be summarised as follows. There is the approach represented by Edna Longley and McDonald which resists the influence of theory and the politicisation of criticism, and opposes any attempt to assemble a narrative (in any conventional sense) or unitary tradition. Attacking the hijacking of Irish writing by political Irishness,

17 Clair Wills, *Improprieties: Politics and Sexuality in Northern Irish Poetry* (Oxford: Clarendon Press, 1993), p. 109. 18 Peter McDonald, *Mistaken Identities: Poetry and Northern Ireland* (Oxford: Clarendon Press, 1997) p. 61. 19 Ibid., p. 80.

Longley espouses an ideal of 'complex diversity', a literary movement which is fluid and unpredictable, and a concept of identity as interactive rather than fixed. This position has found official recognition in the formation of the Government-sponsored Cultural Traditions Group in 1988. 'Cultural Traditions' represents a model of cross-cultural understanding and tolerance achieved through cultural and artistic projects outside the sphere of politics and within a Northern Ireland context. Opposing the idea of a transcendent aesthetic and cultural realm are those, like Seamus Deane, David Lloyd and Terry Eagleton, who insist on the ideological function of art and culture and call for a fully politicised criticism. In Deane's view, even if the writers aren't attempting to engage their readers in an explicitly political manner, their de-politicising strategies themselves represent (consciously or unconsciously) significant political interventions. Critics such as Deane, Lloyd and Eagleton represent a decolonising perspective, and have constructed a powerful and sophisticated interpretative position drawing on the work of post-colonial theorists such as the Palestinian Edward Said and the Indian Homi Bhabha. Feminism also challenges the dominant, hegemonic discourse. Both postcolonialism and feminism, in opposing the grand narratives of colonialism and patriarchy, may be seen as instances of postmodernism. Postmodernism provides another critical paradigm, for it would be impossible for Troubles fiction to escape the global influence of the postmodern revolution. Postmodernism, as formulated by Richard Kearney, provides a framework for accommodating both tradition and modernity through the re-evaluation and re-construction of traditional myth in order to open up new possibilities for the future. One expression of political postmodernism might be seen to be Garrett Fitzgerald's 1983 New Irish Forum, which looked beyond the usual Nationalist and Unionist positions to postulate new configurations of Irish identity. If, as Deane and Eagleton complain, the general application of (postmodernist) theory elides or ignores the specific social, political and historical environment, 'Irish Studies' offers yet another context – a discursive field of pervasive and radical social and political change in Northern Ireland since the late '60s – within which to view the fiction. A more detailed account of these main critical approaches is given below.

LIBERAL HUMANISM AND THE REALIST AESTHETIC

According to the doctrine of Enlightenment humanism, the individual is placed securely in the centre of the universe as the origin and focus of meaning, distinguished from society and given absolute priority over it. Identity – individual, national, human – is understood in terms of a fixed, unchanging essence, a unique consciousness capable of transcending socio-cultural conditions. As elaborated by John Stuart Mill and late nineteenth-century middle-class culture, liberal humanism is associated with faith in historical progress and individual freedom. A belief in rational mind replaces adherence to religious or mythological accounts of a 'magical' universe. Corresponding to humanism's empiricist view that knowledge can be obtained directly through experience, Realism invites its reader to look through the language of the text to see as if directly what is represented there. Language provides a transparent window on the world. Literature penetrates beyond the historically and culturally specific to uncover the universal truths of an essentially unchanging human condition. The emphasis placed on form – the specific features of the literary work – is viewed by some as a deliberate response to the fractured interpretative paradigms produced by a fractured society. New Criticism not only provides a methodology for a liberal construction of an aesthetic and cultural ideal, but in doing so offers an alternative to politics. Liberal criticism, according to Lionel Trilling in *The Liberal Imagination*, is to promote awareness of 'complexity and difficulty':

> ... the culture of a nation is not truly figured in the image of the current. A culture is not a flow, nor even a confluence; the form of its existence is struggle, or at least debate – it is nothing if not a dialectic. And in any culture there are likely to be certain artists who contain a large part of the dialectic within themselves, their meaning and power lying in their contradictions; they contain within themselves, it may be said, the very ... essence of the culture, and the sign of this is that they do not submit to serve the ends of any one ideological group or tendency.[20]

Typically, the liberal humanist avoids extreme political commitment, demonstrating a realistic sense of the dangers of political utopianism, and of how such ideals can lead to violence, anarchy and fascism. Progress is achieved through moral education rather than political revolution. Refusing to be recruited to any party or creed, the liberal humanist privileges individual sensibility and self-fulfilment above all. The individual must be free to choose for himself, and not allow his life to be determined by traditional values or loyalties. However, the values of liberalism that were developed in the Victorian era of technical achievement, expanding capitalism, and social confidence have to fight for their survival in an age which is much more cynical and uncertain, more aware of evil, less confident of the power of reason. The liberal ideal of heroic self-fulfilment is challenged by the political imperative which calls for collective solidarity in time of war. In the North's climate of violent social upheaval, the classic liberal humanist narrative can all too easily collapse into tired resignation or ineffectual withdrawal. The enormity of suffering, the apparent intractability of the situation, undermine faith in progress and humanity. Distrust of politics breeds feel-

20 Lionel Trilling, *The Liberal Imagination* (London: Penguin, 1970), pp 22–3.

ings of impotence. The desire for a free individuality can end in solipsism and soli-
tude. Not surprisingly, the relevance of the liberal analysis is frequently called into question. How can the typically middle-class, educated, liberal writer, physically removed
from the conflagration, understand the underlying causes of discontent or the need
for urgent action? Is he not in the position of Nero fiddling while Rome burns?

The critique of humanism mobilised by Nietzsche, Althusser, Foucault and others
is based on a view of humanism as ideological. The ground of this critique is its rejection of the dominant culture's notions of disinterested aesthetic effects and essential
human values. By universalising the historically specific as the naturally given,
humanism is seen to mask its ideological function of hegemonic control. In a Field
Day pamphlet, Terry Eagleton applies these insights to the Irish cultural debate,
launching a fierce attack against apolitical criticism:

> This is not to say, on the other hand, that the aesthetic as 'disinterested' mythic
> solution to real contradictions is not in evidence in Ireland at all. There are Irish
> critics and commentators who deploy the term today as a privileged mark of
> that decency, civility and cultivation of which an uncouth nationalism is fatally
> bereft. In the stalest of Arnoldian clichés, the poetic is still being counterposed
> to the political – which is only to say that the 'poetic' as we have it today was,
> among other things, historically constructed to carry out just that business of
> suppressing political conflict. Imagination and enlightened liberal reason are
> still being offered to us in Ireland today as the antithesis of sectarianism: and
> like all such idealised values they forget their own roots in a social class and his-
> tory not unnoted for its own virulent sectarianism, then and now.[21]

In the context of Northern Irish fiction, Eagleton, it would seem, calls for a criticism that would be alert to the ways in which the liberal humanist novel, sub-
tending the values of the imperialist centre and supported by a Realist aesthetic,
interpellates the reader to see the Troubles in a 'common sense' way which only
reinforces and perpetuates the dominant perspectives and values of the Northern
Irish statelet, while marginalising or suppressing antagonistic discourses which
cannot be assimilated to the colonial/ liberal bourgeois metanarrative. Of course,
the 'Nationalist' or 'Republican' novel, drawing on a combination of essentialist
national myths ('stalest of Arnoldian clichés'?) and progressive post-Enlightenment
politics and rationality, may equally lay claim to 'imagination and enlightened liberal reason' (the mark of that 'decency and civility' of which an imperialist
Unionism is fatally bereft). The appeal to 'disinterestedness' and 'universal human
values' is not the mark of an exclusively Unionist literary pathology.

21 Terry Eagleton, *Nationalism: Irony and Commitment* (Derry: Field Day pamphlet, 1988), pp 12–13.

Deane joins Eagleton in decrying the residual bourgeois faith in the autonomy of the 'aesthetic' and of the individual:

> To believe that there is such a thing as fine writing, and that it is somehow autonomously separate from a speech by Ian Paisley, John Hume or Margaret Thatcher, is to show that you truly have been brainwashed. It shows that you actually do believe that there is a stable place called 'culture', to which you can retreat from the shouts and cries of the street, from the murder and mayhem that takes place there, and that you can go into that realm of humanist subjectivity in which literature or great art prevails. When you do that you are actually responding to an invention of 19th-century bourgeois culture, the idea of autonomous individual character.[22]

The 'realm of humanist subjectivity' is, for Deane, the realm of illusion, of 'retreat' from authenticity, which is always political. Yet, while it is true that the centripetal forces of the aesthetic (the 'stable place called "culture"') have to contend with the centrifugal forces of history ('the shouts and cries of the street'), the aesthetic may at least still exist as an enabling and assuaging ideal, a momentary stay against confusion. Art may accommodate both a social and an aesthetic demand. This is the message of Seamus Heaney's *The Government of the Tongue* (1986), the title of which signals Heaney's ambivalence: it could refer to the need to subordinate the poet's voice to politics, or, equally, it could affirm the tongue's autonomy. Against Deane's deconstructive levelling of 'art', Heaney reasserts the unique value of the aesthetic. He draws on the biblical story of the woman taken in adultery whom the crowd drag before Jesus demanding that she should be stoned. At the time Jesus was writing in the sand with his finger:

> The drawing of those characters is like poetry, a break with the usual life but not an absconding from it. Poetry, like the writing, is arbitrary and marks time ... It does not say to the accusing crowd or to the helpless accused, 'Now a solution will take place'; it does not propose to be instrumental or effective. Instead, in the rift between what is going to happen and whatever we would wish to happen, poetry holds attention for a space, functions not as distraction but as pure concentration, a focus where our power to concentrate is concentrated back on ourselves.[23]

Ultimately, Heaney aspires to an art that is, paradoxical though it may seem, both socially responsible and creatively free, a double imperative suggested by the double meaning in the title of another essay, 'The Redress of Poetry':

22 Deane, 'Canon fodder', pp 26–7.   23 Seamus Heaney, 'The Government of the tongue', in *The Government of the Tongue: The 1986 T.S. Eliot Memorial Lectures and Other Critical Writings* (London: Faber, 1988), p. 108.

Which is to say that its (poetry's) power as a mode of redress in the first sense – as agent for proclaiming and correcting injustices – is being appealed to constantly. But in discharging this function, poets are in danger of slighting another imperative, namely, to redress poetry as poetry, to set it up as its own category, an eminence established and a pressure exercised by distinctly linguistic means.[24]

As Eve Patten has shown, these oppositions between subjective and objective, private and public, individual and society, form the central thematics of the liberal/Realist Troubles novel. Traditionally, Northern fiction, she argues, relies on a 'determinist formula'[25] whereby the world is divided between a public, political realm which is inferior to, and destructive of, a superior private realm of domestic sexuality and personal realisation. The public and the private are held apart, and only by detaching him/herself from community and politics and escaping into an apolitical privacy can the individual find authentic existential fufilment. Failing this resolution in the private sphere, a tragic closure is inevitable, brought about by bomb, bullet, prison or exile. In offering this conflict as an emblem of the universal human condition, the fiction tends to oversimplify or overlook socio-political identity and the particular circumstances of the Ulster situation:

> Recourse to the juxtaposition of vulnerable individuals with an amorphous and superficially drawn terrorist presence has supplanted the novel's function of critique with a kind of literary compensation: consolatory images which provide for an unreflective but consensual response have obliterated the need to examine the complexity and ambiguity of social conflict, while the elevation of individual sufferings has largely obscured the exploration of community, identity and motivation.[26]

As a result, this fiction is characterised by 'pietistic and complacent narratives'[27] which contribute to fixed perceptions and definitions of the conflict. The pervasiveness of the formula has had the effect of consolidating, legitimating and popularising the dominant perception of the Troubles as an irruption of irrational, aberrant atavism which threatens the sacred realm of private feeling and personal relationships. The charge against the Realist liberal humanist novel is that, under pressure from the Troubles, it abandons both reality and humanity, withdrawing in fear and horror from crucial areas of life into limited, secure areas of experience. It is true that these novelists, unconfident about the possibility of significant action, typically escape into pri-

---

24 Seamus Heaney, 'The redress of poetry', in *The Redress of Poetry: Oxford Lectures* (London: Faber, 1996), p.5.
25 Patten, 'Fiction in conflict' p. 129.   26 Ibid., p. 132.   27 Ibid., p. 146.

vate worlds – sentimental romance (Bernard MacLaverty's *Cal*), solipsism (Jennifer Johnston's *The Railway Station Man*), the idyllic past (Benedict Kiely's *Proxopera*). Yet, as any of these novels would serve to illustrate, Patten underestimates the powerful emotional and moral challenge of the terrorised (liberal) imagination, even if it operates within conventionalised narrative structures. It is to the discourses of postmodernism, postcolonialism and feminism that we must look for new languages and perspectives to understand and describe the North and the Troubles. Influenced by these new cultural paradigms, the fiction re-configures the division between the public (political) and private spheres and modes of discourse. Where liberal humanism enshrines the private realm not only as place of refuge from the incursions of the public world, but as source of truth and authenticity, the new writing reconstructs the relationship between public and private, self and Other, seeing it not as an (essentialist) opposition, but as a (materialist) continuity, each sphere constituted and penetrated by the other.

POSTMODERN HUMANISM

According to the postmodern critique deriving from Ferdinand Saussure and Jacques Derrida, traditional liberal humanism is founded on a 'metaphysics of presence', an ideal of pure, transparent correspondence between consciousness and language, the word and the world. The metaphysician assumes that language – which the postmodernist may fear may be merely 'bourgeois' or 'Unionist' or 'Nationalist' or 'patriarchal' – is an instrument that can enable us to get at or uncover something universal, to grasp at 'real essence'. Postmodernism undermines both the metaphysicians' 'real essences' and the structuralists' systems of binary oppositions which are used to produce unity and determinate meaning. Post-structuralism exposes the artificiality of the binary categories – self and Other, good and bad, masculinity and femininity, private and public – in which one term is always privileged over the other. Saussure's insight that meaning in language is just a matter of difference leads to the Derridean notion that there is no such thing as secure ground, no 'centre', no 'transcendental signified', no 'absolute presence', which could guarantee meaning and truth. Rather, according to Derrida, meaning is constituted by difference and endless deferral or *différance*. One term in an antithesis is always traced through by its binary opposite. The Other cannot be understood without reference to the self: the self can only be defined in relation to the Other. Essentialist notions of self and Other give way to a view of identity and otherness as constructs which, as Edward Said has shown in a postcolonial context, always serve ideological interests. In his seminal work, *Orientalism* (1978), Said argues that the West's construction of the Orient was not based on objective, scientific observation but was, rather, a discourse condensed in binary opposition to that of western consciousness and culture, producing an alien, exoticised, dehumanised and often demonised Other which was more revelatory of the preoccupations and structures of the west than of the Orient it presumed to define. Postmodernism challenges the cultural myths whereby a community seeks to understand and represent itself and others, in order to expose hidden assumptions and alienating content. In doing so, it opens the way for new re-configurations of self and Other, and the relation between them. In a Northern Ireland context, post-modernism offers the possibility of deconstructing the perennial categories of Catholic and Protestant, Unionist and Nationalist; exposing the difference and *dif-férance* within identity; exploring new horizons of identity altogether. Crucially, post-modernism questions the essentialism inherent in revivalist notions of recovery of a pure source, and the totalising tendencies of national mythologising, which, in the opinion of many critics, not only encourage a false consciousness of historical real-ity, but have the effect of contributing to violence.

Thus, Seamus Heaney, in his early archaeological 'place-name' and 'bog' poems, stands accused of failing to confront the reality of violence, of reducing history to myth, and of peddling unreal notions of collective identity. In a now famous *Honest Ulsterman* review of Heaney's *North* (1975), the younger poet Ciaran Carson took Heaney to task for becoming 'the laureate of violence – a mythmaker, an anthropol-ogist of ritual killing, an apologist for "the situation", in the last resort, a mystifier'. Heaney, in Carson's view, stands accused of 'falsifying the issues' and 'applying wrong notions of history instead of seeing what's before your eyes'.[28] Neil Corcoran invokes Carson's review as a turning-point in Northern Irish writing about the Troubles. Carson, according to Corcoran, was calling for an alternative aesthetic to the poetic orthodoxies of Romanticism and High Modernism in order to encode more directly the confusion and shock of the realities of post-1969 Northern Ireland. As a poet of Belfast's 'contemporary disintegration',[29] Carson's rejection of the metanarrative of myth and his construction of 'a narrative of his own' expresses for Corcoran a new 'Northern postmodernism':[30]

> Recent philosophy and literary theory have proposed to us the concept of a cul-ture and a consciousness of the 'postmodern' (whether the term is understood to imply a temporal sequence or a kind of opposition-from-within of moder-nism to its own deepest structures, forms and presumptions). The will to such mythical, trans-historical coherence is castigated in this writing as an ideo-logically fraught 'master narrative' or 'metanarrative', a tale of suspect plenary

---

28 Ciaran Carson, '"Escaped from the massacre"?', in *Honest Ulsterman*, 50 (Winter 1975), pp 183–6. Quoted by Neil Corcoran, 'One step forward, two steps back', in Neil Corcoran (ed.), *The Chosen Ground: Essays on the Contemporary Poetry of Northern Ireland* (Bridgend: Seren Books, 1992), pp 213–33, p. 213.   **29** Corcoran, p. 216.   **30** Ibid., p. 216.

interpretation. An 'incredulity toward metanarratives' is, for Fredric Jameson, the simplest definition of the postmodern; and, in the book Jameson is introducing when he makes this remark, Jean-François Lyotard actually goes further, declaring that the signal of the postmodern is not merely the lack of credibility of the grand narrative but the end of the 'period of mourning' for it.

In the challenge to the earlier phase of Heaney's work represented by Carson's review it is surely possible to see the ground of a Northern Irish poetry of the postmodern beginning to prepare itself.[31]

Notwithstanding Corcoran's, Patten's and Smyth's emphasis on the emergence of a 'Northern postmodernism', first in poetry, then in fiction, Northern Irish fiction since 1969 has, with significant exceptions, been remarkable for the conventionality of its formal procedures. Of course, while there may be no wholesale embracement of a postmodern aesthetic practice, it is impossible to escape the wide sweep of the postmodern condition. Though often understood as representing a radical break with essentialist humanism and with Realism (the logical expression of humanist ideology), postmodernism, as Patricia Waugh argues, need not involve 'a negative evaluation of Realism'.[32] Postmodernism, by engaging dialogically with Realism, can expose the contradictions and illusions of humanism from within. Mikhail Bakhtin's theories provide a useful framework for understanding this postmodern construction of Realism. As Waugh says:

> Bakhtin's dialogism sees knowledge of world, self and other, as always historically situated, relational, open-ended and perspectival, a process of shifting through time and space. None of these categories is a self-sufficient construct, but a relational process anchored in provisional and continuous 'authorships'.[33]

Existing in dialogue with other dominant literary modes, and offering re-examination rather than outright rejection of the humanist concerns of Realism, Northern Irish Troubles fiction may thus be seen to engage with, and can be read through, the concerns of the postmodern. As much of this fiction demonstrates, the traditional Realist or modernist novel is still very much alive, but it is invariably in all kinds of postmodern trouble, having to mediate a sense of multiplicity, pluralism, indeterminacy, fragmentation, instability of meaning, dissensus, dissolution of the grand theories of personal, national and gender identity that prevailed in the past. Contemporary writers are still participating in the Realist and modernist struggle for truth and vision, not adopting the postmodernist preoccupation with mere style, 'just gaming'. Postmodern

31 Ibid., p. 215.   32 Patricia Waugh, *Practising Postmodernism Reading Modernism* (London: Edward Arnold, 1992), p. 58.   33 Ibid., p.59.

strategies of disruption, perspectivism and distancing, when they are employed, do not proclaim the end of humanism or produce an anarchic dispersal: more characteristically, they are strategies to re-imagine self and world, to re-formulate identity, history and agency.

What is common to the whole diverse range of theoretical international postmodernisms is awareness of the breakdown of the grand narratives of the past, what Lyotard calls 'an incredulity towards metanarratives'.[34] Thus, we have Edna Longley, in her essay 'From Cathleen to Anorexia: the breakdown of Irelands', declaring that it is 'time to admit that both parts of Ireland are failed conceptual entities. That is, the ideas that created them and the ideologies which sustained them have withered at the root.'[35] For Longley, mid-twentieth century Ireland was a kind of 'Dark Age' on the painful journey from cultural Nationalism through cultural regionalism to 'civilization'. By mid-century, she argues, Irish literature is largely in 'dissident mode, at odds with the nation',[36] and this 'dissidence', she believes, has proved importantly creative. The 'dissidence' of Northern writing, she suggests, is more complicated than that of the Republic, there being in the North two communities, two major historical narratives to be deconstructed, and a stronger consciousness of multiple perspectives and languages. In Northern writing particularly she detects the evolution of new paradigms of individual and communal identity being advanced against the environing forces of reaction and stereotype:

> Northern writing does not fit the binary shapes cut out by nationalism and Unionism. It trellises the harsh girders with myriad details. It overspills borders and manifests a web of affiliation that stretches beyond any heartland – to the rest of Ireland, Britain, Europe.[37]

Similarly, Seamus Deane, in a 1984 *Crane Bag* essay, 'Remembering the Irish future', urges the need to give up essentialist notions of Irish character and identity: 'if you look, not forwards, but back, to a lost wholeness and then seek to regain that, then you have not only a conservative politics but you have a Romantic literature'.[38] Deane contrasts two modes of figuring Irish identity using William James' terminology of the 'Tender-Minded' and the 'Tough-Minded'. There is, says Deane, a 'Tender' or 'Romantic' construction of identity which is monologic, grounded in concepts like

34 Jean-François Lyotard. 'Answering the question: What is postmodernism?' in Charles Jencks (ed.), *The Post-Modern Reader* (London: Academy, 1992), pp 138–50, p. 138.   35 Edna Longley, 'From Cathleen to Anorexia', in *The Living Stream: Literature and Revisionism in Ireland* (Newcastle-upon-Tyne: Bloodaxe Books, 1994), p. 173.   36 Edna Longley, 'Northern Ireland: poetry and peace', in Karl-Heinz Westarp and Michael Boss (eds.), *Ireland: Towards New Identities* (Aarhus: Aarhus University Press, 1998), pp 103–115, p.108.   37 Longley, 'From Cathleen to Anorexia', p. 194.   38 Seamus Deane, 'Remembering the Irish future', *Crane Bag*, 7, 2(1984), pp 81–92, p. 84.

race, nationality, faith and devotion to the past. The other 'Tough-Minded' or 'Enlightenment' mode respects innovation, change, escape from traditional pieties and looks forward to a pluralistic future. In a spirit of empirical constructivism, Deane calls for a re-assertion of 'Tough-Mindedness': 'If the Irish could forget about the whole problem of what is essentially Irish, if they could be persuaded to see that this does nothing but produce an unnecessary anxiety about a non-existent abstraction, they would have recovered some genuine independence'.[39] Irish people must free themselves from old faiths, myths, dreams, pieties, and tribal allegiances, and realise that identity is here and now, that the future depends on a selective use of the past, not an unquestioning enslavement to it. These ideas are reiterated in an essay, 'Heroic styles: the tradition of an idea', published the following year, where he proclaimed that it was time to leave behind restricted, provincial, stereotypical notions of Irishness: 'It is about time to put aside the idea of essence – that hungry Hegelian ghost looking for a stereotype to live in ... Everything, including our politics and our literature, has to be re-written – i.e. re-read'.[40]

However, these postmodernist-sounding ideas articulated by both Longley and Deane have not formed the basis of any emergent consensus. Each critic reads the other's deconstructive instincts, not as ushering in a postmodern heaven of openness, tolerance, pluralism and heterogeneity, but as re-constituting traditional modes and attitudes. Longley's concept of literature as the dwelling place of the Other in the author, as a site of fluidity and hybridisation, is attained, according to Deane, through an elitist fetishising of civilised form, which effectively de-materialises the work. Her idea of aesthetic order, balance and resolution, says Deane, involves a de-politicisation of art and culture, a re-instatement of a liberal humanist aesthetic and cultural ideal which he interprets as evidence of a re-cycled literary Unionism that is unacceptable in a divided and unstable society. Even while denouncing the outworn binaries of Protestant and Catholic, Nationalist and Unionist, Longley stands accused of wanting to retain another binary which polarises Culture and Politics. On the other hand, from Longley's point of view, Deane's call for a deconstructive re-reading of 'our politics and our literature' only leads to the construction of Deane's 'Derry metanarrative',[41] expressive of traditional Nationalist cultural paradigms, and enshrined in the *Field Day Anthology of Irish Literature*. Where one critic puts the emphasis on art's liberating and transformative power, the other insists on art's situatedness in the world of national and political experience.

---

39 Ibid., p. 90.   40 Seamus Deane, 'Heroic styles: the tradition of an idea', in *Ireland's Field Day* (London: Hutchinson, 1985), pp 45–59, p. 58.   41 Longley, 'Introduction: revising "Irish Literature" ', *The Living Stream*, p. 39.

Postmodernism has both a positive and negative potential. For some writers faced with the breakdown of the grand narratives of the past the situation leads to a sense of deep confusion and powerlessness, sometimes a nostalgic yearning for the old certainties. These feelings can produce a depressed and pessimistic quietism in the face of what is perceived as an indifferent process of exchange and fluidity, or an irresponsible carnival of endless textual play. For others, decentralisation, dispersal and improvisation are invigorating aesthetic opportunities. Where Baudrillard sees the world emptying itself out into the simulacrum, Lyotard sees new possibilities for innovation created out of the breakdown of stable categories of the 'real'. Where Jameson saw the postmodern as the end of all meaningful action, community, historical consciousness, resistance or change, Linda Hutcheon insists on its continued capability to perform the function of critique, its capacity to contest and disrupt centralised, closed systems from within: 'to include irony and play is never necessarily to exclude seriousness and purpose in postmodern art'.[42] This 'postmodernism of resistance',[43] as Andreas Huyssen calls it, is informed by feminism and the women's movement, by anti-imperialism, by growing awareness of other minority subcultures and traditionally marginalised groups. From this perspective, the entire history of Irish literature in English might be construed as a perennial site of the postmodern. Implicit in these positive views of the postmodern is a rejection of binary thinking and a recognition of the need to conceive difference without opposition. In a famous essay, the American novelist, John Barth, suggests how this may be done. For Barth, postmodernist fiction, far from being a literature of exhaustion, clapped-out epigonal decadence or cultural anarchy, is a 'literature of replenishment', which he defines in terms of a productive, contemporary 'synthesis' of previous modes (traditional bourgeois Realism and modernism):

> A worthy programme for postmodernist fiction, I believe, is the synthesis or transcension of these antitheses, which may be summed up as premodernist and modernist modes of writing. My ideal postmodernist author neither repudiates nor merely imitates either his twentieth-century modernist parents or his nineteenth-century premodernist grandparents. He has the first half of our century under his belt, but not on his back.[44]

Brian Friel, following his fellow Field Day founder-member, Seamus Deane, has shown how this synthesising model of postmodernism applies in a (Northern) Irish con-

42 Linda Hutcheon, *A Poetics of Postmodernism: History, Theory, Fiction* (London and New York: Routledge, 1988), p. 27.   43 Andreas Huyssen, 'Mapping the Postmodern', in Charles Jencks (ed.) *The Post-Modern Reader* (London: Academy, 1992), pp 40–72, p. 69.   44 John Barth, 'The literature of replenishment: postmodern fiction', in Charles Jencks, *The Post-Modern Reader*, pp 172–80, p.178.

text. Friel's play *Translations* provides a useful metaphor to understand the political and aesthetic potential of the revisionary, transformative dynamic in postmodern, post-Nationalist culturalism. Translation is a means of acknowledging cultural rootedness without being transfixed by culture. It expresses the simultaneous need for continuity as well as transformation. Translation recognises the way in which the mind is structured through the languages of a cultural tradition, but equally implies that there can be no mindless acceptance of the past, no passive submission to the 'given' reality. It calls for active reworking of the established discourses, a sifting and selecting and rewriting so that what is useful may be retrieved and retained. The stability that comes from a sense of continuity or tradition is valued, but so is the capacity to adapt to new circumstances. There may no longer be available to us a single explanatory myth which we unself-consciously accept, but we may self-consciously manipulate the fragments of a diverse range of myths to open up new possibilities of meaning. The postmodern presents the writer with exciting opportunities for re-mapping identity, re-writing the past, re-centering cultural difference, re-shaping the very notion of 'national' destiny. Salman Rushdie's observation that 'Reality is an artefact, it can also be made well or badly and that it can also, of course, be unmade',[45] suggests the challenge facing the postmodern writer in a post-colonial context: postmodern fictionality may serve either repressive/ regressive or emancipatory ends. The fragmentation of value creates the conditions where, far from destroying our powers of ethical self-determination, actually offers them new opportunities, new forms and contexts, and where, without completely abandoning traditional moral value, we may find release from the prison houses of outworn myths and stereotypes.

The theorist most closely associated with the construction of Irish postmodernism I have been describing is Richard Kearney. Kearney emphasises the way Irish postmodernism problematises dominant values by contesting their codes of representation from within, acknowledging an unavoidable situatedness in the culture, while still finding ways to reformulate its discursive premises and fictional modes. The fiction thus fulfils art's dual function of critique and Utopian or mythic (re-)imagining which opens us to new horizons of possibility. As Kearney explains in his book, *Transitions: Narratives of Modern Irish Culture*:

> Without demythologization, no remythologization.
>
> Postmodern myth invites a plurality of viewpoints. It encourages us to reread tradition, not as a sacred and inviolable scripture, but as a palimpsest of creative possibilities, which can only be reanimated and realized in a radically pluralist culture.[46]

---

45 Quoted by Patricia Waugh, *Practising Postmodernism Reading Modernism*, p. 53.   46 Dublin: Wolfhound, 1988, p. 280.

Kearney claims that Irish writers since the '60s have been required to respond to 'the transitional crisis' of Irish culture, to bear witness to a tension between tradition and modernism.[47] In the wake of the breakdown of the grand narratives of the past, Irish culture, he says, has become 'a complex web of interweaving narratives which refuse the facility of an homogenous totality'.[48] The new urbanised, educated, internationalised generation which grew up in the '60s and '70s are what he calls 'migrant minds'[49] – products of a changing culture where the influence of television, cinema and popular music co-existed with inherited allegiances, tribal atavisms and traditional pieties. Kearney is interested in the way the 'migrant mind', having made the journey away from 'home', whether physically or mentally, returns to see what might be rediscovered and recreated from indigenous, local or traditional cultural resources to contribute to new constructions of Irishness:

> This is where modernity's obsession with absolute novelty and rupture – its frequent repudiation of historical memory – is perhaps tempered by a postmodern awareness that we cannot afford to not know our past. Rupture is complemented by remembrance. Creation ex nihilo gives way to the more playful practice of recreation.[50]

The 'migrant mind', in Kearney's view, demonstrates a capacity 'to translate back and forth between the familiar and the foreign, the old and the new, tradition and utopia, reinterpreting one's own history in stories which address the challenge of change'.[51] In doing so, these stories will continually cross boundaries, blur the distinctions that have been used to construct traditional concepts of identity, and open the possibility of a multiple culture. They will acknowledge paradox, self-division, inner quarrel, and embrace the positive value of confusion, uncertainty and questioning. Kearney is particularly keen to stress that this continual 'questing for another place'[52] does not imply any repudiation of Irishness but rather a more fundamental sense of belonging to a 'native place', a place more personally and communally conceived than the abstract nation.

The postmodernist construct of home, the past, identity, is always fictional and therefore provisional, always subject to further critique and revision. It is when the fiction is taken as reality itself, that, as Hugh says in Friel's *Translations*, we 'can become imprisoned in a linguistic contour which no longer matches the landscape of ... fact'.[53] The resulting absolutism of belief can generate the kind of intransigence and violence that has been all too evident in the North over the last thirty years. As Hugh again

47 Ibid., p.14.   48 Ibid., p. 17.   49 Richard Kearney, *Across the Frontiers: Ireland in the 1990s: Cultural, Political, Economic* (Dublin: Wolfhound, 1988), p. 186.   50 Ibid., p. 186.   51 Ibid., p. 280.   52 Ibid., p. 186.   53 In Seamus Deane (ed.) *Selected Plays of Brian Friel* (London: Faber, 1984), p. 419.

says: 'It's not the facts of history that shape us, but images of the past embodied in language ... and once we cease to renew those images, we fossilize.'[54] By accepting the challenge of 'translating', re-negotiating, re-formulating the old, the Irish writer can creatively reinterpret the past to release new possibilities for the present and the future. The 'migrant mind' will tend to display a characteristically ambivalent attitude to home, a tension between nostalgic desire and the corrosive modern sense of alienation and absence, but, Kearney claims, once the idea of a unique identity is abandoned, the work reveals its Irishness all the more confidently; once Irishness is no longer striven for too self-consciously or too fanatically, it becomes all the more securely apparent. It is precisely at this point that Longley intervenes to identify the old nationalist grand narrative which she believes Kearney's polemic recoups: 'I think that "Irishness", with its totalitarian tinge, ought to be abandoned rather than made more inclusive.' 'To include or exclude' is, in Longley's view, 'a false and sterile alternative'.[55] Political 'Irishness', she believes, should be marked off from culture in Ireland, the latter always resisting unitary assumptions or programmes.

POLITICAL *VERSUS* CULTURALIST PARADIGMS

The 'political' has been variously understood in the context of Northern Irish literature. Clair Wills draws attention to its frequent construction, 'not as direct political intervention, but as the poet's cultural expression of the particular stamp of his or her community, his ability to give voice to its political complexion'.[56] In this interpretation, political responsibility is a function of the writer's rootedness in his community, his understanding of the primitive and atavistic levels of the collective psyche codified in myth. David Lloyd objects to the aesthetic politics of Romantic Nationalism, devoted as it is to the recuperation of an original (fictive) identity which precedes difference and conflict, and which therefore involves the denial of history:

> What may need emphasis ... is the role which a politics of identity has played in producing the form of the current civil war in Ireland. The combined effect of political thinking on each side of the border has been to perpetuate not only nationalist ideologies, but their articulation along sectarian and, effectively, racial grounds. The real basis of the present struggle in the economic and social conditions of a post-colonial state, and the peculiar twist given to class differences by such conditions, has consequently been systematically obscured.[57]

54 Ibid., p. 445. 55 Longley, 'From Cathleen to Anorexia', pp 179–80. 56 Clair Wills, *Improprieties*, p.27.
57 Lloyd, *Anomalous States*, p. 19.

Focusing on Heaney's 'place-name poems' and 'bog poems', Lloyd charges Heaney with reducing history to myth, leaving only the timelessness of repeated fundamental acts. By giving himself over to the establishment of myths and the bourgeois ideal of aesthetic autonomy, Heaney, in Lloyd's view, is unable to critique traditional concepts of national identity or interrogate the nature and function of acts of violence.

Seamus Deane takes an opposite view, claiming that there can be no real understanding of the roots of the conflict in the North unless the work identifies with a national or tribal consciousness, the spirit of the people (as Deane himself does in *Reading in the Dark*). Referring to Heaney, Deane remarked: 'When myth enters the poetry, in *Wintering Out* (1972), the process of politicization begins.'[58] This is not a trend which the liberal humanist can approve of for it encourages a false consciousness of historical reality. Reviewing Heaney's next volume, *North* (1975), Conor Cruise O'Brien complained: 'The area where literature and politics overlap has, then, to be regarded with some suspicion. It is suffused with romanticism, which in politics tends in the direction of fascism ...'[59] Narratives in the 'tragic, heroic mode' are to be particularly avoided, for they can be used to glorify a sordid violence. The liberal humanist insists on rational, ethical critique to unmask alienating mythologies which would merely imprison us in illusion and fantasy. Deane replies by questioning O'Brien's call for critical distance, asking if it wouldn't result in the achievement of a sterile lucidity at the expense of sense of belonging and authentic self-representation:

> But surely this very clarity of O'Brien's position is just what is most objectionable. It serves to give a rational clarity to the Northern position which is untrue to the reality. In other words, is not his humanism here being used as an excuse to rid Ireland of the atavisms which give it life even though the life itself may be in some ways brutal?[60]

In his essay, 'Remembering the future' of nine years later, Deane takes a notably more critical view of atavism when it comes from the Unionist camp. He implicitly concurs with O'Brien's association of atavism with fascism when he alludes to the Civil Rights protest in the North as an expression of Enlightenment libertarianism opposed by atavistic Unionism: 'In the North the opposition of the Civil Rights movement to Unionism is a recent example of the battle between a cosmopolitan liberalism and consolidated native loyalties.'[61] In this essay, the urgent need is to forego

58 Seamus Deane, 'The timorous and the bold', in *Celtic Revivals* (London: Faber, 1985), pp 174–86, p. 179.   59 Conor Cruise O'Brien, 'An unhealthy intersection', *New Review*, 2, 16 (July 1975), p. 7.   60 Seamus Deane, 'Unhappy and at Home', interview with Seamus Heaney, *Crane Bag*, 1, 1 (1977), p. 69.   61 Seamus Deane, 'Remembering the Irish future', *Crane Bag*, p. 82.

the visionary, Romantic appeal of a Utopian future or an Edenesque past, 'to change ground before it opens up and swallows us'.[62] This 'tough' rationalism is carried over into his Field Day pronouncements. Field Day, he says, set out to 'contribute to the solution of the present crisis by producing analyses of the established opinions, myths and stereotypes which had become both a symptom and a cause of the current situation'.[63] Later writings, however, reveal the emergence of more obviously totalising, more strenuously political, ambitions. In his 'General introduction' to the *Field Day Anthology*, he writes: 'There is a story here, a meta-narrative, which is, we believe, hospitable to all the micro-narratives that, from time to time, have achieved prominence as the official version of the true history, political and literary, of the island's past and present.'[64] And in his introduction to *Nationalism, Colonialism and Literature* (1990), he urges the need for the clarity of a political, historically informed, discourse. Postmodernist pluralism and anti-foundationalist relativism must not be allowed to negate the possibility of stable value and thus of any oppositional critique:

> To remove ourselves from that (historical) condition into one in which all these lesions and occlusions are forgotten, in which the postmodernist simulacrum of pluralism supplants the search for a legitimating mode of nomination and origin, is surely to pass from one kind of colonizing experience into another. For such pluralism refuses the idea of naming; it plays with diversity and makes a mystique of it; it is the concealed imperialism of the multinational, the infinite compatibility of all cultures.[65]

Deane is here perhaps reacting against the threat posed by revisionism as practised by historians such as F.S.L. Lyons and Roy Foster and by literary critics such as Edna Longley. Despite Foster's claim that revisionists are opposed to the 'old pieties', not Irish Nationalism *per se*, revisionism has tended to be regarded as anti-Nationalist historiography. History-writing, as the cultural commentator Desmond Fennell says, is always ideological, and is valuable as a way of legitimising and reinforcing a value system which binds a people together and confirms a sense of identity and common purpose.[66] This was the great advantage of 'the nationalist narrative' which told the story of heroic struggle against seven hundred years of English colonialism, a struggle which continues in the North today. However, since the 1960s there has developed another kind of history-writing which Fennell, the sentimental Republican, social conservative and traditional Catholic, sees as antagonistic to a bonding

62 Ibid., p. 86.   63 Seamus Deane, blurb on dustjacket of Ireland's Field Day .   64 Seamus Deane, 'General introduction', *The Field Day Anthology of Irish Writing* (Derry: Field Day Theatre Company, 1991).   65 Seamus Deane, '*Introduction*', *Nationalism, Colonialism and Literature* (Minneapolis: University of Minnesota Press, 1990), pp 18–19.   66 See Desmond Fennell, *Heresy: The Battle of Ideas in Modern Ireland* (Belfast: Blackstaff, 1993).

Nationalist ideology, and which he castigates for its rootless individualism and anti-Catholic, anti-rural provincialism. This neo-revisionist historiography, Fennell claims, is all too ready to accommodate itself to Britain, Northern Unionists and EC Europe, and is fuelled by fears aroused in the South by the deepening crisis in the North.[67] The revisionist endgame, Deane wryly surmised, is to conjure away both 'colonialism' and 'nationalism' altogether.[68] While Deane rails against Foster's and Longley's imperialist revisionism, Longley describes Deane's 'cultural decolonisation' as just another type of revisionism.[69]

So, if all history-writing (and indeed all creative writing) is revisionist, then what matters is the kind of revisionist one is. Eagleton notes that revisionists tend to be anti-Nationalist because Nationalism is 'essentialist', but he goes on to point out that 'nationalist historiography was itself the first great revisionist school in Ireland'. It is the current orthodoxy of middle-class liberal revisionism that Eagleton cannot stand:

> What is wrong with these scholars from a radical viewpoint is not that they are revisionists, but that they are middle-class liberals. And what is wrong with middle-class liberalism is not on the whole its values, most of which are entirely admirable, but the fact that it obliquely refuses to recognise the depth of social transformation which would be necessary for those values to be realised in universal form.[70]

The contemporary revisionists' commitment to sceptical, empirical, anti-teleological, anti-utopian, anti-theoretical historiography which must itself always be subject to further revision is obviously closely allied to postmodernism, which rejects the idea of disinterested historical consciousness, suspects consensus and solidarity as inherently authoritarian, and considers difference to be the sign of authenticity. 'Postmodern culturalism' – the cultural expression of revisionism in the sphere of Irish historiography, and of postmodernism in the sphere of international aesthetics – refers to the movement devoted to cultivating an increased tolerance and appreciation of Ireland's diverse traditions in the realm of culture. But to political critics, postmodern pluralism, diversity and heterogeneity mean very little without a clearly articulated political discourse. Both Eagleton and Deane are fiercely critical of any drift towards postmodern quietism, and cling to a hope of radical political change. Eagleton provides the rationale for giving prece-

67 Fennell, *Heresy*, pp 87–8.   68 Deane, *Nationalism, Colonialism and Literature*, p. 7.   69 Edna Longley, 'Writing, revisionism & grass-seed: literary mythologies in Ireland' in Jean Lundy and Aodán MacPóilin (eds.), *Styles of Belonging: The Cultural Identities of Ulster* (Belfast, Lagan Press, 1991), pp 11–22, p. 14.   70 Terry Eagleton, 'Revising revisionism', in *Crazy Jane and the Bishop:: and other essays on Irish Culture* (Cork: Cork University Press in association with Field Day, 1998), p. 320.

dence to 'politics' over 'culture': having asserted that 'the liberal humanist notion of culture was constituted, among other things, to marginalise such people as the Irish', he continues:

> One can make rational choices between forms of politics, but not for the most part between forms of cultures, so that to redefine the political in cultural terms – to call Orange marches a celebration of one's heritage, for example – is to render one's politics far less vulnerable to critique ... To view the conflict in the North as primarily one between alternative 'cultural traditions' fits well with postmodern culturalism in general, and so sounds reasonably persuasive; it is just that it also happens to be false.[71]

Thus, cultural debate is summarily closed down, replaced by a totalising, omniscient political argument. Instead of the pluralising crossings and fusings associated with postmodernism, the political approach imposes rigid definitions and enforces difference and polarisation. While the 'middle class liberals', 'revisionists' and 'intellectuals' whom Eagleton reviles attempt to encourage open debate and respect for the diversity of cultural tradition, both he and Deane, unashamedly dismissing the liberal humanist ideals of 'fairness' and 'objectivity',[72] insist on the need to make clear choices about identity, politics and modes of historical representation. On this view, 'genuine identity, true difference and authentic pluralism can finally be established only on the basis of political justice and emancipation'.[73]

POSTCOLONIALISM

Postcolonialism, taken not in its chronological sense referring to a post-independence period, but as a description of the various cultural effects of colonisation, provides another critical context for the reading of Troubles fiction. There is, of course, a substantial proportion of the population of Northern Ireland who would dispute the appropriateness of a colonial or postcolonial construction of the present situation. John Hewitt speaks for those who see themselves as neither colonised nor (any longer) as colonist in prose writings such as 'No rootless colonist' and in poems such as 'The Colony' which ends: 'we would be strangers in the Capitol; / this is our country also, no-where else; / and we shall not be outcast on the world'.[74] Nevertheless, for others, postcolonialism offers a valuable oppositional or deconstructive form of reading practice which orders a critique of the hegemonic discourses of British imperialism and

---

71 Eagleton, 'Revising revisionism', p. 326.   72 Seamus Deane, quoted by Nick Fever in 'A kind of life sentence', *Guardian*, 28 October 1996, p. 9 .   73 Eagleton, 'Revising revisionism', p. 327.   74 John Hewitt, 'The Colony', in Alan Warner (ed.) *The Selected John Hewitt* (Belfast: Blackstaff, 1981), pp 21–4.

an uncovering of an emergent counter-hegemony. We have already noted David Lloyd's objection to a poetics of identity whose function is to suggest the possibility of transcending conflict by excluding or integrating difference wherever it threatens the hegemonic image of unity. Moving from poetry to fiction, Lloyd sees the Realist novel as designed to perform a similar colonial integration or harmonisation or hierarchization of sociolects, relegating to the margins those forms which threaten to destabilise the overall narrative structure. Realism's chief function, Lloyd argues, is to tell the story of the individual's quest for self-discovery which is rewarded with social integration, and this narrative of individual self-formation, he believes, mirrors the master narrative of modernity which charts the civilising process whereby a nation is transported from barbarity to civility. However, the purpose of the Realist novel to produce a narrative of reconciliation runs into all sorts of difficulties in a postcolonial context. Joe Cleary examines the way the drive to imagine some kind of reconciliation between the two communities in the North has produced a form of romance which straddles the political divide – the 'romance-across-the-divide' story – which has, he says, acquired the status of a 'master narrative'[75] of the Northern Irish conflict. However, in Cleary's view, the effort to smooth over conflict and difference by suppressing any reference to partition makes the 'love-across-the-divide' story 'an anxious and contradictory literary mode':[76]

> the consignment of state borders to the margins, and the corresponding magnification of sectarian boundaries, is far from innocent: it reflects and sustains a fundamental misperception of the Northern conflict premised on the assumption that the problem of sectarianism can be detached from the question of the existing state order in the British Isles, an assumption that inevitably tends to underestimate the degree to which the sectarian conflict is rooted in conflicting national and state allegiances.[77]

Referring specifically to Joan Lingard's *The Twelfth Day of July* and *Across the Barricades*, Bernard McLaverty's *Cal* and Neil Jordan's film *The Crying-Game*, Cleary notes that the attempt to imagine a reconciliation of the divided communities in terms of a 'love-across-the-barricades' 'master narrative', with the union of the lovers from opposing communities standing as metaphor for a larger social and political reconciliation, can only work if we suppress politics and accept the political and constitutional status quo in Ireland. The Northern Irish 'love-across-the-barricades' story therefore 'cannot emerge as a full-fledged "national romance" celebrating the consolidation of the Northern Irish State unless it takes the form of an explicitly Unionist wish-fantasy and ignores the hostility of Northern nationalists to a "resolution" of

75 Joe Cleary, 'Fork-tongued on the border bit', p. 238.   76 Ibid.   77 Ibid., p. 237.

this sort'.[78] This, Cleary concludes, explains why in so many of the Northern Irish romances the relationship between the lovers from different communities often either fails in the end, or can only be realised in a private sphere where sexuality and politics are dissociated and individual self-realisation counts for more than the claims of the public, political world.

In challenging what is perceived as the misrepresentations and distortions of mainstream fiction, and re-writing the colonial discourse of British imperialism, the narrative of decolonisation is in danger of simply inverting the colonial stereotypes. 'Ireland' and 'England' are, in Declan Kiberd's view, colonial reflections of each other, fictions that each has created in response to precise needs at certain points in their history.[79] Irish Nationalism, grounded in essentialist categories such as 'race', reproduces even as it opposes, imperialism. Deane, in his introduction to *Nationalism, Colonialism and Literature* (1990) explains:

> Irish nationalism is, in fact, in its foundational moments a derivative of its British counterpart. Almost all nationalist movements have been derided as provincial, actually or potentially racist, given to exclusivist and doctrinaire positions and rhetoric ... The point about Irish nationalism, the features within it that have prevented it from being a movement toward liberation, is that it is *mutatis mutandis*, a copy of that by which it felt itself to be oppressed. The collusion of Irish with British nationalism has produced contrasting stereotypes whose most destructive effect has been the laying of the cultural basis for religious sectarianism.[80]

The binary habit of mind produces such essentialist fantasies as Danny Morrison's *West Belfast*, where overcompensation for a perceived process of colonial dehumanisation results in the creation of as unrealistic a character typology as that which obtained in the crassest of colonial narratives. By simply inverting the hegemonic categories, Morrison ends up with heroic Republicans as unbelievably idealised as they once were caricatured, and an enemy, in the form of the British Army, as demonically proportioned as the political terrorist had been in mainstream representations. Morrison's novel is graphic demonstration of the way any counter-hegemonic narrative exists in both parasitic and antagonistic relationship to the dominant discourse, always caught within the dominant culture, always revealing the limiting horizons of the universalist hegemonic perspective, and, torn by tension and internal contradiction, continually straining against the conventions of a traditional Realism. Of course, there may be political advantages in adopting what Gaytari Spivak calls a 'strategic

78 Ibid., p. 239.   79 See Declan Kiberd, *Inventing Irelands: The Literature of the Modern Nation* (London: Vintage, 1996).   80 Deane, *Introduction, Nationalism, Colonialism and Literature*, p. 6.

essentialism', a mode of negotiation in which the decolonising subject, inscribed within the hegemonic system of natural and universal categories, seeks to disrupt it from within. Deane's own writings, as we have already noted, reveal a tension between the post-structuralist urge to dismantle essentialism on one hand, and, on the other, the desire for unifying, motivating concepts within Nationalist discourses. While agreeing that Nationalism mirrors what it opposes, Deane still recognises it as a useful site of resistance and a foundation for the construction of a historical identity in the face of the threats of erasure, elision and 'depthlessness' posed by revisionists and postmodernists.

More explicitly opposed to the oppositional, identitarian politics of imperialism and nationalism are the postmodern postcolonial theories of Kearney (epitomised by his idea of 'migrant minds'[81] traversing the heteroglossic fields of Irish culture) and Lloyd, whose theory hinges on the idea of 'adulteration' as exemplified by Joyce. In a desire to oppose both the constructions of a reactionary bourgeois Nationalism (derived from British nationalism) and those of colonialism, Lloyd, building on the theories of Homi Bhabha, proposes a fragmentary and hybridised discourse between imperialism and nationalism. Acknowledging nationalism's imbrication in imperial forms, he calls for a mobilisation of indigenous forces of anti-colonial resistance. Hybridisation or adulteration ensures against subordination to any hegemonic master narrative of representation, any process of cultural assimilation, any essentialist concept of identity. Rejecting the old Nationalist obsession with an exclusive concept of racial identity, Lloyd recognises instead an Irish postcolonial identity which 'is not a self-sustaining and autonomous organism ... but, rather, at the individual and national-cultural level, a hybridization ... in which antagonism mixes with dependence and autonomy is constantly undermined by the perceived influence of alien powers'.[82] Robert MacLiam Wilson's *Ripley Bogle* and *Eureka Street* (which the author referred to in a *Time Out* interview as a 'Belfast *Ulysses*')[83] are innovative, forceful demonstrations of the potential of the adulterated narrative which is heterogeneous, hybridised, assimilating, disruptive of fixed identities, whether imperialist or nationalist.

WOMEN'S WRITING

There are many different kinds of feminist discourse, from 'revolutionary' or 'radical feminism' at one end of the spectrum to 'liberal feminism' at the other. Where 'revolutionary' or 'radical feminism' implies direct action to bring about a feminist overthrow of patriarchal social structures, 'liberal feminists' believe that equality can

81 Kearney (ed.), *Across the Frontiers*, p. 185 .   82 Lloyd, *Anomalous States*, pp 111–12.   83 Robert MacLiam Wilson, quoted by John O'Mahony, 'Troubles in mind', *Guardian*, 7 July, 1993.

be achieved through reform of existing structures. Other 'feminisms' include 'cultural feminism', 'psychoanalytic feminism', 'lesbian feminism', and 'socialist feminism'.[84] Mary Beckett and Mary Costello might be regarded as writing versions of 'socialist feminism', emphasising the economic base of society, and exploring women's oppressed position in the realms of politics, family and work; a male writer, David Park, explores a lesbian feminist analysis of male power and ideas of sisterhood and women's community as the basis of women's liberation in general; most (though not all) women's writing contributes to the exploration of an alternative women's culture ('cultural feminism'). 'Feminist fiction', as defined by Catherine St Peter, characteristically exhibits at the very least a political awareness and sometimes even a discernible ideological framework that marks it as socially progressive, or as writing that inscribes a journey 'going from here to somewhere else'.[85] While most of the women writers considered in this study challenge the received orthodoxy about women's place and function, and are interested in re-configuring the narratives of female identity and history, they do not necessarily see themselves as pursuing an explicitly political agenda or belonging to a 'women's movement', important though the 1970s Women's Peace Movement, or the Women's Coalition Party founded by Monica McWilliams in 1996 have been in focusing women's issues in the North. For many women writers, even those sympathetic to feminist theory and political practice, art inevitably overspills any of the given categories and will always be subject to new readings and interpretations which may be very different from those which the author anticipated. In taking this line, they are, of course, often accused by 'socialist' or 'radical feminists' of being individualist and elitist, pursuing personal cultural goals, remaining disengaged from direct political struggle, and perpetuating traditional associations of femininity with creativity, emotion, spirituality, peace, and the maternal.

Women's writing, even that which is not consciously combative or political, represents the significant emergence of various forms of 'otherness' in the cultural sphere, which are sometimes perceived as a threat to the stability and sanctity of established authority, canon and tradition. Women's writing as a form of representation which has been denied legitimacy exposes the system of power that authorises certain representations while blocking or invalidating others. Traditionally excluded from representation, women return within it as a figure for the suppressed, marginalised or unrepresentable. This prohibition applies to women as subject rather than object of representation, for there has certainly been no shortage of images of women in Irish tradition, from the 'Hag of Beare' in early Christian times, to the goddess/muse Erin of Aisling poetry, to the whore/hag of the nineteenth and early twentieth cen-

84 Paulina Palmer, *Contemporary Women's Fiction: Narrative Practice and Feminist Theory* (Hemel Hempstead: Harvester Wheatsheaf, 1989), pp 166–9.   85 Catherine St Peter, *Changing Ireland: Strategies in Contemporary Women's Fiction* (Basingstoke: Macmillan, 2000), p. 151.

tury, to the chaste virgin mother, to the suffering pietá of Pearse's 'The Mother' and the old hag in Yeats' 'Cathleen'. In being represented by others, women have been rendered a silence and an absence within the dominant culture. In accepting the challenge of self-representation, they may be seen as part of what Andreas Huysman calls a new 'postmodernism of resistance'.[86] Rozsika Parker and Griselda Pollock suggest that 'feminism explores the pleasures of resistance, of deconstruction, of discovery, of defining, of fragmenting, of redefining'. This 'feminism' of resistance and revision is certainly relevant to much Irish women's writing since the '60s which has, consciously or unconsciously, offered a significant challenge to the grand narratives of the past. Women's writing, itself heterogeneous and varied, may be considered an intrinsic part of the postmodernist critique of representation; women's insistence on sexual difference as an instance of postmodern pluralised thought.

The decolonising discourses used to advance the cause of Irish nationalism entailed the subordination of Irish women. Irish postcolonial 'liberation' did not include women either. As Ailbhe Smyth says: 'The liberation of the state implies male role-shift from that of Slave to Master, Margin to Centre, Other to Self. Women, powerless under patriarchy, are maintained as Other of the ex-Other, colonized of the post-colonized'.[87] Feminism and Nationalism, it is sometimes felt, are antagonistic practices. Edna Longley, for example, suggests that the starved, emaciated figure of 'Anorexia' (symbol of the idealised Nationalist cause of the hunger strikers), rather than Cathleen Ni Houlihan, 'should personify Irish women ... starved and repressed by patriarchies like Unionism, Catholicism, Protestantism, Nationalism'.[88] Yet, says Longley, for many women, mainly from the North, 'Cathleen flourishes abundantly still'.[89] Nor is Ulster Protestantism any less traditionally patriarchal than Catholic Nationalism, Longley continues, though 'Unionism does not appropriate the image of women or hide behind our skirts'.[90] Both Nationalism and Unionism, Longley concludes, 'have distorted ethics, politics, social and personal relations, the lives of women, education, what passes here for religion, and our whole understanding of Irish culture'.[91] It is the role of literature to challenge the anorexic categories, and not only must the new, revisionist ideas of 'nation' and 'identity' be subject to a specifically feminine critique to expose the residues of patriarchy, but even female revisions of Irish tradition must be carefully inspected for the persistence of unconscious Nationalist assumptions which continue to exclude women's lived realities from public discourse. In Longley's view, unitary assumptions about nation and tradition continue to marginalise and scar many Irish women and men: 'Even on her death-bed Cathleen-Anorexia exerts a residual power over the image and self-images of all Irish women'.[92]

86 Andreas Huyssen, 'Mapping the Postmodern', pp 40–72, p. 69.   87 Ailbhe Smyth, 'The Floozie in the Jacuzzi', *Irish Review* 6 (Spring 19890), pp 7–24, pp 9–10.   88 Longley, 'From Cathleen to Anorexia', p. 173. 89 Ibid., p. 173.   90 Ibid., p. 187.   91 Ibid., p. 175.   92 Ibid., p. 186.

In the wider cultural context, other theorists such as Betty Friedan, Kate Millett, Elizabeth Janeway and Ann Oakley have, since the '70s, drawn attention to the oppressive effects of the stereotypical representation of women as sex object, wife and mother, whereby women are relegated to the private sphere of sexual relations and family life. Still others, such as Hélène Cixous, Julia Kristeva and Luce Iragaray have examined the way femininity is constructed through a phallocratic culture's assumption of a set of binary opposites whereby women are identified with nature and the body, and men with mind and culture. Writers such as Jennifer Johnston and Kate O'Riordan have challenged the degrading effects of this identification and explored the self-destructive syndromes in which it entraps women. Their fiction exemplifies the central conflict in women's writing – the collision between the female protagonist's evolving self and society's imposed identity. This writing not only focuses on the oppressiveness of patriarchy and the contradictions which it involves, but suggests strategies of female resistance and challenge. Feminine identity is re-written so that the 'feminine' values of nurture, emotion and sensitivity are re-constructed as the behavioural norm, while the 'masculine' values of aggression and violence are written as deviant and aberrant.

Writing in 1974, Rosalind Miles criticised modern women novelists for their 'parochialism' and 'narrow concentration upon the minutiae of women's lives, the emphasis on domestic difficulties and sexual sorrows'.[93] Miles was not referring specifically to Northern Irish women writers, but clearly women's writing on the North has tended to focus on the 'specifically female' areas such as family, and sexual and marital relations. However, it would be wrong to see this concentration on the personal life as a simple evasion or rejection of politics. As Paulina Palmer explains:

> ... with the rebirth of feminism in the late 1960s, the 'private' domestic area ... has received re-evaluation. No longer can it be dismissed as 'parochial'. The division between the 'private' and 'public' realms has been challenged and to a degree eroded by the feminist focus on sexual politics and the perception, integral to it, that 'the personal is political'.[94]

From this point of view – and as demonstrated by the fiction of Jennifer Johnston, Mary Beckett or Kate O'Riordan – women's 'personal' problems, rather than reflecting their own inadequacies, stem from a social structure in which women are systematically dominated, exploited and oppressed. In the women's fiction considered in this study, the critique of patriarchy is frequently focused through exploration of the family unit, which is invariably constructed as the site of women's enslavement.

---

93 Rosalind Miles, *The Fiction of Sex: Themes and Functions of Sex Difference in the Modern Novel* (London: Vision Press, 1994), p. 197.   94 Palmer, *Contemporary Women's Fiction*, pp 42–3.

The family is not only the arena in which acts of male violence occur, but is also the place where the patriarchal law is inculcated and the positions of masculinity and femininity are learnt.

One of the most trenchant critics of contemporary women's fiction in Ireland is Eve Patten who, in a a hard-hitting essay on women's fiction between 1985 and 1990, complains about its lack of imaginative range, its clinging to Realist and autobiographical modes, its preoccupation with identity, its reliance on a style that is 'never more than one step away from reportage'.[95] While Medbh McGuckian and Nuala Ní Dhomhnaill have extended the language and form of Irish poetry, women prose writers have rarely ventured beyond an aesthetically unadventurous confessional Realism devoted 'not only to telling the story straight, but telling very much the same story: that of the individual struggling against domestic and economic hardship, against sexual repression, against patriarchy'.[96] Patten quotes Ailbhe Smyth's explanation of women writers' lack of stylistic and imaginative development – 'There is too much suffering, violence and anger still to be written over and through. Our troubles are too raw to be denied and there is so much personal history still to be recorded'[97] – but concentrates on demonstrating the loss to women in settling for an earnest, reactionary, even philistine, Realism. The preoccupation with the theme of female identity, Patten argues, is a distraction from the real question of 'the relationship which operates between political reality and fictional narrative'.[98] The biographical novel tracing the individual woman's personal/sexual development promotes an image of a 'definitive' womanhood, a representative female norm. Authenticity is conferred on one kind of woman's experience to the exclusion of others. Patten objects because this kind of writing harbours essentialism and denies the politics of difference. These women-centred novels, Patten continues, are ironically self-limiting in that they simply reproduce the ideology which constructs women as objects: 'in the process of becoming "author"; in the need to "authorise", women writers have reinforced their sex as "object" constructed according to ideological requirements. Is there any real gain in exchanging a masculine-made myth for the "struggling woman" – stoical, angry, victimised – of a new iconography?'[99] Patten's critique of Irish women's fiction in this article is of a piece with her critique of Northern Ireland's Troubles novelists, male and female, in another article 'Fiction in conflict: Northern Ireland's prodigal novelists'. Both articles blame over-reliance on a Realist mode and fetishisation of the liberal humanist aesthetic for 'an abnormally long adolescence'[100] in the development of women's writing, and a 'creative paralysis'[101] in women's and men's imaginative engagement with the Troubles. In both articles she looks for a more intellectually challenging fiction, a fiction which would, through the postmodern aesthetic modes of irony, self-consciousness, per-

95 Eve Patten, 'Women & Fiction 1985–1990', *Krino*, 8–9 (1990) pp 1–7, p. 2.   96 Ibid., p. 1.   97 Ibid., p. 1. 98 Ibid., p. 2.   99 Ibid., p. 4 .   100 Ibid., p. 1.   101 Patten, 'Fiction in conflict, p. 129.

spectivism, and displacement, renegotiate the terms of representation of both women and the Troubles.

If women's writing of the North is overwhelmingly Realist, that may be because it is designed to fulfil a reassuring and supportive function in the field of sexual politics, and to provide Northern Irish women, anxious to recognise themselves amidst the turmoil, with positive images of female identity and women's community. Some writers influenced by deconstructive and psychoanalytic theories – Briege Duffaud, Lionel Shriver, Deirdre Madden – take a more sceptical view of Realism, challenging its assumptions of a unified subject and of the text as a transparent medium reflecting authentic experience. But even these more radically experimental writers, aware that the disruption of the subject and the dispersal of the text can become just another orthodoxy, still tend to cling to some residual sense of the unitary self and the Realist text.

Christine St Peter, in her book, *Changing Ireland: Strategies in Contemporary Women's Fiction* (2000), takes issue with Patten's criticisms of women's writing:

> With particular kinds of male experimentation firmly in mind as model, one will fail to see how women's texts radically de-center and re-center the value structure of the narrative tradition, engendering the subject in language, and creating a wholly new relation among reader, writer and text.[102]

By examining women writers' strategic re-workings of inherited genres such as the 'self-begetting novel' (metafiction in which the writer writes about writing), 'exilic writing', 'historical fiction', 'the *Bildungsroman*', 'fictionalised memoir', 'classic Realism' and 'war literature of the North', St Peter discerns a significant, varied, distinctively female intervention in the literary representation of women in contemporary Irish fiction. Writing from within the language and culture that excludes her, St Peter insists, the woman writer may yet devise strategies of deviation from representational norms, speak through the gaps, exploit the system's internal contradictions. From a position, as Eavan Boland put it, 'at an oblique or disruptive angle to the tradition',[103] the woman writer is well placed to promote new seeing and introduce a subversive potential. In light of St Peter's urgings, we should not underestimate the extent to which Northern Irish women's voices, traditionally subordinated, occluded or marginalised, have managed to intrude new perceptions and values, new feminine forms of subjectivity, as alternatives to the dominant patriarchal, totalising discourses of Nationalism and Unionism.

---

102 Page 15.   103 Jody Allen Randolph, 'An interview with Eavan Boland', *Irish University Review*, 23, 1 (Spring-Summer 1993), p. 130.

Which of these views of the world, of the North, of the Troubles, is the most valid? While I have attempted to provide a map of the various positions which may be taken up in reading and interpreting Troubles fiction, I have no wish to claim an inevitably spurious neutrality on the question of writing and reading the North. All writings and all readings are ideologically conditioned, some more so than others. Traditional liberal humanism, with its roots in Romantic notions of imaginative unity and wholeness and British 'common-sense' empiricism, serviced a backward-looking, imperialist and reactionary view of culture: the powerful new discourses outlined above allow us to examine fundamental questions about identity and subjectivity, the nature of representation, and the processes of history, yet no new theory can expect to accommodate fully the richness, variety and unpredictability of actual life. Certain fictions illustrate certain literary and ideological perspectives, but any fiction may also be read 'against the grain' from critical standpoints based on alternative ideas of history, politics and representation.[104] By mobilising a variety of critical paradigms we can produce alternative readings and problematise received readings; we acknowledge different ways of constructing identity, history, community, nation; we recognise the politics of difference encoded in texts, which might otherwise remain critically disenfranchised, outside the pale of academic study; we are able to see beyond the texts, to see how Troubles fiction functions and can be made to function in ideological or hegemonic ways, for literature is always potentially an apparatus for colonising the subject. Liberal humanism espouses 'timeless' human truths, but the feminist or Republican or Loyalist activist may not see them as such. Rather, these readers may feel that they are being 'colonised' in being asked to accept as universal values which they do not recognise as their own. An eclectic methodology allows for possible crossings of epistemlogical, political and cultural borders, an opening up of new interpretative spaces. It challenges the reader to merge various interpretative modes, to read in a multi-discilplinary fashion and thereby complicate univocal or essentialist notions of identity and meaning. The different theories themselves cross-fertilise each other. Feminist, Marxist, psychoanalytic, postcolonialist, post-

---

104 This obviously has important implications for the organisation of this study. The placing of particular writers and novels under the headings of 'Popular Fiction', 'Liberal Humanism', 'Postmodern Humanism', 'Political Fiction' and 'Women's Writing' can only be regarded as provisional, a matter of critical convenience, for the categories are not watertight. All the writers and novels considered in subsequent chapters could be analysed very profitably under different banners. For example, Danny Morrison's *The Wrong Man* or Colin Bateman's novels might easily have been considered under 'Popular Fiction'; Seamus Deane's *Reading in the Dark* might have found itself in the 'Postmodern Humanism' rather than the 'Political Fiction' chapter; Frances Molloy, Briege Duffaud and Deirdre Madden might have been taken to illustrate aspects of 'Women's Writing' rather than 'Postmodern Humanism'. Benedict Kiely is considered in two different chapters, first as a traditional Realist and then as a Postmodernist.

modernist, historicist, culturalist criticisms have all contributed to their mutual development. My own position embraces all these materialist currents which constitute a major critique of the dominant liberal humanist cultural position, questioning – but not necessarily demolishing – traditional concepts of individual autonomy, the unity and stability of the self, the universality of human values.

CHAPTER TWO

The Troubles as trash

There are a number of reasons for including popular fiction within this study of Northern Ireland's literary culture since the late '60s. The huge sales of popular fiction indicate its importance as a major site of ideological and cultural production. Popular fiction commands a much wider readership than 'serious' literature and so, arguably, has had a much greater influence than 'serious' literature in shaping public perceptions – especially those abroad – of the Northern Irish conflict. Secondly, the fact that popular fiction is genre-based means that the Troubles have been constructed predominantly in terms of the conventions which govern the thriller form. Since the thriller works primarily to evoke feelings of suspense, excitement, exhilaration, fear, other narrative elements, such as complex characterisation or moral conflict, are subordinated to the demands of the genre. The Troubles thriller may create a vivid impression of a world of emergency and danger, but at the expense of other important aspects of Northern Irish experience which remain unwritten – though, clearly, even 'serious' writers have often found the basic format of the thriller a useful framework within which to write the North. Thirdly, the reductive nature of popular fiction, its tendency towards cliché and stereotype, means that the Troubles thriller has shaped, reinforced and given wide circulation to unhelpfully simplified ideas and images of the Northern Irish conflict.

Conventional literary criticism, its assumptions and methodology, is designed to address the question of aesthetic value, to distinguish between 'major' and 'minor' literature. This is never an ideologically-free process, and the procedures of criticism cannot be deployed in any straightforwardly innocent or unselfconscious way. Thus, in the chapters which follow, analysis of 'serious' literature will take account of various reading positions that may be adopted in approaching these fictions, and close formalistic readings of the texts will be informed by consideration of their relationships with social, historical, political and literary contexts. Popular fiction invites an even more deliberately sociological criticism, a criticism capable of showing how popular fiction speaks the history of its time, the tensions and contradictions within society, the needs and interests of its mass readership, though, as the Marxist critic Tony Bennett says, even popular fiction need not simply be 'collapsed back into the conditions of production from which it derives'.[1] The methodology employed in con-

1 Tony Bennett, 'Marxism and popular fiction' in *Literature and History*, 7, 2 (Autumn 1981), p. 151. Reprinted in Peter Humm, Paul Stigant and Peter Widdowson (eds.), *Popular Fictions: Essays in Literature and History,*

sidering specific Troubles thrillers in the second part of this chapter will therefore combine historical and literary criticism in order to demonstrate the specific ways in which the practices of writing negotiate ideology and history by means of the formal strategies peculiar to them.

Following Levi-Strauss' 'The structural study of myth', some commentators have discussed popular fiction as a form of urban myth or folktale which serves an ideological function in resolving contradictions within society. Stephen Knight, in his book *Form and Ideology in Crime Fiction* (1980), comments:

> Social function has been a recurrent theme in recent discussions of cultural products. A crucial notion has been that stories, myth, books, rituals are not so much an answer about the world, but a set of questions shaped to provide a consoling result for the anxieties of those who share in the cultural activity – the audience. Cultural productions appear to deal with real problems but are in fact both conceived and resolvable in terms of the ideology of the culture group dominant in the society.[2]

Knight emphasises the way ideology may be read through form as well as content. According to this argument, the examination of the internal structure of the narratives of popular Troubles thrillers and romances can provide important indicators of dominant cultural and political values. The text need not be taken as offering a simple reflection of external conditions, but, as Pierre Macherey has shown in *A Theory of Literary Production* (1978), may be more appropriately construed as a site of ideological struggle. The narrative, through an ensemble of imaginary processes, seeks to construct a coherent fictional world, smoothing over or magically reconciling ideological contradictions. But these stress-points, Macherey demonstrates, allow us to glimpse the repressed meanings in the text – what Fredric Jameson calls the 'political unconscious' of the narrative.

Macherey's theory of the text's illusory unity and therefore subversive potential contrasts with John Cawelti's emphasis, in *Adventure, Mystery, and Romance* (1976), on the consensual role of the 'formulaic' text of popular culture, which he distinguishes from the function of the 'mimetic' or 'elite' fiction which is to challenge us with representations of life's complexity and unknowability:

> The mimetic element in literature confronts us with the world as we know it, while the formulaic element reflects the construction of an ideal world without the disorder, the ambiguity, the uncertainty and the limitations of the world of our experience.[3]

(London and New York, Methuen, 1986), pp 237–65, p. 250.   2 London: Macmillan, p. 4.   3 Chicago: University of Chicago Press, 1976, p. 1.

This neat division is highly problematic since popular fiction can be anarchic, subversive, and operate at a distance from the dominant ideology, as the example of Colin Bateman's comic thrillers or Ronan Bennett's bleak, existential thriller, *The Second Prison*, would demonstrate. The relationship between popular fiction and ideology operates in a more dialectical fashion than Cawelti's theory implies. In the Marxist functionalist analysis, the question of value is abolished altogether. For Tony Bennett, the need to distinguish between 'popular' and 'elite' is a misplaced bourgeois obsession: 'In place of a theory of value, then, Marxism's concern should be with the analysis of "the ideological conditions of the social *contestation* of value".'[4]

Much of the discussion of popular culture is informed by the Marxist cultural theory of Louis Althusser. Althusser was concerned with the way ideology operates on us at an unconscious level, transforming us into subjects willing to accept our arranged positions in the productive process of society. The dominant culture wins obedience not only through force – the Repressive State Apparatus of police and army, but by seeking consent through the Ideological State Apparatus – the legal and education system, the Church, media, popular culture, the institution of the family. Ideology 'interpellates' or hails the subject to its side through the linguistic, symbolic and discursive order. In this theory, popular fiction may be viewed as a textual operation of 'audience positioning'. Although relatively autonomous, popular fiction nevertheless represents an important social intervention involved in organising and producing individual and social consciousness by naturalising ideology and rendering it as common sense. However, hegemonic control can never be total. There are always emergent forms of consciousness and representation which threaten the hegemonic order. The text, as Macherey emphasises, can become a site of struggle between hegemonic and counter-hegemonic forms.

Where the 'serious' Troubles fiction has been largely the work of indigenous writers – mostly from the North (relatively few Southern writers have been attracted by the subject), the large majority of popular Troubles thrillers have been written by English writers. In the popular thriller's representation of the Troubles, that is, the views of the British cultural and political establishment tend to predominate. Bowyer Bell, in a *Hibernia* review (1978) entitled 'The troubles as trash', presented this composite picture of the Northern Irish Troubles as gleaned from seven Troubles thrillers (Max Franklin's *The Fifth of November*, John Cleary's *Peter's Pence*, John St Jorre and Brian Shakespeare's *The Patriot Game*, Gerald Seymour's *Harry's Game* and *The Glory Boys*, and Jack Higgins' *A Prayer for the Dying* and *The Savage Day*) written between 1973 and 1976:

> The present violence apparently arose from legitimate grievances, not too specifically detailed, of the Catholic community – the Protestant complica-

4 Tony Bennett, 'Marxism and popular fiction', p. 246.

tion is largely avoided. The IRA, however, focuses almost entirely on the struggle for a united Ireland ... As a revolutionary organization no one has much time for the Provos: bloody but inefficient, lacking in vision, heartlessly cruel, redeemed if at all by a few idealists ... The moral nearly every time is that violence corrupts both the cause and the man. The more complex the man corrupted, the better the thriller; but never, never is there an indication that violence in fact may pay decent wages in the coins of political power. The common reader is not yet ready for a politically successful 'terrorist' organization as once he was not for the good red Indian ... Thus in some small strange way the thrillers on Irish matters may have played a part in the British campaign to restore order, if not justice, to Ulster. In bold strokes of black and white, they have painted the jolly ploughboy, the Irish Rebel, the romantic gunman, as a terrorist, futile, brutal, at best misguided, at worse a callous killer. Surely the British could not ask for more.[5]

According to Bell, these attitudes, 'though hardly profound', represent 'the wisdom of the common reader'.[6] It is true that these novels take little interest in the social and political basis of physical force Republicanism in Ireland, and it is true that they generally present the IRA unsympathetically, but it would be wrong to imply, as Bell does, that these are simply the attitudes of British colonialism. Rather, they reflect not just British public opinion but the majority opinion inside Ireland, North and South, if local and national voting figures up to 1990 are anything to go by.[7] On a further point, Bell correctly notes the way the violated moral sensibility takes refuge in the consoling fiction that crime doesn't pay and terrorism is counter-productive. This interpretation of events, however reassuring it may be to the state authorities, is, as Bell implies, questionable, for what history shows is that violence, or the threat of violence, does pay political dividends. Both the twenty-six county Republic and the Northern Unionist statelet were born out of violence in 1921; it was the escalation of violence on the streets in 1972 which forced the British government to meet with the IRA, and it was Loyalist violence in 1975 which scuppered the 'Sunningdale Agreement' .

   Richard Deutsch, in his review, '"Within two shadows": the troubles in Northern Ireland', which appeared three years earlier than Bell's, concentrates on Troubles fiction by Irish writers: W.A. Balinger, Peter Leslie, Martin Waddell, James Carrick,

5 *Hibernia*, 20 January 1978, pp 21–2, p. 22.   6 Ibid., p. 22.   7 The IRA's political wing, Sinn Féin, won 11.3% of the vote in the May 1989 local council elections in Northern Ireland, and 9.2% in the European Parliament election in 1990, while in the Republic of Ireland general election in June 1989 they won only 1.2% of the vote. Subsequent voting figures in the North, however, indicate a steady strengthening of support for Sinn Féin/IRA: in the 1997 election in Northern Ireland, Sinn Féin's vote went up to 16.1% of the total poll, which they improved on again in the 2001 general and local elections.

Terence de Vere White, Shaun Herron, Walter Hegarty, Harry Barton and Joan Lingard. Deutsch sees the Troubles thriller as an extension of folklore and oral tradition which unquestioningly and simplistically reproduces the popular, deterministic view of the conflict as a tribal war: 'For the writers studying this polarised northern society everything is clear cut, and they indulge in a dichotomy which already existed in the mental patterns of their ancestors: a closed society with its two cultures. Sectarianism is part of their identity.'[8] Unwilling to interrogate their own positions, these writers, according to Deutsch, are concerned simply to repeat the myths and values of the cause or community to which they belong. The result is, not surprisingly, 'a somewhat cliché-ridden explanation of the conflict',[9] usually in terms of religious difference. Deutsch's review is an odd, contradictory mixture of fatalistic acceptance of the limitations of this fiction as unavoidable (the fiction is 'clear cut' because the society is 'clear cut' – the writers are only telling it like it is) and a more recognisably literary critical concern with the writers' imaginative failure, their lack of distance, the absence of any exploratory, forward-looking or utopian dimension, the 'narcissistic provincialism'[10] which underlies their assumption of the uniqueness of the Northern conflict.

In his essay, 'Rough rug-headed kerns: the Irish gunman in the popular novel' (1980), Alan Titley, a Dublin critic and broadcaster who writes in both English and Irish, places the popular novel on Irish affairs in a long line of English travesties and traductions of the Irish character from Spenser and Shakespeare to Kingsley and Kipling:

> ... the Irishman as a nasty brutish creature of dim wits, uncouth appearance and, more dangerously, of inexplicable mind is alive and not so well and usually dying in the modern popular thriller thrown up, in the last ten years, by the Northern Ireland conflict.[11]

The IRA gunman is such a stock figure, simplified and diabolised: 'In popular fiction, to be a terrorist is to be completely understood'.[12] With the melting away of the Cold War, Titley claims, the IRA rather than the KGB has supplied the bogeymen of popular consciousness, hate figures who come complete with 'the general xenophobic undertones' of the thriller genre and the traditional 'disdain for colonized peoples, among them the Irish'.[13] In this recourse to stereotype and cliché, Titley says, popular fiction refuses to face up to or to investigate the causes of conflict or the reality of the gunman.

8 In Patrick Rafroidi and Maurice Harmon (eds.), *The Irish Novel in Our Time* (Publications de l'Université de Lille, 1976), pp 131–56, p. 149. 9 Ibid., p. 150. 10 Ibid. 11 Alan Titley, 'Rough rug-headed kerns: the Irish gunman in the popular novel', *Eire-Ireland*, 15, 4 (Winter 1980), pp 15–38, p. 17. 12 Ibid., p. 23. 13 Ibid., p. 26.

> The thriller gives reasons for the horror and the hate, but in the manner of a washing of hands. Ireland is a 'mad' place; the people are 'irrational'; the gunman is 'sick'. Placing all explanations beyond the rational, however, conveniently excuses us from examining the problem any further ... The picture thrillers present of the gunman is not one of a person but of a cipher – a univocal collective symbol of fear and abhorrence. The question of his private complexity, his twisted and holy humanity, is never faced. To aver that the question exists is in itself deemed horrific, illiberal, yet it is the pivotal political and literary problem to have arisen from the Northern Ireland savagery.[14]

What is at issue, in Titley's analysis, is not that thrillers endorse an ideology: all literature does that; but, first, how successful are the writer's narrative methods in embodying that ideology, and, secondly, how successful is the narrative in convincing us of the virtue of that ideology? The 'truth' of the fiction is what guarantees the validity of the ideology.

Joe McMinn, reviewing a further batch of Troubles novels in 1990, noted the remarkable proportion of such novels written by journalists – *Interface: Ireland* (1979) by Kevin Dowling, *Harry's Game* (1975) by Gerald Seymour, *Bitter Orange* (1979) by Des Hamill, and *World without End, Amen* (1974) by Jimmy Breslin. To these names might be added these other journalist-novelists: Jack Holland, Joe Joyce, Eugene McEldowney, Colin Bateman, Martin Dillon, Gavin Esler, Chapman Pincher, Gordon Stevens, Eddie Shah, Tom Bradby and John Cole. One of the common features of the thriller genre is the concern for *verisimilitude*, especially factual or technical accuracy. The journalist has the advantage of being able to draw on privileged forms of knowledge, whether of the inner workings of secret organisations such as the IRA or RUC Special Branch (as in Seymour's *Harry's Game*) or of the main players on the political scene. Yet, for all the documentary realism, these thrillers are often the work of what McMinn calls 'political tourists' who, since they do not write from deep down in the environment, are unable to give a sense of 'a people's experience of the war'.[15] Another kind of Troubles writer is what McMinn calls 'the professional Irishman',[16] authors such as Shaun Herron and T.W. Taggart who, their publishers tell us, have an Irish family connection, a qualification which is meant to vindicate, racially, their account of the situation. Referring specifically to Shaun Herron's *The Whore Mother* (1973) and T.W. Taggart's *The Patriots* (1974), McMinn considers these novels to represent 'the lowest form of social/political awareness in this selection – their values indistinguishable from those of the *Daily Express*'.[17] Yet another kind of Troubles writer who might also be expected to have insider information on the situ-

14. Ibid., p. 31.   15 Joseph McMinn, 'Contemporary novels on the "Troubles"', *Études Irlandaises*, 5 (December 1980), pp 113–21, p. 114.   16 Ibid., p. 116.   17 Ibid., p. 117.

ation is the politician turned popular novelist – Douglas Hurd, Secretary of State in Thatcher's Conservative government and author of *Vote to Kill* (1975) and *The Shape of Ice* (1998); and Danny Morrison former Director of Publicity for Sinn Féin and author of three novels (discussed in Chapter 5). As well as the thriller, McMinn identifies the romance as the other main genre of Troubles fiction. The romance, which often includes elements of the thriller, 'represents the Troubles as a separate but proximate world which impinges on the preference for a private order'.[18] McMinn's chief criticisms are directed against those fictions which refuse to take seriously any kind of historical or political motivation of the Troubles and attempt to confine their explanations to psycho-sexual motives – 'the re-emergence of some dark, mysterious atavism', 'sublimated sexual frustration or criminal deviancy', 'the return of some ancient, irrational curse on the tribe'.[19] He concludes by looking ahead to a novel which will break the mould:

> [I]t will achieve a presently unrealized distance from the values of the media and the reductionist psychologising of the thriller. Its sense of history should be more persuasive and comprehending than anything reviewed here.[20]

Writing from a Republican activist's as well as a scholar's standpoint, Patrick Magee echoes much of the earlier criticism of popular fiction's misrepresentation of the Troubles:

> What is most striking to me about the content generally of troubles fiction is the remarkable uniformity of its underlying assumptions. With few exceptions, the common theme encountered *ad nauseam*, is of Britain's role as honest broker in the North of Ireland, a referee between warring factions, or contending atavisms. Britain is rarely depicted as part of the problem; never mind, as republicans would argue, the problem.[21]

From the Republican viewpoint, the image of the Provo has been reduced to cliché and stereotype, a projection of Britain's demonised Other, the embodiment of all that is evil or villainous in the 'colonial morality tale'.[22] From his reading of Troubles fiction, Magee offers this description of the 'composite Irish republican':

> a Mother Ireland-fixated psycho-killer, aka a Provo Godfather ... The violence attributed to republicans results from an ingrained bloodlust and is not the effect or symptom of a deeper political malaise. And when romantic nation-

---

18 Ibid., p. 119.   19 Ibid., p. 117.   20 Ibid., p. 121.   21 P. J. Magee, *Troubles fiction: a critical history of prose fiction dealing with the conflict in the North of Ireland since the late 1960s,* unpublished DPhil. thesis (Coleraine: University of Ulster, 1999), pp 20–1.   22 Ibid., p. 26.

alism, via Pearse's putative call for 'blood sacrifice' doesn't provide the motivation for violence, then personal aggrandisement and enrichment, often
through drug trafficking, is frequently the slander of next resort ... Gross negatives of the IRA gunmen ... offer non-explanations that befog the issues central to the struggle in Ireland and detract from the search for a just settle-
ment.[23]

Taking a Gramscian point of view, Magee argues that the hegemonic British discourse
is preserved through political and commercial pressures and constraints. Publishers
and the book trade may be reluctant to deal with contentious material. The writers
themselves tend to be middle-class with little experience of either the Troubles or the
Republican movement.

In the light of these theoretical and critical considerations, we may now turn to
examine in some detail a selection of popular Troubles novels, each of which was not
only a best-seller but attained cult status.

Good terrorists and bad terrorists:
Jack Higgins' *The Savage Day* (1972)

This action-packed thriller opens in a prison cell on the Greek island of Skarthos.
There, an ex-British Army major, Simon Vaughan, son of an Irish mother and
nephew of an IRA hero of the 1920s, is visited by Brigadier Ferguson of the British
Army and offered the chance of escape from prison if he agrees to infiltrate the IRA
in Northern Ireland. Vaughan accepts. Under cover of running an arms consignment
from Obban to the north coast of Ireland, Vaughan's real mission is to recover for the
British Government half a million in bullion daringly hijacked and hidden by an
ageing leader of the IRA, 'The Small Man'. Vaughan's contacts are the old man's
niece, Norah Murphy, who has her own reasons for hating the British, and Binnie
Gallagher, a young gunman who idealistically thinks he can fight clean in a dirty war.
Instead of dealing, as expected, with a self-styled 'old-fashioned revolutionary',[24]
Vaughan finds himself confronted with Frank Barry's Sons of Erin, a fanatical splinter group of the IRA, who are also after the bullion. Barry takes Norah hostage, her
freedom dependent on Vaughan and Binnie delivering the bullion safely into Barry's
hands. After a series of adventures the length and breadth of Northern Ireland, on
land and at sea, disguised as British soldiers, Vaughan and Binnie return to Barry with
the bullion only to discover that Norah has been on Barry's side all the time. Norah

23 Ibid., p. 1.   24 Jack Higgins, *The Savage Day* (London: Collins, 1972), p. 166. Hereafter, page references will
be incorporated into the text.

shoots Binnie, Binnie shoots Barry, and Norah dies in a bomb-blast when she attempts to escape with the bullion in Vaughan's boat.

The novel exploits the political situation for thriller purposes. As a thriller, it is a commercial before it is an aesthetic product, and contains many predictable generic ingredients – conspiracies, chases, shoot-outs, explosions, hostage-taking, disguised identities, treacherous females. Beyond the occasional references to 1916, the Black and Tans and the split in the Republican movement into Official and Provisional IRA (which took place in the winter of 1969-70), Higgins' historical contextualisation is remarkably thin. Realism is readily sacrificed to the demands of creating strong atmosphere, high adventure and vivid character. The action proceeds at an unflagging pace and is intended to create constant suspense. Adopting the classic thriller first person narration, the novel encourages us to see things from Vaughan's point of view and thereby to identify with him. Vaughan is a typical thriller hero – the glamorous outsider, defender of the *status quo* against subversives and revolutionaries all over the world. He refuses to be identified with bureaucratic authority or national interest, and is always ready to exceed due process and take the law into his own hands. He says he doesn't take sides and that he doesn't believe in anything. He seems to be motivated by nothing more than professionalism and a vague humanitarian impulse. Like James Bond, he is the special individual, uniquely competent and resourceful, and demonstrates a similar sexual aggressiveness. Typical of Bond's sexual relationships, Vaughan's relationship with Norah begins in hostility and is dubious from the start; the hero remains emotionally unengaged and essentially alone – there is no depth of feeling, the relationship is brief, and the girl turns out to be an enemy agent. By controlling his sexuality, the hero demonstrates his superiority over women, his independence and manly strength.

Like the Bond thrillers, *The Savage Day* occupies the fictional space between actuality and fantasy, the real world and fairy-land. The description of Barry's base, Spanish Head, with its 'battlements and towers black against the night sky, like something out of a children's fairy tale' (130), foregrounds the strong element of Gothic fantasy. In the candle-lit depths of this establishment, Barry keeps his ancient uncle locked away. The uncle, 'Old Lord Palsy' (130) as Barry calls him, is 'a past Grand Master of the Orange Lodge' (130), a ludicrous male version of the mad woman in the attic. What Barry, the fanatical Republican, is repressing is his Protestant, Unionist background.

In accordance with the usually conservative form of the thriller, 'rough justice' is ultimately seen to be done, retribution is carried out, and the world returns, however temporarily, to normal. The novel traces a mythic pattern: social order is disrupted but, through the interventions of the uniquely competent and courageous hero, society's demons are exorcised and order is eventually restored. History and politics are converted to ritual process. In the melodramatic conflict between 'good guys' and 'bad guys', the 'baddies' are easily recognised: Barry who believes in the 'purity of violence if the cause is just' (90); Norah who betrays her uncle and her comrades and is responsible for the death of the saintly Binnie; and Lucas and Reilly, the Provos who plant a bomb which kills women and children. The 'goodies' are a little more ambiguous. There is the hero, Vaughan, whose methods of dealing with subversives in the past are not unlike Barry's, and whose ruthlessness has earned him the soubriquet of 'the Beast of Selengar'. 'The Small Man' is a sympathetically treated revolutionary – 'an old-fashioned kind of revolutionary' (166) who says he'll use force if necessary but would really rather negotiate. He reads Augustine's *City of God*, a counter-revolutionary text which teaches the divine authority of civil government. And there is Binnie who is appalled by the Provos' indiscriminate killing of innocent civilians, but has no compunction about eliminating Provos like Lucas and Reilly, Barry's gangsters, or British soldiers. Throughout the novel, Binnie and 'The Small Man' find themselves acting in concert with Vaughan and the Brigadier against the fiendish Barry. The hero, Vaughan, is continually crossing borders – both literally and metaphorically. While working for the British Army, he eventually finds himself running the gauntlet of British Army checkpoints across Northern Ireland in order to deliver the stricken IRA leader, 'The Small Man', to hospital in the Republic. The blurb on the novel's dust-jacket reads: 'As the story races to its climax, the lines of demarcation between Catholic and Protestant, Englishman and Irishman, even between North and South, begin to blur ... Jack Higgins, himself half Irish, presents with compassion and scrupulous fairness the crisscross of love, hate, cruelty and idealism which make up the situation in Northern Ireland today.' If indeed Higgins' high-minded intention was to affirm a common humanity underlying social division, all that can be said about its fictional working out is that it lacks even superficial credibility.

A central concern is to differentiate between kinds of revolutionaries according to their attitudes to violence. There are 'good' terrorists and 'bad' terrorists. As 'The Small Man' tells Vaughan:

> Revolutionaries, Major, like the rest of humanity, are good, bad and indifferent. I think you'll find that's held true in every similar situation since the war. We have our anarchists, the bomb-happy variety who simply want to destroy, and one or two who enjoy having a sort of legal excuse for criminal behaviour ... We also have a considerable number of brave and honest men who've dedicated their lives to an ideal of freedom (167).

'The Small Man' himself is a type of the responsible revolutionary who uses violence only as a last resort. Vaughan finds him an 'enormously likeable man' (166). Binnie is the idealist who is appalled by the killing of innocent civilians. Vaughan is 'impressed' (80) to hear from Norah about the exploits of 'The Small Man' and

Binnie at the beginning of the Troubles in Belfast when, with a handful of IRA men, the heroic duo prevented 'an Orange mob led by B Specials' (80) from attacking Catholic families on the Falls Road. But when Norah goes on to expand on the revolutionary rationale – 'We have a right to be free ... The people of Ulster have been denied their nationhood too long' (81) – Vaughan recoils from her doctrinaire fanaticism: 'It sounded like the first two sentences of some ill-written political pamphlet and probably was' (81). He is provoked to supply the counter-argument, conceding that what happened in August '69 was 'a bad business', and insisting that political changes were being put in hand and would have worked had not the IRA hijacked the civil rights movement. As well as using Vaughan's reactions to distance Nora's revolutionary attractiveness, Higgins also undermines the force of her political arguments by having her confess that the provenance of her political commitment is psychological rather than ideological. Her hatred of the present political arrangements in the North, she explains, stems from childhood trauma – her rape at the age of thirteen by a B Special. Even 'good' terrorists like Binnie cannot keep 'clean hands', his misplaced idolisation of the unworthy Nora leading him into dishonourable behaviour towards his own side. The lowest form of revolutionary life is that represented by the Provos and the Sons of Erin who have no moral qualms about the use of violence to further their cause. Vaughan sums up the novel's somewhat confused position on the question of political violence:

> Binnie and I had come a long way since that first night in Cohan's Select Bar in Belfast and I'd learned one very important thing. The IRA didn't just consist of bomb-happy Provos and Frank Barry and company. There were genuine idealists there also in the Pearse and Connolly tradition. Always would be. People like the Small Man, God rest him, and Binnie Gallagher. Whether one agreed with them or not, they were honest men who believed passionately that they were engaged in a struggle for which the stake was nothing less than the freedom of their country.
>
> They would lay down their lives if necessary, they would kill soldiers, but not children – never that. Whatever happened, they wanted to be able to face it with clean hands and a little honour. Their tragedy was that in this kind of war that just was not possible. (184-5)

According to the novel's calculus, political violence, as long as it is directed against soldiers, is acceptable. Violence is more likely to be acceptable when it belongs safely in the past and has been vindicated by history. The extreme and indiscriminate nature of contemporary Provisional violence, visited upon civilian and military alike, negates idealism and honour, and debars the Provos from legitimacy. But certain revolutionaries – 'The Small Man' and Binnie – who seem to be aligned with the Marxist-oriented Official IRA, approximate heroic status because their violence is directed against military targets and belongs, so the novel insists, to a time-honoured tradition of political idealism associated with Pearse (though ironically Vaughan inveighs strongly against romantic nationalism and the Irish cult of martyrdom) and Connolly, the champion of Irish socialist Republicanism (though neither 'The Small Man' nor Binnie shows the slightest interest in a socialist agenda).

Just gaming: Gerald Seymour's
Harry's Game (1975)

Harry's Game opens with the assassination of Henry Danby, Secretary of State for Social Services and former Northern Ireland Office minister in charge of prisons, who is shot dead outside his Belgravia home by an IRA man, Billy Downs. The British Prime Minister responds by going against on-the-ground advice from the army and the RUC and authorising an undercover SAS agent, Harry Brown, to go to Belfast to kill Danby's assassin. Prior to the writing of this novel, there had never been a successful IRA attack on a leading government figure during the recent Troubles: *Harry's Game* imagines the carrying-out of such an attack and the consequences it might have. In comparison with *The Savage Day*, in which Higgins' taste for *Boys' Own* high adventure and melodramatic effect betray him into fantasy and unreality, *Harry's Game* exhibits a much greater concern with *verisimilitude* – perhaps as a consequence of the author's journalistic background. The textual surface of *Harry's Game* is freighted with information that locates the reader in a particular urban environment (Anderstown, Falls Road, Broadway, Ardoyne) and a particular socio-historical situation. References to actual incidents such as the interception of the *Claudia* which the IRA was using to run guns from Libya (on 28 March 1973), the IRA's uncovering of British Intelligence's surveillance operation in the Four Square laundry (in October 1972), or the IRA attack on the Catholic magistrate William Staunton (on 25 January 1973) increase the sense of realism and help to establish the exact date of the action (April 1975, by Magee's reckoning).[25] Other incidental social detailing – the references to the Loyalist Tartan gangs which roamed the streets in the '70s or the Long Kesh handkerchiefs sold to raise money for prisoners' families – further helps to root the novel in historical reality. Seymour's professional experience no doubt provided him with useful close knowledge of, for example, the state apparatus and procedures involved in planning security in Northern Ireland, or the inner workings of the IRA's Army Council. The writing style demonstrates a journalistic precision in its notation of people, places and objects (particularly weapons); the precise time of day at which particular incidents take place is carefully documented.

25 P.J. Magee, *Troubles Fiction*, p. 138.

The realism, however, is only superficial. Even at the level of language, Seymour has only limited success in reproducing convincingly Belfast speech idioms, intonations and rhythms. Characterisation still relies heavily on stereotype. The novel establishes what Magee calls 'a moral equivalence' in its representation of the eponymous Harry Brown, an SAS assassin, and his antagonist Billy Downs, an IRA assassin. Both are loners, cut off from wife, family and familiar environment. Both have been singled out by their respective organisations as individuals possessing special talents and potential, and both share a sense of pride in thus being recognised. Neither man has any strong ideological or patriotic motive. Harry 'reckoned he was as disinterested now in the welfare of the great body of society as he had been (in Aden). He had been given a job to do, and he was doing it because someone had to, and by a series of accidents he was better equipped than most.'[26] He doesn't regard his quarry as an 'enemy' – 'just a target' that he has to 'eliminate' (72). Downs uses a similarly depersonalised language. He thinks of the assassination of Danby as 'a job well done' (104). Tasked with another assassination, that of a Special Branch man, Howard Rennie, Downs responds with a chilling professionalism: 'Like a mathematician attempting the answer to a complex formula, he stayed in the chair thinking on the method and manner by which Rennie would be assassinated' (170). He is absorbed only by practicalities, not by morality or ideology or history or personal feeling: 'Others determined the morality. Others had the hatred. Others turned his work into victories. he did as he was told, expertise the trade mark. The soldier in his army' (171). But neither Downs nor Harry is an utterly unfeeling monster. Against his professional judgment, Harry refrains from killing his girlfriend, Josephine, who has come to know too much; while Downs cannot entirely repress his humane feeling and shoot Rennie because he might also kill Rennie's young daughter. But while the two men are given certain similarities, Harry comes out the more attractive and likeable character. Harry has all the attributes of the stereotypical English hero – physical prowess, distinguished military service, bulldog determination. Seymour may be attempting to avoid a crude racial or religious stereotyping by making his hero a Catholic, born and bred in Portadown, but by the end of the story Harry is simply – ironically – 'the Englishman' (270, 272, 287, 289). Downs cuts a less impressive figure. Where Harry wishes his wife knew of his latest secret mission so that she could 'share in his pride' (72), Downs is despised and scolded by his wife for his involvement in the IRA. Having intruded upon the Rennie household, Downs is treated with the utmost contempt by the wife of the policeman he has come to murder: 'You're a rat, a creeping, disease-ridden little rat' (223). Frequently in the novel he is described as a rat: 'Like a rat he was, waiting in a barn with the door shut for the farmer to come' (253); he dies

26 Gerald Seymour, *Harry's Game* (London: Collins, 1975), pp 71–2. Hereafter, page references will be incorporated into the text.

'like a rat in the gutter' (296). Refusing to be intimidated, Mrs Rennie taunts her murderous intruder until 'he knew he no longer dominated the situation' (225). By the end of the story Downs's commitment has been broken. He admits that he has lost his nerve and that he is a failure: 'Failure from the élitist. More important, failure against the enemy' (276). Despairing and lonely, he doesn't care what happens to him: 'I'm finished with it. There'd be a reason to run if I was going on, but I'm not' (288). As the victorious Harry stands over his defeated adversary, Downs appears merely pathetic: 'Harry studied him hard. The other man, the opposition. Dirty, cowed and frightened – is that the terrorist?' (289). In a final ironic twist, however, Harry is also brought down, shot by a British soldier and then finished off by a bullet from his own gun in the hands of Downs' wife. Harry is a victim not only of the 'lunatic' (255) struggle in Ireland, but also of British failures or miscalculations of policy (historically and immediately) in Ireland – as indicated by the additional application of the word 'lunatic' to the in-fighting amongst British government departments and services ('this lunatic fighting between departments' (262)) which has also played a part in bringing about Harry's premature death. But where Downs dies a broken man, Harry dies convinced of the rightness of his actions: 'He (Downs) deserved to die. He was an evil little bastard. He's better off ...' (296). The ending emphasises the pointlessness of all the violence, for nothing has really changed and life returns to the way it was before. Individuals are dispensible on both sides, but the novel assumes an inexorable motion of history in which British physical and moral superiority will eventually reassert itself over an insurgent Irish Nationalism. The novel may thus be seen to reflect the view (current in some quarters in the mid-'70s) that the IRA would be unable to sustain their terrorist campaign. Seymour even ascribes this opinion to the IRA themselves: 'It was acknowledged at the highest levels of the IRA's Belfast Brigade that the campaign was at a crucial stage, the impetus of the struggle consistently harder to maintain. The leadership detected a weariness amongst the people on whom they relied so greatly' (167). It is a view which is reiterated by Mrs Rennie, the RUC man's wife, in her diatribe against Downs: 'There's no future for you boys. Your best men are all locked up. The people are sick and tired of you. You know that. Even in your own rat holes they've had enough of you' (222).

The novel in fact derives from the kind of thriller described by Stephen Knight:

> The international crime version of the thriller (the spy story as it is often and misleadingly called) developed in its first phase the racist and nationalist pattern of true Britons confounding the anti-imperial wiles of foreigners of all kinds. Erskine Childers's *The Riddle of the Sands* was perhaps the most nuanced of these novels; the Bulldog Drummond stories by 'Sapper' (H.C. McNeile) were probably the most overtly Fascist. Transmuted as it has been into the quasi-modern discourse of Len Deighton or Robert Ludlum, and

often revealing failures of faith or loyalty within the Western camp itself, the international thriller remains firmly attached to the cultural and economic wisdom of the 'free West'.[27]

The conservatism of *Harry's Game* is easily discernible in its upholding bourgeois, capitalist values through the actions of its hero who, like Higgins's Simon Vaughan, is a British Army officer drawn out of obscurity to defend the 'free' society against the anti-imperial machinations of the IRA. Yet while remaining attached to 'British' values, the novel's faith in the structures of 'British' power is not unqualified. Included in the novel is a sharp critique of the British establishment, particularly its handling of internal security. It is political interference in operational intelligence matters that condemns the hero to death. The Prime Minister, who is the one primarily responsible for putting Harry's life at risk, is a particularly unattractive figure – ambitious, autocratic, incapable of any real human feeling, always craving personal recognition, adept at cover-up and 'spin'.

But, as Knight also goes on to say, even apparently conservative thrillers can harbour elements of radical critique:

> A lot of malign 'isms' are produced and validated in the mainstream thriller, principal among them capitalism, individualism, nationalism, racism and sexism. Yet these constructs are not generated without conflict, without some challenges to their reassuring resolutions. For a start, a perception of threatening radical possibilities is innate to the role of conservative ideology. But the dialectic character of the thriller includes many other radical elements ...[28]

Knight's point is that even in a conservative thriller such as *Harry's Game* there must be an element of radical critique, a sufficient threat to the dominant society to engage the fears of the reader and activate a narrative process that can produce a consoling resolution. The novel assumes a close connection between author, liberating hero and reader, yet speaks with what Knight calls 'a partly radical voice' (175) in order to realise the very real threat represented by the IRA in the mid-'70s. The 'genuine historical fear and possibility' which *Harry's Game* dramatises is that of a highly organised enemy within the state, challenging its legitimacy and practical viability. The IRA is represented as an internal disruptive potential operating through a tentacular structure of informers, spies, lookouts, enforcers, snipers and special agents, and capable of executing particular acts of 'spectacular' violence as well as prosecuting a long war of attrition against the British colonial presence. Through its depiction of a meeting of the IRA's Army Council, the novel acknowledges a ruthless enemy led by a cold-

27 Stephen Knight, 'Radical thrillers', in Ian A. Bell and Graham Daldry, (eds.), *Watching the Detectives* (Basingstoke: Macmillan, 1990), pp 172–87, p. 173.   28 Ibid., p. 173.

blooded expert in the economy of terror: 'Like some cost-effectiveness expert or a time-and-motion superman, he (the Chief-of-Staff) demanded value for effort' (172). And though the novel rarely articulates the political causes of IRA violence, Downs, in his exchange with Mrs Rennie, gives brief, trenchant expression to the threat represented by Catholic grievance which lies at the heart of the novel:

> 'What do you know of the way we live? What do you know of what support we have? ... You don't know what life is like on the Falls, with murdering bastards like your husband to beat the shit out of boys and girls ... you don't kill the Provos just by locking a few up. We are of the people ... The people are with us. You've lost, you are the losers. Your way of life, God-given superiority, is over and finished, not us ... We're winning ...' (223-4).

The fear which that threat arouses is eventually resolved through the elimination of its human agent – but never completely resolved since, as Downs has just said, the threat comes not from a single agent but a whole community. Since the violence is the product of specific socio-political conditions, it can only be genuinely resolved through social and political reconstruction. The radical element, however, is never strong enough to undermine the conservatism of the form or reshape public opinion to any serious extent. With Downs' death, the narrative returns to a newly established, albeit uneasy, conservative stasis – the 'acceptable level of violence' which the prime minister says he is content to live with.

Harry's Game is a story of political and paramilitary intrigue, secret messages, crossing enemy lines, operating incognito, the narrative an echo-chamber of rumour and report, intelligence and counter-intelligence. Belfast is the physical correlative of the novel's labyrinthine plot:

> When he (Harry) took in the rabbit warren revealed by the reconnaissance photographs he began to comprehend the complexity of the problem. Displayed on his walls was the perfect guerilla fighting base. A maze of escape routes, ambush positions, back entries, cul-de-sacs and, at strategic crossroads, great towering blocks of flats commanding the approaches to the terrorist strongholds. (57)

Amid an atmosphere of constant danger and suspicion, Seymour explores fugitive, alienated modes of existence, the idea of life stripped of all essentialist value and conducted in the simple adversarial terms of a game. The game, Harry explains, has nothing to do with 'Queen and Country ... Forces of Right against Forces of Evil' (188): it is, rather, a simple elemental power struggle, a battle of wills, in which the stakes are life and death:

'They (the IRA) put the glove down, didn't they? That's what shooting Danby was about. To make us react and see how effectively we would counter-attack. They killed him as a test of strength. We have to get the man and the team that did it. Either we do, or they've won. That's the game'. (188)

Harry rejects the grand narratives of 'Queen' and 'Country', 'Right' and 'Evil' in favour of a primitive, anti-intellectual manipulation of combat and survival strategies. That is, the novel plays out, in terms of popular literature, some of the preoccupations and themes of postmodernism: ideas of fragmentation, dissensus and gaming; and these are configured within a cinematic narrative structure of quick cuts from one line of narrative, one locale, one centre of consciousness, to another – a technique which, as well as creating thriller tension and dramatic irony, defines a postmodernist episte-mology of narrative simultaneity, cultural multiplicity and perspectival plurality.

Internationalising the Troubles thriller: Tom Clancy's *Patriot Games* (1987)

The hero, Jack Ryan, is a thirty-one year old Irish American, a former lieutenant in the US Marine Corps and now a naval historian. While on holiday in London with his wife, Cathy, and their four year-old daughter, Sally, he witnesses an apparent kid-napping attempt. Ryan immediately assumes it is an IRA attack. However, the per-petrators are not the IRA but an ultra-left-wing splinter group, the Ulster Liberation Army. Ryan intervenes, killing one of the gang and disabling another. In hospital, Ryan learns that he has saved the lives of the Prince and Princess of Wales and their new baby. His impulsive act of bravery wins him the gratitude of royalty and of the nation. The Queen visits him in hospital and a warm friendship begins between the Ryans and the house of Windsor. But he has also made bitter enemies, and, back home in Baltimore, he and his family become the targets of evil men.

Ryan is the all-American hero – honourable, courageous, loyal, and socially responsible. He functions effectively as part of a collective enterprise (the Marine Corps, the CIA) and demonstrates the classic American virtues of self-reliance, prag-matic resourcefulness and frontier hardihood. He combines man of action and intel-lectual man, as well as being a devoted husband and father. But he's human, suscep-tible to understandable excesses, as when he's tempted to finish off the terrorist who has threatened his family rather than see him brought to justice, or when he expresses outrage at the government allowing Sinn Féin representatives into the United States. His fulsome royalism and his support for the death penalty are further markers of his right-wingism. Indeed, he finds the CIA more 'politically moderate'[29] than he is him-

29 Tom Clancy, *Patriot Games* (London: Collins, 1987), p. 287. Hereafter, page references will be incorporated into the text.

self. He despises terrorism as cowardly, unmanly and un-American, the antithesis of his romantic idea of soldiery:

> To a man, professional soldiers despised terrorists, and each would dream of getting them in an even-up-battle – the idea of the Field of Honour had never died for the real professionals. It was the place where the ultimate decision was made on the basis of courage and skill, on the basis of manhood itself, and it was this concept that marked the professional soldier as a romantic, a person who truly believed in the rules. (514)

He claims to express the revulsion of Irish-America against terrorism. Irish-America, he says, does not have a revolutionary tradition but has, rather, always been identified with state authority, civic values and establishment politics:

> ... your prototypical Irish-American is still a basic police officer or firefighter. The cavalry that won the West was a third Irish, and there are still plenty of us in uniform ... in America we are the forces of order, the glue that holds society together. (48),

Irish-America, Ryan claims, resents being regarded as 'relatives of terrorists' (48). His own father, he protests, was a police officer who spent his life 'taking animals like that off the streets and putting them in cages where they belong' (48). In Ryan's mind, Irish political violence is equated with gangsterism: the attempt to kidnap the Royals takes place 'just like some Chicago gangster movie' (5); like 'something right out of a Dodge City movie' (18); and, in explaining to the Queen why he acted to save the lives of the British royal family, he compares the IRA to the Mafia: 'I guess I understand how Italians feel about the mafia' (48).

Various narrative techniques are used to reinforce and generalise Ryan's deeply hostile attitude to Irish Republicanism. American honour, the novel seems to say, depends on the extirpation of any residual sympathy with terrorists or those, like Sinn Féin, associated with them. In a brief, digressive encounter, Clancy dramatises a fantasy of purgation. The episode involves Ed Donohoe, an FBI man, and his uncle, John Donohoe, a naive Hibernophile who owns the Patriot Club in Boston. Armed with some photographs of victims of terrorist attacks, Ed visits his uncle and, after quickly converting him to a more realistic view of terrorism, delights in seeing uncle John eject a Sinn Féin delegate from the bar. Another digressive encounter occurs at a lecture Ryan attends at Georgetown University. There, he meets Platonov, a Secretary from the Soviet embassy, who is just as anxious as Ryan's Irish Americans to disown the IRA's revolutionary claims:

My country has no business with those IRA madmen. They are not revolutionaries, however much they pretend to be. They have no revolutionary
ethic. It is madness, what they do. The working classes should be allies, contesting together against the common enemy that exploits them both, instead
of killing one another. (426)

Despite the Secretary's anti-IRA sentiments, he is nevertheless allowed to pose some
difficult considerations for Ryan, such as the idea that the early American colonists
were themselves once victims of British imperialism and were prepared to take up
arms in the cause of political and economic self-determination.

Generally, however, Clancy's terrorists are never allowed to attract much sympathy or even understanding. The ULA leader, Kevin O'Donnell, is portrayed as a
megalomaniac, 'the most ruthless chief of security the Provos had ever had' (73).
O'Donnell, we are told, has used his power as counterintelligence boss to purge the
IRA of political elements he disliked, until he himself was ousted from the movement. Sean Miller, who goes after Ryan, has no compunction about shooting a comrade in cold blood for daring to criticise him. Contemplating his would-be abduc-
tor, Ryan thinks of Miller as a psychological aberration, ordinary yet monstrous:

What sort of person, Jack had wondered for weeks could plan and execute
such a crime? What was missing in him, or what terrible thing lived in him
that most civilized people had the good fortune to lack? The thin, acne-scarred
face was entirely normal .... Then he looked at Miller's eyes. He looked for ...
something, a spark of life, humanity – something that would say this was
indeed another human being. It could only have been two seconds, but for
Ryan the moment seemed to linger into minutes as he looked into those pale
gray eyes and saw ... *nothing*. Nothing at all. (121-2).

Animal imagery is liberally used to present the character. In court, face to face with
Ryan, Miller 'looked at Ryan as a wolf might from behind the bars ... he was a predator, looking at a ... thing – and wondering how he might reach it' (133). Re-captured
at the end of the novel, Miller is merely pathetic: 'He still looked like an animal to
Jack, but he was no longer a predator' (600).

Clancy is writing for an international, not an exclusively Irish, readership. He plays
on the exotic appeal of British history and royalty and, ever helpful to his American
reader, provides glosses on local and national terminology, explaining what 'RUC',
'Garda' and 'IRA' mean (though his invention of a Republican splinter group with
the word 'Ulster' in its name – the 'Ulster Liberation Army' – betrays an outsider's
lack of political awareness). The novel sounds a particularly American and – in light
of the apocalyptic events of 11 September 2001 – prophetic note of anxiety about the

threat posed by international terrorism. The ULA is depicted as part of a global terrorist organisation, it uses weapons supplied internationally, it trains in the Libyan desert, and it operates not just in London but in the United States (Northern Ireland does not figure as a location of action at all in the novel). By giving the ULA and IRA a primarily Marxist-Leninist rather than anti-colonialist agenda, he misrepresents militant Irish Republicanism in order to associate it with the 'Red Scare', which would have more relevance to American readers: IRA spokesmen are accused of suppressing their movement's Marxist-Leninist affiliations when fund-raising in America, hiding their ambition to turn Ireland into 'another Cuba' (223). The novel also celebrates a new era of international co-operation to eliminate terrorism. This is clearly an important theme for Clancy as his choice of epigraphs would suggest. The first is from Edmund Burke: 'When bad men combine, the good must associate; else they will fall one by one, an unpitied sacrifice in a contemptible struggle.' The novel is devoted to imagining this desired combination of the forces of good in action: the FBI and CIA working harmoniously together and in close partnership with the British Secret Service and the French counter-terrorist forces – an image of friendly co-operation between sovereign states which contrasts with the petty rivalries and deadly dissension amongst the terrorists. The second epigraph is from William H. Webster, FBI Director, and dated 15 October 1985:

> Behind all the political rhetoric being hurled at us from abroad, we are bringing home one unassailable fact – [terrorism is] a crime by any civilized standard, committed against innocent people, away from the scene of political conflict, and must be dealt with as a crime ...
>
> [I]n our recognition of the nature of terrorism as a crime lies our best hopes of dealing with it ...
>
> [L]et us use the tools that we have. Let us invoke the cooperation we have the right to expect around the world, and with that cooperation let us shrink the dark and dank areas of sanctuary until these cowardly marauders are held to answer as criminals in an open and public trial for the crimes they have committed, and receive the punishment they so richly deserve.

Webster's policy of criminalisation was of course the policy adopted by Margaret Thatcher in 1976 when she precipitated the hunger strikes by declaring Republican prisoners common criminals and refusing them political-prisoner status. It is also the aesthetic policy adopted by Clancy in *Patriot Games*, where he de-politicises the Troubles and reconstructs them as a mythic, moral conflict between 'good guys' and 'bad guys'. The 'bad guys' are not motivated by social or political ideals but are presented as either power-hungry like O'Donnell or psychopathic like Miller. The main action of the novel – Miller's vengeful pursuit of

Ryan and his family – takes place in the States and has nothing to do with the political convulsions of Northern Ireland. Terrorism is just a deadly game. As Robby Jackson, ace aviator and friend of Ryan, says: 'War isn't a game, it's a profession. They (terrorists) play their little *games*, and call themselves patriots, and go out and kill little kids. Bastards' (487). Where Seymour's Harry Brown cynically accepts that he is part of a deadly, amoral game when he comes to Belfast and gets involved in the Northern Irish situation, Ryan clings to an highminded Romantic idealism. Where Harry's actions are, to some extent at least, schematised as mirror images of the terrorist's, Ryan questions the morality of his actions: is he defending his family and serving his country, or is he too starting to play patriot games? The 'all-action' thriller treatment of criminal terrorism as dramatised in *Patriot Games* simplifies both the problem and the solution. In a Northern Ireland context, it promotes the dangerous idea of a purely military solution to the Troubles.

Clancy appears to be using his novel to attempt a rehabilitation of Irish-America, so often accused of a naively romantic attachment to the 'patriot game' back home, and a readiness to give its unquestioning support to the IRA. When the North became an issue for Irish-Americans in the late '60s, Irish Northern Aid (NORAID) was founded in 1969 by the IRA leader Joe Cahill to assist the families of IRA prisoners, but the organisation has often been accused of being merely a front to raise money for IRA arms. In the '70s the Irish National Caucus was founded to act as a pro-IRA pressure group. Amongst the Irish-American community there has been, as Tim Pat Coogan explains, strong sympathy with the physical force tradition:

> Part of the Irish-American scene is extremely radical. The famine tradition, the Fenians, the defeated Republicans of the Irish civil war period, those who emigrated because of unemployment in the fifties, or fled the contemporary Troubles, they all combine to produce a strain of thinking which worries that any tendency towards the ballot box, and away from the Armalite, is heading for a sell-out.[30]

Not surprisingly, certain sections of Irish-America objected to Clancy's version of the conflict in Ireland. He responded with an article entitled 'My views on unity' in the upmarket *Irish America Magazine* where he revealed that his research sources had included the London Metropolitan Police and the British military. No doubt Clancy's representation of the Northern Irish situation was influenced by such a perspective

30 Tim Pat Coogan, *The Troubles: Ireland's Ordeal: 1966–1996 and the Search for Peace* (London: Arrow, 1996), p. 448.

on events emanating from the British security and military establishment. What is not at all discernible in the novel is any evidence of his further claim in his article that while being resolutely opposed to Republican violence, he believed the only possible solution to the Troubles was 'the peaceful reunification of Ireland'.[31]

---

31 Tom Clancy, "My views on unity', *Irish America* (January 1988), pp 15–17. Quoted in Magee, p. 226.

CHAPTER THREE

Liberal humanism and the realist aesthetic: the terrorised imagination

This chapter examines the distinguishing features of the liberal humanist response to the Troubles, and considers the pressures imposed on the Realist aesthetic in dealing with the experience of fracture and breakdown in the social, political and personal spheres. The chapter begins by analysing four novels which focus principally on the victims of terrorism, then two novels which might be termed apologetic explorations of the mind of the terrorist.

VICTIMS

The view from the South: Terence de Vere White's
The Distance and the Dark (1973)

The Distance and the Dark considers the North and its Troubles from a Southern Irish perspective, specifically that of the Southern Protestant Anglo-Irish, who become victims of the terrorist plague emanating from the North. The novel focuses on a sensitive, middle-aged landowner, Everard Harvey, who is unhappily married to Sally, a snobbish Englishwoman, following the death of his first wife Kate. Everard's ancestral home is Mount Harvey, situated near Dundalk, Co. Meath, not far from the border with Northern Ireland. The IRA are active in the area, and, at the instigation of Seumas Gallagher, target Everard and a local man, Maurice MacCarthy, who has been making trouble for them as a member of the Forsai Cosanta Aitula, the Irish Army Territorials. Everard escapes an IRA bomb, but it blows up MacCarthy, Sally's son Michael, and Michael's nurse. Everard continues to attempt to bring Gallagher to justice, and eventually succeeds in having him arrested. Gallagher is acquitted for lack of evidence and released to a civic reception. Everard is assassinated by the IRA but believed to have been killed because of his philandering.

In his book, *The Anglo-Irish* (1972), White defines the Anglo-Irish in these terms:

> It is too broad a view that sees the Anglo-Irish as a race, they were a class ...
> The difference between them and the other Irish is not indifference to Irish
> culture ... Religion marked the dividing line ... By becoming Protestant Irish
> families became indistinguishable from the English in Ireland ... To Irish
> Catholics Protestantism conjures up every injustice that England has ever

inflicted on Ireland. In Southern Ireland because the minority is small it is tolerated; but bigotry is plain to be seen in all its ugly nakedness in the Northern counties.[1]

In the novel, Anglo-Irish families such as the Harveys and their neighbours the Grevilles, are proud of their deep roots in Ireland. Charley Greville, Everard's best friend, distinguishes between himself and bucaneer Englishmen such as the local horse trainer Percy Dalrymple, who have no stake in the country: 'Damn it all', says Charley, 'my people have been here since 1730. Imagine that, say, in the United States. I'd be a national monument' (93). Everard dates his family's arrival in Ireland back to 1639. But apart from Everard, the Anglo-Irish community as presented in the novel are not just indifferent to Irish culture, but positively hostile to it. Sally 'hates'[2] Ireland. Bertha Butcher exhibits the usual colonial attitudes, reserving her particular scorn for Bernadette Devlin. Both she and Charley are dismayed by Everard's 'cranky' (93) liberal opinions, for Everard believes himself to be as Irish as anybody else living in Ireland. As he attempts to explain to Bertha: 'I don't know more than one way to be Irish. We both belong to families that have lived nowhere else for generations ... I won't accept these degrees of Irishness. My family sent members to Grattan's parliament; so did yours, Charley. Why should we let anyone tell us we are less Irish than, say, Mr de Valera, who was born in America of a Spanish father?' (28-9). He regrets the indifference of his father and forefathers, blaming them for 'failure in sympathy' (94), and acknowledges the colonial abuse of power: 'We were like white men in Rhodesia' (94). In Everard's view, which he propounds much to the consternation of the rest of the Anglo-Irish community, there won't be peace in the country until the border disappears. He disapproves of the Republican violence in the North, but understands the reasons for it. Nevertheless, while he may feel part of Irish history and the Irish landscape and share the desire for a united Ireland, Everard is aware of his alienation from the native Irish people. He feels separated from them by 'the rules of caste' (248) which leave him isolated and lonely at the top of the 'feudal pyramid' (249). Everard's Anglo-Irishness is crucially defined by class, not by race or even by religion. As a remnant of a privileged 'caste', he feels especially vulnerable to the forces of change spreading from across the border. Like the other members of the Anglo-Irish com-munity, he sees events in the North heralding the spread of a revolutionary socialism dedicated to the complete extinction of Anglo-Ireland:

> What was the use of holding on? Even if the troubles in the North were patched up, the next state would be class war in the South. Michael would

1 London: Gollancz, 1972, p. 265–6.   2 Terence de Vere White, *The Distance and the Dark* (London: Gollancz, 1973), p. 62. Hereafter, page references will be incorporated into the text.

never be allowed to inherit the land that the Harveys had held for ten generations. (75)

This apocalyptic fear is echoed by Charley's wife, Aileen: 'If these people succeed in the North, they won't stop until they get their way down here. They want to make a Cuba of the country, because only if it were bankrupt would they be able to take it over' (95). Charley sounds a more defiantly belligerent note. Speaking of 'the average farmer' in the South, he says: 'So long as the troubles are confined to the North, they are prepared to take things easy; but they'll sing a different tune, I'm telling you, if anyone comes along and says he wants to socialise the land they've fought for for centuries' (127).

The Northern Troubles bring to the surface other forces in Southern Irish life which threaten liberal Protestant Anglo-Ireland. Directly threatened by the IRA, Everard discovers that the current Southern Government is prepared to connive in an IRA programme of murder, intimidation and ethnic cleansing rather than risk offending the primitive instincts of the Irish people. The Southern Government refuses to take firm action against the IRA and uphold the rule of law and order. There is no justice for Everard's family, or even for the local native son, Maurice MacCarthy, or for the nurse who works for the Harveys. After the deaths of Mac-Carthy, Everard's son, and the nurse, Everard has no one to turn to – not the Guards, not the law, not his wife, not his friends, not those who work for him. He is popular with the locals, but they close ranks against him either because they are frightened of IRA reprisal or because of their 'atavistic loyalties' (166). Yet Everard clings to rational, liberal democratic principles. Neither the personal tragedies he has suffered at the hands of the IRA, nor the failure of the Southern Government to enforce the law makes him any less critical of Northern Unionists, or any more sympathetic towards the Unionist determination to hold on to the reins of power.

In many ways Everard is an idealised Anglo-Irish gentleman, a handsome ex-fighter pilot, courageous, loyal, gallant, rational. His political opinions aren't swayed by personal disasters or by the disapproval of his peers. He rejects the idea of going after Gallagher himself and decides instead to confront him directly with the facts of what he has done. In that crucial interview, Everard delivers the usual liberal humanist response to terrorism, in which the central themes are conscience, law, civilisation, restraint:

> You run a Mafia here. You can laugh at law courts now; but you won't laugh forever. A time will come when my son and the other children and everyone else you have murdered will haunt you. I would really be doing you a kindness if I shot you. I could. I have a gun with me. I had almost decided to kill you. But I shan't. I would rather be Maurice MacCarthy dead than you, Gallagher, alive. (211)

The confrontation highlights the contrast between Everard's dignity and courage, and Gallagher's 'insolence' and lack of human feeling. The confrontation changes nothing but for Everard it is a kind of personal catharsis.

Gallagher is the main IRA representative in the novel, and he is consistently portrayed unsympathetically. His manipulation of MacCarthy is like 'the coils of the snake' (45) encircling its unfortunate victim; in his interview with Everard, his face is a 'sneering mask' (213). He is responsible for at least half a dozen deaths in the course of the novel. But White's language is also always satirically inflected so that the character is seen in a bizarrely comical light: 'his hair was close-cropped in the style of a lavatory brush' (53) More significantly, Gallagher's radical chic is comprehensively lampooned, his politics portrayed as naively doctrinaire and removed from any recognisable actuality:

> He talked of 'the Republic'; but it would have been a mistake to think he was referring to his country. 'The Republic' was a concept, having nothing to do with people or a place. His Presbyterian forbears had come from Glasgow at the beginning of the century to work in the Belfast shipyards. Everard arrived three hundred years before them. But Jimmy, who preferred to be called Seumas, and wrote his name in the Irish fashion ... had no doubt that the Harveys had no right to their land and that when he was in a position of power he would take it off them in the name of the Republic'. (47)

The whole conclave of IRA men to whom Gallagher introduces the hapless MacCarthy is similarly presented in a satirical light.

In the second half of the novel the political theme tends to drop out of the picture as the narrative explores the personal lives of the Harveys and the Grevilles, in particular the love affair that develops between Everard and Aileen. White incorporates several significant, universalising intertextual connections. One is when Everard construes his situation as a Greek tragedy with himself as plaything of the gods: 'the old gods of the Greeks seemed to have taken over his affairs' (299) – and, clearly, Everard's story is strongly determined by the unexpected twists and turns of fate. Another allusion is to *Hamlet*, when Everard recalls Polonius's advice to his son: 'To thine own self be true, /And it must follow, as the night the day / Thou canst not then be false to any man'. White, however, stops short of pointing up the irony of this advice as it might be applied to Everard. Everard has attempted to be true to himself, only to discover that the self is more compex and contradictory than he had reckoned, and that being true to himself can indeed render him false to others, even to his best friend, whose wife he wants to steal. Everard is a basically honourable and responsible man but the gods have conspired against him, leading him into marriage with Kate instead of Aileen and, at the end, into foolish loyalty to Sally when Aileen, whom he really loves, needs and wants him. The rueful lines which he recalls from *As You Like It* are perhaps more relevant to his story: 'Most friendship is feigning, / Most loving mere folly' (316). At the end, on his way to meet Aileen and clear the situation one way or another he is gunned down by the IRA. We are told of this event indirectly, through a conversation over lunch in the Garrick in London between two minor characters, the Englishmen Peter Cooper who is an old flame of Sally's, and Laurence Wyndham, whose uncle knew the Harveys. The shift in narrative perspective is an ironic decentering device which turns Everard's death and the Irish Troubles into marginalia, topics of casual gossip, stories of peripheral interest which take place in the distance and the dark.

'The distance and the dark' also characterises a corrupt modernity. The first of White's epigraphs, from Browning's *The Ring and the Book*, expresses longing for recovery of a prelapsarian innocence – 'That still, despite the distance and the dark,/ What was again may be ...' The second, from Stevie Smith's *Novel on Yellow Paper*, reaffirms the central values of liberal humanism in a fallen world: 'Now I say. How difficult is life nowadays. But there must be freedom and generosity and truth and candour. There must be love and wisdom and honour. Nothing must prevent this, there would better be death'. In the story of Everard Harvey these grand liberal abstractions – freedom, generosity, truth, love, wisdom, honour – are put to the test in both private and political life. While staring into the dark, the novel still concentrates on man as the source of meaning and value.

Manichaeism and melodrama: Eugene McCabe's *Victims* (1976)

Victims, a story with a strong topical appeal, tells of a ruthlessly planned hostage-seizing operation involving five IRA operatives – Leonard, the silent, 'ice-cold'[3] leader; Lynam, a female member of the team; the psychopathic Gallagher; and the two half-wit McAleer brothers. Their victims are an Anglo-Irish family – Colonel Armstrong, his wife Harriett and their daughter Millicent – and their friends who happen to be spending the evening with them – Canon Plumm; Dr Cardwell an American military historian; and Alex Boyd-Crawford, a dissolute Unionist MP and Harriett's ex-lover. These are cultured and complex individuals who find themselves suddenly – dangerously – involved in a conflict from which they had always thought themselves removed.

Victims is the quintessential liberal humanist novel, centred on 'character' and involved with liberal values. One of the central themes of the liberal humanist novel is the crisis of liberal humanism in a world where the individual is increasingly subject to external controls, whether from a bureaucratic state, the pressures of the industrial

---

3 Eugene McCabe, *Victims: A Tale from Fermanagh* (London: Gollancz, 1976), p. 108. Hereafter, page references will be incorporated into the text.

urban environment, the conditioning influences of late capitalist society, or, as in this novel, the encroachments of revolutionary politics. In *Victims*, humanist values, vested in a social élite, the Big House family and their friends, are under siege, forced to confront the knowledge that society is not static and that the forces of dehumanisation are abroad, bent on cleansing the world and imposing their conception of moral order upon society. Articulacy and complexity of mind are the properties of this liberal élite. Like Beckett's characters, McCabe's victims are waiting for the end, but not as near sub-human, ruined creatures talking themselves into non-being; rather, McCabe's victims are dignified individuals capable of heroic acceptance of their fate. They represent an individualism which, unlike American versions, is not that of the isolated hero asserting himself in the face of a hostile world, but an individualism which is placed in dialectical relationship with a complex social and moral order, and seems doomed to tragic defeat.

W.J. Harvey's book *Character and the Novel* (1965) suggests the ideological implications of the centrality of character:

> We may fairly say that the novel is the distinct art form of liberalism, by which I mean not a political view or even a mode of social or economic organization but rather a state of mind. This state of mind has as its controlling centre an acknowledgement of the plenitude, diversity and individuality of human beings in society, together with the belief that such characteristics are good as ends in themselves. It delights in the multiplicity of existence and allows for a plurality of beliefs and values ... Tolerance, scepticism, respect for the autonomy of others are its watchwords; fanaticism and the monolithic creed its abhorrence.[4]

As a novel of character, *Victims* dramatises this liberal, pluralist world-view and its abhorrence of the kind of fanatical commitment to a monolithic belief system which characterises the IRA revolutionists. At the same time, the liberal view comes under pressure. The political activists in the novel would be unlikely to accept Harvey's statement that liberalism is 'not a political view or even a mode of social or economic organization' (though to call liberal values or aspirations 'political' does not make them any the less real or valid). Repeatedly, McCabe's Provos voice their condemnation of a colonial reality of racist exploitation and dispossession which masquerades as liberal respect for other people, uncontaminated by ideology. Canon Plumm is included as immediate, living proof of the outrageous bigotry that can lurk behind the civilised, liberal facade, though at the end, even he displays a heroic dignity, a genuinely Christian forgiveness ('I want you ... all of you to understand that while I

4 London: Chatto and Windus, 1965, p. 24.

abhor your methods profoundly and dislike your politics, I hold no hatred in my heart', 114), and is given the large and luminous insight that all are victims – 'we are what we are because of history' (114). The terrorists never pose any serious moral challenge to the liberal humanist world-view, not least because they are constructed in the very terms of that world-view. As such, they (with the exception of Lynam) are never granted a full humanity but presented in the reductive terms of stereotype and cliché. To the violated liberal humanist sensibility, the terrorist represents all that is taboo, beyond reason, inadmissible, unrepresentable. In an influential essay, 'Against dryness', Iris Murdoch wrote: 'Real people are destructive of myth, contingency is destructive of fantasy ... Literature must always present a battle between real people and images; and what it requires now is a much stronger and more complex conception of the former.'[5] If McCabe's portrayal of victims – and that includes Lynam – incorporates a sense of the impenetrability and unpredictability of real life which resists appropriation, whether political or aesthetic, his portrayal of the committed revolutionist is notable for the way it subdues the contingency of life to rigid authorial manipulation. His terrorists remain creatures of myth and fantasy. Lynam is the only one who becomes a real person because the author understands the reluctant terrorist's horror of killing, her self-doubt and scepticsim about the value of revolutionary struggle much better than he understands the motives of the serious and committed activist.

Camus has said: 'We are in a world where we have to choose between being a victim or a hangman – and nothing else.'[6] Camus' logic of the excluded middle produces an extremist, essentially melodramatic view of life, and it is largely such a view which obtains in *Victims*. Melodrama reduces life to a manichaeian struggle of good and evil (though Camus avoids such absolute moral values). The terrorised imagination finds its natural expression in the terms of melodrama – strong emotionalism; moral polarisation and schematisation; extreme states of being, situations and actions; overt villainy; persecution of the good; rhetorical extravagance; intrigue and suspense. Evil, fully personalised, and strongly but but not neccssarily complexly characterised, controls the plot. From the moment the IRA gang arrives at Inver House the victims are reduced to passivity, and we are drawn into the experience of nightmare. Good and evil are experienced largely as affect. As in that sub-species of melodrama, the Gothic novel, *Victims* recognises the diabolical forces which inhabit the world and, in bringing them to light, dramatises the anxiety caused by the apparent triumph of the darkness. Frank O'Connor's classic hostage narrative 'Guests of the Nation' breaks down the divisions between victims and executioners, English and Irish, the political and the personal, to propose a liberal vision of richly realised humanity and universal

5 In Malcolm Bradbury (ed.), *The Novel Today* (London: Fontana, 1975), p. 24.   6 Albert Camus, *Carnets 1942–1951*, trans. Philip Thody (London: Hamish Hamilton, 1966), p. 71.

brotherhood. When trust and friendship are betrayed and the narrator at the end confronts the eternal silence of the infinite spaces, the story is turned into a modern myth of disorientation and failure. In contrast, McCabe's novel, adhering to a structure of bipolar moral absolutes, apprehends a complex world in terms of intense and primal conflict, and strives to affirm, despite the irruptions from the demonic depths, the existence of a moral universe.

The Colonel, patriarchal remnant of Anglo-Ireland and head of Inver House, is first seen in the context of the Inver agricultural show which takes place each year under the Colonel's patronage. The Colonel operates under the banner of British imperialism and Unionist hegemony: 'On a pole above the marquee a Union Jack flapped in the south wind. From it triangular bunting in red, white and blue stretched round the enclosure ... Across the entrance from the road an embroidered cloth read: WELCOME TO INVER SHOW GOD SAVE THE QUEEN' (7). The music blaring from the speakers is 'Land of Hope and Glory' (7) and 'The Eton Boating Song' (15). The presence of British soldiers, including 'a tall limber Negro' (13), based nearby are further reminders of British imperial power. However, ominous signs appear within the field of carnival. A horse has broken its leg and 'will have to be destroyed' (8); the show is infiltrated by the two IRA conspirators, Leonard and Lynam, plotting to take the Colonel and his family hostage; in the enclosure 'the green sward pulsed with a violence that forced him (Leonard) to look away' (8). In this opening section, the Colonel is established as an essentially benevolent individual: he has to remove a tinker woman, but does so in a kind and courteous manner; he distances himself from the bigotry of George the blacksmith, and can understand the dilemma of Aiden O'Donnell, a Catholic barrister who feels hypocritical having to argue for justice in a social system which he considers unjust. The Colonel demonstrates the typical liberal instinct to see both sides of the question and avoid dogmatism.

Inver House, the domain of the novel's social élite, is a large, impressive lake-side Tudor house. Conversation amongst the Armstrongs and their friends is freighted with references to the rich archive of English cultural history – Shakespeare, Wilde, Wordsworth, Lamb, Shelley, Dylan Thomas, Elizabeth I; Harriett's mother played Chopin with Padereweski; Harriett is like 'an El Greco portrait' (89); the living-room is hung with Armstrong ancestral portraits; the book-case declares a proud colonial background: '*The Un-finished War*, by Eric Moore Ritchie ... The drama of Anglo-German Conflict in Africa in relation to the future of the British Empire ... includes campaigns in Africa, Cameroons and Togoland' (68). Reading this, the barbarian Gallagher delights in deflating colonial pretension: '"Or: who owns the Nig Nogs, their nuts and their nickel"' (68). Looking at another title, '*Pig Sticking or Hog Hunting*, by Sir Robert Baden-Powell', he is roused to more savage expression of colonial resentment: 'Nothing in our culture to match that ... makes you feel inferior ... humble ... we've a long way to go ... we bog, we pig-in-the-parlour Irish' (68). The

Colonel, however, insists, that his family has always represented a benign colonialism. The title of a lecture he once gave to Clogher Historical Society was 'The Armstrongs in Ulster: The intruders who contributed'. He resists the imputation of colonial exploitation, at least as far as his own ancestors are concerned: '"All so unfair", the Colonel said, "We were never absentees, my grandfather cut rents to half and nil during the famine, mortgaged the estate to feed tenants, Catholic and Protestant, one of my cousins signed the treaty for the Irish side, Harriett's father was related through marriage to Lloyd George ..."' (82). Harriett recalls both her and her husband's anger after Bloody Sunday: 'After Derry I wept, you know, and Nobby was overwhelmed ... true ... he's human ... all of us ... very human ... so terribly sad what we do to each other don't you think? He tried to 'phone Frank Carrington' (91). Entombed in the darkened living-room of Inver House, the victims demonstrate their rich humanity. Like so many sensitive, educated liberals who have appeared in previous literature, they may lack vitality and have withdrawn from the real struggles in the outside world, but their belief in freedom, reason and the rights of the individual make them protest courageously and passionately against the revolutionary zeal of their invaders. Harriett, broken by alcoholism and disappointment in marriage, detects in the terrorists' will to change the world a cruel intransigence: 'I can understand those who want to kill themselves, not those who kill others ... Hatred is so sad ... personal hatred I know only too well, but to hate an entire people, race, sect or class, is so blind, so stupid, so unending, so universal, it makes one despair' (93). Nevertheless, she recognises Lynam as 'a feeling girl' (92) – a very different assessment from that of Lynam's comrades: ' ... calculating as a cat ... makes love with her eyes open ... Christ knows what she thinks or believes' (14). These two characters, Lynam and Harriett, are united in despair, Lynam eventually discovering a stronger bond with her victim than with any of her accomplices or even her own mother: 'In ten minutes she (Lynam) seemed to understand the oblique confusion and compassion of this strange woman's mind better than she had ever understood her own mother' (94).

Contrasting with Inver House is the terrorists' base, a small two-storeyed Monaghan farmhouse with its own antithetical symbolism and iconography. The kitchen is painted brightly in green, white and gold, and is decorated with pictures of the Sacred Heart, John F. Kennedy and Roncali. Presiding over this household is Mrs McAleer, 'an Irish Queen Victoria, with De Valera's nose and Churchill's mouth' (32). Mrs McAleer is the allegorical matriarch of Republican tradition, the figure of Mother Ireland who demands the blood sacrifice of her sons: 'Above a bedside commode a frail madonna stared upwards in tears, her heart transfixed by a sword. Beside the madonna, a calendar print of Padraig Pearse, his head in a halo of flames. Underneath someone had printed in red biro, his poem "The Mother"' (32-3). Pervading this tacky Republican shrine is 'a personal fishy smell, mixed with Lysol and deodorant'. The language is calculated to alienate the reader and undermine the explanatory, legitimising and cohesive force of national myth.

Equally emblematic is the presentation of Jack Gallagher: about him hung 'the black flag of violence and death' (40). Even his colleagues recognise him as 'paranoid, schizoid' (46), 'inhuman, a mindless killer' (111). To Lynam, he is the very spirit of anarchy, 'a natural mechanism of terror and disorder' (107). He boasts about his killings and his sexual conquests. He is repeatedly associated with animals: 'Every now and then his pistol wrist gave an involuntary twitch like the tail of a caged tiger' (63); he is 'like a dog who has scented quarry and waits for it to break' (78). Gratuitously, he throws Alex's hearing-aid to the floor and smashes it, and viciously strikes Harriett when she asks about Alex. Listening to Gallagher's ravings, the Colonel comments: 'A spitting mini-Hitler ... pointless to argue with such hysterical hatred' (103). Gallagher's speech, forced to melodramatic excess, is pure self-expression, the venting of what he is; it is never anguished or self-questioning. By dismissing the character as irrational and insane his motives require no further examination.

Leonard is a cold and calculating leader who at the end strikes a deal with the British army whereby he succeeds in securing the freedom of three particularly valuable IRA prisoners, but at the price of sacrificing three of the comrades with whom he has carried out the hostage-taking mission. Usefulness to the cause is the only criterion he uses for deciding who should be handed over and who should go free. His professionalism, he believes, is what distinguishes him from Gallagher. He takes no pleasure in killing, unlike Gallagher. Gallagher, he believes, could never be a leader because he is 'too personal' (111). Leonard requires reasons for what he does. He needs 'to justify in advance, to cancel fear and doubt' (43). Thus, he attempts to rationalise his actions by repeating over and over to himself that 'the wealth and privilege of the Armstrongs in these islands and Europe had been gained by force and fraud, sanctioned and maintained by Church and State for centuries ... If London refused to negotiate they would have to kill and be killed' (43). Once he has convinced himself, nothing can shake him.

Lynam, in contrast, is a more complex creation. She is wracked by doubts. She feels 'sick' and 'odd' (9); she trembles, suffers from nightmares, feels 'ashamed' (99). She has no respect for the IRA, no patriotic feeling, no belief that revolution can effect any really meaningful change in life. She envies the victims' dignity: 'She had joined with executioners, the army of the damned' (110). Her motives for joining are unclear, even to herself: 'She had chosen freely the waking nightmare of action, the comradeship of men whose vivid words, aims and violence seemed more attractive, honest and hopeful than the hollow crafty manoeuvrings of politicians' (26). But the salvationist glamour of direct action is not the only reason she joined for later she confesses to Harriett that personal 'rejection' (93) lies behind her political commitment. 'Rejection' seems to be the story of Lynam's unhappy life: she repeats her family's rejection of her by rejecting her own child which she has had aborted, and, ironically, at the end she is rejected by her terrorist family when Leonard decides to hand her over to the British authorities. Political commitment is a symptom of psychological trauma.

While arousing some interest in the character of Lynam, McCabe's primary objective is to make us participate in the dilemma of the hostages, to view them with sympathy. Plumm recognises the failure of Christianity to provide answers, though his *Selected Sunday Readings* supplies a ritual language of dignity and comfort, and his proffered handshake demonstrates Christian forgiveness. Harriett and the Colonel re-affirm 'friendship' which is 'much better than love' (109). At the very end, Harriett finds some answer in simple connection with her environment, affirming the healing and beneficent influence of the countryside, albeit in a somewhat abrupt and generalised language. The idea of progress is in suspension. On awakening from the nightmare, only the most tentative affirmations seem possible. The novel has nothing practical to offer to efface the impressions of evil beyond simple Christian truisms of forgiveness and friendship, and Harriett's facile assertion that 'The world is still beautiful' (128). Nevertheless, if the novel is unable to complete the ritual process which sees anarchy expunged and traditional moral order confidently restored, it allows us to see the kinds of problems we must face and the resources we have to deal with them. *Victims* forces us to confront the abyss, to assume the burden of consciousness, while refusing false hopes of reconciliation to a metaphysical order (the role of tragedy) or the vision of a new society (the role of comedy).

Nativist piety, civilised outrage: Benedict Kiely's *Proxopera* (1977)

From White's Southern Protestant Anglo-Irish and McCabe's Big House Ulster Unionists, we move to another kind of terrorist victim in Benedict Kiely's *Proxopera* and Brian Moore's *Lies of Silence* – the cultivated bourgeois Northern Catholic. In Kiely's novel he originates in a traditional, rural world, in Moore's he is a mobile cosmopolite. Both novels are versions of the suborned proxy bomber narrative. *Proxopera* tells the simple, stark story of an old man, Mr Binchey, whose house is invaded by three masked IRA men who force him to drive a live time-bomb to the home of a local, fair-minded judge, while they hold the old man's family hostage. The narrative is presented largely from Binchey's perspective which, one assumes, is very close to Kiely's own. Binchey is a respectable, middle-class schoolteacher of history, Latin and English literature, a man who clearly prizes civilisation and education, who is deeply attached to place and community. From such a point of view, terrorist violence is simply desecration, and the terrorists simply 'animals'[7] (14), figures out of nightmare (35), the threatening 'other' who are ready to destroy all that Binchey holds most dear – family, friends, home, civilisation.

The novel begins with elemental landscape, with Binchey's perceptions of a timeless, magical world of nature, a legendary, fairy-tale world presided over by the goddess of the lake. Kiely uses Binchey to articulate a Heaneyesque sense of place. In his essay 'The sense of place,' Heaney tells of how in his childhood he experienced a sacral world which still retained 'some vestigial sense of place as it was experienced in the older dispensation.'[8] Heaney's totemistic, hieratic, magical landscape, 'instinct with signs' of folkloric belief, is the Celtic Eden which Kiely reproduces in his novel. This sense of place, as Heaney suggests, is 'the foundation for a marvellous or a magical view of the world, a foundation that sustained a diminished structure of lore and superstition and half-pagan, half-Christian thought and practice'.[9] Inscribed in a traditional rural culture and a pagan, Catholic metaphysics, Binchey is equally aware of loss and change, and his narration is largely expressive of a 'backward look' that is both nostalgic and elegiac. His early reference to the water-skiing on the lake initiates the opposition between an old sacral sense of nature shaped by myth and legend and the modern technological, leisured world:

> Water is a sort of god. Or at any rate a goddess. That's what people thought long ago, they called rivers after goddesses.
>
> The lake for sure had been a goddess on the day of the water-skiing. Never had he thought that he would see on his own lake the sort of thing you saw on the movies or television: Californian or Hawaiian beaches, galloping rollers, bouncing speedboats, composed naked young women on surfboards, Arion on the dolphin's back ... (4)

The refrain that runs throughout Binchey's narrative is 'the lake will never be the same again' (3, 25, 27, 93), with its variations: 'that pub would never be the same again': (68), 'that spring will never be the same again' (76), 'the world will never be the same again' (34). Binchey laments a lost golden time, a vanished innocence: 'Once upon a time a creamery can had been a harmless or lovely, even a musical object' (50). Now it contains the bomb that will destroy the town.

The central trope of modernity is the political violence that threatens and disrupts originary, formative, communal ground, but cannot ultimately annihilate it. Antaean Binchey, connected to roots and absorbed within a female, pagan, earth-orientated

---

7 Benedict Kiely, *Proxopera* (London: Methuen, 1988), p. 14. First published London: Gollancz, 1977. Hereafter, page references will be incorporated into the text.   8 In *Preoccupations: Selected Prose 1968–1978* (London: Faber, 1980), p.133.   9 Ibid.

rural and mythological order, is dispossessed and expelled from home. The three invaders are denied a human face – quite literally in that they remain hidden behind their masks, but also narratively in that they are always seen from the outside, at a distance. Terrorist violence is taken out of a political context and treated meta-physically, as the manifestation of evil and madness. By the end, the process of demonisation is complete, and Binchey curses the evil spawn to hell: 'And even if every blade of grass were an eye watching me, to hell with them, let the grass wither in the deepest Stygian pits of gloom, and blast and blind the bastards and Bertie Bigboots and Mad Minihan and that creepy half-literate Corkman' (77).

What is interesting is Kiely's re-working of the traditional nationalist trope which understands the roots of the Troubles in terms of a struggle between a mythic mother-land and a historical, imperial masculinity. Heaney has described the traditional idea as follows:

> To some extent the enmity can be viewed as a struggle between the cults and devotees of a god and a goddess. There is an indigenous territorial numen, a tutelar of the whole island, call her Mother Ireland, Kathleen ni Houlihan, the poor old woman, the Shan van Vocht, whatever; and her sovereignty has been temporarily usurped or infringed by a new male cult whose founding fathers were Cromwell, William of Orange, Edward Carson, and whose godhead is incarnate in a Rex or Caesar resident in a palace in London. What we have is the tail end of a struggle in a province between territorial piety and imperial power.[10]

In Kiely's novella the colonial intruders have metamorphosed into terrorist despoilers; 'territorial piety' struggles, not with 'imperial power', but with a Gothic Provo-vandalism. The myth of motherland, enshrining the desire for a primordial natural-ness and rootedness, is disrupted by the incursion of the arbitrary and alien forces of history in the form of the three gunmen. Kiely's novella is premised on the conservative Nationalist, anti-modernist mythic or epic construction of Irish history as the adulteration of a pure (Irish) essence by an alien intruder, but radically ironises the traditional narrative by making militant Irish Republicanism, not the forces of British colonialism, the alien intruder.

In his essay, 'Feeling into words', Heaney tells of wanting to develop a poetic response to the Troubles which would include not just the critical perspectives of 'a humane reason', but also an understanding of the tribal passions which give the conflict its 'religious intensity'.[11] (19). Heaney's nativist piety includes a strain of tribal bitterness and resentment that comes into conflict with humane reason. He can

10 Seamus Heaney, 'Feeling into words', in *Preoccupations*, p. 57.   11 Ibid.

imaginatively identify with the killers while another side of him condemns the killing. Much of his best poetry derives its power precisely from this tension. Kiely, however, refuses to enter this difficult terrain. There is no attempt to analyse the motives of the terrorist. The novel is, in fact, in retreat from the world of ideological and sectarian conflict altogether, seeking escape in the primordial, timeless world of nature and the private world of family relationships. In the end, Binchey symbolically hands the whole situation over to the authorities by driving his deadly load off the road, running the dangerous new technology to ground in the mythical, Gaelic bog, and requiring the help of the British soldiers to escape from the wreckage.

As part of his narrative procedure, Kiely makes liberal use of references to Irish and popular song, mythological, legendary and historical material, and other literature of all kinds, but (to continue the metaphor) he stops short of driving his narrative into an intertextual bog of endlessly ironic textual play. The diverse allusions and quotations may be psychologically explained in terms of the free-associating activity of the narrator's intellectually well-stocked and creatively expansive mind. Whatever disruptions threaten the desired dreamland of original piety and civility, the narrative point of view is founded on the firm belief that there *is* a correct way of seeing and behaving, there *are* permanent values, there *is* consistency of character. Kiely's powerfully nostalgic and elegiac tone bespeaks a novel which hasn't got beyond the stage of mourning the passing of the grand narratives of the past.

The moral thriller: Brian Moore's *Lies of Silence* (1992)

Lies of Silence is concerned with the way innocent and uninvolved civilians are caught up in terrorist action. Moore tells of the origins of the novel in an actual event that took place when he was in Belfast in July 1987 to receive his honorary doctorate from Queen's University:

> I was in the Wellington Park Hotel, near Queen's University, and we had a bomb scare in the middle of the night. We were all put out in the street, and I saw these French tourists there. I was listening to them, and they hadn't the slightest idea what was happening. So I thought about what happened and wondered about what it would have been like if they were killed and they didn't know who killed them.[12]

Moore has also spoken of another kind of victimage which is explored in the novel - 'the whole question of hostages ... you never hear one interview with, or one word

---

12 Quoted in Denis Sampson, *Brian Moore: The Chameleon Novelist*, (Dublin: Marino Books, 1998), p. 276.

of, the hostages and that's the silence I was interested in'.[13] In the novel, the central victims are a middle-class Catholic couple, Martin and Moira Dillon, whose home is invaded one night by a unit of masked IRA men. Dillon is ordered to take a bomb in his car to the hotel where he works, while Moira is held hostage. Faced with a decision between raising the alarm and saving the lives of a lot of people he doesn't know or keeping quiet and ensuring his wife's safety, Martin decides to defy the terrorists and contact the police. Having inexplicably escaped the attention of the terrorists, Moira also decides to break the silence and speak out against the IRA in the newspapers and on TV. Although Dillon remains apolitical and leaves Belfast to go and live with his Canadian girlfriend, Andrea, in London, he agrees to help the police by identifying Kev, whom he recognised as one of the IRA intruders. A Catholic priest who has links with the IRA warns Dillon against making the identification, and both Andrea and Moira, recognising the danger he is in, also attempt to dissuade him. At the end, when he is about to phone the police we are unsure whether it is to agree to continue with the identification or to back out of it altogether. Before we can find out he is silenced by an IRA gunman who has tracked him down through the priest.

The significance of the title is highlighted in the following passage which is focalised through Dillon as he contemplates the youthful terrorists who have broken into his home:

> Dillon felt anger rise within him, anger at the lies which had made this, his and Mr Harbinson's birthplace, sick with a terminal illness of bigotry and injustice, lies told over the years to poor Protestant working people about the Catholics, lies told to poor Catholic working people about the Protestants, lies from parliaments and pulpits, lies at rallies and funeral orations, and, above all, the lies of silence from those in Westminster who did not want to face the injustices of Ulster's status quo. Angry, he stared across the room at the most dangerous victims of these lies, his youthful, ignorant, murderous captors. What are they planing to do today, what new atrocity will they work at to keep us mired in hate?[14]

Dillon's anger and despair at the 'terminal illness of bigotry and injustice' in Northern Ireland echoes Moore's own direct statements which he made in an essay, 'Bloody Ulster', written at the outbreak of the Troubles in 1970. As Moore himself has indicated, he identifies closely with the character of Dillon, who stands at an oblique angle to the situation in the North: 'I felt as an expatriate that I wasn't the person to

---

13 Quoted in Sampson, p. 276.   14 Brian Moore, *Lies of Silence* (London: Vintage, 1992), pp 69–70. First published London: Bloomsbury, 1990. Hereafter, page references will be incorporated into the text.

write the big Northern Ireland novel, so I made the hero someone like me, who doesn't want to be in Northern Ireland, who left it, and just has no desire to go back there, hates the place, and then I'll be able to identify with him, and so that's how it came about.'[15] Dillon articulates the political view of the apolitical bourgeois liberal humanist who claims to represent 'ninety per cent of the people of Ulster' (69), Protestant and Catholic. It is a view which is vague and generalised in its analysis of the social causes of 'the injustices of Ulster's status quo', and remarkably clichéd in its picture of the terrorists as hate-filled, deluded 'victims of these lies'. In an extremely critical review of the novel, Seamus Deane doubted that 'any deep morality is involved in bearing witness against the IRA or against a corrupt system' and pointed to a number of 'improbabilities' – an IRA unit going to the trouble of making a hit in London; the closeness of the relationship between the Catholic priest and the IRA. 'The lies of silence', Deane argues – in an echo of the theorist Pierre Macherey – 'are in what this novel does not say about the North'.[16] For Deane, as for Macherey, the chief task of criticism is to articulate the silences and absences that the novel embodies. Thus, at crucial points, we might observe, such issues as the motivation of the IRA men, the inner life of the volunteer, and the legitimacy of what Foucault calls 'the discourse of the Law', are largely elided. In his book, *Crime and Ideology*, Leo Radzinowicz summarizes the liberal theory of the social causation of crime in these words: 'Society carries within itself, in some sense, the seeds of all the crimes which are going to be committed, together with facilities necessary for their development';[17] and contrasts this view with the conservative belief that criminals are born not made. Moore acknowledges the liberal view ('he stared across the room at the most dangerous victims of these lies ...'), venting his liberal outrage at the horror of the terrorist acts of transgression while remaining silent on questions about the causes of those acts or the legitimacy of the social order which is transgressed.

Moore seems to want to give the idea of 'lies of silence' as wide an application as possible. They are not only a feature of successive British governments who have refused to face the manifest injustices of the Unionist Stormont hegemony, or of the Christian Churches, or the labour movement; the 'lies of silence' are also the 'unsayable' of the terrorised Northern liberal experience – the lies of silence enforced by paramilitary terrorism and intimidation. If Dillon breaks his silence and raises the alarm, Moira will pay with her life. 'You speak to nobody' (74), he is warned by his captors: 'When the police ask you questions about us, we're all wearin' masks, you don't know names, or what we look like, nothin'. Remember, we'll know what you told them. And that goes for that wife of yours. If you value your life, you'll make sure she keeps her mouth shut' (77). At the centre of the novel is a moral debate

15 Quoted in Sampson, p. 277.   16 Seamus Deane, 'In the firing line', review of *Lies of Silence* in the *Times Literary Supplement* (20–26 April 1990), pp 430.   17 Leo Radzinowicz, *Crime and Ideology* (New York: Columbia University Press, 1966), p. 35.

between silence and safety or speaking out and putting life – others' as well as one's own – at risk. Though Dillon, on an impulse, breaks the silence and warns the authorities about the bomb, he is opposed to his wife's decision to propagandize against the IRA in the media. The lesson Moira says she has learnt is that 'You can't avoid responsibility by pretending things aren't there' (133). From the beginning, she has shown more courage and fighting spirit than her husband, making an escape bid out of the bathroom window and provocatively challenging her captors:

> 'You're not fighting for anybody's freedom. Not mine, not the people of Northern Ireland's, not anybody's. The only thing you're doing is making people hate each other worse than ever'. (62)

Moore uses her as a mouthpiece to unleash a series of tirades against the IRA:

> 'It's people like us who're the only ones who can stop them. And we're not going to stop them by letting them run our lives. Do you know what I should do? I should tell the whole world what happened to us last night. I should tell the way they treated us. I should come out into the open and say this is what happened ... We should stand our ground. And then, if we're shot, the whole world will know why we're being shot. And I don't think even the most stupid of the people who back the IRA would say that it was fair'. (137)

However, in the end she performs a dramatic *volte face* by urging Dillon not to agree to identify the terrorist for fear of reprisal. She comes to eptomise a demoralised and defeatist liberalism which withdraws into passivity and silence. Dillon, meanwhile, finds himself plunged ever more deeply into a nightmare world of not knowing: 'That was the real damage in all this. Never to know ... Not to know. That is the real fear' (192). He enters those frightening metaphysical zones with which readers of Moore's other fiction will be familiar – a realm of uncertainty, anxiety and existential dread where nothing is as it seems. 'It was a world of men in masks whose true identity could not be guessed' (187). The culture of terrorism finds its natural expression in the genre of the thriller, which is designed to surprise, mystify and thrill the reader. Unlike the typical thriller, *Lies of Silence* doesn't focus on one isolated crime or series of crimes which has to be solved. It isn't a conventional whodunnit: its concern is not with discovering what happened, but creating tension about what is going to happen. Nevertheless, it demonstrates many of the usual ways in which the thriller writer manipulates reader response – from the techniques of withholding as well as of giving information, to the melodramatic division of characters into victims and villains, to the provision of false clues to intensify suspense and indicate the protagonist's growing paranoia. Yet Moore does not exploit linear narrative in order simply to stimulate the reader's desire to discover the final outcome, in the way Barthes describes the working of the *texte de désir*.[18] Barthes excludes thrillers and other forms of popular literature from his *textes de plaisir* category on the grounds that they possess none of the verbal excess or play of the text which is the mark of a *texte de plaisir*. Indeed, the thriller, in Barthes' view, seeks to propel the reader as forcefully as possible from beginning to end without interference from digressive effects or ambiguities. But clearly the action in Moore's novel is continually being delayed by a variety of devices and diverting features that are experienced as pleasureable in themselves, chief amongst which are the intellectual interest of the on-going moral debate about silence or speaking out, the psychological interest of Dillons' vacillating mind, and the sub-plot love-interest of his and Andrea's affair. The effectiveness of the novel depends as much on these elements as the novel's teleological urgency. In Chapter 3, Moore devotes a lengthy passage to the description of Dillon's journey in his bomb-laden car from his home to the hotel – an obvious example of a delaying tactic necessary for the generation of suspense. But the passage also has a number of clearly discernible, intrinsically significant and pleasureable aesthetic functions: the recitation of placenames, landmarks and street names grounds the action in a specific place, thereby increasing the illusion of reality. By giving the journey an historical as well as spatial dimension, Moore places the present action in the larger contexts of both the city's troubled history and the protagonist's past life.

Finally, Moore would seem to be concerned with 'lies of silence' in the private as well as the public sphere – though it is unclear exactly what the basis of this continuum or parallel is supposed to be. The protagonist's private life – his relationships with wife, lover, parents and in-laws – is marked by various forms of (masculine) emotional and communicational withholding. Dillon's marriage is based on lies of silence. He doesn't tell his wife about his affair, nor of his intention to leave Belfast and move to London with Andrea. Though Moira probes him about his feelings about their marriage, he remains evasive, unwilling to hurt her by telling her that he doesn't love her. When he joins her in bed 'he kissed her, a traitor's kiss' (39). Language becomes smokescreen, not a medium of genuine communication. He tells Moira that he has decided to move to London out of fear for his life: he says nothing to Moira of his real reason for going, which is to be with Andrea. And he is no more candid with his father:

> 'How does Moira feel about going?'
> 'I don't know yet', he lied. (174)

Even his dealings with Andrea are ambiguous. He promises her he will tell his wife of his affair and of his intention to go off to London with Andrea, but he never does

---

18 See Roland Barthes, *The Pleasure of the Text*, trans. Richard Miller (London: Cape, 1976).

so, until Moira unexpectedly turns up at the hotel and discovers them together. He promises Andrea that he will forget about Belfast and the past and start a new life with her in London, but her efforts to make him sever all connections with Belfast and his past and to tell the police he is too afraid to identify Kev make him uneasy: 'I don't want to be a coward. I don't want to let them frighten me' (247). Andrea, he feels, threatens the very foundations of his identity: 'he would lose for ever something precious, something he had always taken for granted, some secret sense of his own worth' (250). Moore's ambiguous ending leaves us wondering if Dillon's final phone call to the police, which he insists he wants to make in private, is to agree or to refuse to co-operate. His action suggests a desire to create a space, free of Andrea's influence, where he can be his own man. In the public mind, 'lies of silence' indicates key categories in the cultural meaning of 'maleness', and the importance of notions of masculinity in Moore's novel is apparent in the characterisation of Dillon. *Lies of Silence* may thus be read as a critique of the masculinist cultural paradigms which are habitually applied to Northern Ireland. In his poem, 'Whatever You Say Say Nothing', Heaney refers to 'The famous / Northern reticence, the tight gag of place / And times'; 'Smoke-signals are loud-mouthed compared with us' in this 'land of password, handgrip, wink and nod'.[19] Heaney's characterisation of a victim Catholic Nationalist culture in a Protestant Unionist state mutates in Moore's novel to a more generalised image of Northern Irish cultural victimage – discernible in political, religious, social and personal spheres – which has fatal consequences.

TERRORISTS

A compulsive literary stereotype associated with the liberal humanist cultural philosophy is the romance plot involving retreat from the conditions of history into the superior world of private feeling and self-realisation. Two popular Troubles novels which have adopted the romance narrative are Maurice Leitch's *Silver's City* and Bernard MacLaverty's *Cal*. Both novels present sympathetic portrayals of the terrorist. Silver is a former Loyalist paramilitary, Cal has been connected with the IRA. Cal is sympathetic to the extent that he disowns militant Republicanism, attempts to escape into an antipolitical privacy, and accepts the status quo. Silver is a sympathetic figure for two contradictory reasons. First, to the extent that he too struggles to escape from the entanglements of a reactionary, sectarian politics and embrace the superior values of the personal life; and, second, to the extent that he re-politicizes himself in progressive, non-sectarian, working-class terms. Unlike Cal, Silver never entirely

---

19 Seamus Heaney, 'Whatever You Say Say Nothing', *Opened Ground: Poems 1966–1996* (London: Faber, 1998), pp 131–2.

repudiates politics. Curiously, it is the Protestant Loyalist (Silver), not the Catholic Nationalist (Cal), who is committed to the cause of revolutionary social change in Northern Ireland, even though one might think that the Nationalist would have more to gain from the overthrow of the status quo and the Loyalist who would fight to defend it. In both novels, history threatens identity, morality and life itself, but cannot be escaped for long. On the other hand, the world of romance is no less illusory: while offering an escape from the alienating, impersonal, public world, it too involves loss of identity, a rejection of full social and historical being. In both novels, the masculine world of history ultimately overcomes the feminine sphere of private feeling and personal fufilment.

The terrain of nightmare: Maurice Leitch's *Silver's City* (1981)

Silver's City paints a vivid, naturalistic picture of a sleazy underworld of Loyalist drinking clubs, massage parlours, racketeering, abduction and murder. The book is governed by the conventions of the thriller, and opens with a brutal murder (that has little bearing on the rest of the action), then moves to describe the abduction of Silver from his hospital bed, Silver's giving his Loyalist minders the slip, Silver being pursued, Silver finally stabbing his assailant to death. These lurid events occur against a backdrop of urban decay and desolation. Leitch powerfully evokes a dark, brooding *film noir* atmosphere, a sense of pervasive evil. He takes his epigraph from St Augustine: 'The Devil hath established His cities in the North'. Silver's city ultimately belongs not to history but religious allegory. The frightening, labyrinthine under-world through which Silver moves is 'the true terrain of nightmare'.[20] It could be exchanged for any other version of a threatening social milieu without doing serious damage to Leitch's central thesis. Here, violent action has a hallucinatory intensity:

> The man above stared at his bandaged hand moving the safety catch, then he turned and began scrambling back up the stairs. He was panting and falling, as if the carpet had become slippery. Galloway's first bullet hit him in the upper part of his legs, yet he continued sculling with his arms. He didn't cry out, Galloway noted, but just went on clutching at the banisters ... He raced up the stairs, mounting their soft treads, and, at close range, poured three more shots into his victim's back and neck. Warm blood stippled the gun and the hand that held it. He looked down at the bright freckles, like paint. His skin stung, as if he was wounded. (4-5)

20 Maurice Leitch, *Silver's City* (London: Abacus, 1983), p. 93. First published London: Secker & Warburg, 1981. Hereafter, page references will be incorporated into the text.

LIBERAL HUMANISM AND THE REALIST AESTHETIC / 83

Our attention is removed from the human agony to aesthetic contemplation of design and colour. The episode is described largely from the point of view of the killer, the narrative concentrating on Galloway's sensations and perceptions. The victim is viewed externally throughout. Visual impressions are all-important. Every detail of the scene is recorded with preternatural clarity, as if through a camera's lens: 'He stared at the heap on the stairs, looking for answers. Old enough to be his father, a bit of a paunch, one hairless leg, bare to the knee. There was a flattened blob of chewing gum on the heel of his right slipper' (5). There is reference to the daughter's horror, but it is distanced: 'Her cries seemed to come from behind a closed door' (5). In typical hardboiled thriller fashion, atrocity is stylised, objectivised, kept at a safe distance, while the narrative exploits the thrills and excitements of explosive violence. To Galloway's accomplice, Tweed, the incident is like something 'he'd only ever seen in films before' (6): 'Meanwhile, in the car, Tweed still looked on aghast. Such behaviour was beyond him. Stories about that one out there, legs apart in that cowboy fashion, hadn't prepared him for any of this' (6).

The sense of unreality in this opening chapter pervades the whole novel. The eponymous protagonist is a Loyalist terrorist who has spent ten years in prison for killing a Catholic gun runner. Silver is a hero, his name spelled out on gable walls and toilet cubicles. He was 'loved for being the original' – the original sectarian killer. But Silver is unhappy with his hero status, and is troubled by the media's continual distortion of the facts. He feels trapped in the unreality of a fictional past and an equally fictional present. Ten years ago he was put away for firing the first shot in the bloody sectarian war, but his motives for doing so are unclear even to himself. The action of burning the chemist out of his house and then shooting him seemed unreal to Silver even at the time: 'The rest hung there as though seeing a performance on a bright screen which they must watch to its conclusion' (124). Truth has been obscured by the interventions of the media and the politicians, and by the need for heroes:

> All those years locked away, he had of course realised that his reputation and exploits had become popular property. Any man would have found some of that to his taste. Propaganda value was an important aspect too, of course. Early on, he had recognised just how desperate the craving for symbols and symbolism could be. In his own way he himself had become one of those, without being consulted. (75)

Only Silver, it seems, cares about the truth any longer. Belfast is no longer 'Silver's City'. It has become the 'property' of racketeers: 'The scripts were different these days' (40). Reincarnated as a militant Marxist, Silver represents a threat to the new generation of venal paramilitary godfathers. This brave new world into which he has been liberated is 'a savage, unreal world' (72), a world in which he was finding derangement in almost everything'(72). He is referred to throughout as 'the prisoner', as if in recognition of the Foucauldian notion that society as a whole – the Ulster madhouse outside the literal prison – is carceral: 'The prisoner somehow took comfort from that fact, that he was not like the others, these new men with their toupées and identity bracelets and hard, modern manner. They had modelled their image on what they saw on television' (38). Only in the strictly controlled environment of the prison did Silver feel at home:

> But gradually, as time passed in that enclosed existence, he had changed, he knew he had, the outside world seeming further and further away, alien in its irregular daily pulse, its lack of inevitability. It began to seem like a crazy planet out there, beyond the chicken wire, with politicians roaring on, off, hot and cold, ordinary people in the grip of violent and unreasonable action for its own sake. (75-6)

Reality, it seems to Silver, has been displaced and usurped by the image: 'The newspapers and the television do all your thinking for you ... Journalists either lie or exaggerate. I think I blame them almost as much as I do politicians. For what's happened' (108-9). Silver's city has become Simulation City, in which Silver finds himself alienated and bewildered, participating in a 'hyperreality' of self-referential signs.

Ordering the contemporary metropolis are paramilitary godfathers such as Mr Wonderful and Billy Bonner, reinforced by unpredictable and violent maverics like Ned Galloway. In the character of Galloway, Leitch presents the short, unhappy life of a psychopath. Galloway, in his pathological addiction to violence, his self-hate and desire for power, his modelling himself on TV gangsters and wild west gunmen, his complete lack of any serious political commitment, prefigures Eoin McNamee's 'Shankill Butcher', the 'resurrection man' Victor Kelly – with this difference, that where killing is a sacred act to Victor, Galloway is a paid assassin who kills for money and fun. Part of the fun is the sexual thrill which Galloway finds in violence. He kills to compensate for sexual inadequacy. Prior to murdering Silver's girlfriend, Nan, Galloway trashes her flat in a frenzy of violence – 'The feeling was almost sexual' (154). His own death at Silver's hands is the ultimate sexual act in the novel, its narration focalised through Galloway in a prose of 'slo-mo', dreamy power:

> Almost lazily then he looked down and watched the point of his own knife going in cleanly and neatly at the slight upward angle that the training manuals recommended. There was no pain, just a warm damp sensation like bed-wetting. He put his arms on this man's thin naked shoulders, drew him close, wanting to tell him, oh, tell him so much, but all he could manage was, 'Not worth it. A huer ... All of them ... huers' then the sound of someone panting harshly grew louder and louder until the room filled with it. (179)

Billy Bonner represents another kind of terrorist – the racketeer businessman. Bonner works for Mr Wonderful, and it is Mr Wonderful who articulates the economic rationale of terrorism:

> People believe everything they read in the history books. You must have noticed that, but you won't find us there. However, take it from me, behind every single event of importance – ever – someone was calling the tune because he was in charge of the finance. (158)

Bonner's racketeering and violence, like Galloway's psychopathic tendencies, derive from a sense of personal and sexual inadequacy and a desire for power. Nan, recovering from Bonner's violent bullying, wonders 'how she could ever have been frightened of this pocket edition of manhood, this sorry little fashion-plate, this budgie', and tells him to 'push off and do your James Cagney imitations somewhere else (49).

Silver's critical and self-reflective detachment, his political idealism, and his capacity for love, set him apart from all the other paramilitaries in the novel, but he, too, is included in the novel's critique of the contemporary crisis in masculinity. Nan recognises that Silver is tainted by misogyny and by a corrupt and dangerous *machismo*, from which she tries to save him: 'It's not a man's world any more, you know ... Where you come from it still is though, isn't it? Boys' town' (142). Detaching himself from the urban nightmare, from politics and ideology, and returning to nature, Silver, like Cal, attempts to recreate himself through love. The beach house, provocative of childhood memories, is the place of nostalgia, warmth, love, trust; it is Silver's 'dusty cave' (164). But Silver, a product of the city, is reluctant to accept the reality of Nan. She's a dream figure, a *femme fatale*, with her 'movie-star's nails, glistening ovals, blood red' (56): 'Could he seriously believe that she wasn't party to the plot against him?' (56). However progressive his reconstructed social politics may be, Silver's sexual politics remain rooted in a reactionary puritan fear of femininity: 'Everything about this outside world was cock-eyed, he told himself, including the roles of the men and women in it. He was looking about for the towel while prising this woman's flesh from his own, conscious of its potency to ensnare ...' (61). Fatalistically, he surrenders to Nan's charms. As if to remind himself of the illusoriness of their seaside retreat, Silver calls it 'Our babby house' (126). In the end, the emissaries of the public world track him down and, breaking in upon his private space, convince him that he has been betrayed by love. He kills for a second time in his life and faces the realisation that he has also killed his dreams of the future: 'He had forfeited all future rights, all future dreams' (180). The novel ends on a deeply pessimistic, reactionary note: both the personal and the political life have failed – 'the city always made you pay for your dreams' (181).

Leitch's Belfast – what he calls 'the true terrain of nightmare' (92) – is an unstable fictional space which has absorbed a number of other writers – Ciarán Carson, Glenn Patterson, Robert MacLiam Wilson, Eoin McNamee. *Silver's City* marks a shift away from earlier Realistic representations of urban alienation (Michael McLaverty's *Call My Brother Back*, 1939; Brian Moore's *The Lonely Passion of Judith Hearne*, 1956) and prefigures more recent versions of the city as metaphor for an accelerated postmodern cultural expansion and diversity. For the new, younger writers the city is the site of a disturbing, complex, ambiguous, fragmented, transcultural other. The work which in mood and atmosphere most strongly resembles Leitch's novel is McNamee's *Resurrection Man*, published just over a decade after *Silver's City*. Both novels incorporate elements of Gothic horror and *film noir* to convey a dark and brooding sense of place, both present a contemporary metropolis disrupted and destabilised by violence, and both set out to explore the forces of terror and destruction which stalk the urban wasteland. Of particular interest to both Leitch and McNamee are their protagonists' feelings of disorientation and loss of power in a city which no longer provides the reassurance of a familiar world:

> He (Silver) knew such streets well; nothing had dimmed their image from the past. They existed out there reassuringly, whenever he had cared to think about them in that other alien world of wire mesh and dog patrols. But this was the true terrain of nightmare, fixed in its horrible aftermath. A vista of bricked-up doorways and windows stretched for as far as the eye could travel, for it was one of those immensely long, slightly curving streets, artery for all those little side streets which, together on the map, went to make up a defined city-area with its own nickname and loyalties. But all that was dead and done, merely a memory now. (92-3)

– lines which are echoed by McNamee in *Resurrection Man*:

> He (Victor Kelly) sounded surprised as if he had suddenly discovered that the streets were not the simple things he had taken them for, a network to be easily memorized and navigated. They had become untrustworthy, concerned with unfamiliar destinations, no longer adaptable to your own purposes. He read the street names from signs. India Street, Palestine Street. When he spoke them they felt weighty and ponderous on his tongue, impervious syllables that yielded neither direction nor meaning.[21]

21 Eoin McNamee, *Resurrection Man* (London: Picador, 1994), p. 163.

But though both novels are concerned with the way the 'real history' of the Troubles is manipulated by the media, politicians, racketeers and paramilitaries, *Resurrection Man* is even more comprehensively inscribed in postmodern (inter)textuality, its style more closely approaching pastiche, its methodology more evidently self-conscious and self-reflexive, its city space more ideologically defined and fragmented. In *Silver's City*, the protagonist, despite his past, emerges as the source of a beleaguered moral order, a doomed champion of justice and authenticity in the nightmare metropolis.

Catholic guilt: Bernard MacLaverty's *Cal* (1983)

Silver's City also bears close comparison with *Cal*. Cal is younger and less experienced than the veteran Silver, but both wish to escape their past, and both are pursued by their former paramilitary confederates as well as the state authorities. Leitch, like MacLaverty, uses his eponymous protagonist to de-mythicise and de-mystify the terrorist and present him as a man not a monster: both Cal and Silver are clearly differentiated from the other terrorists in their respective stories – the psychopathic Galloway and the cynical Bonner and Mr Wonderful in *Silver's City*, Skeffington and Crilly, the two noxious IRA men in *Cal*.

When we first meet Cal, he is in retreat from the threatening masculine world of the abattoir, the IRA terror squad and the neighbourhood gang, withdrawn into the private world of his bedroom and his music. His father complains about his son's lack of masculine potency when Cal loses his job in the abattoir to Crilly: 'It sticks in my throat that he got the job that you gave up because you hadn't a strong enough stomach.'[22] Our attention is focused on Cal's refined sensibility and traditional wifely role, doing the cooking and looking after the home that he shares with his father. One of the main traits associated with Cal is passivity, displacement of the self into seeing, thinking, dreaming; into internal confusion and uncertainty. Cal exists in a world which bears down heavily upon him, and denies the authority and validity of the subject. It is a world of random victimisation and institutionalised discrimination and oppression. Cal has no job and no prospects to confirm some positive sense of self. With Marcella, he tries to create a type of regenerative space cut off from the unreasonable threats of the public world. It is in the relationship with Marcella that Cal discovers an emotional and sexual fulfilment previously denied. But while MacLaverty celebrates the intensity of feeling between the two lovers, he also reveals its limitations and impermanency. The romantic alternative is illusory, a merely imaginary answer to historical reality. Marcella is entirely a male fantasy figure, erotic, attentive, understanding, compassionate, receptive, amenable. She is Cal's fairy-tale 'Sleeping Beauty' (124). Marcella gets him a job on the Morton estate and a cottage for him to live in, visits him in his rural hideaway, invites him into the Morton home when the rest of the family are away, sleeps with him in her husband's bed, gives him her husband's clothes. Cal's forest cottage is the counterpart of the seaside retreat to which Silver and Nan repair. Removed from the ugly realities of the outside world, Cal and Marcella make love in the snow-bound forest depths. It is a chocolate-box scene of bucoclic bliss. But there's a price to pay. Under Marcella's influence, Cal surrenders the last vestiges of his own identity, symbolically dressing in her dead husband's clothes, and regressing to a state of foetal helplessness: 'Tired of pacing, he lay down on the floor with his knees to his chest for warmth. He lay inert on broken glass, his eyes open to the night, and saw again the terrible thing he had done' (83). His final, decisive action to inform on Crilly and Skeffington and save Marcella's library might be interpreted as assertion of a recovered masculine authority, a recon- structed social self. But there is no unambiguous emergence from narcissism, passivity or ivory towerism. To the very end Cal remains committed to the dream. Lying in bed beside Marcella, he thinks of her as 'the Sleeping Beauty of his fantasy' (154), and it is she who acts to expel him from the womb-like sanctuary of their union: 'He reached out his hand and touched her moistness but she grumbled in her sleep and jack-knifed, closing him out' (154). With Marcella's unconscious action, Cal is effec- tively expelled from the womb-like conditions of their union. The promise of life and hope implied by the closing references to the winter 'thaw' and Christmas Eve is a further cruel irony, for all that's left to comfort Cal is the certainty of final retribution at the hands of the authorities. The novel's concluding paragraph confirms the protagonist in the role of archetypal helpless victim: 'The next morning, Christmas Eve, almost as if he expected it, the police arrived to arrest him and he stood in a dead man's Y-fronts listening to the charges, grateful that at last someone was going to beat him to within an inch of his life' (153).

MacLaverty handles the political theme with as little regard for realism as he does his romance theme. Where the romance relies on fairy-tale, the political relies on carica- ture and satire. Adopting a highly critical attitude towards the paramilitaries, he stages a number of confrontations between Cal and the novel's two IRA men, Skeffington and Crilly, always to highlight the inhumanity of Skeffington the ideologue and the barbarity of Crilly the active volunteer. Skeffington is ruthless, devious and dangerous, disdainful of his foot-soldiers, devoted to an abstract cause regardless of the human cost, and given to speaking in clichés and euphemisms. When he says that getting rid of the British army from Ireland is 'like sitting in a chair that squeaks. Eventually they will become so annoyed they'll get up and sit somewhere else,' Cal insists that he confronts reality: ' "How can you compare blowing somebody's brains out to a squeaking chair", said Cal'. Crilly is the one who carries into action Skeffington's lethal

22 Bernard MacLaverty, *Cal* (London: Penguin, 1984), p .20. First published London: Cape, 1983. Hereafter, page references will be incorporated into the text.

philosophy. Crilly, like Galloway in Leitch's *Silver's City*, Gallagher in Eugene McCabe's *Victims*, and Victor Kelly in *Resurrection Man*, is a mindless, brutal monster. For all these writers, terrorist action always contains an element of the pathological and the demonic, a motive that is anterior to, more fundamental than, the political.

Cal's own involvement in paramilitarism is pictured, not as heroic revolt, but transgression, and confirmed as such by the force of his contrition. In his depiction of the material conditions of Cal's existence, MacLaverty gives full weight to the economic deprivations and religious discrimination that one might expect to be powerful forces in politicising a disaffected, identityless, alienated, Northern Irish Catholic youth like Cal. Living in a Protestant estate, he feels 'excluded and isolated' (9), unable to think of his environment as home. He inhabits the kind of con-temporary society Michel Foucault describes in his book, *Discipline and Punish* (1975), a disciplinary, highly regulated society which relies for its success on its capacity to produce people who subject themselves to its terms. Cal constantly feels under surveillance, from the RUC, the British army, his Protestant neighbours:

> As he turned into his street he felt the eyes on him. He looked at the ground in front of him. The eyes would be at the curtains or behind a hedge as a man paused in his digging. He could not bear to look up and see the flutter of the Union Jacks, and now the red and white cross of the Ulster flag with its red hand. (pp 8–9)

When he goes to work on the Morton estate, he still feels watched – by the Orange foreman, Cecil Dunlop. Foucault describes the panopticon – a building which revolutionised the nineteenth-century prison system of surveillance – as a mechanism which made possible the 'automatic functioning of power'.[23] The panopticon was a central watch tower surrounded by a series of individual cells which were separate from each other but always visible from the central tower. The central tower could be seen from the cells, but not the watcher in the tower. Through this technique of surveillance, assessment, supervision and correction, the individual feels that he is being continually watched – regardless of whether or not he really is – and so even-tually comes to regulate his own behaviour in accordance with the demands of the dominant society. As Foucault puts it, 'A real subjection is born mechanically from a fictitious relation.'[24] Power is not simply operated by a central repressive apparatus or regime, but rather invested in each individual who in turn assumes responsibility for the constraints of power. On a Foucauldian reading, the panopticon of Ulster Protestant power produces the type of society and the type of (Catholic) subject which MacLaverty depicts in *Cal*.

23 Michel Foucault, excerpt from *Discipline and Punish* (1977), in Antony Easthope and Kate McGowan (eds) *A Critical and Cultural Theory Reader* (Buckingham: Open University Press, 1997), p. 85. 24 Ibid., p. 86.

Cal, through the mechanism of Protestant power, is produced in terms of a traditional Catholic victim psychology:

> Later in the day Dunlop told Cal to muck out the byre and because it was something he could do he went at it with a will. As he scraped and shovelled the slabbery dung he remembered: 'For too long the Catholics of Ulster have been the hewers of wood and the drawers of water'. (68)

His humiliation continues with the beating he takes from the gang of local Loyalist thugs, soon after which he and his father are firebombed out of their home. Yet, none of this makes the ideology of militant Republicanism an attractive option to Cal. If, after his confrontation with the Loyalist gang, he longs for revenge – 'He fantasized about having Shamie's gun, went again through the lead-up to the incident, only this time he produced the revolver and blew the big one's head apart' – these are simply understandable feelings of resentment and anger in the face of discrimination and violence. Cal's initial involvement in the IRA stemmed not from ideological conviction but a sense of personal obligation to those who had supported him and his father when they were intimidated out of their home before. In conversation with Marcella, he admits to being 'very anti-British' and says he 'would like to see a united Ireland' though he hasn't 'decided the best way to go about it yet' (118). One thing he is sure of is that terrorist violence is not the way to accomplish these ends. That, he tells Skeffington, 'goes against my conscience' (148). Cal reacts instinctively and angrily to personal injustice, but then feels guilty at having allowed himself to be used to strike against the system that oppresses him, finally wanting to escape altogether from any further active involvement. As Joe Cleary remarks, the novel reflects the contradictions in contemporary Northern Irish Nationalism, acknowledging the oppressiveness of the Northern Irish Protestant state and Catholic indignation against it, but recoiling from the violence that sets out to overthrow the oppressor, thereby reluctantly conceding the state authority.

The novel suppresses or marginalises the political theme. The romance narrative, as developed by MacLaverty, does not exactly reproduce the 'national romance' as defined by Joe Cleary[25] and Gerry Smyth.[26] It might seem that MacLaverty is going to develop a 'love-across-the-barricades' story, in which a Protestant/Catholic love relationship would be used to model a desired harmony in the political sphere. But instead of that, MacLaverty makes Marcella an Italian Catholic, thus opening the possibility of a consolidated Catholic front against the forces of an oppressive

25 See Joe Cleary, '"Fork-tongued on the border bit": partition and the politics of form in contemporary narratives of the Northern Irish conflict' in *South Atlantic Quarterly*, 95, 1 (Winter 1996), pp 227–76.   26 See Gerry Smyth, *The Novel and the Nation* (London: Pluto Press, 1997).

Protestant hegemony. However, he doesn't take that road either, preferring to push Cal and Marcella into an emphatically anti-political privacy with all its potential for pathos if not tragedy. Rather than a political novel, *Cal* is a blend of fairytale, and, as Neil Corcoran observes, 'a deeply Catholic study of guilt, expiation and desire for confession',[27] supported, we might note, by an emphatically Catholic intertextual field which includes frequent references to Matt Talbot, Maria Goretti, and Grunewald's picture of the crucified Christ. Relying on a predictable plot and stereotyped emotional configurations, MacLaverty indulges an unhealthy appetite for victimage, passivity, and masochism.

The fiction considered in this chapter constitutes a classic demonstration of what Eve Patten calls the 'novelistic obligation to offer a consensual (and usually apolitical) liberal humanist comment on the predicament'.[28] It is fiction marked by a moralistic, sometimes hysterical, reaction to Republican and Loyalist violence and displays little interest in the material and political factors that have conditioned paramilitarism on either side. Ideology and politics are summarily dismissed or ridiculed, regarded as a form of false consciousness, an effacement of reality. Attention is focused on individual sufferings within a degraded and destructive political context. The complexity and ambiguities of social conflict are subordinated to the fiction's psychological interest. Historical determinism occludes historical process. As Joe McMinn notes, the implied 'typicality' of the (anti-social, anti-historical) action perpetuates an unhelpful literary convention which masquerades as universal truth. McMinn's conclusion – that such novels 'deserve to be taken seriously in artistic, if not political, terms'[29] – is well judged. While they may reveal a basic conservatism of form as well as feeling, they nevertheless demonstrate a skillful deployment of literary convention.

---

27 Neil Corcoran, *After Yeats and Joyce*, p. 157.   28 Eve Patten, 'Fiction in conflict, pp 128–48, p. 131.   29 Joe McMinn, 'Contemporary novels', pp 113–21, p. 121.

CHAPTER FOUR

Postmodern humanism

A younger generation of writers who were born in the 1960s and grew up during the Troubles have sought to explore new literary ground. Their work marks a break with past attitudes and ways of seeing. The dislocations, fragmentations and recon-figurations of the postmodern era are reflected in this new, young writing both in terms of style and attitude. These writers represent a strand of self-reflexive writing which is critical of Realist premises and deconstructs the usual relationships which exist between text and reader, language and reality, fiction and history. The processes and possibilities of writing are no longer taken for granted. Where older writers such as Moore, McCabe and MacLaverty sought to reveal the universal truth of specific individuals' struggle in a hostile world, the new writers challenge the very foundations of accepted notions of what constitutes the individual and his world – not to demolish the concepts of the individual, society or humanity, but to re-define them. By developing an existential aesthetics which draws from, while remaining critical of, both Realism and Postmodernism, they experiment with the possibilities of re-mapping identity, re-writing history and re-inventing the language of the Troubles. Confronted with the contemporary crisis in the North, with the cultural logic of Late Capitalism and the proliferating new rhetorics of youth, feminism, anti-colonialism, socialist revolutionism, counterculturalism, these writers look for positive new ways of living in this world of breakdown and dissensus. Their response articulates a new 'postmodern humanism', the term used by the anthropologist Richard Shweder who, seeing a world in which diverse cultures and symbols are flowing together in curious ways, proposed a concept of 'universalism without the uniformity':

> The unity of human beings is no longer to be found in that which makes us common and all the same, but rather in a universal original multiplicity which makes each of us so variegated that 'others' become fully accessible and imaginable to us through some aspect or other of our own complex self.[1]

While still writing from deep down in their own environments and cultures, the postmodern writers inhabit the 'global village' of modern capitalism and technology, keeping on the move between alternative cultural worlds, open to new

---

1 Richard Shweder, 'Santa Claus on the cross', in Walter Truett Anderson (ed.), *The Fontana Post-modernism Reader* (London: Fontana, 1996), pp 68–74, p. 74.

experience, continually border-crossing. For unlike the modernists, who escaped into an elitist aestheticism, these new writers, while pursuing their epistemological concerns or giving vent to their sceptical individualism, have continued to engage with history.

We begin, however, with a couple of older writers, Francis Stuart and Benedict Kiely, who have produced work which is clearly influenced by the postmodern outlook. Stuart was seventy-five and the author of a score of novels going back to the 1930s when his remarkable novel of the North, *A Hole in the Head*, was published in 1977. Yet the later Stuart has more in common with the emergent young writers than with those of his own generation (Liam O'Flaherty, Sean O'Faoláin, Kate O'Brien, Jennifer Johnston, Edna O'Brien, James Plunkett, John McGahern, Brian Moore) who were more or less content to work within the structures of classic Realism. The later Stuart continues what Richard Kearney calls the 'counter tradition'[2] initiated by Joyce and Beckett, and coming down through Flann O'Brien to John Banville in the contemporary period. It therefore seems appropriate to consider Stuart's work in the present chapter under the postmodern banner. Kiely also had an established reputation as novelist, short story writer, travel writer and critic when, at the age of sixty-seven, he published *Nothing Happens in Carmincross* in 1985. Though usually associated with a flexible Realism, an old style Nationalism, and a nostalgic sense of place, Kiely in this novel, under pressure from the Troubles in the North, deconstructs an entire literary tradition, while registering a dazed determination to create new meanings out of the experience of fragmentation and discontinuity.

The anthropology of terrorism: Francis Stuart's *A Hole in the Head* (1977).

> There is an Amazonian tribe that punctures the skulls of its children in the belief that the perforations give access to both good and evil spirits, thus widening the range of perception.[3]

These, the concluding lines of Stuart's novel, foreground his anthropological approach to self and society in the wake of the breakdown of bourgeois liberal humanism, which manifests itself in terms of both a personal and political derangement. The lines reiterate his concern with psychic and mystical forces that influence perception and open up new liberating ways of seeing and thinking beyond the limits of conventional morality. Not surprisingly, therefore, the narrator values the 'aberrations' (99) of his own psychosis as proof of his creative and imaginative

2 Richard Kearney, *Transitions: Narratives in Modern Irish Culture* (Dublin: Wolfhound, 1988), p. 83   3 Francis Stuart, *A Hole in the Head* (London: Martin Brian & O'Keefe, 1977), p. 215. Hereafter, page references will be incorporated into the text.

vitality. Linked to his personal derangement is the political turmoil in the North. This, too, is interpreted anthropologically as a tribal war, an irruption of dark, irrational, atavistic energy. But in contrast to the usual liberal humanist denunciation of atavism, Stuart welcomes its primitive, demonic passion, elaborating a basic opposition between elemental, instinctual life on one hand, and the deformed conscience of so-called civilised society on the other.

At the centre of the novel and absorbing everything in it, is the ongoing drama of the self, the radical search for personal truth. The narrator, Barnaby Shane, aka H, is a writer, recovering from marital failure, mental breakdown and a self-inflicted injury to the head. Barnaby comes North in search of imaginative and artistic revitalisation. In the first part of the novel, his muse, Emily Bronte, is a very real presence to him. She is a figure of the artist he would like to be – one who probed the dark depths of consciousness and had the courage to write directly and honestly out of her own passionate, obsessive nature: 'I looked at one whose imagination was a severed artery draining her life into her fiction' (64). There is a thin dividing line between creativity and insanity. Barnaby is convinced that 'nothing of any moment could happen outside my heightened imagination' (34), and dismisses 'medium-mix-fiction' because it lacks passion. But to fail to distinguish between imagination and reality is madness, which is related to his failure as a writer. Emily reminds him that passion and obsession have to be controlled and are valuable only when they have been transformed into artistic form: 'One day you'll transform these passions into a legend, but meanwhile bear them in patience and silence' (91).

In the second part, when Barnaby can distinguish more clearly between hallucination and actuality, Emily, though less corporeal, remains his intimate spiritual confidante. There is considerable confusion arising out of the narrative disruptions and the constant blurring of the line between fact and fiction, but the first part detailing the narrator's alienation from the social world is more convincingly worked than the second part dealing with his self-realisation in the wider world of morality and politics. The presentation of the external world is notably lacking in coherence and detail, and appears more like a dreamscape than actuality. Despite the topicality of the Ulster setting, Stuart distances himself from historical reality – presumably to avoid limiting the novel's range of applicability – through the use of such gratuitous codings as 'Belbury' for Belfast, and 'B.A.M.' ('Belbury Association of Militiamen' (183) and 'L.D.F.' ('Loyal Defenders of the Faith' (68)) for more familiar Loyalist paramilitary acronyms. The description of Belbury as 'this northern town at the edge of beyond, with occasionally the clatter of distant gun-fire ... and a murky pink flicker on the low clouds from a burning building' (113) has an emblematic, apocalyptic force, in keeping with the novel's general tendency to privilege symbolic or mythic suggestion over realism and analysis. Belfast, the North, the Troubles, politics, the external world generally, have a primarily interior significance. There is only superficial concern with verisimilitude and credibility, as may be illustrated by the way Stuart involves Barnaby in the Northern conflict: paramilitary boss, Arnold Grundy, anxious about the safety of his two children, Sandra and Len, who, along with a politician, are being held hostage by two terrorists from 'two hostile tribes' (194) in an incredible joint Loyalist/Republican operation, recruits Barnaby, the drugs- and alcohol-fuelled recovering psychotic, to act as mediator. Barnaby agrees because, as he puts it, his intervention 'gave me a kind of alibi, absolved me in a way from complicity in what was going on' (207). What was going on was 'the obscure tormenting of the innocent' (210). Obsessed by the world's evil, Barnaby cannot condemn the terrorists: their terrorism is the expression of a betrayed and wounded innocence. Christian Combermale, his wife's new boyfriend, enunciates the romantic view of the terrorist as artist *maudit*: 'A flood of energy with nowhere to go except into fighting and clowning, apart from the occasional one of you who tries his hand at fiction or poesie' (185). Barnaby ponders Combermarle's words: ' "Fulfilment denied results in violence", yes, but only when fulfilment is desired fiercely enough. Then you have the terrorist or, more rarely, the imaginative artist' (185). Thus, the narrator aligns himself with the innocent children, Sandra and Len; with anguished writers such as Emily Bronte and Dostoyevsky; with terrorists such as Sammy the 'iron man' who is still 'an ardent boy' (189). These are the victims of a debased civilisation, which Barnaby 'dismisses' in a whimsically arbitrary tirade: 'Dismissing such minor matters as the blinding of rabbits during tests for the marketing of more-and-more competitive cosmetics, I am looking through the huge patchwork screen of sex, drugs, ball-games, package-tours, gourmandising, collecting, speeding, surfing, and, most opaque of all, piety' (207). The politician taken hostage in Saville Street is forced to listen to tape-recordings of the cant and lies he has purveyed; his blindness to his own culpability mercilessly mocked. Barnaby quotes the psychologist Anthony Storr's cynical assessment of politicians as individuals driven to seek power by inner insecurity, and to substitute extroverted activity for the self-knowledge that comes from cultivating personal relationships. The narrative is littered with references to all kinds of texts – newspaper reports, literary reviews, popular fiction, Communist Party posters, street songs – and both 'official' and 'popular' language is always suspect. Condemnations of the kidnappers from state and church authorities 'grew the more solemn and the diction more artificial as the distance between denunciator and Saville Street increased' (155). The narrator ponders the adequacy of the newspapers' term 'thug' to describe Grundy the paramilitary: 'But now I had grasped that while he might be a thug (a term, when used by the writers of leading articles in the news-papers, I took to indicate anyone whose policies were seen as a danger, however indirect, to the pontifical power of these editors) he was something else as well' (128–9). Words such as 'law-and-order', 'liberty', 'Christian values', 'democracy' have become mere 'catchphrases' (198). Only the words of a spiritual aristocracy of artists and visionaries, especially those who have intimate knowledge of suffering – Tennyson, Blake, Rosetti, Clare, Shakespeare, Yeats, Dostoyevsky and, above all, Emily Bronte – can satisfy Barnaby's demand for truth.

The novel is a chronicle of self-recovery and the creation of 'new gods': 'Did you know that members of a certain tribe whose deities have deserted them can, in states of frenzy produced by magic potions concocted from herbs and fungoids, persuade new gods to undertake their salvation?' (210). Art, like terrorism, is an expression of this desire for magical, frenzied transformation of a debased reality. The 'new myths' (208), Stuart makes clear, lie not in the public events of history but in the 'hidden, unpublished history', not in 'the great design' but in 'sexual memories' (210): 'The new myths, if there can ever be any, in order to redeem will deal with events of utter obscurity' (208). What Stuart proposes is a radical re-ordering of the relationship between life and art, narrative and truth. His comment on the contemporary predicament, as on most other things, is aggressively individualistic and non-consensual, expressive of a profound suspicion of any kind of official ideology, orthodox faith or conventional moral judgment. The 'new myths' will be born of guilt, shame, obsession and personal suffering, so that the bounds of tolerance, compassion and understanding can be extended, and hypocrisy and banality overcome. The artist is not merely the harbourer and explorer of 'secret or shameful passions' (82): he also has a social role, that of healer. The narrator, faced with the challenge of explaining his vision of the world to the two children, Sandra and Len, realises 'I had to risk all in a start that healed their ravaged nerves' (88): 'Here was the dilemma of the fiction writer in miniature' (87). Coming to the close of his story of the Bugaboo that drains people of their vital energy and ensures the 'spread of faith and conformity' (89), Barnaby is aware that he has worked himself into a state of creative frenzy, enacting in miniature the business of the fiction writer: 'But I couldn't immediately switch off the flights of fancy that, with the stimulus of the fever, I'd worked myself up to for the sake of the children' (90–1).

As might be expected of a narrator who is recovering from mental breakdown, given to drugs, alcohol and sex, who is by his own admission an obsessive personality and unable to distinguish between dream and reality, the 'record' of his experiences is fragmented and discontinuous, and highly problematic. By establishing an intimate, confessional relationship with the reader, Stuart forces us to share the narrator's confusions and tensions, the struggle to make sense of potentially anarchic experience. We are continually kept aware of the narrator's interpretative activity, his processing the narrative through the controlling medium of his language. When Sandra says she prayed for Barnaby to turn up, he comments: 'Prayed? To what? To the wounded, white unicorn sheltering in a stormy thicket somewhere near the centre of the galaxy (my interpretation)' (194). He is open about the self-serving, therapeutic function of his narrative: 'I had to disillusion her (Sandra). And, at the same time, for my own private record (and this report) present my side of the situation' (198). By continually 'baring the device' of his narrative procedures, he reminds us that the 'report' is an imaginative enterprise – the writing of a self. The novel, which has been unable to provide a logical, sequential record of events, nevertheless ultimately affirms an artistic order and control over intractable materials. Stuart has said in a *Crane Bag* interview: 'I have an obsession with Art as one of the few hopes in a darkening world ... I'm not interested in the normal work of fiction ... the work that never sets out to do more than tell a story, entertain, give a twist, give facts';[4] while in another interview, he speaks of the need for the artist to be 'a prophet'.[5] At the same time, the refusal of resolution or closure at the end of *A Hole in the Head* is recognition of the limits of fiction: there is no final essentialist heaven, no transcendental self.

Postmodern irony: Benedict Kiely's *Nothing Happens in Carmincross* (1985)

In a postscript to his best-selling novel, *The Name of the Rose* (1983), which is often taken to exemplify postmodern literature, Umberto Eco presents his own ideas about the postmodern attitude, which he believes combines the two modes of parody and transcendence:

> The postmodern reply to the modern consists of recognizing that the past, since it cannot really be destroyed, because its destruction leads to silence, must be revisited: but with irony, not innocently. I think of the postmodern attitude as that of a man who loves a very cultivated woman and knows he cannot say to her, 'I love you madly', because he knows that she knows (and that she knows that he knows) that these words have already been written by Barbara Cartland. Still, there is a solution. He can say, 'As Barbara Cartland would put it, I love you madly.' At this point, having avoided false innocence, having said clearly that it is no longer possible to speak innocently, he will nevertheless have said what he wanted to say to the woman: that he loves her, but he loves her in an age of lost innocence. If the woman goes along with this, she will have received a declaration of love all the same. Neither of the two speakers will feel innocent, both will have accepted the challenge of the past, of the already said, which cannot be eliminated; both will consciously and with pleasure play the game of irony ... But both will have succeeded, once again, in speaking of love.[6]

4 Ronan Sheehan, 'Novelists on the novel', interview with Francis Stuart and John Banville in *Crane Bag*, 3, 1 (1979), p. 76.   5 Bill Lazenbatt, 'A conversation with Francis Stuart', in *Writing Ulster: Francis Stuart Special Issue*, 4 (1996), pp 1–17, p. 16.   6 Umberto Eco, '"I love you madly," he said self-consciously', in

Eco's remarks have a particular relevance to *Nothing Happens in Carmincross*. Like Eco's novel, which transcends the boundary between 'high' and 'low' culture, and parodies the popular detective novel (a genre expressive of modern man's search for truth), Kiely's novel also combines 'high' art and popular culture, and parodies the picaresque novel (Neil Corcoran calls Carmincross 'postmodern picaresque'[7]) and traditional narratives of homeland and exile's return (by forcing a reconsideration of the idea of origin and originality). Following Eco's notion of the postmodern, *Nothing Happens in Carmincross* is written out of a sense of lost innocence. Kiely accepts the challenge of the past – not the negation of the already said, but its ironic rethinking. The central character, Mervyn Kavanagh, through whom the events of the novel are focalised, explains early on:

> [E]very experience takes the form of a quotation ... every experience is a quotation and ... every quotation is renewed experience, a light switched on again in a darkened room to reveal familiar objects. Mervyn recalls that Marx suggested that history repeats itself, second time as farce. Marx was too kind. History is farce the first time.[8]

Self-reflexive strategies such as quotation, allusion, parody, borrowing of styles become ways of freeing narrative from existing values and investing it with new possibilities of meaning. By taking context and situation into account, Kiely moves beyond the grand narratives of the past that have sought to 'totalise' Ireland, and, through a logic of poststructuralist absence, recognises the fragmentariness of the modern world. But as well as unmasking illusory representations of reality, he also, through a residual faith in traditional liberal humanist assumptions, and in the Romantic concept of imagination and individual vision, also reasserts the possibility of transcendence of experience. The bombs are unable to erase completely the life-affirming ebullience of the narration.

Mervyn Kavanagh, a middle-aged man who has been living and teaching in America, returns to his childhood home for the wedding of a favourite niece. Traversing the Atlantic and Ireland to Carmincross, the small Ulster town where he was born, Mervyn encounters people and events from his own and his country's past, while the constant flow of news of the contemporary Troubles infiltrates his consciousness more and more insistently. On the journey to Carmincross, he is witness to the terrorist ambush of a British army checkpoint which leaves one soldier dead. Shortly before the wedding is due to take place, Mervyn's niece, Stephanie, is killed in a Provo bomb blast, and an old friend, Cecil Morrow, a serving Protestant RUC

The Fontana Post-modernism Reader, pp 31–3, p. 32–3.   7 Neil Corcoran, *After Yeats and Joyce*, p. 158.   8 Benedict Kiely, *Nothing Happens in Carmincross* (London: Methuen, 1986), p. 39. First published London: Gollancz, 1985. Hereafter, page references will be incorporated into the text.

man who rescued Mervyn's mother from the blast, is shot by the Irish Liberation Army: 'As far as is known, the killing of Cecil who rescued my mother seems to have been their only contribution to any form of liberation' (250). The novel is bitterly angry, sometimes comic, and deeply troubled by events in the North. Written with great energy and brio, it is garrulous, rambling, loosely and episodically constructed, shifting constantly between memory and actuality, history and fiction, past and present. For its composition, it draws on multiple texts and countertexts derived from official and unofficial histories, folklore and oral tradition, books, photograph albums, yearbooks, magazines, human 'posters', the Bible, poems, political speeches. Events in the present are interpreted in terms of prior texts. The relationship between Mervyn and his old flame Deborah, who is pursued by her jealous husband Timothy, is underwritten by the story of Diarmuid and Gráinne who were fugitives from Fionn. Mervyn is also known as Merlin the wizard, in recognition of his role of sage and seer, the hugely knowledgeable and widely-read impresario of the novel's multiple intertexts. The contemporary landscape still bears the vestigial signs of a folkloric, magical, pagan past, and is shadowed by past events, invariably violent: 'In Ireland there's precedent for everything. Except commonsense' (75). Mervyn supplies the legendary paradigm for the Northern Troubles:

> Mervyn, who is good at such things (after all they gave him money for it in the USA), can provide the relevant text: 'Twas a day full of sorrow for Ulster when Conor MacNessa went forth to punish the clansmen of Connacht who dared to take spoil from the north. For his men brought him back from the battle, scarce better than one that was dead: with the brain ball of Mesgedra buried two-thirds of its depth in his head ...' (77)

But in an age of lost innocence, the romanticising, heroicising rhetoric of the ancient Irish legends is subject to a withering irony. Mervyn's 'relevant text' is immediately re-written by the notoriously cynical Jeremiah Gilsenan: 'He (the old patriot they have visited on their travels) is Conor MacNessa sitting up there with the past buried like a brainball in his head. Up in the north the lads with the bombs instead of brainballs don't give a continental bugger who they throw them at. And King Connor goes on ranting for ever about the glorious dead' (78). Traditional Irishry is continually being debunked: 'Health and long life to you, land without rent at you, the woman of your choice at you, and death in Ireland. That last being the greatest of all possible blessings that an Irishman can bestow on another Irishman or on any variety of a man anywhere' (215–6). The account of the terrorist killing of a mother in front of her three year old child in their caravan home near Middletown in Co. Armagh is interwoven with snippets of old folksongs – 'the raggle-taggle gipsies, oh', 'It's my own Irish home, no matter where I roam my heart is at home in old

Ireland in the county of Armagh', 'the boys of the county of Armagh', 'Beside your caravan the campfire's bright', 'at night when you're asleep, into your tent I'll creep' (149) – to emphasise the point that it is no longer possible to speak innocently. Jeremiah is preparing a *Revised Irish Minstrelsy* to replace the revivalists' false innocence with songs more truly reflective of Ireland's contemporary degradation. Jeremiah's revisionism, which is typical of Kiely's narrative mode generally, exemplifies the American philosopher Richard Rorty's concept of postmodern ironic 'redescription'. Postmodern ironists, says Rorty, reject 'final vocabulary' and notions of 'intrinsic nature' or 'real essence'. They are the ones 'never quite able to take themselves seriously because always aware that the terms in which they describe themselves are subject to change, always aware of the contingency and fragility of their final vocabularies, and thus of their selves'.[9] Kiely, through the self-conscious, self-reflexive, self-mocking mode of his narration, demonstrates this anxiety about having been 'taught to play the wrong language game',[10] of having to accept the loss of 'reality', 'real essence', ultimacy.

Aware of inhabiting the new universe of simulacra, Mervyn repeatedly compares himself to the 'fall-guy from the audience' (29) who tries to clamber into the on-screen action: 'The clown from the real world is there all the time, falling over himself, miraculously dodging disaster, nobody seeming to be aware of his existence' (29). Reality is forever elusive, stories about stories. Image becomes inseparable from reality. Musing on how 'the media does so much for us', Mervyn is aware of a kind of technological take-over: 'So many people you never heard of become part of your life, sit at table with you, walk to work with you, come in the evening between you and the book you read' (60–1). We are all 'fall-guys' of the telecommunications revolution, members now of a global village: 'Never before in what we call history has it been so possible for everybody to become part of the action everywhere. So that the world can go mad together and for the same reasons' (97). Consequently, Northern Irish terrorism is continually placed in larger contexts of international terrorism. The narrative zaps from one news-flash to another, from here, there and everywhere. The last chapter, entitled 'The Rock', comments ironically on notions of unshakeable and eternal foundation ('Rock of Ages') in an imperialist context by focusing on the British army's construction of a model 'Ulster village' (for purposes of training British soldiers before they are sent to Northern Ireland) on the Rock of Gibraltar, itself the site of a model 'little England' on foreign soil. Without a firm 'rock', reality is only ever virtual, a series of proliferating refractions of other images in other symbolic systems, problematising the possibility that value can exist at all. These ideas relate in obvious ways to Kiely's

9 Richard Rorty, 'Ironists and metaphysicians', in *The Fontana Post-modernist Reader*, pp 96–102, p. 97.
10 Ibid., p. 98.

view and treatment of narrative. Instead of an originating creative act, there are inter-texts deriving from diverse cultural texts. To create is inevitably to re-create signs of past culture. Instead of dealing with some prior reality, art actually deals in 'myths of origin'. Kiely's 'Ulster village' on the 'Rock' is, as Baudrillard said of Disneyland, 'a perfect model of all the entangled orders of simulation':[11]

> But deep down in the belly of an Iberian rock those fine British boys search a car for Irish bombs. And a real-life drunk abandons all Hope and Anchor and staggers out to ask them, in what the newspaper calls a passable Irish accent: What are ye bastards doing over here?
> – But a real Irish accent would have said: What in the name o' Jasus ...
> – He pesters them, the paper says.
> – Then they beat him up the balls.
> – No, being of their own he is exempt. He is but a pretending Paddy.
> (263–4)

We read the novel's version of a newspaper's version of a series of non-real events which happened. The question asked by the 'real-life drunk' who is one 'of their own' and only 'a pretending Paddy' echoes an earlier question in the novel when a man called Timoney, to whom Mervyn and Deborah gave a lift on their way to Carmincross, tells them his story of being accosted in the long grass of his own back garden in Co. Tyrone by 'a black nigger in British uniform' who demanded, 'Man, what are you doing here' (196); to which Timoney replies: 'what in the name of the merciful Jasus are you doing here?' (197). The 'Ulster 'village', with its not quite Irish-sounding names for pub ('Hope and Anchor. A fine old English inn'), church ('St. Malachy's R.C. church ... in the North, without being told, most would know that St Malachy was an R.C.') and shops ('Tom's Chippy. Rather more Coronation Street than North Irish') is an image of reality conceived of as an endless interplay of textual paradigms, a parody of both colonial assimilationism and the Realist attempt to represent the truth.

Kiely highlights the bankruptcy of the totalising narratives of the past, and he considers the situation of the human individual inhabiting a world of endless, inescapable simulations, climbing in and out of the screen like the 'absurd comic' who is aware of, yet never quite part of, the action. However, the potential for nightmare does not overhaul an unquenchable optimism, a deeply rooted confidence in humanity, and a sense of a fundamentally beneficent creative force. Like Eco, Kiely also succeeds in speaking once again of love. His search for a better 'final vocabulary'

11 Jean Baudrillard, 'Simulacra and simulations', in David Lodge (ed.), *Modern Criticism and Theory* (Harlow: Longman Pearson, 2000), pp 404–12, p. 405.

than the one in current use is dominated by metaphors of making rather than finding, of diversification and innovation rather than convergence to the antecedently present, symbolised by the return to Carmincross. Kiely's 'final vocabulary' is a poetic achievement, the construction of a 'supreme fiction' based on an historicisation of the aesthetic rather than on notions of eternal verities and aesthetic autonomy.

Remythologising Protestantism: Glenn Patterson's *Burning Your Own* (1988), *Fat Lad* (1992), *The International* (1999)

In his influential book, *Imagined Communities* (1983), Benedict Anderson propounds the idea that communities, including nations, are not the result of a people wakening to self-consciousness: rather, they are inventions. 'Community' is a relational term; like any sign, a community exists by virtue of its difference from the others. The concept belongs to the realm of semiology or signification, not to the external, referential world. Communities and nations have no essential or intrinsic properties; they are discursive constructs dependent on 'the style in which they are imagined'.[12] Communities are imagined because their members are not in constant contact with each other, as members of a family, tribe, village or parish might be: members can only know each other imaginatively. There is a direct relationship, Anderson stresses, between the use of nationalism and the spread of print culture. The 'imagined community' is maintained by a wide variety of discursive institutions, including myths and folklore, works of literature, and mass media representations, along with periodic communal rituals through which the community recollects itself in terms of idealised self-images, though of course all areas of economic, political, cultural and discursive life are communally and nationally inflected. The value of community to the individual is that it offers a sense of identity and continuity.

Referring to 'the litany of dates (for instance 1690, 1798, 1916) and the communal affinities that surround them', Richard Kirkland describes Northern Ireland as 'a mythologised community'.[13] In *Burning Your Own* (1988), Patterson explores a social group's need for a communal set of images, a tradition of mythic idealisations whereby it can represent itself to itself and to others. Set around the 12th of July, the novel focuses on the ritual process of ideological self-representation and recollection of sacred foundational acts (notably William of Orange's defeat of James I at the battle of the Boyne in 1690) whereby the residents on the Protestant estate of Larkview seek to preserve a sense of their communal Protestant identity. However, these mythologised narratives of identity and nationality are also shown to be susceptible to deceit, alienation and intolerance. They function in a reactionary and socially conservative

12 Benedict Anderson, *Imagined Communities* (New York: Verso, 1991), p. 6. 13 Richard Kirkland, *Language and Culture in Northern Ireland since 1965: Moments of Danger* (London: Longman, 1996), p. 5.

fashion, opposing themselves to pluralism and permissiveness, intolerant of what is marginal, different or alien. From the long process of mythic accretion flows much of the barbarism that takes place in the novel – swaggering triumphalism, hawkish paramilitarism, opposition to moderate Civil Rights protest, eviction of Catholic families from Protestant estates, and, most conspicuously of all, the demonisation of the local Catholic boy, Francy Hagan, who is transformed into a figure of mythic proportions, a young Lord of Misrule.

Burning Your Own is set in the 1960s, a period of growth and prosperity, when Unionist hegemony in the North began to be challenged by a new young generation of Nationalists, inspired by the Civil Rights movement in America. The narrative is also conditioned by a defamiliarising perspective which views the world through the eyes of a ten year old boy, Mal Martin, who is caught between conforming to the values of his Protestant community and following his own conscience. Patterson presents Mal as a product of a specific social environment and upbringing, but also exploits the opportunities offered by a child narrator for exploring a view of the world which is still fresh and relatively open and receptive. Mal's own perspectives undergo constant challenge and development in the course of the novel, through his inter-actions with others, especially the Catholic boy Francy Hagan, his several symbolic re-locations, and his experience of the wider world accessed through television.

The novel charts the friendship which grows between Catholic Francy and Protestant Mal, who is the only one in the story to regard Francy as a human being. Ironically, Patterson is not able to see Francy as a real little boy either, burdening him unconvincingly with all kinds of symbolic significance. Francy is a precocious sage, a priestly possessor of tabooed or forgotten or 'dangerous' knowledge. One of Francy's prophetic functions is to articulate a sense of the lubricity and duplicity of received social meanings. Seeing Mal's discomfort at not knowing what 'Home Rule' means, Francy declares: 'Ach, don't be worried not knowing what it means ... Sure, who the fuck knows what anything means? They tell you one thing one day and something else altogether the next. Fucking beans means Heinz now.'[14] Dissociating himself from the dominant culture of sectarian division, Francy establishes an alternative space in the depths of nature, beyond the dump. In Francy's domain, language and meaning become fluid. A flower urn off a grave is 'a spiturn': as Francy explains – 'their rules ... stop at the fence. When they dumped those, it ceased to mean anything but what I wanted it to mean' (61). Francy is the spokesman of unorthodoxy and alternative morality, of freedom from the given reality. He represents a discomfiting, subversive, postmodern energy which undermines all certainties, defamiliarizes a comfortably familiar world, refuses single, definite meaning. He opens up unsettling new

14 Glenn Patterson, *Burning Your Own* (London: Minerva, 1993), p. 217. First published London: Chatto & Windus, 1988. Hereafter, page references will be incorporated into the text.

perspectives for Mal beyond the simple sectarian attitudes of Mal's Protestant friends. He is, in symbolic terms, Mal's alter ego.

Francy's destabilising influence is further evidenced in his account of the history of the Catholic chapel lying in ruins in the woods. The traditional Protestant narrative which Mal has been brought up to believe is one which appropriates the chapel as an emblem of Protestant power: William of Orange destroyed it on his way to the battle of the Boyne. However, Francie unearths a more factually accurate version of events. Producing the evidence of dates on stones and photographs, he dates the chapel back to 1875, not 1690, and constructs a very different narrative: the chapel was built by the combined efforts of Protestants and Catholics, and used by both communities, until the time of Home Rule when a group of Protestants, objecting to the building as 'one great Papish insult', razed it to the ground, thus dispelling what might have been a narrative of exemplary ecumenism.

Patterson's narrative itself seeks to undermine fixed positions and uncover internal contradictions. The physical environment of the novel reflects a process of accelerating change as new housing developments spread across rural terrain, Catholic estates encroach upon traditionally Protestant areas, and a dispersed provincial population shifts to urban and suburban centres. In re-writing the ruined chapel as a polysemic signifier of both ecumenism and Protestant bigotry rather than a simple sign of traditional Protestant supremacism, Patterson deconstructs Protestant history, unmasking mythic memory. Likewise, he foregrounds the centrifugal forces which subvert the possibility of unified identity for community or individual. The central event of the book, the building and lighting of the 12th of July bonfire, takes place without a proper 'centrepole'. Despite the plea, 'let's have no more fighting among ourselves', which ironically comes from the super-bigot, Bobby the binman, what should be the occasion of communal celebration turns out to be a time of marital breakdown and internal dissension and violence. Individual identity is a site of contradiction and contestation. Uncle Simon has no hesitation about taking on the job of building a new Catholic housing estate and speaks disparagingly of Orange parades and bonfires especially when they interfere with making money, yet he is quick to agree with Paisley's estimate of the Civil Rights campaign and summarily dismisses an employee who has been involved in civil protest. The central consciousness of the novel – Mal – is similarly conflicted and complicated. He befriends the Catholic boy, Francy, and feels more at home in Francy's company than with his parents or his own gang, yet shares many of the prejudices of his group, siding with Andy against the Catholic boys who want to join the game of football. He participates unquestioningly in the atavistic burning of images of the pope and Gerry Fitt on the 11th night bonfire amid the cheers and whistles of sectarian bitterness, yet, a little later, looking down on Belfast from his uncle's back garden, he voices new awareness of the interdependency of the different parts of the city. Protestants and Catholics alike, he concludes, 'If they could only see the city from where he saw it, could see how it was linked, built up, each part depending on the others, they wouldn't cause trouble anywhere, knowing that if they did they put everything at risk' (115). Happily, Patterson resists turning his ten year old protagonist into a fulsomly idealised hero, a mouthpiece for his own didactic purposes. Preserving a realistic approach to psychological and social process, he makes Mal's achievement of new awareness a tense and faltering process, and balances it with sympathetic understanding of the attractions of communal solidarity, the human desire to belong, to be part of a group.

Mal's new awareness is a matter of larger perspectives, the attainment of an enabling distance from which to interrogate the nature and meaning of home: 'in the shadow of Cave Hill, overlooking the city, he (Mal) had wondered why people didn't pull together a bit more to sort everything out; but what he hadn't seen was how easy it was to think such things up there at his aunt and uncle's house, with its patio and breakfast bar and long, long garden' (201). The lesson in perspective is reiterated later in the novel, when Francy tells Mal about his potentially vicious confrontation with the incensed Protestant youth, Mucker, whose 'centrepole' Francy has destroyed. Disappointing Mal's expectations of a violent showdown, Francy explains: 'we're not talking John Wayne films here ... all these years, they'd been filling our heads with that much shit, it was starting to get into our eyes. We were seeing things; seeing big men when we weren't any sort of men at all – just two wee lads squabbling over a dump and a frigging bonfire. They weren't worth killing for ... So, I dropped the hatchet' (208). Here, Mal learns a crucial lesson about the dangerously alienating content of the dominant narratives of masculinity and community, and about the value of defamiliarising perspectives. This is the significance of the repeated references to the televised moonshots, which serve to place the sectarian feuding on the streets of Belfast in a larger narrative of human destiny. Mal's and Francy's enlightened perspectives do not in the end prevail, but the important thing is that the apparently monolithic, hegemonic mainstream narratives have been interrogated and exposed, and an agenda of redefinition has at least been set.

Patterson tells of how the writing of his first novel, *Burning Your Own*, benefited from his own position at 'a historical and geographical remove' from what was essentially the circumstances of his own childhood. Living in England, he says,

> I was given an insight into the tensions which surfaced in Northern Ireland when I was a child of eight. By the same token, I hoped that by exploring in novel form territory that existed at a historical and geographical remove I might be able to find new perspectives from which to view events that were, in 1986–7, in every sense much closer to home.[15]

15 Glenn Patterson, 'I am a Northern Irish novelist', in Ian A. Bell (ed.), *Images of Nationhood in*

With the escalation of the Troubles in the 70s, he continues,

> The city was changing day by day, its buildings were being erased, its roads rerouted, its territorial boundaries redrawn. While there can be no denying the destabilizing effects, social and psychological, of all this (I choose the words deliberately) deconstruction and revision, it nevertheless contains within it a certain liberating potential. In particular it resists the closure of traditional interpretations in which one unchanging territory is endlessly contested by two mutually exclusive tribes: the old politics of one thing or the other. Identity becomes dynamic rather than birth-given and static. Concepts like flux and exchange replace the language of original states.[16]

The words Patterson chooses so deliberately ('deconstruction', 'revision') are designed to intrude the city into the textual arena. They turn the city into a metaphor for change. As Richard Kirkland explains, 'Belfast has been, until recently, an unwritten city placed beyond the process of metaphoric displacement by its own self-evident physicality ... To write the city, to make it *visible*, is to stress its place in spatial territory yet also to perceive its contemporaneity through narrative within the process of a fragmented history.'[17]

Patterson's second novel, *Fat Lad*, writes the city as part of a rapidly metamorphosing, postmodern culture, from the point of view of twenty-six year old Drew Linden, a thinly veiled portrait of the artist as a young man. Returning from England to take up a position as assistant manager of a city centre bookstore, Drew is not a little disoriented by the experience of a city redefining itself in terms of an advanced, globalising consumer capitalism:

> The Belfast he had left, the Belfast the ex-Pats foreswore, was a city dying on its feet: cratered sites and hunger strikes; atrophied, self-abased. But the Belfast he had heard reports of this past while, the Belfast he had seen with his own eyes last month, was a city in the process of recasting itself entirely. The army had long since departed from the Grand Central Hotel, on whose levelled remains an even grander shopping complex was now nearing completion. Restaurants, bars and takeaways proliferated along the lately coined Golden Mile, running south from the refurbished Opera House, and new names had appeared in the shopping streets: Next, Body Shop, Tie Rack, Principles.[18]

Contemporary British Fiction (Cardiff: University of Wales Press, 1995), p. 150. **16** Ibid., p. 151. **17** Richard Kirkland, *Literature and Culture*, p.34. **18** Glenn Patterson, *Fat Lad* (London: Minerva, 1993), p. 4. First published London: Chatto & Windus, 1992. Hereafter, page references will be incorporated into the text.

These transformations imply renewed confidence and hope for the future, but they have meant that the old reassuring landmarks and defining boundaries have been erased:

> It was a twenty-minute walk from his flat into town. Malone Road, University Road, Bradbury Place, Shaftsbury Square ... Buildings appeared to him one at a time, stripped of context, jutting into space, as though craning their necks. Where the fuck are we? ... Dublin Road, Bedford Street, Donegal Square – West, North – Donegall Place. (12)

The reconfiguration of the city tends to produce a disorientatingly homogeneised culture, which yet does not completely obliterate the past: ghostly palimpsest that the city is, it continually betrays the ineradicable vestiges of 'the old politics', of tribal conflict and territorialism. Belfast becomes a paradigmatic site of the postmodern, as described by Richard Kirkland :

> Belfast itself becomes through *Fat Lad* a city of flux and commercial modernity displaced within itself by multinational trading interests and observed with the sour dislike of an exile. The city no longer represents essence but becomes a constant second-order simulacra of itself ... Belfast, as Patterson and Carson recognise, is no place; displaced by the all too evident signs of social disruption it becomes endlessly open to appropriation and analogy ... If Belfast used to function under a sign of perpetually missed opportunity it now, as *Fat Lad* demonstrates, operates within a specious internationalism which questions perhaps the most important affective myth of its inhabitants: that Belfast is a special place apart.... yet it is also a city haunted by myth, a city anxious to find significance in narrative, and a city condemned to endlessly reconstitute its past.[19]

Belfast is an inherently unstable city. Built on 'slobland' – 'stolen land' reclaimed from the sea – it is testimony to the human struggle to create order out of chaos, to impose the structures of civilisation upon the flux of nature. Kay Morris, the architect, is the inheritor of this pioneering entrepreneurial zeal and the novel's principle exponent of this perpetually creative and self-creative spirit:

> The battle between destruction and construction, Kay told him, warming to her guide's role, was the oldest battle in Belfast. The congenital predisposition of various of its inhabitants for dismantling the city had been matched at

19 Richard Kirkland, *Literature and Culture in Northern Ireland.*

every turn by the efforts of those who, against this and other, even more elemental enemies, had struggled throughout its history to build it up. Men (for men, in the past they invariably were) who had looked at mudflats and seen shipping channels, had looked at water and seen land. Belfast as a city was a triumph over mud and water, the dream of successive generations of merchants, engineers, and entrepreneurs willed into being. They had to build the land before they could work it. Dredging, scouring, banking, consolidating, they fashioned a city in their own image: dry docks, graving docks, ships, cranes, kilns, silos; industry from their industry, solidity from the morass, leaving an indelible imprint on the unpromising slobland. (204)

Counterpointing this vision of material progress is a counter-text of failure and violence which includes the hubristic folk memory of the Titanic, and the account of city centre bomb which, at the end, wipes out the bookstore.

Patterson emphasises the variety, heterogeneity and contradictoriness of the forces that constitute identity and produce a multi-textured, plural culture. Refusing to settle for any consistent, linear, unambiguous account of events, he unfolds the story gradually, through a fragmented, episodic narrative that keeps looping back in time, shifting from one perspective to another, offering different interpretations of the same data. The result is a gapped, elliptical text, one marked by guilt. The narrative is mainly focalised through Drew Linden, who since childhood has borne a burden of irrational guilt for the Troubles, and even for having been born. His narration speaks his guilt through its repressions and withholdings, its circlings and silences. What Drew cannot admit to consciousness, others tell us about. History is displaced across a range of narratives and we gradually piece together the diverse bits of information, sharing in the process whereby Drew himself gradually confronts his past. He is a fluid character in perpetual motion, refusing to be trapped into any given identity, especially that of Ulster Protestant. He travels through a variety of geographical locations – Belfast, Manchester, Dublin, Paris – transforming and re-inventing himself, seeking self-definition through a labyrinthine excavation of his own and his family's histories. Without stable reference points, Drew is continually open to possibility but, equally, incapable of commitment. His girlfriend, Melanie, discovers in one of Drew's many notebooks the observation that 'Duplicity is the Northern Irish vice. We are always (at least) two people and always false to (at least) one of them' (214). Melanie also knows that however fluid Drew may like to think his identity to be, he is still obsessed with origins. The book's central symbol of the goldfish swimming round and round in its bowl obviously applies to Drew. The fish is too large for its bowl, just as Drew has found Belfast too confining an environment to live in. When his sister Ellen attempts to free the goldfish into the larger waters of the bath, it continues to swim round and round in the small circles it had got used to in its bowl. Her attempts to encourage the fish to widen its horizons only result in its death. Drew, too, despite flight to England, has been unable to swim clear of the confinements of his home place, until the end of the book, when he looks forward to a new job in Paris, and there is the suggestion that he may at last escape from the fish-bowl.

Anna is another character anxious to find significance in narrative, condemned to endlessly reconstitute the past. As she ponders the circumstances of her young husband's violent death, trying to construct a narrative that would explain it, she comes up agains the painful, postmodern realisation of the ever absent or elusive centre: 'it was like trying to hold a pattern in a kaleidoscope, one tiny chip slipped and the whole configuration changed. There was always at least one more factor to be taken into account and the heart of the matter, she came to see, was that there was no heart of the matter; or else (which amounted to the same thing) many millions of hearts' (248). 'Love', like 'Belfast', belongs to a common narrative of heroic struggle to affirm and construct. This is made explicit in the description of Anna and Drew's lovemaking, a blissful moment snatched from the wreckage of both their lives:

> What was involved was a supporting cast of family, lovers, friends disposed collusively about this island and the next and the continent beyond; a conspiracy of events both local and global. What was involved was generations of groundwork, courtships enacted, marriages contracted, births, deaths, and all that fell in between, small happinesses and big fears, modest achievements and heroic failures, titanic struggles, stacked odds, seismic change, adaptability, elation, boredom, certainty, doubt, resignation, restlessness ...
>
> Vast movements of peoples were communicated in the silence of a single kiss. Borders were crossed, identities blurred. Land masses rose and fell with their bodies. (249)

In the structuring of his novel, Patterson reflects this sense of the inexhaustible hinterland of a given moment. The quest for self-identity involves a re-insertion of self into a complex historical and geographical network of human relations. The bomb blast with which the novel ends represents an ultimately futile attempt to coerce the swarm of heterogeneous life into reductive categories, to impose narrative closure and silence all opposition for good.

The International is set in 1967, thirty years before it was written, a time of optimism, growth, prosperity and economic development, when Belfast was on the verge of an accelerated modernisation:

> Only in recent years had the journey on foot from southern tip to northern fringe – from extreme east to far west – ceased to be a comfortable stroll, even now few people I knew missing their last bus home would have dreamed of

taking a taxi. The B.U.M. (Belfast Urban Motorway) was to change all that, of course. The B.U.M. was to give us four-lane, six-lane carriageways in the sky, primary distributor routes, ring roads – inner, outer, and intermediate – with flats where there used to be ratty houses, growth centres where now there were small outlying towns. We were going to be modern tomorrow, but for today the city was little different from the city I was born into ... I reckoned there were probably better places to live and probably places a whole lot worse.[20]

It was also the time directly before the city erupted in sectarian hatred and violence. The novel is set on a precisely specified day – the last Saturday of January 1967; and in a precisely specified place – Belfast's International hotel which 'stood on the south side of Donegal Square, directly behind the City hall', and which, Patterson informs us in an 'Author's Note', was an actual hotel in Belfast until it closed in 1975. In an interview, he further tells us:

> I wanted to write something that would be set on the weekend when the first civil rights meeting took place in this hotel ... It was just something that happened, and there were lots of other things happening ... it's more of an inquiry into how exactly things proceed.[21]

There is a Joycean meticulousness in both the locational and historical detailing, which forms the authentic ground of Patterson's affectionate, elegiac re-imagining of an ordinary day in Belfast before innocence was lost. The novel is a poignant evocation of the end of an era. Patterson's allusion to the next day's inaugural meeting of the Northern Ireland Civil Rights Association in The International is an historical marker of new social and political developments. He makes us aware of brewing civil unrest on the streets outside through the references to the UVF shootings of four of the International's barmen in a Malvern Street bar off the Shankill Road seven months before, while the opening description of an accidental fire in Brand's Arcade serves as a grim foreshadowing of events to come. But Patterson's main objective is, as he says, to give the impression of 'lots of other things happening'. He wants to affirm life's rich diversity, its complexity and contradictoriness, its intransitivity, its resistance to the efforts of the system-makers, ideologues and terrorists to impose their brand of order and authority upon it. The narrative strategies which he employs are designed to resist single meaning, simple linear progression and authoritarian narrative control. Rather, they express plurality, multiplicity and fluidity.

20 Glenn Patterson, *The International* (London: Anchor, 1999), p.62. Hereafter, page references will be incorporated into the text. 21 Glenn Patterson, in interview with Esther Aliaga, in Jacqueline Hurtley, Rosa González, Inés Praga and Esther Aliaga (eds.), *Ireland in Writing: Interviews with Writers and Academics* (Amsterdam: Podopi, 1998), p. 96.

The pre-Troubles setting allows him to marginalise the Troubles, for the essential character of Belfast and its people, he wants to show, cannot be defined in terms of the Troubles only. The 'lots of other things happening' include anti-Maoist revolt in Shanghai, Ronald Regan being sworn in as governor of California, the first appearances in the UK charts of Cream, Jimi Hendrix and the Monkees, the fire on board Apollo 1 at Cape Kennedy, all brought into the Belfast world of the novel through the mass media of newspapers and television. But the chief means whereby Patterson achieves a notable perspectival openness and fluidity is through the creation of 18 year-old Daniel Hamilton as his narrator. Through Danny, Patterson reverses the stereotype of the Ulster character as dourly fixed and inflexible. Continually referred to as 'Danny Boy', the narrator is clearly intended as a symbolic figure, representative of the honest Ulsterman shorn of his traditional bias and bigotry. Danny explains his freedom from sectarianism by telling us of his family background:

> Andy and Edna, my father and mother ... outstanding in only one respect: in this most God-obsessed of cities they had lost their religion. It was not that they were atheist, or even agnostic, at least not actively; one had been born Catholic, the other Protestant – in the absence of grandparents I was never quite sure which was which – but it was as though when they met their native faiths had somehow cancelled each other out. No church marked my arrival into the world and I have left instructions that none is to mark my leaving.
>
> My schooling was, it's true, Protestant, in so far as it had any religion at all, but even that struck me afterwards as simple expediency, the local State primary being a mere two-minute walk from our flats. (41–2)

Danny's narrative weakens the hold of religion on the Ulster character and mocks the absurdities of sectarianism and the bigotry of political leaders such as Ian Paisley:

> Ian Paisley was basically a joke that became less funny each time you heard it. In fact he was so unfunny now it was starting to hurt, very badly. Whether he was dropped on his head when he was a baby or what, his eyes saw catastrophe at every turn; catastrophe for Ulster that is, or more particularly, catastrophe for the Protestant people of Ulster. The Papist hordes were closing in. Our Prime Minister, Terence O'Neill, who had once visited a Catholic school and spoke meekly of reform, was the arch-traitor. Paisley marched around the country trying to convince the Protestant people of Ulster that they were in need of his salvation ... and, while most ignored him, not a few of them came along every Sunday to the church he had built for himself to be scared more. (88–9)

The International itself stands apart from the increasing polarisation and rigidity of the larger society outside its doors. One of the most tensely defined moments in the book is that following Jamesie the barman's reference to Danny as a 'Prod':

> *Prods?* The word caught me like a sharp stick under the ribs. No one in The International had ever made such direct mention of religion to me. (255)

Danny insists he is not a Protestant, and Jamesie, 'annoyed with himself', submits: 'I forgot, we're none of us anything … We're International barmen' (256). The world of the novel is 'international', as opposed to the dark forces of tribalism lurking outside the hotel, and Danny resolutely refuses ready-made, parochial identities, his bi-sexuality further emphasising his resistance to conventional categorisation.

'Internationalism' co-exists with, and illumines, local attachment. Danny's distance from his community gives his perception of Belfast life a greater freedom and variety. The novel, largely constructed out of Danny's point of view, is made up of multiple, interwoven strands which present a multifaceted, kaleidoscopic picture of 1960s Belfast. Freely crossing temporal boundaries, shifting between past and present, Patterson excavates private lives, explaining characters' present circumstances in terms of past events. The narrative is deliberately destabilised. We are repeatedly reminded of the fictionality of what we read. Danny openly admits the limits of his knowledge and indicates explicitly when he relies on surmise, speculation and interpretation to produce a coherent and satisfying narrative: 'I wish I could tell you I got Stanley's story straight from his own mouth. I wish I could tell you a lot of things I can't' (207); 'I know I said I'd take liberties telling this story, but maybe that's taking one liberty too many' (263); '… or maybe I'm losing the run of myself again' (267); 'Ingrid it was who told me all that I have written here about him (Stanley)' (308). At times, Danny hands the narrative over to other characters, such as Jamesie in Chapter 15 or Marian in Chapter 17. In the last chapter, he appears as a forty year old in modern-day Belfast, looking back at the intervening years. Despite violence and death, Danny's final message is one of resignation and hope. He refers to Gusty Spence's comments on the UVF ceasefire of 1994, and recognises him as the man who in 1966 allegedly had been involved in the shooting of the International's four barmen in the Malvern Street bar:

> At the end of his short prepared speech that morning in Glencairn, Gusty Spence engaged the cameras and spoke of the abject and true remorse of the Loyalist terror groups on whose behalf he was speaking.
> It took me a while, but I believed him. (317)

The novel closes with Danny's eulogy to his dead workmate, Peter Ward:

> I can't tell you much else about him, except that those who knew him thought the world of him. He is, I realise, an absence in this story. I wish it were not so, but guns do that, create holes which no amount of words can fill.
>
> We're powerful people for remembering here, I hope that's one thing we don't forget.

With these words, Patterson expresses his recognition of the limits of fiction, while paradoxically affirming its potential for a positive and creative 're-membering' of the dead. Much modern Northern Irish fiction is a remembering; and, as this fiction demonstrates, much remembering is fiction, which may serve either reactionary or progressive ends.

Antic dispositions: Robert MacLiam Wilson's *Ripley Bogle* (1989), Eoin McNamee's *Resurrection Man* (1994)

Polonius's advice to his son – 'To thine ownself be true' (*Hamlet*, 1, iii) – seems like sound common sense. It accords with generally held moral and religious values and has the ring of proverbial truth. However, its assumption of the existence of an inner, single self to which one can be true is not something that is any longer taken for granted. Postmodern psychology dispenses with the concept of the unitary self claiming that identity is a series of masks which one puts on in response to different situations and different people; and, as the psychologist Kenneth Gergen says, 'Once donned, mask becomes reality'.[22] Hamlet's announcement that he 'perchance, hereafter, shall think meet/To put an antic disposition on' recognises the polymorphous self, and indicates that the 'antic disposition' need not be seen as pathological, but as a functional or strategic style of identity necessary for survival. According to the Hamlet paradigm, the 'antic disposition' is a feature of historical periods that are 'out of joint', the recourse of those who find themselves disenfranchised, powerless or under threat within their society. Rather than judge it simply as a sign of psychological disturbance, it might be more correctly understood as adaptive or even innovative. Hamlet, with his interest in acting, is an adept at wearing masks, and in Act 1 scene 5 he gives notice of new, fluid, personal boundaries which may be liberating, revitalising or self-protective, and which those around him may find threatening or confusing.

22. Kenneth Gergen, 'The healthy, happy human being wears many masks', in Walter Truett Anderson (ed.), *The Fontana Post-Modernism Reader* (London: Fontana, 1996), p.138.

Hamlet's shifting, unstable self and social role-playing represents a style of identity that is prominent in our own period of rapid social and technological upheaval. Writing in 1968, the psychiatrist Robert Lifton dubbed it the 'Protean style'. 'The protean style of self-process, then, is characterised by an interminable series of experiments and explorations, some shallow, some profound, each of which can readily be abandoned in favour of still new, psychological quests'.[23] 'Protean man' is to be distinguished from older definitions of identity: 'For it is quite possible that even the image of personal identity, in so far as it suggests inner stability and sameness, is derived from a vision of culture in which man's relationship to his institutions and symbols is still relatively intact – hardly the case today.'[24] And hardly the case in Wilson's *Ripley Bogle*, or McNamee's *Resurrection Man*. The protagonists of these two novels illustrate many of the key features of Lifton's 'protean man'. Among these are: 'a profound inner sense of absurdity which finds expression in a tone of mockery', and which, as Lifton explains, stems from 'a breakdown of a fundamental kind in the relationship between inner and outer worlds'; a feeling of guilt – 'hidden guilt: a vague but persistent kind of self-condemnation ... a sense of having no outlet for his loyalties and no symbolic structure for his achievements'; a feeling of being 'uncared for, even abandoned', which prompts protean man to respond with 'diffuse fear and anger'; a pervasive 'nostalgia' for 'a mythical past of perfect harmony and prescientific wholeness', combined with 'massive disillusionment'.[25] As Lifton recognises, the condition of 'Protean man' is close to the influential Erik Erikson's concepts of 'identity diffusion' or 'identity confusion': a state of bewilderment, usually associated with the young, at the lack of a stable sense of self. However, Lifton is anxious to stress the positive as well as negative sides of the protean style. 'Protean man' is driven by 'strong ideological hunger. He is starved for ideas and feelings that can give coherence to his world, though here too his taste is toward new combinations'.[26] The capacity for change always contains the possibility of renewal: 'The principle of death and rebirth is as valid psycho-historically as it is mythologically'.[27]

The term 'antic disposition', as used by Hamlet, refers to behaviour which, from the point of view of the social centre, is considered aberrant, grotesque, subversive. Transposed to an Irish context, its connotations of strangeness and oddness are readily recognised as elements of the traditional colonial discourse: English colonialism justifies itself by invoking the Irish racial 'antic disposition', the Other of itself, which needed to be civilised. Wilson's postmodern *Ripley Bogle* deconstructs all such binarisms as the 'civilians and barbarians' opposition, all totalising explanations of history, society or identity, and looks to the potential of protean, hybridised consciousness to produce the plural self in 'new combinations'.

23 Robert Jay Lifton, 'Protean man', *Partisan Review* (Winter 1968), pp 13–24. p. 17.   24 Ibid., p. 13.   25 Ibid., pp 22, 24, 25   26 Ibid., p. 21   27 Ibid., p. 27.

Lifton also recognises a tendency which seems to be precisely the opposite of the 'protean' style – a 'closing off or constriction of self-process … a straight-and-narrow specialization in psychological as well as in intellectual life, and … reluctance to let in any "extraneous" influences'.[28] This kind of constricted or 'one-dimensional' self-process is identified as essentially 'reactive and compensatory', requiring deliberate effort 'to fend off protean influences which are always abroad', and not to be confused with Riesman's concept of the 'inner-directed' man or with earlier essentialist notions of the self. The type of man Lifton recognises is what we might call 'fossilized'[29] or rigidified man, those people who are 'fixed' rather than 'flowing', who have closed themselves off to the complexity and contradictoriness of life. Such is McNamee's Victor Kelly, the 'resurrection man', who, in a bid 'to fend off the protean influences which are always abroad', has closed himself into the claustrophobic world of Loyalist gangsterism and its cult of violence, seeking transcendence in, as Lifton puts it, 'the way mystics always have, through psychic experience of such great intensity that time and death are, in effect, eliminated'.[30]

In these two novels we have two versions of the contemporary crisis of identity. Together they highlight some of the difficult challenges facing (post)modern man: How independent or autonomous can the self be from its given culture, environment, society? How can it engage with external reality without being only fluid and protean? How can it engage with external reality without losing itself in that reality? How can the self pursue its own realisation without losing itself in its own desires?

In *Ripley Bogle*, the 'antic disposition' is an effect of the narrator's radical displacement and alienation: situated on the margins of society, distanced geographically, intellectually and ideologically from his West Belfast, Catholic, Nationalist, working class origins. Throughout his life he has known homelessness of one kind or another. Rejected by his family and peers, he describes himself in these significantly textualising terms: 'I was merely ignored, neglected, edited, tippexed really.'[31] Seeking escape from his community and culture altogether he goes up to Cambridge, but his misconduct leads to expulsion and a return to life on the streets of London, which he finds more agreeable anyway.

Ripley Bogle would seem to be the latest in a line of Irish tramps going back to Yeats, Synge and Beckett. In his Introduction to the *Selected Plays of Brian Friel*, Seamus Deane, alluding to the 'deep-rooted sense of inherited failure' in Irish life, remarks:

28 Lifton, 'Protean man', pp 20–1. 29 See Hugh's warnings against the dangers of 'fossilization' in Brian Friel's *Translations*: 'It is not the literal past, the "facts" of history, that shape us, but images of the past embodied in language … we must never cease renewing those images; because once we do, we fossilize'. Brian Friel, *Translations*, in *Selected Plays*, ed. Seamus Deane (London: Faber and Faber, 1984), p. 445. 30 Lifton, 'Protean man' p. 24. 31 Robert MacLiam Wilson, *Ripley Bogle* (London: Picador, 1989), p. 12. Hereafter, page references will be incorporated parenthetically into the text.

Since the beginning of this century, Irish drama has been heavily populated by people for whom vagrancy and exile have become inescapable conditions about which they can do nothing but talk, endlessly and eloquently and usually to themselves. The tramps of Yeats and Synge and Beckett, the stationless slum dwellers of O'Casey or Behan, bear a striking resemblance to Friel's exiles.[32]

At first glance, Bogle might seem to be such a figure of Irish dispossession and exile. Indeed, this is the way – or, rather, one of the ways – in which he likes to see himself:

The world did me wrong by making me an Irishman. I've kicked hard but Micksville packs a boot like a donkey. When you think about it, I'm practically faultless – a victim of circumstance, timing and nationhood. It's Ireland's fault, not mine. (272)

But try as he may to present himself as a kind of Joycean victim enmeshed in the nets of nationality and religion, his situation is much more complex than that of simple 'victim of circumstance, timing and nationhood'. The course of his life is seen to be determined by his own actions and decisions at least as much as it is by social and historical factors beyond his control. His life is inscribed within a system of representation which Bogle exuberantly writes as much as he is written by. He certainly acts the part of the 'boor' (190) or barbarian, but resists any simple essentialist labelling. If he is tramp and boor, his character is not to be read in terms of natural degeneracy or colonial stereotyping, but in terms of mockery, parody and menace: as both recognition and disruption of colonial authority.

Through the figure of *Ripley Bogle*, Wilson reproduces a type of colonial subjectivity which is characterised by ambivalence, mimicry and hybridity. Boglean identity is heterogenous, changeable and ambivalent, split by othernesses within, and hybridized through contact with the external Other. As Homi Bhabha explains: 'The fantasy of the native is precisely to occupy the master's place while keeping his place in the slave's avenging anger. "Black skin, white masks" is not a neat division; it is a doubling, dissembling image of being in at least two places at once.'[33] Wilson follows Bhabha in re-configuring monolithic categories such as race and class in terms of crossings, interstitial spaces, splits and joins, and using notions of plural identity and cultural hybridity to challenge the oppositional, identitarian politics of both nationalism and colonialism.

Bogle delights in evading all fixed positions. His entire career is characterised by a resolute refusal to conform to any social institution or communal organisation,

32 Seamus Deane, 'Introduction', *Selected Plays of Brian Friel*, pp 14–15.   33 Homi Bhabha, 'Interrogating

whether family, school, or Cambridge. Early on he lays claim to a hybrid identity that cannot easily be accommodated within any of the existing formulae. On his first day at school this 'all-inclusive type of chap' insists on calling himself 'Ripley Irish British Bogle' in the face of coercive social forces and more straightforward categorisation: 'She stressed with some vigour that no matter what anyone else were to call us, our names would be always Irish' (14). Bogle's hybrid parentage is 'part Welsh and part Irish', and this, he says, is 'a fucking dreadful thing to be' (7). Whatever the positive possibilities of such hybridity, it also leads to the absurd situation where his 'maternal grandfather was having his legs and most of his testicles blown off at Passchendaele while fighting for the British nation against the German Army – while his brother (my greatgranduncle?) was having his head blown off in O'Connell Street while fighting for the Irish nation against the British Army in the Easter Rising' (7).

The first part of Bogle's narrative adopts the child's fresh, defamiliarising perspective, from which events are emphatically human before they are political. As Eve Patten remarks, 'the stoning of army vehicles is experienced as schoolboy entertainment long before it is perceived as political activity. Set-piece descriptions of a soldier being shot by a sniper and of a local girl tarred and feathered for consorting with British soldiers are presented in vivid cinematic detail, but in the context of childhood horror and voyeurism rather than adult condemnation'.[34] Bogle's memories of Internment Night are informed, not by political outrage, but a child's excitement, especially at the sight of a West Indian British Army soldier standing in his kitchen: 'Boy, was I chuffed or what!' (27). Internment Night 'was all much too good to miss' (28). By adopting the point of view of a young child, Wilson cuts beneath conventionalised ways of seeing, displacing the received Irish Catholic Nationalist perceptions of Internment Night, and offering an alternative narrative of the Troubles composed of elements which have been suppressed or marginalised in the official Nationalist discourse. These new perceptions, conveyed through a detailed Realism, emphasise a child's sense of the force and wonder of the actual. This play with viewpoint is one of a range of narrative strategies whereby Wilson attempts to break down fixed boundaries and create a MacNiecean world in which 'the walls are flowing,[35] a world 'suddener than we fancy it/ … crazier and more of it than we think/Incorrigibly plural'.[36]

Adopting the exile's perspective and a superior attitude, the narrator challenges the fixed identities and received narratives and histories of his benighted homeland. He reduces the historical process to the stark outline of tragic farce in which Protestants and Catholics, IRA, UDA and British army are all ridiculed:

identity: Franz Fanon and the postcolonial prerogative', in *The Location of Culture* (London: Routledge, 1993), p. 44.   **34** Eve Patton, 'Fiction in conflict, pp 128–48 (pp 136–7).   **35** Louis MacNeice, 'Variation on Heraclitus', *Collected Poems* (London: Faber and Faber, 1966), p. 502.   **36** Louis MacNeice, 'Snow', *Collected Poems*, p. 30.

What you must remember is that our particular generation of Irish folk were born into all that crap. We knew nothing else. Think about it. Picture it. The mid-sixties, the birth of Maurice and myself. There aren't actually many bombs and guns around as yet – just a lot of jobless Catholics getting the shit kicked out of them and having their homes burnt down on Protestant feast days, adding to their well-stocked catalogue of hatred and injustice.

Soon, however, will come the Civil Rights marches. The Protestant lot will get annoyed. They (reasonably, I feel) would rather like their civil rights to remain exclusively Protestant. So, the British Army will be drafted in to protect the Catholic minority from the brutality of their Proddie countrymen. Maladroitly enough, the British Army will then shoot a little bunch of unarmed Catholic civilians, clerics and toddlers on Bloody Sunday. In their turn, the Catholics grow rather peeved and start exterminating a whole plethora of soldiers, policemen, prison officers, UDR men, Protestants, Catholics, English shoppers, Birmingham pubgoers and men who make the mistake of editing the *Guinness Book of Records.*

Tsk, tsk, tsk! What chance did we ever have? For a piece of normality? Not much. (83)

Bogle's satiric denunciation of the dominant discourses of Ireland continues through parody and pastiche, which simultaneously remind us of the constructed nature of the novel as a series of literary conventions. His Deirdre story is an ironic re-writing of both the *Book of Leinster* and Joan Lingard's *Across the Barricades*; his Maurice Kelly story is a deliberately exaggerated imitation of a Troubles thriller; the opening account of Bogle's birth in 'It Begins' echoes the depressed Beckettian narrative of birth and childhood beginnings; the account of Bogle's hallucinatory encounter with the four brothers and a 'Harridan' in a Kilburn pub plays intertextually against Joyce's 'Night-time' episode in *Ulysses* and Flann O'Brien's ironic treatment of the themes and tropes of Irish revivalism in *At-Swim-Two-Birds*. Bogle reacts particularly venomously against the conventionalised and sentimentalised discourse of Romantic Nationalism, which he brands as a thorough-going American- and academic-bred lie:

All that old Irishness crap promoted by Americans and professors of English Literature. Menace and cupidity. All balls...

Our Ireland is a lovely place,
A supergroovy nation.
Bigotry is her pastime
Death her occupation.

POSTMODERN HUMANISM / 119

> What is it about Ireland the Irish love so? What makes them guff on so endlessly about their country? Is it the pain and the poverty, the death and danger? Is it the spite, hatred, treachery, stupidity, vice, inhumanity or the comfortless despair? (160)

The narrator's re-location to Cambridge University allows him to switch attention from one of the categories of colonial subjectivity – 'Irishness'- to the other – 'Englishness'. He offers his assessment of Cool Brittania, as he did of his Irish background, from a liminal position that is both within and without the object of his scrutiny. England, which historically has constituted Irish identity in the demeaning terms of the barbarian 'other', is itself now seen, as a site of constructed identity, to be vulnerable to post-colonial manipulation. Post-imperial England, Bogle opines, is in a state of terminal decline, 'Remote, impersonal, disengaged. Easy pickings for the dark, concocted vitality of the Celt (i.e. me)' (171). The English are a race drained of power and vitality. Traditional English values and institutions, as presented by Bogle, are hopelessly degraded, disfigured by an encroaching popular culture and blighted by an endemic violence and racism. Yet Bogle's narrative is always ironically self-subverting and ambivalent. He himself is culpable of the most horrifying violence (as in his account of the fight with another mad, drunken derelict who accosts him in Hyde Park), and, for all his disaffection with Cambridge, he freely admits his susceptibility to English 'charm', personified by fellow student, Laura, an idealised image of bourgeois Englishness, as inspirational a symbol as Petrarch's muse: 'For a time, for a very short time, she made me a little like her. She dragged me halfway up to meet her. By jiminy, it was awfully nice up there with all that charm and discernment. I'm grateful for the jaunt' (228). He may savagely mock 'Englishness', but his consciousness is shaped and stocked by the Golden Treasury of English literary culture, from Dickens and Orwell to Shakespeare, Shelley and T.S. Eliot. Following Hugh's advice to his Irish-speaking peasant students in Friel's *Translations* – 'We must learn these new names ... We must learn to make them our own. We must make them our new home'[37] – Bogle's bravura polyvocal discourse is a powerful representation of counter-domination: yet behind the impressive verbal display lies a contradictory mixture of feelings, among them uncertainty, self-consciousness and inferiority as well as defiance and self-assertion.

Bogle, like Dr Aziz in Forster's *Passage to India*, Dr Veraswami in Orwell's *Burmese Days* or Ralph Singh in V.S. Naipaul's *The Mimic Men* is a 'mimic man'. For Bhabha, mimicry is ambivalent because it requires both similarity and dissimilarity: 'a difference that is almost the same, but not quite'.[38] Irish Bogle is like the English

---

37 Brian Friel, *Translations*, in *Selected Plays*, p. 444.   38 Homi Bhabha, 'Of mimicry and man: the ambivalence of colonial discourse', in *The Location of Culture*, p. 86.

coloniser but remains different. Bogle's near-duplication of authority, in Bhabha's analysis, might be construed as oppositional to the extent that it contains within it uncertainty and the threat of subversion. Mimicry disturbs by displacing and problematising the coloniser's 'essence' or 'authenticity'. Bogle's double vision (both Irish and English) makes him a figure of suspicion, but the challenge he poses to the power and difference of authority pushes beyond mimicry and mockery to explicit menace:

> I kept chancing my arm. I pushed my luck, shoved my fortune and jostled my fate. I persisted in going too far. I picked fights, skipped lectures, told lies, got pissed, taunted dons and made fewer friends. I fucked everyone off in a big way ... At the Boat Club Dinner (I crashed) I chatted up the master's wife in rough-house manner and got chucked out. On another drunken occasion I made a pass at our dodgy Franciscan Chaplain ... (206)

As Bhabha notes: 'The ambivalence of colonial authority turns from mimicry – a difference that is almost nothing but not quite – to menace – a difference that is almost total but not quite'.[39] This is the menace confronted by Dr Byron, the senior tutor, before whom Bogle is arraigned for his insubordinate behaviour. Byron attempts to neutralise the menace represented by Bogle by stripping from him the mask of rebel and misfit: 'Things are changing here but neither quickly nor, I'm glad to say, a whole hell of a lot, Much, thankfully, stays the same. Whether you like it or not, when you came to Cambridge you signed yourself up as a member of an elite ... Egalitarians don't come to Cambridge. Not real ones' (211). Colonial control relies on the capacity of the master class to accommodate difference, to appropriate the Other, and to produce the colonised as entirely knowable: 'His (Dr Byron's) little smile was full of kindness and the promise of future kinship. Inclusion. It made me want to puke' (211). Refusing to assimilate, Bogle resists the colonialist discourse as he had resisted the dominant narratives of decolonisation: he prefers to continue to occupy an interstitial position from which he can interrogate both Englishness and Irishness. Following Bhabha, David Lloyd and Luke Gibbons, Wilson elaborates a displaced postmodern discourse of fragmentation and hybridisation in preference to a totalising narrative which aims for traditional effects of unity, identity and closure. Boglean postmodern post-colonialism is characterised by what Lloyd calls 'adulteration' (similar to Bhabha's 'hybridity' – a 'stylisation of the hybrid status of the colonised subject as of the colonised culture'[40]) and by what Gibbons calls 'allegory' (the articulation of 'a fugitive existence on the margins between the personal and the

---

39 Ibid., p. 91.   40 David Lloyd, 'Adulteration and the nation', in *Anomalous States: Irish Writing and the Post-Colonial Moment* (Dublin: Lilliput Press, 1993), pp 88–124 (p. 110).

political'.[41]) Eschewing the abstraction of essences and a classical dualistic logic, Wilson emulates Joyce, the master of heterogeneity, parody, 'adulteration', and 'allegory', whom Wilson has acknowledged as a mentor. Wilson's text is contentious because its ambiguity is disruptive of fixed identities, whether colonialist or nationalist.

'Ripley Bogle' refers to both an individual and a novel. Identity is an ever-revisable script, subject to 'revision', 'erasure', 'arbitration' (269–70) and other kinds of radical fictionality and textual play. Bogle's narrative is full of omissions, suppressions, evasions, deviations and additions. He indicates explicitly those stress-points where he was 'spoofing' and candidly considers his reasons for playing games with his reader. 'I wanted you to like me', he confesses. By suppressing certain facts and inventing others, he seeks to construct a more sympathetic, more romantic, even heroic, narrative of himself; but at the end, he re-writes his story, hoping to attain 'some kind of wisdom' (270). The novel, in its picaresque form and subversive comedy, is a carnivalised text. Bogle, through his behaviour and language, undercuts the established order and asserts an unruly, carnivalistic energy. But at the end Bogle arrests the carnivalistic play by confronting the need for an authentic textuality. The novel, as Bakhtin would say, is a site of conflict, a heteroglossia of contending voices and identities. In Bakhtin's model, the text is in a state of internal tension between centripetal and centrifugal forces, the centrifugal forces dispersing and destabilising the text, the centripetal forces acting to press it towards closure, unity and confirmation of consensual cultural values. Wilson favours the centrifugal tendencies, decentering authority, upsetting hierarchical orderings, and subverting official systems of life and thought. He does so by adopting the narrative perspective of the indecorous Beckettian tramp situated on the extreme margins of the official world, by constructing Bogle's narrative out of a profoundly self-conscious speech diversity (which even involves crossing the usual genre boundaries to incorporate elements of drama text, film-script and verse), and by turning Bogle into a playfully unreliable narrator. Bogle is an impresario of alternatives and false identities, his masquerade functioning both as survival technique and virtuoso display of his own creativity. The danger is that in assuming and discarding many masks he loses any sense of a coherent self. So, working against the centrifugal energies are centripetal forces which finally require honest self-confrontation and an end of 'evasion'. At the end, the narrator, a kind of 'resurrection man', experiences a momentary epiphanic, Zen-like quietude, in which the value and beauty of the material instant make themselves fully felt. 'Starved for ideas and feelings that can give coherence to his world', he looks forward to an authentic existence founded on 'new combinations':

41 Luke Gibbons, *Transformations in Irish Culture* (Cork: Cork University Press, 1996), p. 145.

That's it. The end. I'm glad it's over. I was running out of evasion. I've sown up all my pockets and I've nowhere left to put my bullshit. I produce the last of my cigarettes. I take it slowly, savouring the process. My last match flares bright and sudden in the mist and I ignite successfully. My exhaled tobacco breath is indistinguishable in the moist fumes of the coiling, weary air. I sit up a little and press my eyes into gazing service. Empty-bellied, I tremble with meagre content. I smile without reason. Things aren't so bad. Perhaps the situation may be resurrected. (272)

Bogle is not passive and helpless. Though he likes to blame his present situation on his Irish background, this notion of historical determinism is counterpointed by the sheer energy and variety of his linguistic performance, which constitutes a graphic assertion of the self's essential freedom from the environing pressures. *Ripley Bogle* is a statement of both the positive and the negative potential of an aesthetics and politics of postmodern fictionality. The novel's concept of textuality dismantles oppressive hegemonic discourses and suggests the positive possibilities of post-colonial political and ethical revisionism and reconstructivism. However, a text where all meaning is seen to be an effect of rhetoric, where there is no stable condition of identity, may also be considered as demonstration of the postmodern capitulation to performative pragmatism. The novel affirms the transformative power of the creative imagination to reshape the ostensibly fixed material world of history in order to produce new identities for human beings, but there is little reason for seeing its celebration of artifice, its self-reflexivity, its ideological fluidity, as anything more than a manifestation of an immature and irresponsible ethical relativism, the triumph of the culture of the simulacrum.

Eoin McNamee's *Resurrection Man* is based on Matthew Dillon's *The Shankill Butchers*, a documentary account of the Loyalist killer gang which terrorised Belfast in the 1970s. McNamee takes the historical personages and the actual events which Dillon presents objectively and factually and tries to understand and explain the perverse impulses and fantastical violence that lie beneath the orderly surfaces of civilised life and seem to defy all rational explanation. The focus of McNamee's attention is Victor Kelly, a character based on the real-life gang leader, Lenny Murphy. McNamee's opening gambit by way of explaining Kelly's behaviour is psychological rather than political. Although ostensibly sectarian – Protestants killing Catholics – the violence is not seen as deriving essentially from religious bigotry. Some of the most brutal acts of savagery in *Resurrection Man* are perpetrated by Protestants on other Protestants. Clearly, McNamee wishes us to consider other more fundamental factors involved in accounting for violence of such extreme savagery. Thus, the novel opens as ironic *Bildungsroman*, sketching Victor Kelly's family background and the circumstances of his childhood. Victor, we see, is not only socially disadvantaged, but also psychologically deformed. The relationship between mother and son is unhealthily close. His Oedipal mother-fixation prevents him from forming normal relationships with other women. His father is a silent shadow whose most significant contribution to the family has been to burden them with a Catholic surname.' Identity, whether afforded by family name or street name, becomes Victor's dangerous obsession: uncertainty about his own identity is what drives him to the violent assertion of one.

Declan Kiberd, drawing on examples from the writings of Joyce, Synge, O'Casey, Kavanagh and Pearse, shows that 'the Irish father was often a defeated man', and that the 'over-intense, clutching relationship between mother and son' often implied 'something sinister about the Irish man, both as husband and father. Women sought from their sons an emotional fulfilment denied them by their men'.[42] The constant preoccupation with father-figures, Kiberd continues, 'is the tell-tale sign of a society which is unsure of its ultimate destiny. Its rebellions are conducted not so much against authority figures as against their palpable absence. These gestures rehearse not the erosion of power so much as the search for a true authority'.[43] Victor exhibits this 'constant preoccupation with father-figures': as a child, we are told, he 'always took up with older boys, men sometimes, who were not concerned about his moral welfare'.[44] Eventually he finds a father substitute in the manipulative Nazi sadist, Billy McClure, the man who pretends to become his minder, and betrays him to his death. Through violence Victor seeks 'a true authority', a sense of self, in a world of 'palpable absence'. The knife attacks involve the most hideous mutilation of the tongue ('the root of the tongue had been severed'), as if in revenge against the failure of the silent father whose throat the son would like to cut when he's shaving him at the end.

Kiberd's Freudian account of psychological forces at work in the production of rebel sons would seem to be relevant to the presentation of Victor Kelly:

> Children with problems have traditionally been described as mother-dominated, but such problems may often be attributed to the father's refusal to assume full responsibility ... By asserting his due authority over his children, the father allows them to explore their own anger until they can control it at will and learn to stand up for themselves. Even more importantly, the father teaches the child that other people have needs too, and that everyone functions as a member of wider and wider groups. When such family authority is not asserted, the child may become a self-indulgent subversive with no respect for the configurations of the larger community ... in other words, a rebel ... If

42 Declan Kiberd, 'Fathers and sons', in *Inventing Ireland: The Literature of the Modern Nation* (London: Vintage, 1996), pp380–94, pp 380–1.   43 Ibid., p. 389.   44 Eoin McNamee, *Resurrection Man* (London: Picador, 1994), pp 7–8. Hereafter, page references will be incorporated parenthetically into the text.

the father does learn to assert himself ... the child can begin the task of achieving a vision of society as a whole and the even more exhilarating challenge of framing an alternative.[45]

Without benefit of any positive example of manliness, Victor emerges as a 'self-indulgent subversive' not a revolutionary imbued with a vision of an alternative society. His actions serve only personal needs, not any kind of social project. Trapped in the mirror-phase, and with no defined centre of self, he looks to popular culture to provide him with a repertoire of desirable identities, heroic images of masculinity, such as those portrayed by James Cagney or Edward G. Robinson, on which he can model himself: 'Before they got in bed he took out his big gun he had stuck in his belt and spun it around in his hand all the time watching himself in the mirror on the wardrobe with an expression of being somewhere else completely' (44).

Victor is a typical product of the contemporary postmodern culture of the simulacrum, and, as Frederic Jameson remarks, 'the disappearance of the individual subject, along with its formal consequence, the increasing unavailability of the personal *style*, engender the well-nigh universal practice today of what might be called pastiche.'[46] Extending beyond the characterisation of the protagonist, the stylish depthlessness of postmodern culture characterises the whole world of the novel. McNamee foregrounds the interetextuality of 'real' life through pastiche of a range of popular forms and genres, including the American gangster thriller (in his use of the figure of the lonely investigator single-mindedly hunting down the bad guys, and a narrative voice modelled on a characteristically understated Chandlerese), the comic-strip (as in the comic-strip names of Victor's gang members – 'Hacksaw McGrath', 'Flaps McArthur', 'Biffo Barnes', 'Big Ivan'), children's television programmes (in recreating the 'Romper Room' as the gang's interrogation and torture room), *film noir* (from which he takes his imagery of urban desolation and the pervasive atmosphere of doom and darkness), and Gothic horror stories (in his conception of Victor and his gang as 'resurrection men').

Victor's simulacral, pastiche 'self' is also a 'performing self'. In the scene in the Pot Luck bar where Frames McArthur is executed, terrorism is theatre. Victor makes a dramatic entrance, approaches 'the cone of light in which the chair sat' (164) and adopts the language and style of an evangelical preacher: 'He was talking in a style that his audience were accustomed to. The preacher's formal madness. The voice pitched and commanding. The vocabulary of flood and plague. The audience swayed now' (165). To McClure, the scene 'seemed distant, a televised roadside execution coming intact from a far-off war': it has no more reality to Victor: 'This must be a simulation of death, a poor rehearsal'. After Victor leaves 'the stage', the rest of the

45 Kiberd, *Inventing Ireland*, p. 391.   46 Frederic Jameson, *Postmodernism, or The Cultural Logic of Late Capitalism* (London: Verso, 1991), p. 16.

onlookers, disoriented by Victor's departing from the expected script and actually killing Frames, 'exchanged puzzled glances then moved to do as he said, standing for a moment to gaze on Frames' unconvincing corpse' (166). Victor experiences his own death as an aestheticised reality coded in terms of the gangster films he has seen, and he is perplexed by the way reality contaminates the simulacrum. Leaving his mother's house and returning to his hide-out, 'he felt an expression cross his face like in a film, something's wrong'. Victor 'knew the moves', but the reality – less romantic, less poignant, less aesthetically satisfying – doesn't quite match the familiar script:

> He wanted them to be serious-minded men who shouted out a warning. He wanted words full of allure and danger to shout back. Never take me alive. The rifle fire had a flat industrial sound. Victor felt the bullets force him back against the door. Victor knew the moves. Struggle to raise the gun. Clutch the breast and lean forward in anguish. His face hit the pavement. He did not see one of the men leave cover and walk over to him and put his foot in his neck and shoot him through the back of the head with a snub-nose revolver. There were no words, got him at last. No last rueful gangster smile, goodbye world. (230)

'Thus perhaps at stake has always been the murderous capacity of images, murderers of the real, murderers of their own model',[47] writes Baudrillard. So the reality of Victor's death quickly loses out to its representation, and is converted to 'an "esthetic" hallucination of reality'.[48] Watching news coverage of Victor's death on television later the same night, Heather 'felt as if she was watching something old-fashioned. Archive footage ...' (231). She reacts to the death now as 'a staged murder, a minor spectacle with themes and digressions' (232). Similarly, the earlier episode when two of Victor's gunmen burst into the Shamrock Bar to exact reprisals for an IRA attack on a Protestant filling-station is presented in terms of Baudrillard's 'precession of simulacra': the shots 'did not fit into the perceived idea of gunfire'; 'a whole glamorous ethic was missing from this scene'. In other respects, reality lives up to fiction: the barman 'started to fall, tumbling down the stairs in a graceful, cinematic manner' (140). Back on their own territory, the gunmen 'were like heroes from a film with John Wayne' (141). As with Victor's death, the narration passes directly from the event to its re-presentation on the television news. Again, McNamee focuses on what occurs in the mediating process, this time indicating a displacement of the real into the modalities of Gothic Horror: 'There was an atmosphere of disinterment, grim cloaked figures working by lamplight, poisonous graveyard vapours' (142).

47 Jean Baudrillard, 'The evil demon of images and the precession of simulacra', in Thomas Docherty (ed.), *Postmodernism: A Reader* (Edinburgh: Harvester Wheatsheaf, 1993), pp 194–200, p. 196.   48 Jean Baudrillard, extract from *Simulations*, in Patricia Waugh (ed.), *Postmodernism: A Reader* (London: Edward Arnold, 1992), pp 186–9 (p. 186).

Both the perpetrators of violence and the newspapermen who write about it are disturbed by the unreality of the media reports: Victor 'became distrustful of the narrative devices employed ... He heard accounts of events he had been involved in which conflicted with his experience' (39). The violence, we are told, 'had started to produce its own official literature' (92) – sanitised versions of events that diverged from actuality. Ryan notices 'how newspapers and television were developing a familiar and comforting vocabulary to deal with violence ... Atrocity reports began to achieve the pure level of a chant. It was no longer about conveying information. It was about focusing the mind inwards, attending to the durable rhythms of violence' (52). Events are converted to text; the city to the giant ordnance survey map which covers Ryan's desk, and the internal street-map which Victor carries about in his own head: 'he felt the city become a diagram of violence centred about him' (11). Reality becomes its representation. To know the real is no longer to know something stable.

Just as Victor recognises the mismatch between actual occurrence and representation, so he is aware of a gap or slippage between external reality and his own perception of it. At the end, his weakening influence is indicated as an increasing disorientation in a rapidly changing world:

> They (street names) had become untrustworthy, concerned with unfamiliar destinations, no longer adaptable to your own purposes. He read the street names from signs. India Street, Palestine Street. When he spoke them they felt weighty and ponderous on his tongue, impervious syllables that yielded neither direction nor meaning.

The street names become 'untrustworthy' because they imprison the citizens of Belfast 'in a linguistic contour which no longer matches the landscape of ... fact' [49] (the history of Empire which they tell), and can no longer be relied upon to delineate the contemporary narrative of Belfast: the remapped city no longer corresponds to the deeply etched topographies of Victor's racial memory. His topographical disorientation betrays a deep uncertainty about identity, the authority of the self, the relation between self and world; and to ward off these troubling feelings, the names of Belfast streets are intoned like a mantra.

Robert Lifton has the following observation to make on the 'profound psychic struggle with the idea of change itself' which 'Protean man' (whether the willing or the reluctant role-master) experiences:

> He is profoundly attracted to the idea of making all things, including himself, totally new ... but he is equally drawn to an image of a mythical past of perfect harmony and prescientific wholeness ... Moreover, beneath his transforma-

---

49 Brian Friel, *Translations*, in *Selected Plays*, p. 419.

tionism is nostalgia, and beneath his restorationism is his fascinated attraction to contemporary forms and symbols. Constantly balancing these elements midst the extraordinarily rapid change surrounding his own life, the nostalgia is pervasive, and can be one of the most explosive emotions. This longing for a 'Golden Age' of absolute oneness, prior to individual and cultural separation or delineation, ... sets the tone for the politically Rightist antagonists of history.[50]

Victor, too, while being attracted to the 'contemporary forms and symbols' of popular culture, longs for a 'Golden Age' of old Belfast:

> Victor found that he could see faint outlines of the old streets on the ground. If he squinted his eyes he could almost see the streets themselves, windscoured and populous. The coopers on the quay, the ropeworks, the bakery, men selling milk from the tin, the honey-wagon from the abattoir ...
>
> But these were not his streets and he found himself drawn back to the night-time rides ... and the sense that he had created a city-wide fear and put it in place and felt it necessary to patrol its boundaries. (202)

Situated midst 'the extraordinarily rapid change surrounding his own life', and caught between his 'restorationist' and 'transformationist' impulses, Victor finds that he has, quite literally, no ground to stand on. The landscape itself is imaged in terms of instability and danger. Victor's mother 'had told him that the city stood on a former marsh', and Victor grows up nourishing himself on dreams of mastery and stability:

> When he was young his ambition was to be a doctor curing people with wisdom and touches of his admirable hands. He would tell the world how much he owed to a firm upbringing in the absence of a father. He would buy his mother a house on high ground away from the threat of the eternal damp. (160)

Later, in his hideout in Sailortown, when he looks out over the docks, his thoughts again return to his mother's obsession with life's threat:

> He watched the channel buoys at night. Their alternate flicker, green-red, seemed faulty, short-circuited by some deep wildness in the tidal mass. Dorcas had warned him about the lough as a child; the sudden squalls, fast currents,

50 Lifton, 'Protean man', pp 25–6.

> sucking undertows. The sea to her was deadly and graceless – full of shifting bars and ancient murks that required a wariness beyond comprehension. (202)

The view over the city is equally demoralising. Even the city landmarks are unreliable and susceptible to change:

> A different territory now that he was looking at it from this height, seeming unreliable with slithery, grey rooftops and the dominating bulk of the city hospital looking prone to moodiness, as if it were at any moment liable to become detached from its surroundings and begin a surly flotation seawards. (203)

For Victor, who experiences himself in a postmodern fashion – ungrounded, decentred, defined through others, lacking agency – violence offers the possibility of full presence. The outbreak of the Troubles in 1969 does not politicise him so much as allow him to complete an already ongoing 'self-process': 'In 1969 the streets began to come alive for Victor' (27). Where other writers such as Benedict Kiely (in *Proxopera*) and Bernard MacLaverty (in *Cal*) show that self-fulfilment and self-expression can only be realized in a private sphere of sexuality or domesticity dissociated from, although constantly threatened by, the world of political violence, McNamee explores the possibility of authentic existential fulfilment through violence. The private relationship between Victor and his girlfriend, Heather, reads almost as a parody of the romance plot as found in *Cal*. Victor, like Cal, is a version of frustrated and disaffected youth, but where Cal escapes into a passive and apolitical privacy, Victor asserts himself through acts of outrage and transgression, thereby seeking to transform himself from victim to 'victor'. *Cal* is a 'Catholic' novel of guilt, anguished conscience and penance, but in the nightmarish world of *Resurrection Man* murder has a salvationist glamour, an invigorating and transfiguring attraction. The 'antic disposition', with its capacity for violent transgression, becomes the basis for a projected authentic selfhood.

The newspapermen, Coppinger and Ryan, who follow the knife-murders, emphasise the uniqueness of these new forms of violence. Ryan imagines the strange new killer as 'an evangelist with burning eyes, a seeker after fundamental truths' (3). The violence 'declared itself different ... demanded a new agenda' (147). In the investigations of the first murder, they note that 'the root of the tongue had been severed' (15). This sentence is repeated at the end of Chapter Two:

> There was a certain awe in his (Coppinger's) tone. There was someone out there operating in a new context. They were being lifted into unknown areas, deep pathologies ... They both felt a silence beginning to spread from this one. They would have to rethink procedures. The root of the tongue had been severed. New languages would have to be invented. (16)

What McNamee does so effectively is convey the sheer excitement and attraction as well as hideousness of violence. In writing of hallucinatory power, he conveys a sense of contemplativeness, of dreaminess at the heart of the action. The unswerving, Hemingwayesque attention to objective detailing is accomplished with journalistic precision and vividness, without any explicit authorial attempt to guide or influence the reader. At the same time, the language, grounded in simple Realism, gestures towards mysticism. Killing has both an aesthetic and religious potential. This is violence with 'a dark and thrilling beauty' (34). Victor's showdown with Darkie Larche is like 'choreographed movements leading to a duel' (41). McClure discovers 'the transcendent possibilities of silent suffering' (30); when Victor raises his gun, his victims 'looked like the members of a sect devoted to moments of urgent revelation' (48); Heather notes the 'mystic zeal' (135) in his eyes, and the effect he has on his followers: 'She had a sense of the huge faith they had invested in him. A devotion almost religious in its intensity. They carried it about with them like a relic' (93); the Resurrection Men 'were seen as favoured and visionary. Defenders of the faith' (145). When Victor confides in Heather, he speaks of the deep need that violence satisfies:

> He said little about the killings themselves but he managed to convey the impression of something deft and surgical achieved at the outer limits of necessity, cast beyond the range of the spoken word where the victim was cherished and his killers were faultlessly attentive to some terrible inner need that he carried with him. (174)

This is the 'need' of the man with no inner self who requires others to confirm his existence. Uniting the erotic, the sacred and the diabolic, Heather describes him as searching for 'design', some secret significance in life: 'Suddenly she pictured him crouched over a corpse holding a knife. The same intentness on his face that she saw in bed, seeking the pattern, the deep-set grain, with dreamy inventive movements' (175). Through violence, Victor momentarily obliterates doubt and uncertainty, and achieves order and control; his acts of torture and killing 'had formal structure' (29); a set of new knives is 'a rapture of design'(48). To the man who 'knew that ordinary speech was inadequate to the occasion' (52), violence offers him a more meaningful form of self-expression, a way of writing himself – literally – on the body of the Other. The identification of knife and word is made explicit when Victor sees Willie Lamb's butcher knives: 'they looked like something inscribed on the counter, a word or versatile phrase of extinction' (132). Looking at photographs of Victor's victims, Heather notes that 'many were marked with knife-wounds on the torso and limbs, the marks regular, like the script of some phantom tongue' (197).

Ironically inscribed within the narrative context of 'slippage' are the figures of Victor and the resurrection men. Victor's situation is not quite as Gerry Smyth defines it – a protagonist who 'lacks any sense of self' inhabiting an essentialist world of 'evil, unchanging and elemental':[51] rather, he is a protagonist who, lacking any sense of self and inhabiting a shifting postmodern world, searches for a transcendent, essential self through monstrous violence. His fanatical, monomaniacal commitment to this project of resurrecting himself from the fallen world of the simulacrum turns him into a grotesque – not a Christ-figure, more a body-snatcher. Reacting against the protean forces, he prefers the 'imprisonment' of fixed outlines. He is happiest in prison:

> The prison building was a geometric expression of rigorous morality ... He was at home in closed societies with their stringent and predictable codes of behaviour. At this time he felt his most powerful. His life was a thing hedged with magic and the possibilities of renewal. (70)

Withdrawn from a changing world, the resurrection men are characterised in terms of fixity and timeless recurrence. Part One ends with a description of Victor and Biffo doing look-out duty on the roof of their hut in Long Kesh.

> They were given the evening shift and sat in silence, wrapped in blankets and watching the sun set like some vengeful fixture of the November sky, the landscape before them reddened with foreboding. Often they stayed up after nightfall, refusing Glennie's order to descend. Their shapes were visible from the other cages, posed on a bleak and landlocked terrain, motionless figures acquiring a permanence which seemed impervious, amoral, immune to entreaty. (113–14)

Like John Montague's 'old people', these latter-day resurrection men 'pass/Into the dark permanence of ancient forms.'[52] They are creatures of myth not history, marooned amid the postmodern flux, monumental, unchanging, unable to keep up with the flow: 'Enchanted to a stone/To trouble the living stream ...'[53]

The novel's original (and originating) 'resurrection man' is of course the author. 'Resurrection' considered as a form of 'restoration' or 'reproduction' gestures toward Baudrillard's idea of the 'hyperreal' where images replace the real and determine the real. McNamee 'resurrects' the historical figure of Lenny Murphy, through the mediation of a complex network of media references, including Martin Dillon's book; through a range of 'resurrection' intertexts – the Gospels, historical accounts of Burke and Hare, the myths of Orpheus and Odysseus; and through contemporary representational forms. But 'resurrection' also has a 'transformational' connotation: it also

51 Gerry Smyth, *The Novel and the Nation*, pp .121–2. 52 John Montague, 'Like Dolmens Round my Childhood', *New Selected Poems* (Newcastle upon Tyne: Bloodaxe Books, 190), p. 12. 53 W.B. Yeats, 'Easter 1916', in A. Norman Jeffers (ed.), *W.B. Yeats Selected Poetry* (London: Macmillan Ltd., 1975), p.93.

expresses a concept of magically reconstituted self-presence, an idea of escape from (cultural and technological) determinism and the sepulchre of the simulacrum. In this sense, the author need not share Baudrillard's notion of a purely reproductive economy of the sign, but use the aesthetic (parody, allusion, quotation, borrowing of styles) as a way of freeing cultural forms from earlier identities and investing them with new possibilities. The author himself becomes Lifton's protean man whose 'innovations' may be thought of 'as new combinations of old modes'. These redemptive possibilities of the aesthetic are twice hailed in the novel: 'The root of the tongue had been severed. New languages would have to be invented' (15, 16).

McNamee's 'new language' challenges the traditional discursive premises of 'Troubles fiction', undermining 'reflectionist' or Realist conventions of literary form and the usual account of history as 'mirror' or 'reflection' of a reality which precedes it and determines the form of its representation. It problematises the epistemological grounds of texts and, by insisting on the postmodern awareness of the absence of centre or source, expresses the constant slippage and unreliability of meaning. But even more striking and controversial is its treatment of the violent 'antic disposition'. In adopting a narrative stance very close to that of his protagonist, McNamee runs the risk of encouraging the reader to identify the author with the character. At first reading it might seem, as Lionel Trilling said of Isaac Babel's collection of short stories, *The Red Cavalry* (1926), that the writing of *Resurrection Man* is itself 'touched with cruelty'. McNamee deals with extreme violence, yet describes it, as Trilling believed Babel did, 'with a striking elegance and precision of objectivity, and also with a kind of lyric joy, so that the reader cannot be sure how the author is responding to the brutality he records'.[54] As one reviewer described *Resurrection Man*: 'This horrible, brilliant book allows us both to condemn and also to understand the awful addictive excitement of violence, the bloody poetry of it.'[55] The relentless detailing of mutilation and murder ultimately evokes the predictable human feelings of shock, horror and moral outrage all the more powerfully precisely because of McNamee's controversial postmodern style – its ironic detachment and objectivity, its apparent indifference to 'depth', 'meanings' and 'values', its refusal of explicit human sympathy, its mechanistic psychology and choreographed horror.

Border-crossings: Dermot Healy's *A Goat's Song* (1994)

In *A Goat's Song*, written from a perspective south of the border, the Northern Troubles are viewed as a manifestation, in the socio-political sphere, of the experience of division which Healy presents as the basic fact, not just of history, but of the

---

54 Lionel Trilling, 'Introduction', *Isaac Babel: Collected Stories* (London: Penguin, 1961), p. 10.   55 See Picador, 1994 edition of *Resurrection Man*. No page number.

human condition. Focusing mainly on the relationship between Catholic Jack Ferris, whose roots are in Co. Mayo, and Protestant Catherine Adams, whose early child-hood was spent in Co. Fermanagh, Healy puts their affair under all sorts of social and political pressures but insists in the end that the decisive factors involved in the breakdown of the relationship are mysterious, disruptive, natural forces, which he commonly represents in the image of the sea. *A Goat's Song* is thus ultimately con-cerned with projecting a tragically deterministic metaphysical and existential vision, which the fissured society of the North, as much as the lovers' broken relationship, is used to exemplify.

The novel in fact moves between several locales: the Mullet peninsula in Co. Mayo, Dublin, Co. Fermanagh, Derry and Belfast. The central metaphors are of crossing bridges and borders of all kinds, the emphasis on journey, transit and travel reflecting a world of both increased mobility and rootless confusion. As a novel of the postmodern condition, *A Goat's Song* explores the experience of flux, change and instability. It plays with distanced, displaced, ironic perspectives. Identity is no longer fixed by social role or tradition but individually constructed from a range of elements across a wide cultural field. Morality no longer derives from a single cultural heritage but is produced from the choices individuals make as they stand on an ever-shifting cultural ground of diverse traditions, rituals, myths and styles. A gap opens up between language and reality, a disjunction which the protagonist, Jack Ferris, is determined to exploit in his re-writing the past in Section I (though the novel generally conforms to a fairly conservative naturalism).

The novel is in four sections. It opens on a wind-battered cottage in Co. Mayo where Jack is waiting for his lover Catherine, who never comes. The disjointed, episodic narrative reflects Jack's broken, restless state. He is always on the move, walking from his home in Aghadoon to the Adams' cottage in Corrloch to the Erris Hotel in Belmullet. He takes a bus to Ballina, and a train to Dublin, in quest of Catherine. In a drunken stupor he imagines he's in a New York taxi. He's taken home in a police-car. His days are a series of chance encounters with people he doesn't know. He has lost all certainty about himself and his world, and feels tormented by a 'perverse self-consciousness'. Eventually, he signs himself into Castlebar psychiatric hospital, his 'Shangrila', where he begins 'the other life, without her'.[56] Section I ends with Jack's decision to write the story of himself and Catherine as a kind of therapy or exorcism: 'The minute he put a word on the page he would stop loving her. Once it became a story it was over. Some other person would materialize.' Nevertheless, Jack takes up the challenge of shaping a new life for himself through a reformulation of the old. He proposes an aesthetic rooted in the past, but, through a process of

---

56 Dermot Healy, *A Goat's Song* (London: Harvill, 1997), p. 51. First published London: HarperCollins, 1994. Hereafter, page references will be incorporated into the text.

symbolic transformation, capable of transcending the experience of failure and breakdown :

> Now he had to live in a different world. To transcend. To enter a new story. She must be imagined. He opened a spiral-bound notebook and thought. Here it begins.

Section I ends with this hope that, even if love has failed, art may yet confirm the meaning and value of experience. However, the novel's overall structure enforces a bitterly ironic vision of endless circularity, rather than a sense of transcendence. Section II initiates a flashback which, as we proceed through sections III and IV, simply moves forward in time to the depressed situation presented in section I. The novel's end is in its beginning, its beginning in its end.

Section II crosses the border, moving from Co. Mayo to Co. Fermanagh, and returns to the time when Catherine was thirteen years old. As Jack summons up Catherine's past, he finds that he is also calling up her whole family history, including that of her father, Jonathan Adams. Adams is introduced as in many ways a stereo-typical Northern Irish Protestant, strict, dour, convinced of the objective and universal truth of his beliefs and, as a Sergeant in the RUC, an enforcer of the Northern, Protestant, Unionist state authority. Healy, however, treats the character with as much understanding and compassion as he does criticism. His intention is to expose the reductiveness of the stereotype and to demonstrate the way in which life always overflows the usual categories of identity. Adams' characterisation is based on an elaboration of internal contradictions, splits, tensions, paradoxes and ambi-guities, which subvert any notion of unitary or monolithic identity. An RUC man for thirty years 'yet he had never managed to develop a policeman's bearing' (98). To his colleagues he is 'an oddity, an outsider' (107). He is 'a church-goer who seldom went to church, a reader of odd doctrines'. He loves words and books, but exhibits a puritan distrust of literature: 'Fiction for him was irreligious, the act of imagination itself was a door opening onto the void' (116). Always harbouring a deep suspicion of Catholics, his best friend and his best man is Catholic Matti Bonner. Matti, we are told, was 'the only kind witness to his (Adams') other nature' (136). The first major assault on Adams' complacency comes after he is forced to take an objective view of his actions during a Civil Rights march in Derry on 5 October 1968. At first he is 'battle-weary and fiercely satisfied' (118) by his day's work in Derry. He takes three days' leave with his wife and daughters in Co. Mayo: 'With a sense of pride Jonathan Adams flashed his identity card as they entered the Republic' (118). However, from the defamiliarising perspective of a bar in Belmullet, where the events in Derry come up on the television, his actions appear to him in a new light:

He saw the mad look of fury in his own eye. He looked round the bar but no one was taking any notice of him. His chin began shaking. Then he shook uncontrollably.

'Bastards', said someone.

Jonathan Adams slipped away.

Next morning at six they left Mayo without breakfast. They were on the road in the dark. He brooked no complaints. And this time he kept his head down as they crossed the border lest anyone might recognize him. (121)

Adams is forced to confront his fallen nature, his own capacity for irrational and vicious cruelty. No longer can he claim a simple, rational, Christian self: he is shocked and ashamed by the discovery of the demons within. Identity is more inconsistent than he would ever have allowed. Back in Fermanagh, he is a different man. He wants out of the police force and takes early retirement. One of his last acts in the RUC is to salute the passing coffin of an IRA man.

Adams is, in several ways, encouraged to adopt larger perspectives than those of his strict Northern Protestant heritage. His education began when he married Maisie, a Southern Methodist from Co. Limerick, who diffuses some of his more virulent Northern prejudices against both Catholics and the South. Maisie even manages to persuade him to buy a house in Co. Mayo. He expects to find the South an alien and inhospitable place, but instead he finds himself and his family beneficiaries of countless anonymous little acts of kindness and friendship. Prejudice is gradually eroded: 'People called out to them and they called back. It was a new experience. To find they could befriend Catholics without appearing Fenian-lovers. It was a great release that first summer'. Soon he regards Co. Mayo as his spiritual home, and it is in the violent North that he feels 'an outsider' (136), and increasingly 'disorientated' (140). He learns Irish in order to pursue his studies of the Protestant past in Belmullet, and starts reading the Irish mythological tales. He is engaged in 'a search for some marvellous reconciliation' – of North and South, past and present, Protestant and Catholic, the various components of the self. His heterogeneous, transcultural identity emerges in a contradictory and ambivalent space between North and South, Unionism and Nationalism.

Section II takes its title from the tale of the Salmon of Knowledge. Jonathan Adams's story, that is, is caught up in the archetypal master narratives of the ancient Irish legends. The salmon's knowledge is 'a knowledge that concerns itself with the duality of things, the elemental going away and the eternal return ... All knowledge, says the salmon, is a journey' (194). In making the journey from Fermanagh to Mayo, from the strict fundamentalism and regimentalism of his life as a Northern Protestant RUC man to the fabulous world of Irish folklore and poetry, Adams, in his mythic quest for wisdom, demonstrates the salmon's capacity to pass between worlds. But, as the story of Fionn emphasises, pursuit of the salmon of knowledge can lead to a total diffusion and dissolution of self. Of Fionn, we are told; 'He shall never know human shape again. He may turn into what he is not. That, the knowledge will allow. He can be a girl today, a bird tomorrow. A fir tree the day after. He can exhaust all possible shapes but can never return to be a man again' (197). The story of Fionn rehearses the dangers of displacing the originary ground of identity. Robert Lifton, drawing on classical rather than Celtic legend for his exemplar of (post)modern identity, refers to a similar problem:

> We know from Greek mythology that Proteus was able to change his shape with relative ease from wild boar to lion to dragon to fire to flood. What he found difficult, and would not do unless seized and chained, was to commit himself to a single form, a form most his own, and carry out his function of prophecy ... Just as elements of the self can be experimented with and readily altered, so can idea systems and ideologies be embraced, modified, let go of and reembraced, all with a new ease that stands in sharp contrast to the inner struggle we have in the past associated with these shifts.[57]

As an individual in constant process of negotiating new social roles, Adams approximates Lifton's description of 'Protean man', the new kind of individual which Lifton sees as having emerged amid the uncertainties of our time. But Adams never quite reaches that condition of 'polymorphous versatility' which Lifton identifies as characteristic of 'Protean man'. Healy concentrates on the 'inner struggle' involved in making these shifts of allegiance and outlook because he has not given up entirely on essentialist notions of the inherent authenticity of the self. Adams' life as a social being is shown to be based on adjustments to shifting contexts and the need to accommodate divergent – even competing – commitments, but as part of a process of expanding and enriching 'a form most his own'. The novel's identitarian pre-occupations may thus be seen to illustrate the principle of transgression, instability, anomaly or impropriety, while at the same time avoiding a dangerous slide into relativism by confining the play of identity within (and thereby making it complicit with) the traditional frameworks of Protestant/Catholic, Unionist/Nationalist, Northern/Southern.

The problems of 'protean' identity identified by Lifton are more evident in the love-story of the younger generation, Jack Ferris and Catherine Adams, which is told in Sections III and IV. Section III inverts the situation in section II. Where in section II the South is constructed from an alien Northern, Protestant, perspective (that of Jonathan Adams), section III constructs the North from the perspective of a

57 Lifton, 'Protean man', pp 16–17.

free-thinking, free-wheeling, 'protean' Southerner (Jack Ferris). Both Adams and Ferris are seen as products of particular social and historical circumstances – Adams of a divided, over-determined Northern Irish cultural history, Ferris of a post-Nationalistic, post-Catholic, post-ideological Southern culture. Through Adams, Healy shows the dangers of an older generation's fossilisation in traditional prejudiced formulations, and through Ferris, the risk of the non-identity of pure fluidity which threatens a younger generation. In the relaxed and peaceful environment of Co. Mayo, Adams manages to free up and extend his identity, but in the rigidly anta-gonistic environment of Belfast, Ferris finds his life frustratingly constrained, eroded and even threatened. Unaware of, or indifferent to, tribal divisions, he puts his life in jeopardy by innocently befriending both RUC men and Republicans. He crosses back and forth between two sides of town (teaching Irish in Conway's Mills on the Falls Road and living in Protestant My Lady's Road), between two traditions, two languages, two communities, attempting to resist the conditioning forces and life-denying fixities. At home, when Catherine asks him to read the part of 'a woman who agrees to go undercover for the RUC' in her current play, Ferris's reply – 'Oh yeah? ... It's getting that I don't know who I am anymore' – expresses something of the unease he feels at other people's (including Catherine's) attempts to dictate his identity and control his actions.

The novel outlines a sharp contrast between its two main locales: the rural, elemental, Gaelic, pagan/Catholic, folkloric world of the west of Ireland, and the urban wasteland of Belfast, deeply scored by sectarian division. Catherine can feel at home on neither side of the border. She ends up a figure of the deracinated indivi-dual, the perpetual exile, adrift in a world of flux and change. In Belfast 'she was growing away from herself and all the sad conspiracies of the beleaguered city... After a while in Belfast you grew tired' (345). But she now feels equally alienated from the west of Ireland:

> She'd wonder was it possible that she could live that sort of life, out there on Mullet. She read of the neighbours arguing over land, sales in Penney's, ceili music in Tubbercurry, prayers for the dead, set-dancing workshops; and she thought: where do I fit into all of this? It was not only that all this had happened a long time ago in another dimension, that it was rural and unsophisticated. Not even that it was Catholic, with pages of newspapers given over to novenas and mindless prayers.
> It was foreign, and at peace.
> That was what alienated her most of all....
> As she crossed the border at Blacklion she felt like a deserter. (346–7)

What gives purpose to her life is her career as an actress, as professional shape-changer and improviser of different roles. Her breakthrough on the stage comes with a role which Jack wrote for her in his latest play, but, ironically, instead of bringing them closer together, the role takes Catherine further away from Jack, separating her from him in Mayo while she goes into rehearsal and then production in a Dublin theatre. Jack, as playwright, is also an adept in creating new worlds and identities, while, like Catherine, not believing in anything much either. But, without any stable identity, he begins a slide towards total disintegration, a process exacerbated by his isolation and alcoholism. So great is his desire for Catherine that 'he felt for a moment that he had become the woman beside him' (320). Crossing gender boundaries, he momentarily assumes the identity of Catherine; he is 'grateful when his own identity was restored, for he had not the courage to sustain that rootless feeling a moment longer' (321). Even when he retreats to the rural quiet of his home place in Co. Mayo, his breakdown accelerates. His sense of alienation produces a feeling akin to Camus' 'nausea': 'the same mental gap opened again. But this time the wrench was longer and more frightening, for now all natural things – grass, birdsong and sea air – were becoming objects of horror' (383). Worst of all is the feeling that there is no language to express this radical dislocation: 'It seemed to him, just then, that every person knew this, this loss of self, but it could not be told. It was an opening into a non-world' (381). This 'non-world' or existential void acquires a distinctively postmodern inflection in the episode where he takes the disk containing the text of his play to be edited by the computer operator. Here, the writerly imagination is overwhelmed by a new hi-tech 'magic':

> He looked over her head and saw with relief whole pages being erased. Nights and days of work were disappearing. Characters, lines and moments went off the screen like magic. This gave him a crazy sense of satisfaction.
>
> He would like to have leaned in and pressed the erase button so that the entire play would be wiped from the memory. That would have been the business! Leave nothing, nothing at all!
>
> He watched enthralled as the voices of people he had invented sped by like trains into the night. One press of the button and another whinge disappeared into the void. (379)

In this uncertain, accelerated world, Jack and Catherine look to each other for stability and support, but find that trust is continually compromised by disruptive, elemental forces, both internal and external – the dislocating elements of subjectivity, unruly libidinal and neurotic energies, Jack's alcoholism, the separations enforced by space and time. Their vow of fidelity to each other, though repeatedly broken, is an attempt to arrest flux and uncertainty. Healy's imagery continually emphasises their struggle to maintain balance amidst the elemental flux:

> The sea was thunderous. They walked out along the pier. Midway it became dangerous to go any further because the sea every few seconds was breaking across it. They stood watching the seas meeting. Then Jack suddenly, during a lull in the mountainous waves, ran to the far side. He called to her to follow him. But she couldn't hear him. He waved her over. *Come on! Come on!* But she was too afraid to follow him. So he ran back to her. He took her arm. Count three, he said. The waves leapt the pier again. No, she screamed. Then he pulled her across with him. They continued on to the end of the pier with the sea breaking behind them, and each side of them. (367)

Their relationship throughout is figured as a series of crossings back and forth, two lovers constantly reuniting and separating. Repeatedly, they are presented calling to one another across the thunderous seas, or over the sound of boat engines:

> 'When do I see you again?' she called.
> 'The weekend after next in Belmullet.'
> 'What?'
> 'Belmullet!' he shouted over the roar of the engines. 'In Belmullet!' he roared through cupped hands (360);

or over a crackling ship's radio:

> 'What did you say? Can you please repeat the message, Catherine? Over.'
> 'I can't hear you properly. I'm going now.'
> 'When will I see you? Over.'
> 'I'll be down next weekend. I'll leave a letter in the house.'
> 'See you, then. Over.'
> 'Goodbye, Jack. Over.'
> 'Goodbye, Catherine. Over.'
> When her call ended, the skipper started the engine up again. They went on. She was never mentioned. It was as if a fantastic sea-animal had been sighted. They had circled it. Then it dived. Then they went on. (407)

The normal lines of communication are broken and never reliable: Jack receives Catherine's letters too late; he is unable to reach her in Dublin on the telephone; their relationship disintegrates while she holidays without him on the island of Cyprus.

The title of the novel highlights the tragedy of division and separation. The word 'tragedy', Jack informs Catherine, is derived from two Greek words, *Tragos* meaning goat and *Oide* meaning song. According to Jack, Greek goatherds used to separate their herds by putting the bucks on one island and the nannies on another. The bucks, not being able to swim across to reach the nannies, raised 'a mournful cry' (227). *A Goat's Song* is such a tragedy of desire, a 'mournful cry' raised against boundaries and 'big seas' that cannot be crossed. The novel's tragic fervency, anguished questing, and despair at the absurd, constitute a rather different kind of writing from the cool, ironical detachment that is usually associated with the postmodern attitude. Lengthy, rambling, garrulous, lyrically expansive, *A Goat's Song* is an extravagant novel, extravagant in the root sense of the word – roaming outside and beyond the usual structures of language and literary form. Its destabilising and re-writing of fixed notions of identity, community, the past, are conducted through a process of fictional dialogism whereby the terms of 'the search for some marvellous reconciliation' (between freedom and order, subject and object) are revised and revitalised. At the same time, despite the fragmentation and digressiveness of the narrative, it never roams far enough away into such radically displaced and self-reflexive forms as would seriously challenge the Realist's notionally pre-existing unity of an imaginative and aesthetic Utopia.

Historiographic metafiction: Briege Duffaud's *A Wreath upon the Dead* (1993)

The context of Duffaud's novel is the contemporary Irish historiographical and cultural debate which is reflected in the novel's treatment of themes of nationalism, revisionism and modernisation. Duffaud takes a place with John Banville (*Doctor Copernicus, Kepler*), Brian Friel (*Making History*) and Seamus Deane (*Reading in the Dark*) as a writer writing about the writing of history. Commenting on the ideological and political crisis in the North, *A Wreath upon the Dead* makes its own contribution to 'historiographic metafiction'. The crisis in the Northern statelet's political authority is mirrored in the novel's crisis of historiographic and intellectual authority. The surfacing of submerged subversive forces in the political sphere produces the crisis in authorial authority in the literary sphere. Maureen Murphy wants to write a national romance based on the story of two nineteenth-century figures, one a distant relative, Cormac O'Flaherty, and the other, Marianne McLeod, the daughter of a Scottish landlord, who lived in the townland of Claghan in south Armagh where Maureen herself had been brought up. However, Maureen finds that as this discursive field becomes increasingly complicated by her historical research and by her personal memory and experience, she is unable to write their story. The past, she discovers, is a web of competing, jostling narratives. There is no such thing as a single, transcendent concept of historical truth.

The opening chapters introduce the author, Maureen, and her range of sources – the Rev. Richard Flowerdew's book *The Beauties and Miseries of Our Sister Isle* (1840),[58] 'Minutes of evidence taken before Select Committee on Outrages 1852' (128), Peter

Maguire's booklet, *The Forgotten Hero* published in 1930 by the Catholic Truth Society, Thomas O'Flaherty's *Memoir* – 'Publ. Portnafinn Press 1855' (139), contemporary poems, ballads, letters, oral tradition, newspaper reports and, most important of all, Marianne McLeod's journal which stops a few years before the Famine. Like all the other versions of past events, this journal is an openly contested text. The local historian, Dr McCormack, claims it is a 'forgery' (9), the work of a later date, penned by 'an old drunken crook in the McLeod family' (9): but McCormack's opinion is later contemptuously rejected by Eric McLeod, the local schoolteacher and a descendent of Marianne McLeod's. Maureen surveys both 'official history' – the history based on official records which tends to be narrowly political and fulfils a hegemonic function, and 'unofficial history' – the history embodied in memory, journal, letter, ballad and folklore, which is a popular or subaltern history that tends to be de-legitimised as 'mythology'. All these histories, Maureen discovers, serve vested interests, and she despairs in the end of the possibility of a legitimate literature or history-writing.

In showing Maureen's difficulties representing the past, Duffaud sounds out the contemporary critique of the rhetorics of both Nationalism and Unionism. Like O'Faoláin famously before her, she challenges the traditional association of Nationalism and race – the idea of 'Irishness' as a racial inheritance and native culture as a manifestation of an underlying racial or national 'character'. The irony of this form of cultural exclusivity is that it is not indigenous to Irish culture at all but derives from scholarship of the Romantic period and, more specifically, from Ernest Renan's *The Poetry of the Celtic Races* (1896) and Matthew Arnold's *The Study of Celtic Literature* (1912), and is represented in the novel by the Scottish and English landlord class, including Marianne, whose construction of the Irish peasantry in her journal is based on anthropological notions of Irish distinctivenvess: '... reality here is a vast body of people ... moving through our rooms, across our land, speaking an alien language, locked in an alien world whose key is hidden from us' (94). Transplanted to 'a wild, foreign country' (60) and surrounded by the descendents of 'mythical, ruined aristocrats' (92), Marianne finds the peasants 'more interesting' than the people of her own class 'in spite of their disordered imaginations – or because of them' (93). Her journal and letters elaborate the stereotypical mystique of the Celt:

> They laugh and joke and sing. They sing! And they dance. Weddings, baptisms, feast-days, they all gather in barns and they dance their extraordinary dances. All night long the men drink themselves into senselessness with raw home-made spirits. Then magically next morning one sees them toiling up the mountain again, greeting one another, laughing, calling a blessing ... (95)

58 Briege Duffaud, *A Wreath upon the Dead* (Dublin: Poolbeg, 1994), pp 6–6. First published Dublin: Poolbeg, 1993. Hereafter, page references will be incorporated into the text.

Seamus Deane has explained how this stereotyping initiative undertaken by the coloniser defined an Irish otherness in terms of a 'supplement' or 'transfusion of energy' which the English considered necessary for their own survival. The Irish, accepting the stereotype of themselves as wild, poetic, imaginative, spiritual, exploited it for their own purposes, constructing a self-identity founded on notions of radical racial difference:

> [T]he Irish ... finally took possession of the stereotype, modified the Celt into the Gael, and began that new interpretation of themselves known as the Irish literary revival. The revival, like the rebellion and the War of Independence, the treaty of 1922 ... and the subsequent civil war, were simultaneously causes and consequences of the concerted effort to renovate the idea of the national character and of the national destiny.[59]

In the historical trajectory of Duffaud's novel, covering the period from the 1840s up to the present Troubles in the North, she traces the process whereby a potentially liberating Nationalist politics is produced from the forces of colonial suppression. The 'Gaelic' or 'Celtic' stereotype was a means of fixing Irish identity, thereby making the Irish more easily manageable, but as well as performing this colonial function the idea of an Irish 'essence' had its attractions to those native Irish looking for a distinctive cultural identity and a rationale for anti-colonial rebellion.

Duffaud writes the usual revisionist opposition to the grand narrative of Gaelic identity. Through the rich diversity and ironic contradictoriness of her characterisation of 'Irishness' in the novel she shows the limitations of any attempt to impose an ideological or racial uniformity on Irish identity and culture. Writing in 1944, O'Faoláin observed that the Gaelic mystique is 'the opponent of all modernisations and improvisations – being by nature, in its constant reference to the middle-ages – terrified of the modern world, afraid of modern life, inbred in thought, and so, utterly narrow in outlook'.[60] Duffaud reproduces O'Faoláin's critique of the myth of the Gaelic past in her excoriation (through the adolescent Maureen) of Pakky O'Flaherty's obsessive, backward looking Nationalism:

> Yes, yes, we know, she was thinking, we all know you came down in the world, Pakky. We all know your birthright was stolen by Cromwell or John Joe McCormack or some crooked solicitor. We all know that if the Wild Geese hadn't flown you'd be entertaining me with lavish wealth in Claghan Hall, but for once just for once would you let me pay a visit to your daughter

59 Seamus Deane (ed.), *The Field Day Anthology of Irish Writing*, p. 13   60 Séan O'Faoláin, quoted by Seamus Deane, 'Challenging the canon: revisionism and cultural criticism', in *The Field Day Anthology of Irish Writing*, p. 561

> without deafening me with your holy martyred ancestors? I come into Quarry
> Street, I walk the four flaming miles of an August Sunday afternoon for no
> other reason than to listen to records with Kathleen, I'm a *teenager*, did you
> never hear tell of a teenager, Patrick, a girl of my age doesn't want to hear an
> old beardy man telling her some daft yarn about rotten potatoes and emigrant
> ships and murder. (116–17)

Pakky is shown to be not simply a victim of British imperialism but of inherent deficincies in the native tradition, namely his father's drinking, which lost the family their seat in Claghan Hall. Duffaud's critique of the Gaelic cult derives from a view of Nationalism as hopelessly lost to the past, unable to adapt or modernise. She insists on the disruption of the continuum of tradition, the absurdity of the idea of recovering a Gaelic golden age. Pakky's primary text – his 'Bible' (358) – is Patrick Maguire's *A Forgotten Hero*, a highly influential work endorsed by the Catholic hierarchy through publication by the Catholic Truth Society. But Maguire's messianism and elaboration of a sacrificial cult of violence are undermined by another historical text, Thomas O'Flaherty's 1855 first-hand account of his nephew, in which Cormac O'Flaherty is no hero, rebel, poet or romantic lover but a greedy, ruthless philanderer who never 'interested himself greatly in the misfortunes of his people' and 'had little real physical courage' (143). Nevertheless, the fusion of mysticism, violence and Catholicism in Maguire's history is identified as a driving force of Nationalism over the centuries. Nationalism founded on myth, violence and Catholicism becomes the antithesis of a liberal, modernising society. By reading back from the present-day Troubles, Duffaud's revisionist perspective uncovers a monolithic Catholic Nationalist tradition, immune to cross-cultural influences and social change.

Yet Duffaud refuses to embrace any straightforward revisionist historiography for her character. Modernity may be associated with such positive developments as pluralism, Civil Rights and secularisation, but it has also resulted in the shame, hatred and contempt that Maureen feels about her Claghan Bog origins, or her old school-friend Kathleen O'Flaherty feels about her family home in Quarry Street. Modernity has the admirable aim to escape from a deadening Catholicism, poverty, sectarian hatred, enslavement to the past; but only to propel the individual into a superficial cosmopolitan materialism. Tradition may be associated with Gaelic chauvinism, sentimentalism and authoritarianism, but it provides a framework of values and a common history that can contribute importantly to a stable and coherent sense of self. Maureen also realises that however insular, illogical, atavistic or narrow-minded Nationalist mythology may be, it cannot be expunged from an 'honest' history:

> I'll have to keep in mind, she thought, that I'm writing for modern readers
> who most definitely do not want the stage-Irishry of tyrannical priests and

dead men in bogholes. Yes, but if I'm going to be honest, she thought? Could you leave out the folklore and be honest? (111–2).

The 'folklore' is the narrative of the dispossessed, as opposed to the 'truth' of the official, hegemonic history.

> A tragedy so complete and so far-reaching could not surely be regarded as folklore, Maureen was thinking ... We did suffer, that's true enough. We were forced to live on potatoes, and they failed, and a good many of us died. It took generations for us to recover from it. Maybe we've never recovered. Maybe it explains Bobby Sands and the rest, explains our neuroses, our shame of birth, our easy acceptance of death? That's why I have to keep apologising for being objective. Martin McCormack thought it was disloyal of me to want to be objective. Given, he said, the continuing circumstances. Anyone in Claghan would say the same. Because we *did* suffer and that does, surely, set us apart. Justify us. Does it?
>   Could it? (113–4)

Momentarily, Maureen submerges her bourgeois revisionist desire to make Ireland seem modern and civilised to the outside world, and acknowledges the depth of the colonial 'tragedy'. Whatever 'folklore' may have grown up around the Great Famine, no-one can deny the suffering; however much the gombeen Irish had themselves to blame, that cannot take away from the scandal of colonialism which deprived Irish people of the right to political self-determination. She questions the appropriateness of a clinically objective language to normalise or evade such traumatic past events. The idea of writing an 'objective' history, purged of ideology, myth and utopian teleology denies the existence of those subaltern groups for whom the current dispensation has no legitimacy.

And yet Maureen acknowledges that the subaltern folklore, in pursuit of its own social and political ends, can make a mockery of historical fact. The death of Kathleen O'Flaherty's daughter, Sarah, is a case in point. Having discovered that her father is Eric McLeod, Sarah and her boyfriend abduct Eric and hold him in a house in Quarry Street that is rumoured to be used by the IRA. When Sarah is shot by the British army, her distant relative, the Yank O'Flaherty, wants to turn Sarah into a Republican martyr, though there is no evidence that she has ever had any political loyalties:

> They'd say anything around Claghan, Maureen agreed. But gradually the sensational stories were forgotten and the Yank O'Flaherty's version accepted: Sarah as heroine and victim. Sarah, direct descendent of Cormac O'Flaherty,

striking a blow against the cynical McLeod who, years before, had her family evicted so that he could construct a monument to the glorious memory of Protestant landlordism. 'But everyone in Claghan knows that's just not true!' Maureen protested. (463)

Refusing any simple tradition/modernity opposition, Maureen recognises a cultural heritage that is inclusive rather than exclusive, 'both/and' rather than 'either/or'. The Irish past is multifaceted and contradictory. In this truly pluralistic spirit, she continually subjects her own revisionism to revisionist critique. All history-writing, Maureen concludes, is subject to mythic appropriation and penetrated by fiction and ideology. All history is perspectival, subjective, partial, unstable. 'There is no true story', she says to husband Trevor, 'it's just a mess of ambiguities and lies and more or less guesses. And it doesn't matter, it doesn't change a thing. Claghan will make up whatever truth suits it. Don't we all?' (466). Maureen's own version of Cormac O'Flaherty and Marianne McLeod is shown to be strongly conditioned by her own childhood, by her own experience of Claghan and the wider world, and indeed much of the novel is devoted to specifying Maureen's authorial-position in terms of this network of social, historical and political relations in which she is inscribed.

All of the book's micro-narratives – the historicist narrative of Nationalism, Eric McLeod's dream of the Marxist union of Protestant and Catholic working classes, the narrative of Ulster Unionism, Maureen and Kathleen's narrative of absolutist individualism – are refused closure and moral resolution. Duffaud's fragmented anti-narrative writes the impossibility of making any of these histories 'realistic'. Maureen's failure to write the book she had planned betokens the breakdown of the liberal humanist metanarrative of modernity founded on reconciliation and Enlightenment ideas of progression from barbarity to civilisation. There is no master narrative of the past, metalanguage or omniscient narration such as Realism implies. Not even the fiction of a coherent narrative viewpoint can be sustained. For almost one-third of the novel we are led to think that this is Maureen's story of her book-project. However, the novel's centre of consciousness is a shifting signifier: the narrative perspective moves from Maureen and events are focalised through a series of other characters – Lizzie, Kathleen, Eric, Sarah. The result is a radical de-centering (if not quite the 'death') of the fictional author (Maureen). As well as this, the novel's conflicted semiosis, which incorporates historical and pseudo-historical as well as literary discourses, and at several points crosses the generic boundary between prose and drama, produces a radically unstable narrative. The novel rejects the possibility of Realism with its totalising ambitions, its reflection of comparative social stability, and, instead, demonstrates a postmodern insistence on complexity, ambiguity, plurality, heterogeneity and discontinuity. Duffaud is clearly indebted to the tradition of Realism of O'Faoláin and O'Connor and the aesthetic politics of social and political critique of the earlier generation, but she also reacts against the Realist orthodoxy in her reflexive experimentalism. This aestheticism undercuts any communal identification or political purpose. Her metafictional experiment, combining a humanist individualist episteme and a postmodern culturalism, is therefore quite different from that of more obviously political writers such as Seamus Deane in *Reading in the Dark*. Duffaud recognises that the control of meanings is social and political power, but shrinks from any attempt to politicise the polyphony of the signified. The plurality of meaning is never more than a matter of infinite play. The novel's turn from the political world signifies a disillusion with politics and the possibility of change. It suggests a debilitating determinism. Seamus Deane sums up the kind of revisionism Duffaud's novel exemplifies in the 'General introduction' to his *Field Day Anthology*:

> [I]n those 'revisionist' periods, when the myths are dismantled and the concept of 'objectivity' rules, there is often an anxiety to preserve the status quo, to lower the political temperature and to offer the notion that historical processes are so complex that any attempt to achieve an overview cannot avoid the distortions and dogmatism of simple-minded orthodoxy.[61]

Against Duffaud's postmodern scepticism, politically-minded critics insist that not all versions of the past are of equal value, and that choices must be made between one version and another. As Terry Eagleton says: 'It is not true that there is nothing to choose between one political reading and another .... it is not a choice between the factual and the political, but between the sorts of political frameworks which allow us access to the facts, and the sorts which do not'.[62] He warns that if the postmodern 'language of difference and identity is abstracted from this political context, it will end up short-circuiting the very political conditions necessary for its realisation'.[63]

Four trauma narratives: Deirdre Madden's *Hidden Symptoms* (1986) and *One by One in the Darkness* (1996), David Park's *The Healing* (1992) and *Stone Kingdoms* (1996)

The case for considering Deirdre Madden under the 'Postmodern' banner has already been made by Michael Parker in his essay 'Shadows on a glass: self-reflexivity in the fiction of Deirdre Madden' (2000). Describing her as 'a highly sophisticated, very contemporary writer, one who is alert both to changes in the practice and theory of fiction in recent years', Parker declares that 'from the first, her texts have exhibited many of the features of metafiction', amongst which he numbers 'extreme self-con-

---

61 Seamus Deane, 'General introduction', *The Field Day Anthology of Irish Literature*, p. xxiii. 62 Terry Eagleton, 'Revisionism revisited', pp 308–27, p. 323. 63 Ibid., p. 327.

sciousness about language, literary form and the act of writing fiction'; 'a pervasive insecurity about the relationship of fiction to reality'; a 'questioning not only of inherited pieties and verities, but also of the authority of art itself'; 'self-reflexive references, allusions to writing and other kinds of texts'; 'constant shifts in focalization, perspective and chronology, which destabilize the narrative'; 'the conviction that crucial data is being withheld'; and characters' consciousness of themselves as 'plural texts'.[64] In this section I shall attempt to illustrate a progression in Madden's work. Conceived within a context of social, psychic and epistemological rupture, Madden's fiction may be seen to move from a pessimistic to a more optimistic view of the postmodern. In her first novel, *Hidden Symptoms*, the postmodern writes itself in terms of copies without originals, textuality, loss, self-reflexivity; in her subsequent novel, *One by One in the Darkness*, the postmodern offers possibilities of authentic self-expression through restructuration of indigenous or traditional resources.

Hidden Symptoms is a subtly probing study of the experience of loss and absence. Theresa, a student at Queen's is struggling to cope with the loss of her twin brother, Francis, who was an innocent victim of a random sectarian murder two years previously. Belfast and its Troubles are directly responsible for Theresa's grievous and far-reaching sense of loss. Belfast, having cast aside its mask of 'normality' which 'had always been forced, a prosperous facade over discrimination and injustice',[65] reveals itself as a site of unreason and Gothic horror:

> Just as when she was small she (Theresa) had been very ill and the doctor diagnosed the illness as measles (for some reason the spots had failed to appear), Ulster before 1969 had been sick but with hidden symptoms. Streets and streets of houses with bricked-up windows and broken fanlights, graffiti on gable walls, soldiers everywhere: Belfast was now like a madman who tears his flesh, puts straw in his hair and screams gibberish. Before it had resembled the infinitely more sinister figure of the articulate man in a dark, neat suit whose conversation charms and entertains; and whose insanity is apparent only when he says calmly, incidentally, that he will club his children to death and eat their entrails with a golden fork because God has told him to do so. (13–14)

The language of Madden's description of Belfast invites a 'symptomatic reading' of the novel to explicate its latent or concealed meaning, to fill in the gaps and to expand upon the partial explanations provided by the text in order to make it whole and complete. This, according to Pierre Macherey in *A Theory of Literary Production* (1978), is the primary function of criticism as it is traditionally practised:

---

64 In *Irish University Review* (Spring/Summer 2000), pp 82–102, p. 83. 65 Deirdre Madden, *Hidden Symptoms* (London: Faber, 1988), p. 13. First published Boston and New York: Atlantic Monthly Press, 1986. Hereafter, page references will be incorporated into the text.

> For there to be a critical discourse which is more than a superficial and futile
> reprise of the work, the speech stored in the book must be incomplete;
> because it has not said everything, there remains the possibility of saying
> something else, *after another fashion*. The recognition of the area of shadow
> in or around the work is the initial moment of criticism.[66]

The danger in this approach is that the critic usurps the role of author, turning
the text into something which it is not. Thus, Macherey argues, the critic's task is
not to smooth over or resolve the problems which the text raises, but rather to
expose them so that the conditions of the work's literary production, ideology and
history may be revealed. For Macherey, the meaning of a literary work is not contained simply in what it says, but is rather produced in a relationship between
what it says and what it does not say, between the visible and the hidden, between
the explicit and the implicit. The critic's task is to probe the hidden symptoms of
the work's unconscious: 'In its every particle, the work *manifests*, uncovers, what
it cannot say. This silence gives it life'.[67] This silence or absence at the work's centre
constitutes its radical otherness, and as the work's unconscious it contains all that
is banished, repressed, consigned to the margins so that the conscious project can
be realised. But as there is no guarantee that the repressed will stay repressed in
Freudian theory so, for Macherey, the return of the repressed may be brought
about by a reading practice that concentrates on the gaps, omissions and silences
within the text.

In Madden's novel, Belfast is an unstable Machereyan or Derridean text through
whose fractures and stress-points the otherness it had attempted to conceal – its
'political unconscious' – erupted in 1969. What was silenced or negated in the
interests of holding in place a singular, positive, authoritative city/text incubated
hidden symptoms of revolt. Belfast as text is no longer single and fixed, but broken,
written over, traversed by conflicting forces, its inherent contradictions exposed by
the return of the repressed. It is the site of discontinuities, omissions, absences, partial
explanations; of that which remains unspoken, secrets that can only be guessed at. It
is haunted by secret organisations which occupy the social margins and whose acts
of terror remain hidden and untold. Neither Theresa nor her mother knows exactly
what happened to Francis. To Theresa's assertion, 'They just killed Francis because
of his religion, he had no choice', her mother replies: 'How do you know?' (42). Like
the circumstances of Francis's death, the identity of his killer(s) remains in 'the area
of shadow', masked and hidden. Theresa finds that the frustration of being denied
full truth distorts and clouds her whole attitude to life: 'Every stranger's face was a

66 Pierre Macherey, 'From *A Theory of Literary Production* (1978)' in Antony Easthope and Kate McGowan
(eds.), *A Critical and Cultural Theory Reader* (Buckingham: Open University Press, 1997), pp 21–30, pp
22–3.   67 Ibid., p. 21.

mask, behind which Francis's killer might be hiding ... She could not conceive of Francis's killer as an individual ... but only as a great darkness which was hidden in the hearts of everyone she met' (44). Repression is not only a foregrounded feature of narrative style and plot construction, but also of character presentation. Theresa consciously adopts a strategy of dissimulation as a way of speaking. She wants no-one to be told about Francis's murder for reasons which the novel never explains, beyond the authorial statement: 'It was almost as if she were ashamed of what had happened' (25). Why Theresa should feel 'ashamed' is unclear. As well as the unusual passion she displays for her dead brother, there is some minor textual detailing which may be intended to raise suspicions in the reader's mind about 'what had happened' between Theresa and Francis in the past. Theresa remembers the time she and her brother came upon 'a little Lugano fountain' and 'they dipped their hands in the cold water and accidentally their fingers touched', an occurrence which is followed by her reference to the fountain bowl as 'tainted' (87). Or there's the time when she pays a drunken visit to Robert and he has to carry her forcibly into his bed, 'when he put his arm around her waist to heave her into the bedroom, she hadn't even known who he was. Three times she had called him "Francis"' (108). The veiled hints of a repressed incest narrative (which are reinforced by a reading of Madden's second novel, *The Birds of the Innocent Wood*, 1988) would explain Theresa's anxiety to place the memory of Francis under taboo and envelop it in the unspoken. Theresa's student friend, Kathy, also experiences the return of the repressed in the form of her absent father who, she discovers, is not dead as her mother has always told her, but had deserted the family years before. The effort to interpellate the father's originary presence only confirms his absence: 'She (Kathy) could not talk about her loneliness, and so translated it into anger' (122).

The novel's 'symptomatic' preoccupations are further emphasised in Theresa's thought that 'her iceberg mentality' may be a condition of existence: 'was it common to feel that only a tiny facet of one's self was exposed and communicable to others, with the rest locked in ice, vast, submerged and impossible?' (82). The past, Theresa feels, also lies 'submerged and impossible' in memory. On awaking from a dream of the school she attended with Francis, she wonders: 'was her waking memory accurate, or had the dream been the truth rising to the surface now after the passing of years? Everything was confused: never again would she be able to picture the school to herself with any confidence; now all was a jumble of dream and supposed reality' (31–2). Francis thus becomes an imaginary, ghostly imitation of the lost original: 'She was alone now, and at the mercy of her own memory and imagination' (33), aware that she can produce only distorted copies of the unknowable reality.

Theresa despairs because she is aware of the alienation of the subject from its object. The death of her brother stimulates her anguished awareness that the subjective world, constructed in language, is always necessarily at a remove from reality. The human subject, as the novel demonstrates, is always denied unmediated access to the real, is always frustrated, always exiled from an Edenic or heavenly imaginary of real presence which can only be envisaged through the language of loss, absence and bereavement. This is the Platonic philosophical inheritance and, as Stan Smith explains, neoplatonism has always had two main inflexions:

> The positive inflexion concedes that the things of this fallen world are mere copies of eternal, ideal Forms, but takes consolation from the existence of those Forms: somewhere, they really exist, sustaining, casting their shadows onto, the fallen world of mortality. The extreme version of such optimism is Sir Philip Sidney's assertion, in *An Apologie for Poetrie*, that art in general and poetry in particular offer truer versions of the ideal forms than our transient time-bound histories permit, offering, in his memorable phrase, 'a golden world for nature's world of brass'. The pessimistic strand of neoplatonism, however, represented in our time perhaps by Jacques Derrida, insists with melancholy frequency that the world we know is unreal, a phantasma, or, in Baudrillard's idiom, a mere 'simulacrum' of the true, which we can never apprehend, so that we are permanently exiled among *disjecta membra* which are the relics, in the empirical world, of those ideal and inapprehensible Forms.[68]

Theresa recalls Francis telling her how he gained a sense of self-presence from the conviction that he existed in the eye of God. Francis takes comfort in the way the divine transcends any merely human gaze which is 'never perfect, never total' (54). Contemplating Michaelangelo's Pietá in the Vatican, Francis says: 'People do not look for God, they only look for bits of metal and stone and glass. They come for art's sake; they don't believe' (55). Theresa understands Francis's desire to be 'stunned into ecstasy by union with God' (55), but 'she could not fully share that desire and it frightened her' (55). Following his death, however, she feels an overwhelming sense of dispossession, loss and exclusion, of displacement into a fallen world felt to be unreal, and she is filled with nostalgic longing for the absconded reality that was Francis. She seeks comfort in ancestry, in 'an eclectic array of photographs of her father', attempting 'to pluck and save her father from the flux of time' (67). The essence of her father, she feels, lurks somewhere in the 'fuzzy little snaps'. A ghostly paradigm must somewhere invest the simulacra of the real. But she cannot make the scattered photographs cohere into a convincing narrative. She is aware that what she sees in the photographs and what she hears from her mother about her parents'

---

68 Stan Smith, 'The twilight of the cities: Derek Mahon's Dark Cinema' in Elmer Kennedy-Andrews (ed.), *The Poetry of Derek Mahon* (Gerards Cross: Colin Smythe, 2002), pp 219–41, pp 228–9.

honeymoon in Clifden is only partial truth: 'She (Theresa) accepted her mother's evocation of Clifden as she accepted Dostoyevsky's Petersburg. Each place was conceived in the memory, language and discourse of others, then took life in her own imagination' (70). Through the delusion of memory, Francis becomes an originary and foundational presence of which the surrounding world is an unhappy copy. She remembers holidaying with him in Venice where 'all seemed fused to timeless perfection': 'There were many people there, mostly tourists, all strangers; and then suddenly she had seen Francis's face materialize out of the crowd, as familiar to her as her own foot or finger. This was what she had been seeking, and the faces of all those other people were masks, dross, distortions, faces which were wrong; suddenly the only right and real face in Venice had appeared' (85).

Theresa's memory contrasts with another epiphanic moment associated with the young writer, Robert. Sitting in his darkened room watching the 'perfect image' of himself and the room reflected in his window, he finds the idea of this shadow world 'liberating'. He sees it as an alternative to the tyranny of what is: 'Too much reality was hard to bear' (89). Where Theresa's vision of Francis in Venice was a quasi-mystical revelation of the real, Robert longs to be evacuated into a virtual reality where the struggles of historical and social life are transposed to spectacle and he can be 'dissolved into nothingness'(88). The 'reflection' imagery reappears in Theresa's memory of Francis's funeral: 'His coffin had been carried a short distance and then placed in the hearse. Theresa and her mother had found themselves looking at their own reflections, ghostly and bloodless as photographic negatives, cast upon the glass behind which lay the solid coffin and a few bright wreaths of flowers' (124). The glass of the hearse gives back a ghastly image of material existence as itself insubstantial and unreal. In the dying moments of the relationship between Robert and Kathy 'As night fell, he (Robert) could see the ghostly room begin to crystallize behind the dark glass' (131). Now, however, the reflected world 'unsettled him' and he lowers the blinds as if to close it out and consolidate what's real. When he goes to Theresa's house to explain how he discovered the secret of her brother's death, he sees himself and the room reflected in a mirror in the parlour, and thinks of how the scene finds its own reflection in the scene painted by van Eyck in 'The Arnolfini Marriage': 'He remembered from the painting trivial domestic details – a little dog; some oranges; a pair of slippers carelessly tossed aside – and as he thought this he noticed that Theresa was wearing the most absurd bedroom slippers he had ever seen' (135). Robert inhabits a 'hyperreality', a world of self-referential signs engendering a reality more real than the real itself. The novel's manifold intertextual hauntings reinforce this sense of reality's construction through a system of signs which no longer necessarily refer to anything outside themselves. The novel ends with Theresa catching sight of her own reflection in the same mirror and realising the unbridgeable distance between subject and its reflection. At that moment she experiences the anguish of recognising presence that marks only absence: 'Could there be anything more wearisome, she wondered, than to stand alone, alone, alone before a mirror? How long would it be, she wondered, until she could go beyond reflections? For how long would she have to continue claiming the face in the mirror as her own? When would there be an end to shadows cast upon glass? (141–2).

Theresa's raising these questions of authenticity obviously relates to her ideas about art and religion. She longs for the fulness of self-presence, union with the absolute, the age-old desire of Plato's troglodytes only ever able to watch a reflection of the real thing flickering on the walls of the human cave. Early on she declares her artistic commitment to the 'absolute': 'I write about subjectivity – and inarticulation – about life pushing you into a state where everything is melting until you're left with the absolute and you can find neither the words nor the images to express it' (28) – part of her aestheticist manifesto in which an artist is simply 'a person who composes or paints or sculpts or writes' (28). In this vein, she condemns the drunk playwright who champions 'useful art' (26). Shortly after, however, we find her vehemently resisting any notion of aesthetic autonomy and berating Robert for his declared lack of interest in politics. By the end, her distrust of art is complete: 'These people of marble and bronze were first an image of the body which lay beneath, but soon became a dishonest distraction, attempting to belie the hidden bones and dust. Whited sepulchres. Futility' (123–4). Her melancholy conclusion is that perfection lies in death not art: watching Francis's burial 'she believed that her brother was now perfected' (124)

Similarly, the loss of her brother precipitates a crisis of faith in the devoutly Catholic Theresa. She continues to believe in God because the assumption of an eternal, spiritual world allows her to believe that Francis is not gone from her forever. Christianity, she says, is 'the religion for victims and failures ... People who can see below the surface of things, and who have difficulty in accepting their own existence' (128). Hers is a religion which allows her 'to glimpse perfection and know that that was the state to which one had to aspire, only suddenly to see it offset by the immense imperfection of one's self'' (129). Her faith is something to hold against the postmodern flux and the inescapable fact of mortality, but it is remote from human actuality and gives her no joy and little reassurance. Ultimately, the novel itself, with its complex symbolism, ambiguity and dislocated patterning bears a closer resemblance to dreams than to the familiar substantial reality we think we know.

One by One in the Darkness covers a week in the lives of the three Quinn sisters and their mother in the summer of 1994 shortly before the declaration of the first IRA ceasefire which also marked the twenty-fifth anniversary of the outbreak of the Troubles in 1969. The youngest sister, Sally, is a teacher in the same school she attended as a child and lives with her mother, Emily, in the family home near Toome in Co. Antrim; the middle sister, Kate, works on a fashion magazine in London and has come home to tell her mother and sisters that she is pregnant; and the eldest,

Helen, is a solicitor on the Falls Road in Belfast, specialising in terrorist cases. *One by One* is essentially biographical fiction, the assembling of a family archive. In constructing a context for the lives of these women, Madden interweaves personal life and public events, emphasising the impact of the public on the personal. She also intercuts past and present, incorporating flashbacks to different periods in the 1960s and '70s which the characters recall in strongly nostalgic and elegiac tones. These retrospective chapters, though narrated in the third person, are focalised through each of the women, thereby enforcing a sense of the primary reality of personal perception and personal feeling; they help to develop a sense of the women's embeddedness in a particular locale, landscape, community and history; and they are used to highlight contrasts between the sense of security and plenitude associated with the past and the feelings of loss and anxiety which pervade the present. Both Patricia Craig and Carlo Gebler criticise the novel for its lack of continuity in treating the public world of Northern Irish politics, Craig referring to Madden's 'vagueness'[69] and Gebler to the 'insufficiency of material' to join up 'the dots'.[70] Both, however, praise the author's descriptive skill in rendering domestic detail and the inner, psychological life of her characters. In Craig's words, 'Her (Madden's) approach to the terrorist element in Northern Irish life is the opposite of a thriller-writer's: she takes no interest in the mechanics of plot-making ... what saves her as a writer, and makes her novels likeable, despite their refusal of qualities such as charm, high spirits, robustness and aplomb, is a formidable descriptive gift which is harnessed to the small-scale and quotidian'.[71] Even more enthusiastic was Maxine Jones: 'No other book has left me with such a lasting impression of the hurt of Northern Ireland'.[72] The 'hurt of Northern Ireland' is also, of course, the theme of *Hidden Symptoms*, but the degree of abstractness in the early novel provides justification for Jones' elevation of the later one.

In *One by One* the 'hurt of Northern Ireland' is represented in various ways: a neighbour of the Quinns, Tony Larkin, blows himself up while planting a bomb in Magherafelt; Uncle Brian, an outspoken Republican, is harrassed by the security forces; Emily remembers growing up in Protestant Ballymena and realising as she listens to the drums on the 12th July that she is hated because she is a Catholic; Civil Rights marchers in Derry are treated brutally by the police. But the shattering event at the heart of the book is the Loyalist shooting of Charlie Quinn, Emily's husband and the sisters' beloved father. Like *Hidden Symptoms*, *One by One* is a trauma narrative exploring the effects of violent death on those closest to the victim. It is concerned with the struggle of the four women to recompose themselves after the Troubles have

69 Patricia Craig, 'A cabinet in Co. Clare', *Times Literary Supplement*, review of *One by One in the Darkness*, 24 May 1996, p. 26.   70 Carlo Gebler, 'Specifically Personal', review of *One by One in the Darkness*, in *Fortnight*, May 1996, p. 36.   71 Patricia Craig, 'A cabinet in Co. Clare', 24 May, 1996, p. 26.   72 Maxine Jones, review of *One by One in the Darkness* in *Tribune Magazine*, 26 May 1996, p. 20.

invaded the vulnerable space of family and ordinary life. Structurally, everything in the novel takes place under the sign of absence, loss and violence. Charlie's death is the central event, but it remains repressed for most of the narrative: reference to it is made early on, and thereafter further information is gradually filtered in, but allusions are glancing, evasive, circling. Only at the end Helen brings herself to confront the full horror of what actually happened. The incident is always strongly mediated: at no point does the narrative escape from the consciousness of the four women to present the facts of Charlie's death directly as simple third person Realistic narration. Madden's interest is not in the act of violence itself but in the psychological effects of violence. More specifically, she is interested in the ways in which traumatised characters represent violence to themselves. Beyond this subjective problematic, she is interested in the ways in which violence is represented in public, institutional arenas such as the mass media and the law.

The recent work of Cathy Caruth on the relationship between trauma, narrative and history in the twentieth-century provides a useful context in which to examine Madden's novel. Basing her findings on historical narratives of such experiences as the First World War, the Holocaust and the Bomb, Caruth demonstrates that only after the event, in the process of telling it and incorporating it into their own personal and historical contexts, do those who have direct experience of violent events, whether as perpetrators, victims or witnesses, manage to deal with it:

> Trauma is described as the response to an unexpected or overwhelming event or events that are not fully grasped as they occur, but return later in repeated flashbacks, nightmares, and other repetitive phenomena. Traumatic experience, beyond the psychological dimension of suffering it involves, suggests a certain paradox: that the most direct seeing of a violent event may occur as an absolute inability to know it; that immediacy, paradoxically, may take the form of belatedness.[73]

This subjective processing of trauma does not produce a rational, linear narrative, nor a model of history that, as Caruth puts it, is 'straightforwardly referential'.[74] Instead, history emerges out of the complex relation between knowing and not knowing. It is an interpretation of the past, a reconstruction that makes use of all kinds of fictive strategies, and is always subject to the distortions of memory and imagination.

Thus, the narrative of *One by One* is shaped by the psychological processes of repression, displacement, condensation and transference, whereby the subject attempts to avoid direct confrontation with the traumatic event in the past or to achieve some kind of psychic control over it. Dreams and nightmares, which are a

---

73 Cathy Caruth, *Unclaimed Experience: Trauma, Narrative, and History* (Baltimore: Johns Hopkins University Press, 1995), p.91.　74 Ibid., p.11.

prominent element of the text and often transcribed in detail, encode the tensions of the characters' psychic lives. Emily tells of a dream she had in which she and her family were on a raft heading for a waterfall and disaster. Under these exacerbated conditions, she sees her family, especially her mother with whom she has never got on, in a new light. Emily feels 'transformed by the spirit of compassion and forgiveness'.[75] The dream allows her to achieve some kind of control over her life: 'She couldn't change the fact of things but she could change how she saw them, and in that way she could determine the effect they had on her' (125). This reconciliation dream is immediately followed by her account of another dream she had: 'She was standing in Lucy's kitchen, and at her feet was a long thing over which someone had thrown a check table cloth. There were two feet sticking out at one end, wearing a pair of boots she'd helped Charlie to choose in a shop in Antrim. The other end of the cloth was dark and wet; there was a stench of blood and excrement' (125). Also present in her dream is the cowering, crying figure of 'a skinny, shivering boy in jeans and a tee-shirt' who pleads with her: '"Please, Missus", he kept saying to Emily, "please, Missus, I'm sorry for what I did, I'm sorry, so I am, please, Missus ..."' (125) – an intertextual echo of Michael Longley's poem, 'Wounds', which describes the terrorist murder of a Belfast bus conductor 'shot through the head / By a shivering boy who wandered in / Before they could turn the television down / Or tidy away the supper dishes. / To the children, to a bewildered wife, / I think "Sorry Missus" was what he said'.[76] Emily again attempts to assert some control over circumstance by dreaming a killer of pathetic and penitential demeanour from whom she withholds the comfort of her forgiveness. This is not, however, the reality for, according to Helen at the end of the novel, 'as they (the killers) ran out of the house, one of them punched the air and whooped, because it had been so easy' (181), and Emily herself recognises that her inability to forgive is not the sign of power but of the loss of her own humanity – of a 'heart ... forced shut': 'To be a woman in her late sixties, to have prayed to God every day of her life, and to be left so that she could feel no compassion, no mercy, only bitterness and hate, was a kind of horror she had never imagined' (125).

Each of the daughters has been forced to re-think her life in the wake of the father's death. The novel opens with the word 'home' and proceeds to elaborate what 'home' used to mean, and what it means now, to the three sisters. The opening paragraph presents Kate's view:

> Home was a huge sky; it was flat fields of poor land fringed with hawthorn and alder. It was birds in flight; it was columns of midges like smoke in a

75 Deirdre Madden, *One by One in the Darkness* (London: Faber,1997), p. 124. First published London: Faber, 1996. Hereafter, page references will be incorporated into the text.   76 Michael Longley, 'Wounds', *Poems 1963–1983* (London: Penguin, 1985), p.86.

summer dusk. It was grey water; it was a mad wind; it was a solid stone house where the silence was uncanny. (1)

Home is what is distinctly unhomely or 'uncanny' – a place haunted by the return of the repressed. In his discussion of Heaney's ambivalent attitude to home, Richard Kearney invokes Freud:

> In a study entitled *Das Unheimliche* (translated as the 'unhomely' or 'uncanny'), Freud explores the paradox that the '*Unheimliche* is the name for everything that ought to have remained hidden and secret and has become visible'. This study, which has become something of a *cause celèbre* for post-structuralist critics, reveals that while the term *unheimliche* refers ostensibly to what is unfamiliar or un-known, it also carries the opposite connotation of what is intimately familiar and homely (*heimlich*).... The extension of the linguistic usage of *heimlich* into its opposite, *unheimlich*, is thus explained by the curious fact that the 'uncanny is in reality nothing new or alien, but something which is familiar and of old established in the mind and which has become alienated from it only through the process of repression.[77]

The uncanny return of repressed memories observed by Freud is also a key motif for Madden. But the 'uncanny', as Kearney goes on to show, is not only 'a psychic experience of the unconscious' as described by Freud, but 'an existential experience of Being' as described by Heidegger:

> Heidegger isolates the experience of 'uncanniness' as a distinguishing feature of modern man's sense of 'uprootedness' and 'estrangement' . Our being-in-the-world is authentic, writes Heidegger, to the extent that it faces up to the 'nothingness' which informs our contemporary relationship to Being. We are no longer at home in our world; we reside between two worlds, being 'too late for the gods and too early for Being'.[78]

Madden's sisters experience something of Heaney's paradoxical feeling about home, his awareness of the impossibility of ever really returning 'home' to rediscover there some harmonious unity. Returning home means facing the demons of violence and terror, recognising the strangeness of the familiar world. Homecoming is to experience the loss of home, to approach the existential awareness of death. After her father's death, Kate's old sense of her own 'invincibility', her old 'confidence', disappeared:

77 Richard Kearney, *Transitions: Narratives in Modern Irish Culture* (Dublin: Wolfhound, 1988), pp 113, 115
78 Ibid., p. 119.

> In the past, she'd felt invincible. It wasn't that she didn't think about whether or not disaster might befall her; she did think, and decided that it couldn't. Her life was charmed. When she was a teenager, she would shelter under trees during thunderstorms, sure that she was safe. A train or a plane couldn't crash if she was on board ... For years she believed she could have absolutely anything she wanted in life. Her family hadn't been able to understand where it came from, this ... confidence, she'd called it then. Arrogance, she called it now. It had left her that night in October over two years ago, when Sally rang and told her what had happened. (2–3)

The novel expresses intense nostalgia for a lost home, a lost past, a lost childhood. The childhood home has been both centre and sanctuary, a known world of calendar customs and natural pieties.

> For the pattern of their lives was as predictable as the seasons. The regular round of necessity was broken by celebrations and feasts: Christmas, Easter, family birthdays. The scope of their lives was tiny but it was profound, and to them, it was immense. The physical bounds of their world were confined to little more than a few fields and houses, but they knew these places with the deep, unconscious knowledge that a bird or a fox might have for its habitat. (74–5)

However, the sense of an organic community can only be preserved by ignoring the political and sectarian fault-lines that traverse their terrain: 'And yet for all this they knew that their lives, so complete in themselves, were off centre in relation to the society beyond those few fields and houses' (75). The novel's concern with the sisters' personal sense of dispossession is placed in the context of the larger collective sense of dislocation which the Catholic Nationalist community feels in Protestant Ulster. The sisters' attempts to recover a sense of home is parallelled by the Northern Irish Catholic community's attempts to reclaim a lost heritage and identity through Civil Rights protest and then terrorist violence.

Kate has years ago fled from the massacre in the North, re-invented herself as 'Cate', re-located herself in the English cosmopolitan centre, and become the exponent of glamorous modernity as fashion editor of a glossy magazine: her 'very career and standing with her colleagues depended upon her ability to read the signs of the times more quickly and fluently than most, and to endorse them with enthusiasm' (86). Despite this, she remains umbilically attached to home. She is shocked to discover how little family means to her colleagues in London. She resents the changes that her uncle Brian and aunt Lucy have made to their home, for they erase the memory of the Edenic as well as the demonic past:

The changes meant that Cate didn't imagine her father lying murdered on the floor, as she had feared, but it also meant that she couldn't imagine the nut-cracking either. She had always thought of her childhood not principally in terms of time, but as a place to which she could always return. Now that was over. What was the word Lucy had used two years ago? 'Desecrated'. That was it. The place was desecrated. (143)

Standing preparing a stir-fry, she listens to the news of a man found shot dead in south Armagh 'seeping from the radio into the bright warm kitchen' of her London apartment and 'she didn't know why, but she wanted then to be home' (141). On her visits home she spends her time 'driving for hours through the countryside alone, trying to fathom Northern Ireland' (82). Her memory of driving through the Ulster wasteland – 'Swatragh and Draperstown; Magherafelt and Toome; Plumbridge and Castledawson' (82) – evokes Heaney's similar progress, 'driving, / Saying the names / Tollund, Grabaulle, Nebelgard, / Watching the pointing hands / Of country people, / Not knowing their tongue / Out there in Jutland / In the old man-killing parishes / I will feel lost, / Unhappy and at home'.[79] Homecoming can exist only as memory or desire, no longer as fulfilment. For both Heaney and Madden's fictional character, the sacramental sense of landscape has been fractured and foreclosed. Home is most fully appreciated when it's lost: Kate 'was even a bit ashamed to realise how much she'd taken for granted, how unremarkable she'd found the tremendous warmth and love in which she had grown up' (88). It remains a potent memory. Kate, whose private life in London leaves her 'increasingly dismayed as, time and again, things fell apart' (147), wonders if the intense happiness she enjoyed as a child has disabled her for life in the adult world: 'Was it possible to have too happy a childhood, to be loved too much?' (148). Disoriented by the death of her father, acutely aware of life as 'a finite thing, an illusion' (93), and burdened by a Heideggerean sense of homelessness and the 'uncanny', she finds comfort in the prospect of motherhood: 'I wanted something real' (93). Kate's embracement with 'a rush of pure delight' (93) of the role of unmarried mother, and her own mother's conscientious struggle to adapt to changing times represent a radical re-writing of the traditional narrative of the Irish family. Kate's re-negotiation of the past is represented in two key images. Early in the novel, she is absorbed by a bird's egg, wondering 'what it would be like to be in an egg, shut up in a tiny space hardly bigger than yourself, knowing nothing but that you had to tap and tap and tap until you broke into the light and fell out uncoiling yourself' (19). By the end of the novel, she proposes another image which both acknowledges the past and re-affirms her conviction of the need to break out of the confinements of the past and look beyond immediate concerns to future horizons of

79 Seamus Heaney, 'The Tollund Man', *Opened Ground: Poems 1966–1996* (London: Faber, 1998), pp 64–5.

possibility. Unlike the egg, a natural given thing, the image she now proposes is something that has to be designed and constructed, but it is something, she believes, which would represent an appropriate 'memorial' to all the victims of the Troubles:

> She imagined a room, a perfectly square room. Three of its walls, unbroken by windows, would be covered by neat rows of names, over three thousand of them; and the fourth wall would be nothing but window. The whole structure would be built where the horizon was low, and the sky huge. it would be a place which afforded dignity to memory, where you could bring your anger, as well as your grief. (149)

For the eldest sister, Helen, going home is 'entry into a danger zone' (24) because it is to re-enter the past and to re-activate memories of what has been lost. Her life away from the originary home has an air of impermanence, provisionality and rootlessness. She lives in 'a development of upmarket townhouses' (44) and 'grew to appreciate the very sterility of the place ... it was, psychically, a blank' (44). She chooses a neutral space without memories or associations. In Helen's memory, home is closely associated with the loved father who is remembered as a powerfully sustaining and nurturing presence, a quiet, dignified figure of exemplary reasonableness and fairness. His compassionate understanding and supportiveness of children, wife and deranged brother are continually in evidence. He epitomises the 'oul' decency' to which Heaney pays tribute in his elegy for Sean Armstrong in 'A Postcard from North Antrim'.[80] Indeed, as my remarks so far would suggest, Heaney is an exceptionally strong presence in Madden's novel. Charlie is a Heaney reader: 'Helen remembered her father taking her along to hear Seamus Heaney read in Magherafelt ... He'd bought at that reading one of the several collections of Heaney's poems which he owned' (27). The Quinn family inhabits the same world around Toome and Magherafelt on the shores of Lough Neagh as Heaney did, and this landscape is evoked in the novel with a Heaneyesque archaeological interest and sacramental regard. Heaney's affectionate, heroic image of the father in poems such as 'Digging' or 'Follower' ghosts Helen's memories of her father. Recalling a day at the carnival when she was terrified by the deranged and drunken antics of her uncle Peter and by Tony Larkin's reckless behaviour on the swingboats, 'Helen didn't know why what she had seen made her feel so strange, so confused. She only knew that she wanted her father, and when she suddenly saw him coming through the gate into the field again, she ran over at once, and buried her face in his jacket' (70). Helen presents her father, as Heaney presents himself, as custodian of the past, excavator of the national landscape. Helen remembers her father taking his children to see the elk that Heaney

---

80 Seamus Heaney, 'A Postcard from North Antrim', *Field Work* (London: Faber, 1979).

wrote about in 'Bogland', and sets up further echoes of Heaney in the references to her father's interest in local hoards of ancient coins, excavations of Viking swords and Iron Age canoes. Her memories of a half-pagan, folkloric world of miraculous cures, Holy Wells, a 'Mystery Man' who haunts the woods, and halloween festivities further beds Madden's fictional world into Heaney's poetic locale. And just as Heaney's father is turned into a spirit of land and place associated with ancestral figures such as the servant boy or martyred Tollund Man, so, too, the sisters' father becomes a mythic figure of 'tradition' and 'nature', the lord of their first world, a doomed god. The night after Belfast is torn apart by multiple bombings and nine people are killed, Helen comes upon her father crying in the darkness of their kitchen:

> She knew now, all in a rush, what he was thinking, and there, in the darkness, it was as if she had already lost him, as if his loved body had already been violently destroyed. They clung to each other like people who had been saved from a shipwreck, or a burning building, but it was no use, the disaster had already happened. All over the country, people were living out the nightmare which she now dreaded more than anything else. (130)

The scene reverberates poignantly against earlier occasions when the father figured as powerful protector. That night, we are told, Helen 'gained a dark knowledge ... which would never leave her' (131).

Helen's discourse of dispossession extends beyond her personal sense of loss of home and father to include her postmodern sense of displacement into language. The theme is introduced when Helen recalls as a schoolgirl going off to start her homework essay on 'Narrative point of view in *Great Expectations*'. She is enraged by the way her father's death has been treated in the media – 'the death was reported coldly and without sympathy, much being made of Brian's Sinn Féin membership, and the murder having taken place in his house. The inference was that he had only got what was coming to him' (47). Her conversations with her journalist friend, Dave, are used to explore the issues: '"But there's something about the whole nature of it", Helen argued, "about taking things and making stories about them, and that's all it amounts to: making up stories out of a few facts, and presenting them as though that interpretation was the absolute truth. That's what I can't stand"' (50). Here, Helen expresses her awareness of being caught in a conflicted discursive field of manipulable facts and uncertain truth where, she says, the media are unable to deal with 'complexity', 'paradox' or 'contradiction' (51). But, as Dave points out to her, Helen herself is implicated in the processes of institutionalised distortion in defending Oliver Maguire, the killer of a Protestant taxi-driver. She sits down to watch a TV documentary marking the twenty-fifth anniversary of the start of the Troubles and is struck by the inadequacy of the (significantly) 'black-and-white' media images:

It made Helen feel sad to look at the images on the screen. It had been like that, yet not like that: the pictures told only part of the story. She remembered the austerity, even though she hadn't been aware of it at the time, and she wondered how you ever got to the essence of things, of your time, your society, your self. It struck her as strange that out of her whole family, she, the only one whose life was supposedly dedicated to the administration of justice, was the only one who didn't believe in it as a spiritual fact, who perhaps didn't believe in it at all. (60)

At the end Helen is forced to admit that her attitudes to terrorists 'were inconsistent, perhaps even hypocritical'. The novel closes with Helen's vision of an absurd and empty universe with 'no pity, no forgiveness, no justification'. The childhood sense of wonder, continuity and an ordered world is replaced by the 'cold light of dead stars; the graceless immensity of a dark universe' (1). Hers is a disconsolate narrative of Catholic grievance, of Civil Rights hopefulness collapsed into confusion and carnage. Exiled from Eden into a dark and cruel world, the old certainties fragment, the family atomises: 'One by one in the darkness ...' (181).

The third sister, Sally, has never moved from home. She 'felt loyal to home' (139) and was afraid that if she did move away she'd be lost and discontented forever. After her father's death she admits that she would like to have left, but duty to her mother prevented her from doing so. She looks forward to the birth of Kate's baby, but cannot say this as that would be to reveal how fraught and unfulfilled her own life has been: 'To say how much she felt the family needed something like this would have been to point up how haunted and threatened she had felt herself to be over the past two years' (145–6).

The novel is pervaded by the 'sense of an ending', illustrating the disruption, disintegration and dispersal of a 'centre' or 'dominant', defined by Jakobson in an aesthetic context as the 'focusing component of a work of art' which 'rules, determines and transforms the remaining components'.[81] Jameson has applied this formal notion of the 'dominant' to his theory of historical change: 'Radical breaks between periods do not generally involve complete changes of content but rather the restructuration of a certain number of elements already given'.[82] In *One by One*, the figure of Charlie, like John McGahern's Moran in *Amongst Woman*, though lacking Moran's iconic charisma, functions as both artistic 'dominant' and a symbolic historical 'dominant' whose death precipitates a necessary 'restructuration' of identity. Madden's fictional daughters, like McGahern's, all face the challenge of renegotiating the past in order to deal with the present. In *One by One* the 'dominant' is constructed

81 Roman Jakobson, quoted by Patricia Waugh, *Practising Postmodernism Reading Modernism* (London: Edward Arnold,1992), p. 38.   82 Fredric Jameson, quoted by Patricia Waugh, *Practising Postmodernism Reading Modernism*, p. 38.

in terms of an entirely benevolent patriarchy, in contrast to the figuration of Moran as a site of tension. There is no sense in which Charlie blights social, personal and sexual development in the way Moran does in *Amongst Women*. Charlie stands for traditional notions of rural life, family, religion, sexuality and politics, at a point of cultural transition when the pressures of modernity are also making themselves felt in terms of the increased social mobility and independence of women, Helen's rejection of religion and marriage, Dave and Steve's gay sex, Kate's pregnancy outside marriage, the mass media culture of the simulacrum, and the new peremptory politics of terrorism. In my reading, Madden's excision of the redemptive trope of rural Ireland inherited from the Revivalists and epitomised by the father is replaced by the alternatives of a depressed (post)modernist scepticism (Helen), an equally depressed ancestral dutifulness (Sally) and regenerative reappropriation of a redundant ideology and its projection into a tentatively hopeful future (Kate). In a novel so centrally concerned with the father, Madden's own literary genealogy deserves comment. Thomas Kinsella remarked that 'the Irish writer, if he cares who he is and where he comes from, finds that Joyce and Yeats are the two main objects in view, and I think he finds that Joyce is the true father'. Joyce is the 'true father' because he combines 'Irish tradition' while simultaneously admitting 'the modern world'.[83] Madden may be seen to do this too.

David Park's *The Healing* tells the story of a boy, Samuel Anderson, who witnesses the death of his father, an RUC man, shot dead by terrorists as he and his son work together in a field near their home. The boy and his mother, both devastated by their sudden bereavement, hope for a new start in life by moving to the city. Their new next door neighbour, Mr Ellison, forms a close bond with the boy. The old man keeps a record of all the tragic deaths in the Troubles by saving newspaper cuttings in a ledger. He believes the boy has been sent by God to help him lead a movement against the world's evil and to bring 'healing' to the province. However, 'healing' does not take the expected form. The old man, discovering that his son is involved in paramilitary executions, kills him in order to save the lives of others. And the boy, who since his father's death has been unable to speak, ultimately finds healing in the redemptive power of words.

The novel opens with the child in nature. But this is a child re-visiting the scene of his father's murder, a child who is traumatised and paranoid, a primitive, fugitive life form moving across the terrain: 'Silently, and face down, he scuttled like a rat along the damp course of the ditch.'[84] Bearing the dedication 'For the children afflicted by

83 Thomas Kinsella, 'The Irish writer', in Thomas Kinsella and W.B. Yeats, *Davis, Mangan, Ferguson?: Tradition and the Irish Writer* (Dublin: Dolmen, 1970). **84** David Park, *The Healing* (London: Cape, 1992), p. 1. Hereafter, page references will be incorporated into the text.

dreams', the novel continues a tradition of fiction writing, exemplified by writers such as Hemingway and Twain, which narrates the experience of growing up with violence and desperately trying to cope with it and survive. Samuel, like Twain's Huck Finn or Hemingway's Nick Adams, is a casualty of violence and evil – sickened, scarred, very nervous, continually in flight, afflicted with insomnia and nightmares, withdrawn from society. Moreover, the style which Park develops to embody his character's struggle to maintain emotional and psychic control is strongly reminiscent of Hemingway's:

> He had not gone far when he crouched and listened. Somewhere on the road ahead was a car. Its sound sent a surge of panic through him. On either side unbroken hedgerows fenced him in. He looked behind, but the gate into the barley field was too far away and the ditch had disappeared. They were coming. They were coming back. He was trapped. (3)

The narrative, which is mainly focalised through the boy, is composed in a terse, factual, repetitive style using a common diction and short, declarative sentences. Events and sensations are recorded as if unmediated by any ordering mind, unmixed with authorial comment or explanation. The impression is of intense objectivity. The economy and narrow focus of the prose create the sense of a severely delimited area of consciousness. To venture beyond these carefully guarded limits would be to risk losing control of himself. The refusal to comment, elaborate or be discursive is an expression of the need to repress difficult memories. In Hemingway's story, 'Big Two-Hearted River', Nick Adams' anxieties are projected onto the physical landscape in terms of the burnt ground around the town of Seney, and the dark and treacherous waters of the river which he has come to fish. Reading about Nick watching the trout 'keeping themselves steady in the current',[85] we realise that Nick, like the fish, is struggling to keep himself steady in his own stream-of-consciousness as he tries to come to terms with the traumatic past. The echoes of Hemingway are unmistakeable in the way Park writes terror into his protagonist's perception of familiar surroundings:

> Reaching the stream he (Samuel) knelt down and pushed his hand against the current, letting the cold water foam about his fingers. He spat and watched it float away. The water's edge was pock-marked with the hoof prints of cows. He wondered where the herd was now. The slaughterhouse and the butcher's knife. He thought of their yellow-skinned carcases hanging from shiny metal hooks, tiny drops of blood dripping on to sawdust floors. He imagined their blood flowing into the stream, turning it red, then snatched his hand out of the water and wiped it repeatedly on his trousers. (5)

---

85 Ernest Hemingway, 'Big Two-Hearted River: I' in *The Essential Ernest Hemingway* (London: Triad Grafton, 1988), pp 340–58, p. 341.

Like Nick Adams, Samuel cautiously 'circles' the dread moment in the past which is the source of terror:

> As more days and weeks went by, he found himself beginning to think of it. Not all of it, but just the small parts he could control, the parts he could rearrange into new shapes. At the start his whole being had sought to deny his memory, refusing to accept his own experience, but now he crept lightly towards it, ready at any moment to flee its grasp, ready to block it out once more with disbelief ... Cautiously, he circled the moment, always keeping it at a safe distance. (83)

The sense of dislocation is structurally represented through various 'circling' devices. The narration is throughout deeply fractured, shifting suddenly from one time, locale and point of view to another, and it is only gradually that the reader pieces together the events of the past into a coherent narrative.

After the boy, the old man, Mr Ellison, is the novel's chief focaliser. If Samuel's literary antecedents are those young boys of American fiction who have been traumatised by violence such as Huck Finn and Nick Adams, the old man's fictional precursors are the lonely, obsessive, fanatical grotesques we find in Sherwood Anderson's stories of mid-west small-town America in *Winesburg, Ohio* and in Flannery O'Connor's and Carson McCullers' fiction of the Deep South 'Bible-belt'. Mr Ellison, conscious of his own inadequacy, looks to the boy to speak his message to the people. What exactly that message might be, or what form it might take, is never specified. Park seems to try and make up for the vagueness with a repetitive and overloaded Biblical rhetoric designed to imbue the old man's mission with significance and urgency, while at the same time critically undermining the old man's self-conceived prophetic role. The irony in *The Healing* is that nobody understands the old man's strong, true purpose, least of all the boy Samuel who, the old man believes, has been sent by God to be his 'helpmate' (117). Samuel is in fact conspicuously lacking in qualifications to be the old man's chosen mouthpiece: not only does the boy say that he hates God, but he has been struck dumb as a consequence of his own traumatic experience. Mr Ellison thinks of himself as an Old Testament patriarch who has been divinely called to oppose a decadent modernity, and in the end he is prepared to sacrifice his own son, Billy, as Abraham was prepared to sacrifice Isaac: 'No other way, no lamb in the thicket' (168), Mr Ellison thinks to himself, as he pulls Billy, onto the knife he is holding. The old man illustrates the dangers of religious fanaticism. His alienation from the real world of society and politics leads to such extreme individualistic actions which, however courageous and well-meaning, are nevertheless criminally anarchic.

The characters of Park's novel belong to a community which views the Troubles, not in political or historical terms, but as the manifestation of a metaphysical and social malaise. The pastor speaks of 'a spirit of evil loose in this land' (7). To the old man, the Troubles are but one manifestation of a corrupt and corrosive modernity, and he refers to a 'darkness all around' (16), a 'creeping sickness spreading out and infecting more and more' (51), 'a plague' (51), a 'great sickness' (108). There is a general feeling that the institutions of Church and State are unable to offer protection against the 'sickness'. The pastor prays: 'The forces of government and state have deserted us and, in this our hour of need, we turn to You for our succour and deliverance. Pour down Your wrath on those who daily sow the seeds of death and destruction and confound their evil schemes' (10). Samuel's widowed mother refuses to accept the assurances of the representatives of the British government who tell her that her husband's death was not in vain. She is equally unconvinced that medical science can help her son: 'I know you mean well, Doctor, and I know you can heal many sicknesses nowadays, but only God's peace can heal my son now' (64–5). In their despair at the failure of society, people rely on extreme, non-official modes of response such as those offered by fundamentalist religion or by the paramilitaries.

The boy Samuel, however, ultimately finds healing in 'words'. The novel insists on the duplicity and divisiveness of words. 'Words aren't worth shit' (140), says Billy to his father. For Billy, 'healing' can only follow extirpation of the enemy through violence. Words themselves can be weapons: as Samuel listens to the argument between Billy and his father, 'their voices grew louder – vicious volleys of words' (141). Moving around the city, the boy is aware of the ubiquitous grafitti of hate: 'every-where there was a wall, or square of concrete, the spider writing spread its messages of warning and hate. The words spat at him, hissing white-teethed whispers' (82). Religious words offer no meaning or solace either. Listening to the pastor pray, Samuel 'shut his ears against the words, heard only the whispering voice telling him to block out the screams, to hide in silence' (11). The words of the preacher in the mission-tent only serve to oppress and ensnare the boy's natural spirit: 'He felt like a little bird trapped in the great dome of the tent, desperate to break into the safety of the sky. The words were the bars against which his wings beat frantically until they were bruised and broken' (69). To Samuel, the old man's words are 'inexplicable riddles which made no sense' (85). On the street, the old man is assailed by a caco-phony of different voices 'as they urged their particular brand of false salvation ... It was as if each one was building a miserable little Tower of Babel, each speaking a language that no one else understood' (127). The novel becomes a comprehensive and complex image of disconnection and discontinuity, amplified by a Biblical intertext which links contemporary Ulster to the plight of the Israelites wandering aimlessly in the wilderness. After his father's death, the boy experiences the world as an 'unhomely' place, whether in the city or in the country: 'He didn't want to go back, but he didn't want to stay. Instead, he wanted to live in some different place, but he didn't know where that place was. He wanted to find some secret door and pass through it into some safer, better world' (155). The boy recognises that he, his mother, Mr Ellison, Billy, all inhabit a broken world. He feels his mother's disappointment in discovering that places like Portrush and Belfast are not at all as she had once known them. The old man yearns for the loss of his wife and the son he once played with. Just as Mrs Anderson realises that the memory of her husband will soon be forgotten, so the boy, perusing the faces of the victims in the old man's ledger, 'tried to know them, but they had faded like their stories into the past' (177). Against these recognitions of violence, confusion and mutability, the boy discovers the positive potential of words. He tears up the old man's ledger, throwing it to the winds, but finds that 'the print would not come off his hands' (178). He cannot escape words, but instead of simply hoarding the past he can re-work it and thereby gain imaginative control over it. The novel ends with a great surge of forward movement and energy. The boy is born again: 'He crawled out of the crevice, his legs stiff and awkward at first, then clambered over the stone to the top of the outcrop' (179). No longer seeing himself as simply a victim of circumstance, he occupies a position of dominance, looking down over the sick and troubled city. He has achieved distance from the events of the past and now aspires to a bird-like freedom through the power of words and their capacity for imaginatively transcending the tyranny of fact. He appropriates the old man's prophetic idiom, but for young Samuel healing lies in the religion of art, not in fundamentalist Christianity:

> And as he lifted his face words faltered in the fiery flux of his throat, each sound a tiny flame which seared the softness of his being. They stuttered brokenly to his lips, melting at first into nothingness like snow falling on water, but he forced them forward until at last they broke free. His voice rang out raw and strange, but he shouted again and again, calling the world to look, and as he hung trembling on the air, the wind scattered the words like seed. (180)

This epiphanic conclusion is a transformative, redemptive moment outside time, a re-working of Christian mysticism in which the protagonist is rapturously restored to a state of primordial unity with the world. Samuel's 'intolerable wrestle with words',[86] to use T.S. Eliot's words in *Four Quartets*, implies some degree of aesthetic self-consciousness and self-referentiality: but the impulse is still towards transcendence. If the metaphysical framework of Idealist (Christian) thought has collapsed, there survives a post-Christian, post-Romantic sense of the word as ontologically distinct from the world as well as being embedded in it. In *The Necessary Angel*, Wallace Stevens argues that 'modern reality is a reality of decreation in which our revelations are not the revelations of belief, but the precious portents of our own powers'.[87] Samuel learns that we create our own realities through reformulation of the existing discourses. 'The old man had spoken of a cure', Samuel thinks, 'but maybe it had existed only inside his head, buried amidst the tangle of words' (179). The 'healing' the novel emphasises is that which comes from realisation of our own God-like imaginative power, albeit provisionally and ironically.

Writing about the Northern Irish Troubles novel in 1976, Richard Deutsch had this to say: 'Perhaps the main criticism of this form of literature is that it sinks into narcissistic provincialism. Writers assume with pride this civil war, it is theirs and it is unique. There is little influence from abroad, or any comparison with some countries ravaged by the same problem today or in the past (Cyprus, Holland).[88] Park's third novel, *Stone Kingdoms*, which views the Northern Irish crisis through disturbing perspectives that derive from foreign African culture, is a powerful refutation of Deutsch's conclusion. The novel illustrates 'the overdue exploitation of literary strategies such as perspectivism, ambiguity and displacement'[89] which Eve Patten mentioned as characteristic of a new, postmodern generation of writers. 'The introduction of a degree of distance into the novelistic vision', Gerry Smyth says, 'can be physical (as with the introduction of geographical perspectives from the rest of the British Isles, Europe and beyond) or discursive (as for example with the use of irony, parody and other defamiliarising devices'.[90] Park follows Robert MacLiam Wilson, Glenn Patterson and Briege Duffaud in adopting a displaced geographical and discursive perspective which allows him to destabilise the usual configurations of 'home', identity, belonging, the past, the Troubles. By exploring the double vision of a narrator who sees the North from an African perspective and Africa from a Northern Irish perspective, he re-works a literary convention which, as Patten remarks, 'pandered to the isolation of Northern Ireland as a stagnant and erratic phenomenon'.[91] The manipulation of huge geographical and cultural distances inevitably produces striking ironic effects but, like Wilson and Patterson, Park also transcends irony to affirm a reconstructed humanism deriving from a fresh approach to Realism and the transformation of exhausted provincial clichés and pietistic, complacent or nihilistic narratives.

Both *The Healing* and *Stone Kingdoms* are transformations of yet other kinds of prior narratives. Both are ironic re-tellings of Old Testament stories. The Bible story of God calling the boy Samuel to be his servant reappears as a mad old man's presumption that the boy who is his new next-door neighbour has been sent to him by God to speak his message to the world. But where the biblical Samuel is an example of obedient service to the divine will, Park writes his boy Samuel as a self-creating,

86 T.S. Eliot, 'Four Quartets' *The Complete Poems and Plays of T.S. Eliot* (London: Faber, 1969), pp 169–98.
87 Wallace Stevens, *The Necessary Angel: Essays on Reality and Imagination* (London, Faber, 1951), p. 175.
88 Richard Deutsch, '"Within two shadows", p. 150.   89 Patten, 'Fiction in conflict', p. 129.   90 Gerry Smyth, *The Novel and the Nation*, p. 116.

existentialist hero. The biblical Naomi who promises that she will never leave nor forsake the foreigner Ruth is refigured as the Donegal Naomi, the narrator of *Stone Kingdoms*, whose relationship with the African girl, Nadra, constructs an image of liberating and supportive lesbianism. This kind of intertextuality reflects these texts' ambiguity – their belonging to, and distance from – the Ulster Protestant 'Bible-belt'.

Stone Kingdoms begins in Africa with the highly traumatised heroine, Naomi, recovering from injuries sustained in an unspecified African war (Rwanda?), then the story abruptly loops back a little in time to Naomi teaching in Belfast, conducting a class on Golding's *Lord of the Flies* and the children acting out Golding's story of schoolboy savagery on a tropical island. The novel develops an anthropological view of the Northern Irish Troubles, relating them to the conflict between the two gangs in Golding's fable, which itself is modelled on the dynamics of African tribal society. One of the children, Daniel McCarroll, understands why the boys paint their faces in Golding's story: 'Because it helps them lose their inhibitions, because they're able to hide behind a mask, behave in a way that's different from what they're normally like'[92] – an ironically prophetic insight, given the part which Daniel plays later as one of the mob which savagely kills the two CID men caught up in a Republican funeral cortège on its way to Milltown cemetry in West Belfast: 'The crowd is driven by its own collective frenzy; hungry, atavistic, each man outdoing the other' (65).[93] The schoolchildren's glosses on *Lord of the Flies* suggest a view on the Northern Irish crisis, and articulate a moral perspective as applicable to Park's as to Golding's 'book':

> This book provides an insight into good and evil in the world. It shows that there is good and evil in every person and in certain situations this evil escapes and takes control of the person. It was the boys' own evil which brought the images of beasts and their own fears which made it real to them. (49)

On her way to school, Naomi reads the newspaper headlines in the newsagents telling of 'some far-off tribal war' (53), but the same savagery is enacted daily on the streets of Belfast outside the school. Like Friel's association of the tribal dancing of the Ryangans with the Celtic rites of Lughnasa and the irruption of wild, libidinal energies in the repressed Mundy sisters in *Dancing at Lughnasa*, Park emphasises the link between so-called primitive and civilised societies, as when Naomi shows her class 'pictures from magazines of shadowy faces, painted sports fans, an African tribe performing a dance, the stone statues of Easter Island, a dark figure wearing a combat

91 Eve Patten, 'Fiction in conflict: Northern Ireland's prodigal novelists', p. 146. 92 David Park, *Stone Kingdoms* (London: Phoenix, 1997), p. 49. First published London: Phoenix, 1996. Hereafter, page references will be incorporated into the text. 93 Park refers to an actual incident which took place in 1988 three days after the Loyalist gunman, Michael Stone, attacked the mourners at the funeral of an IRA unit shot in Gibraltar.

jacket and a balaclava silhouetted against some Belfast gable wall' (49). Naomi recognises that as a schoolteacher she is 'driven by the unbearable zeal of the missionary'
(57): 'I clutched the spurious belief that I could alter what I conceived then as the
narrow limits of their existence'. But Naomi's naive Arnoldian belief in a perfectable
human nature and in the power of culture to bring 'sweetness and light' to the anarchic masses is put to the test in both Belfast and the African refugee camp of Bakalla
where she works as a schoolteacher. Daniel, the boy in whom she has taken a special
interest, seems perversely resistant to her civilising efforts, indistinguishable from
Golding's boy savages chanting 'Kill the pig! Kill the pig!' (48). She goes to Africa
'partly because of a boy' (264), partly because the violence in Belfast has ruptured any
sense of home, ultimately her belief in civilisation itself. Her experience epitomises
the trauma of the liberal humanist in a barbarous world:

> 'Why did you come to Africa, Naomi?'
> How can I start to explain? How can he understand? I would have to begin
> with a feeling which belongs in a city I once thought of as home. It is a sense
> that we are slipping closer to the abyss, that with each new atrocity comes the
> frightened knowledge that all semblance of restraint, of the accepted para-
> meters of barbarity, has gone, and that there is nothing to stop us slipping
> over the edge. (64)

The reader at first is made to feel the insignificance and pettiness of the Northern
Irish Troubles when they are set against African conditions of famine, barbarity and
utter degradation, but Park repeatedly insists on the similarities between the two
theatres of conflict, evoking an overwhelming sense of universal cruelty and inhumanity before which the forces of civilisation are pathetically ineffectual. His
description of African society, reminiscent of Heaney's version of the Viking ethos in
'North', resonates with local relevance:

> Great fault lines slowly began to open in the camp. Ancient feuds that had
> lain dormant long enough for some to believe they had been forgotten, started
> to move and shift. A fight at one of the wells, some stolen cattle, a dispute
> over a sack of grain, the body of a young man found on the river bed with his
> throat cut. Accusations and counter-claims, funerals and calls for vengeance,
> the re-formation into tribal enclaves. (172)

Naomi, disillusioned by civilisation, rejects the simple binary opposition of civilian
and barbarian. In an ironic inversion of the usual colonial stereotypes, it is the native
girl, Nadra, who upholds the value of the rational ideal represented by 'books and
education, schools and universities' (234), and Naomi who insists that Nadra under-

stand the powerlessness of education to overcome 'magic and dreams ... history and the past' (234). Superstition and barbarism, Naomi maintains, are as much a part of the First World as the Third World: 'I come from people who worship stone statues they think can move or cry tears, people who believe it pleases God for them to climb mountains in their bare feet. And in the north of my country people kill each other because they belong to a different tribe' (234). Western liberal humanism, institutionalised in the form of the international relief Agency, is depicted as ludicrously powerless to deal with the succession of corrupt and bloody African regimes of power. The Agency's cynically pragmatic administrators have no influence beyond their capacity to bribe the local factions for permission to continue offering humanitarian aid. Its workers form a forlorn band of disillusioned and demoralised doctors, nurses and teachers whom the natives regard with suspicion as an unwelcome neo-colonial presence. Nevertheless, despite their cynical or self-serving motivation, these volunteers embody a residual idealism which, to Naomi, makes individuals such as Rollins a more compelling example of human 'goodness' (151) than her self-righteous clergyman father.

Naomi, the narrator, is an outsider, a displaced person, in relation to both the Northern Irish situation and the African crisis. Park's 'African' discourse inverts the colonial stereotype so that instead of black skin adopting white mask, we have white woman adopting (literally) black mask, refusing the reality and identity provided by colonialism, even though this means consigning herself to the role of fugitive in the new postcolonial (dis)order. There is no more secure place for her in the 'Belfast' discourse. Driving to visit Daniel's home, she thinks: 'It makes me nervous driving into territory which is foreign, paranoia generating a fear that I am clearly recognizable as an outsider, a member of another tribe' (84). Her perspective on the Troubles is from outside the North, yet even as a Protestant living in Donegal she has been an outsider: 'We are outsiders in the community we live in, part of the declining Protestant population' (12). 'An only child', she says, 'I am often alone' (12). Her femaleness accentuates her isolation and vulnerability in this strongly gendered narrative which, like the Golding intertext, reflects a solidly male world characterised by tribalism and violence. Like young Samuel in *The Healing*, Naomi is brought to the edge of annihilation and, just as Samuel re-constitutes himself through the healing power of the word, Naomi is re-born into a native, female world of love and kindness. The women of Bakalla help her to escape the soldiers by ritualistically preparing her as if for the grave:

> Then, as I started to grow faint and think that I would suffocate, I suddenly felt hands opening the shroud and heard voices talking to me. They helped me sit up and washed and dressed me but let me drink only a little at a time. A damp cloth was pressed against the back of my neck and hands helped rub

the circulation back into my arms and legs. I tried to stand up but my legs buckled under me and then as they continued to minister to me I looked round the women's faces. (188)

Hiding among the sunflowers, re-absorbed in nature, she longs for physical contact with Nadra: 'Her (Nadra's) absence had freed the truth', though the voice of her upbringing, of her dead father, of the Christian God, tries to obstruct the process of self-discovery:

> Sometimes words came to my lips, words that came from somewhere I didn't know, but I stifled them and pushed them back into a nervous silence. For there was another voice, a voice like the one my father used when he spoke for God, and it warned and mocked what it insisted was an unutterable foolishness, perhaps even the greatest and most dangerous of all ... But sometimes, too, that grip would slip and I fastened only on the blink of her eyes, the white whorled skin on the tips of her fingers, the electric rustle of her hair, and I would feel the life that coursed through all my being. (205)

Repeatedly in the novel, femininity is constructed as a source of nurture, practical assistance and healing. As fugitives from the soldiers, Naomi and Nadra are helped by the women of the villages which they pass through, though the non-ideological sphere of native female influence is always subordinate to the tribal patriarchy from which the community's final decisions emanate. Nevertheless, the novel demonstrates how male military and sexual threat galvanises a consolidated feminine resistance, epitomised by the interracial bond between Nadra and Naomi. For Naomi, the prototype of female kindness and courage is her mother – 'My mother is the kindest person I have ever known' (18). The childhood memory of her mother's courage in standing against a menacing group of men taunting another man on the streets of Derry returns to Naoimi in Africa when her own courage is put to the test. A feminist reading would focus on the novel's suggestion of a strong feminine alternative to counteract the degraded male order of institutionalised cynicism and emptiness (the Camp Leader Charlie Wanneker, the veteran medic Rollins), cold rectitude (Naomi's father) and tribal barbarism (the McCarroll males, the IRA, the macho African fighters); and on Naomi's struggle to escape from patriarchy (her father, Wanneker, Medullah the tribal holy man, the village guide whom she kills in self-defence) and evolve a new radical lesbian-feminist identity. Queer theory's concern with crossing lines of difference meshes with postmodernism. 'Queer', according to Suzanne Walters, is 'the perfect postmodern trope, a term for the times, the epitome of knowing ambiguity'.[94] On a 'queer theory' reading, Naomi's acts of resistance to normative social and cultural constructions of sexual identity may be seen as part of a larger dissatisfaction with the received categories of identification. She undoes or 'queers' not only the established categories of sexual identity but disturbs the straightforward binary polarities of civilian and barbarian, coloniser and colonised, home and exile, Protestant and Catholic, the North and the South. Ultimately, she calls into question the very ground of liberal humanist orthodoxy – the essentialist opposition of 'good' and 'evil' – as when she remembers Daniel's last words to her in the Young Offenders' Centre:

> 'Everything's simple to you. You want everything simple like it's those two gangs of kids on that island, and one's led by Ralph and one's led by Jack and you want to be in Ralph's gang and everybody you don't like is in Jack's.'
> 'Maybe it is simple, Daniel.' As soon as I've said it it sounds stupid, pathetic, but it's too late. (260)

Like *The Healing, Stone Kingdoms* never gives up on the re-integrative and trans-formative powers of the imagination or on the Romantic faith in the life-force. While Naomi awaits a second re-awakening and the removal of the bandages from her eyes, she finds consolation in thinking about the ocean which claimed her father's life – 'It is the ocean I think of now, the memory I cling to more than any other' (9). Her submarine visions are not of despair and drowning; they are of a magical, colourful, serene, fecund and regenerative place, thinking about which 'My whole body feels liquid, alive, more fluent than I have ever known it' (10). The organic, natural image with which the novel closes emphasises hope and renewal, life's continual re-assertion of itself in the face of death and destruction:

> I try to stem the pain, imagine a pink slick of sperm trembling in the water, then some time in the darkness a glint of coral starting silently through the currents. Swimming through the dangers, swimming until it finds the safety of the reef where it grows and renews what has been destroyed. I think, too of a city which petrifies on its own calcerous skeleton, but the memory fades and there is only this other world, fragile and strangely strong, full face to the ocean, a rampart against the ceaseless beat of the waves. (278)

---

94 Suzanne Walters, 'From here to queer: radical feminism, postmodernism, and the lesbian menace (or, why can't a woman be more like a fag?)', *Signs: Journal of Women, Culture and Society*, 21, 4, (1996), p. 837.

The carnivalised text: Frances Molloy's *No Mate for the Magpie* (1985),
Lionel Shriver's *Ordinary Decent Criminals* (1992), Colin Bateman's
Divorcing Jack (1995) and *Cycle of Violence* (1995), Robert MacLiam Wilson's
Eureka Street (1996)

Any language, any speech, reflects the attitudes and values of the person using it, the person's social and cultural position, his or her relationship to a particular regional and social community; whether the speaker is in authority or is in some oblique or oppositional relation to authority. Issues of language and of voice are raised from the outset in Frances Molloy's novel, *No Mate for the Magpie*. The novel is colonised entirely by a strongly dialectal voice from the margins of rural Co. Derry, and by placing this voice in charge of the text, Molloy forces the reader to engage with it as an important part of Northern Irish culture. What we hear is not the standard, educated, genteel voice of formally written or spoken discourse, but a voice that works against socio-political and cultural centralisation, signalling from the beginning the importance of class, hierarchy and status – and therefore issues of power and authority. The dialectal and idiomatic vitality of the narrator's speech represents a straining away from a closed or centralised system, an officially recognised 'unitary' or 'monoglossic' language expressive of an official set of class, cultural or national values. The narrator speaks as a female, as a child (at least for the first half of the novel), as a member of an oppressed minority (that is, as a Roman Catholic growing up in Protestant Ulster in the 1950s and '60s), as someone from a poor and underprivileged family who has little education or social status, and who occupies a series of menial or vulnerable positions in society (nanny, nun, mental patient, factory machinist, bacon slicer, priest's house-keeper, unqualified nurse, prisoner in the Bridewell jail in Dublin) in which she is subjected to all kinds of indignity, exploitation and manipulation. She speaks a language which, both consciously and unconsciously, parodies, criticises and generally undermines the authority of the dominant society and any cultural pretensions it might have towards a unitary language. In favouring this voice from the margins, Molloy asserts a commitment to social diversity and change rather than to fixity and the hierarchical.

The preference for 'low' language over 'high' goes hand in hand with the narrator's temperamentally subversive nature. The opening lines of the book emphasise difference –

> Way a wee screwed up protestant face an' a head of black hair a was born, in a state of original sin. Me ma didn't like me, but who's te blame the poor woman, sure a didn't look like a catholic wain atall.[95]

95 Frances Molloy, *No Mate for the Magpie* (London: Virago, 1983), p.1. Hereafter, page references will be incorporated into the text.

- not merely difference from the dominant bourgeois society, but also difference from mother, family, (Catholic) community, and even self, thus setting the scene for the highly individualistic, irreverend and transgressive perspective on the world which the novel presents. The idea of conflict here may be related to Bakhtin's notion of the tension between 'centripetal' and 'centrifugal' forces within literary works, and in the way the works relate to their cultural contexts. The 'centripetal' forces press towards closure, centralisation and canonisation, while the 'centrifugal' forces seek to dislocate and disturb the movement towards a unified and monoglossic discourse:

> [A] unitary language gives expression to forces working toward concrete verbal and ideological unification and centralisation, which develop in vital con-nection with the processes of sociopolitical and cultural centralisation ... Alongside the centripetal forces, the centrifugal forces of language carry on their uninterrupted work; alongside verbal-ideological centralisation and unification, the uninterrupted processes of decentralisation and disunification go forward.[96]

Ann's 'low' language offers a challenge to 'high' cultural pretensions and is instru-mental in the (characteristically) comic upsetting of official systems – the educational system which puts children in the care of mad women like Mrs Greene; the local council; the 'welfare' system which threatens to break up the McGlone family; the religious order of the convent; the systems of medical and psychiatric institutionalisa-tion; a social order characterised by sectarianism, bigotry, and a fetishisation of bourgeois respectability; a political system which treats the minority community of the North as second class citizens; and a penal system in the South which is every bit as repressive as that in the North. While there are times when the challenge to the official systems is presented quite seriously (as in the account of the Derry Civil Rights march on 5 October 1968 and the Belfast-to-Derry student march on 1 January 1969, which leads to confrontation with Paisleyites and police at Burntollet Bridge), laughter is more generally the weapon used to bring down various forms of authority in the novel.

The comic effects suggest a carnivalistic element in *No Mate for the Magpie*. Carnival is probably Bakhtin's most influential concept. Drawn from the medieval ritualistic festival practice, carnival represents a kind of 'licensed misrule', a disruption of normal hierarchical structures and the blurring of divisions between 'high' and 'low'. During the carnival celebrations, the high and mighty were ridiculed, the mockery directed primarily against the Church and civic authorities. Carnival allowed for the uninhibited, joyful expression of an unofficial folk culture which was opposed

---

96 M.M. Bakhtin, excerpt from *The Dialogic Imagination* (1934) in Philip Rice and Patricia Waugh (eds), *Modern Literary Theory* (London: Arnold, 1999), pp 256–64, pp 256–7.

to all forms of authority and pretension, and for a free and familiar mingling of all types of people. Molloy's use of the picaresque form, with Ann meeting a wide variety of social types as she moves from job to job, place to place, from one kind of lodging to another, helps develop a carnivalised plot, and by using humour the author undercuts the hierarchic values of the culture, Ann's vernacular voice all the time asserting the carnivalistic displacement of 'respectable' modes of discourse.

Authority is decentred through laughter, and Ann's indecorous voice opposes and undercuts, or — to use Bakhtin's term – 'dialogises' the voice of authority. Thus, in what Bakhtin calls 'double-voiced discourse', Ann's speech disingenuously parodies that of the nun who is instructing her in her novitiate:

> The nixt mornin' after mass, the mother of novices took me inte hir office an' toul me te kneel on the floor, so a did. Then she started te list off all the rules of the convent te me. The first wan was custody of the eyes. That meant that a was te learn to be shifty an' niver te look at a body if a was talkin' te them but te look at the floor instead. Then she toul me the rule a knew about any-way only she called it custody of the lips. That meant that a was not only to be shifty but a was te walk right by people without even botherin' te pass them the time of day. (76)

The humour arises from the de-privileging of religious discourse, as the nun's life of Christian submission to God is, through Ann's reductive language, made into something 'shifty', unfriendly and downright rude. When Ann refuses 'Reverent Mother's' 'pile of blood-stained cloths' (76) to take care of her period, Molloy again dialogises 'Reverent Mother''s sanctimonious response, rejecting its validity, by re-processing it through Ann's pragmatic and parodic vernacular:

> Well, she (Reverent Mother) didn't take that very well atall an' she launched inte me way a new lecture as long as the day an' the morrow, about learnin' obedience an' humility an' how self-will hinders the search for perfection an' holiness an' how a must learn te turn away from all earthly desires an' give mesel' over completely to god. She said that a must always bear in mine how great an' manifole were the gifts that god bestowed on them that loved him.
>
> A allowed that at that rate of goin' these nuns musta loved god a quare good bit because it appeared te me that the seven poun' that a had brought them for sanitary protection was a great an' manifole gift indeed considerin' what they were sellin'. (77)

Ann's narration throws into question the whole meaning of Christianity as it relates to everyday life, but her speech also reveals her own lack of confidence in her own perceptions. It is only because her mental health has already been officially checked out by the authorities that Ann can believe that it is not her, but 'Reverent Mother', who is 'insane':

> Before ye go away te be a nun ye have te go te a doctor to have yer head examined te see if ye'r mental, an' if ye happen' to be foun' to be mental, the nuns will have nothin' atall te do way ye. Now it was just as well that a'd had me head looked at before a went inte the convent because if a hadn't have, a would of been askin' mesel' questions about me own sanity, for here was this woman standin' in front of me, flayin' hersel' way a whip, an' me kneelin' there watchin' hir doin' it way the blood runnin' down me thighs. (77)

At this point, Ann is, to some extent, a naive narrator. When she speaks of the bishop 'barberin'' her, and how the two of them 'confabbed away in Latin' (81) during the ceremony of her 'gettin' married te Christ', she is unaware of how her language is in competition (both linguistically and ideologically) with the language of the Church. The naive narrator defamiliarises the world of social conventionality, forcing us to see it in new ways, taking nothing for granted, making us question conventional judgment. Thus, of one of her Belfast flat-mates, Ann says: 'A don't know whether the other girl who lived in the flat was beautiful or not because a niver got a good enough look at hit. She kept hir face hidden away all the time behine a heavy mask of make-up' (106). Ann reports directly and literally what she sees, in a language that is unaffected by conventional social valuation or colouring. Make-up is viewed, not in the way it usually is, as an aid to beauty, but as a cover-up which makes it impossible to tell whether or not a face is beautiful. Here, in miniature, we have the novel's central principle, its valuation of the natural above the artificial or 'civilised'.

The narrator, Ann, demonstrates a limited self-awareness, and a limited confidence in her own judgments and instincts. It is her father, not Ann, who is prepared to take a more outspoken line with 'Reverent Mother' over the way his daughter has been treated in the convent. For most of the novel, Ann's consciousness and speech are profoundly shaped by feelings of inferiority and powerlessness: a shopkeeper who threatens her father's job as binman is 'a wile big important high-up man that always carried the canopy at the chapel whinever the Blessed Sacrament was bein' brought up an' down the aisle' (23); the doctors in the mental institution are 'a whole lot of big important high up lookin' people ... Some of them looked at me an' some of them didn't' (95); the Protestant girls in the factory invite her to come along to an Orange Hall where 'some wile shockin' big important high-up man be the name of the Reverent Ian Paisley was comin' to make a speech' (108–9). But if Ann's contestation of authority is at first hesitant and unsure, she is firmly planted on a narrative path leading to radical transformations of subaltern (female, Catholic) roles, mentalities and identities.

The authorial handling of Ann's metamorphosis is not altogether successful. In attempting to turn her heroine into a strong, self-assertive subject, Molloy is led into gross exaggeration and unreality. The account of Ann's acts of defiance of priestly authority during the brief time she works as housekeeper for a parish priest stretches the bounds of credibility too far, as does the description of her relationship with the superior and puritanical Dublin landlady, Mrs McBride, whom Ann makes a fool out of with her fantastic stories. Ironically, and sadly, the naivety which, when projected onto the narrator, had produced such richly subversive and sophisticated comedy, becomes towards the end of the novel the mark of the author's own burlesque style.

Nevertheless, *No Mate for the Magpie* represents a significant experiment in deflating the traditional pieties and allegiances in the North, Catholic as well as Protestant. Opposing itself to any kind of essentialism, the novel emphasises instead the way identity is socially produced. Ann, finding herself the centre of attention in a Protestant factory, has to pretend to her work-mates that she herself is a Protestant:

> To begin way, a had to be very careful not te say the wrong thing in case they twigged on that a was a catholic, so a limited mesel' te repeatin' verbatim what the dreadful catholics from our town said about us protestants, an' only repeatin' some of the better known anti-catholic slogans, but as me confidence increased, a got te enjoy the part a was playin' so much, that a became more excessive an' outspoken than any of the others in me 'scarhin' criticism an' condemnation of fuckin' popish scum. (108)

The carnivalesque humour dialogises the standard sanctimonious discourse in which the sectarian conflict in the North is usually inscribed. Moreover, the Northern situation is viewed as neither special nor unique, but merely part of a larger national and international malaise. From being a Civil Rights marcher in Derry, Ann becomes an anti-Vietnam war protester in Dublin. Re-located in the South, her narrative registers another equally virulent set of social problems – Dublin society's obsession with bourgeois respectability, sexual and emotional repression, rampant racism, venal materialism, narrow religiosity, petrification of the spirit, joyless and humiliating conformism. The novel closes with a series of disconsolate vignettes of Dublin's poor and destitute, children neglected and abused, foreigners who are rejected and despised, drug addicts wandering the streets, nuns who have removed themselves from normal human contact. Despite her experiences of the corrupt and oppressive hegemonic regime in the North, and the social problems of the South, Ann remains free of ideological entrapment, in close touch with real life. Refusing to be controlled, to allow her own consciousness to be shaped by the language, perceptions and values of others, she insists on seeing for herself and expressing herself in her own idiosyncratic way. Suspicious of all systems, she is figured as a lone, fugitive, homeless spirit, the titular magpie – a bird traditionally regarded as uncanny. In a parody of Joyce's flight from Dublin, Ann also takes her leave, carried along by the mythic force of Joyce's female muse, Anna Livia, the river of Life, 'bringer of plurabilities': 'A could see "Anna Livia" movin' beneath me, resolutely, determinedly, headin' outa Ireland, an' a knew then that a too must do the same an' go to a place where life resembled life more than it did here' (170).

Ordinary Decent Criminals was originally published in the USA and it was no doubt on account of her intended American readership that Shriver included the 'Glossary of Troublesome Terms',[97] in much the same way as Maria Edgeworth appended her 'Glossary' to *Castle Rackrent* to explain Irish terms and dialect to her English readers. In her Glossary, Shriver explains that 'Ordinary Decent Criminals' is 'an official term in the Northern Irish prison system, used to distinguish offenders with political motives' (422). The novel, she further clarifies, is fiction 'set within a real political context', a mixture of the invented and the actual. The novel's references to a 1988 Border Poll and the conference held to marshal support for it are fictional, though there had been such a poll held in 1973 to determine whether the people of Northern Ireland wished to remain in the UK. Since the 1973 poll was boycotted by most Catholics the referendum was never re-activated. The remaining events, Shriver claims, 'would have taken place more or less as described, from late 1987 through 1988' (416).

These events are, however, rendered through a distinctive narrative mode – a highly carnivalised writing which upsets conventional boundaries, and overthrows the firm structures which define the different communities, systems and ideologies – whether those of Republicanism, Loyalism or bourgeois liberalism. Satiric humour is the primary technique used for the de-privileging of discourse and decentering of authority. The notions of masquerade, festival and joyful disruption associated with carnival are given vivid expression in the episode describing the street disturbances in response to yet another unpopular political development: 'The South had just extradited Robert Russell over the border today, and it was a perfect excuse for a party' (251). The barricade is 'magnificent' (250), 'the atmosphere was festive' (251), a boy is barbecuing chickens on steering columns over a burning City Bus, a visitor begs the lads to hijack another lorry or two so that he can get a good photograph – 'but the hijackers were all anxious to get home in time to catch their barricade on the BBC' (253). This happy subversion of 'British' law and order is itself subjected to a second-order verbal disruption through the prevailing ironic tone of the narration. At other times, West Belfast's Republican discourse is undercut by being voiced through a

---

97 Lionel Shriver, *Ordinary Decent Criminals* (London: Flamingo, 1993), pp 415–27. First published New York: Farrar, Straus & Giroux, 1990 under the title *The Bleeding Heart*. Hereafter, page references will be incorporated into the text.

collection of drunken wasters in the Green Door 'blattering out tales' (33) of Republican derring-do, always 'whining' about the Brits – 'all those shoe shops in the town:
more rape of our culture' (343) – and 'sounding ferocious' – 'Look at Enniskillen: the
Provos bow and scrape how it was a mistake, but I say it was fuckin' brilliant!' (343).
These are the 'bullshitters' (344). Their actions on behalf of the motherland are
rendered as farce. 'The Pints of Shearhoon', a parody of the sentimental patriotic
ballad, commemorates a Republican volunteer ('National self-determination/Was
dear to old Shearhoon') who, intent on bombing the refurbished Crown Bar which
he now finds 'too smarmy', is refused admittance by the bouncer, gets drunk, and
blows himself up by mistake. The elegy concludes with:

> We'd yet buy Guinness for the bastard –
> He didn't have to die,
> If he hadn't of been plastered,
> Or he'd only worn a tie. (354)

Another young volunteer, emerging from the toilet after planting a bomb in Union
Jackie's bar in Loyalist Belfast, is shocked to find that the bar has been evacuated and
the doors locked. Irish language, even in West Belfast, is also subject to carnivalised
overthrow. Clive, the American visitor and Irish culture vulture, may not realise the
'bullshitters' are taking a hand out of him –

> '*Luchann alaibh*, Michael,' said Damien, kicking Callaghan and jerking his
> head toward Clive. '*Ta Americanle. Ar freisin drinkoine. Te understandua,
> eejiteanna?*'
>   'Ach, right! *Ard fheis! Ard Chomairle! Bus Eirreann!*'
>   '*Chucky arla. Slantia ceili an phoblacht.*'
>   '*MacStoafain o'muillior sinn féin! Fianna fail fine gael charlie haughey RTE.
> Clannad gay burn aer lingus.* Yeats! GAA! Och! Um, och … (165)

but the authorial comment immediately following turns the satiric whip away from
the naive American and back on the local 'bullshitters': 'At one time the Green Door's
loos were labeled in Irish, but the signs had to be changed because the customers kept
going in the wrong bog' (165).

The forces of de-centralisation and displacement in the novel are chiefly mobilised
through the three main characters – the American visitor Estrin Lancaster, and the
two champions of a new power-sharing executive, Catholic Farrell O'Phelan and
Protestant Angus McBride. Together, these three characters mediate an alienated,
carnivalising point of view which consistently undermines the dominant discourses
of 'Orange' and 'Green' in this deeply divided society. But since the views of these

three characters merge and overlap so much, and since their language and voice –
whether American or Northern Irish, Protestant or Catholic, male or female – are
virtually indistinguishable one from another, there is insufficient variety of character
to convey a sense of real life. Ideas and attitudes are more important than fully
rounded characterisation, which consequently tends towards caricature.

Estrin, an author surrogate, is a version of the classic American romance hero
involved in anxious quest, daughter of Captain Ahab, Huck Finn, Isabel Archer and
Augie Marsh. She is a transworld easy-rider, rootless and restless, the not-so-innocent
abroad who casts a cold eye on both her native land and her adoptive home in Belfast.
In comparison with other American fictional negotiations of the North and its
Troubles, Shriver offers something quite different. Her satirical American character,
constructed on the edge of mainstream society and based in Republican West Belfast,
contrasts sharply with most previous representations, such as Tom Clancy's all-
American hero in *Patriot Games*, who becomes the darling of the British royal family
and leads the fight against IRA-fronted international terrorism. Estrin's shrewdly
observant, irreverent outsider's perspective on the Troubles has a striking freshness,
free as it is from the usual indigenous attachments and pieties. Ever-alert to contradiction and absurdity, she responds to the North with an acerbic wit and an
unillusioned affection. Her point of view is that of the itinerant, the natural decon-
structionist, one who is drawn to mavericks, misfits and subversives – 'people who
are obstreperous, inconsiderate, abusive, and nonplused. Card-carrying assholes' (25)
– of whom, it is clear, Belfast is blessed with an abundance. The Troubles are precisely
what makes Belfast interesting. Much preferable to bland bourgeois heaven are the
massive Republican murals in West Belfast and the flaming orange edifice of King
Billy on Sandy Row, the vicious political graffiti, the paramilitary funerals with gloves
and berets and Armalite salutes, the hijackings and burnings that go unchecked, the
racketeering, soldiers stalking the streets 'like an episode of The Dirty Dozen' (254),
bomb scares and bomb disposal, dirty tricks, reports of men's bloody deaths. 'Estrin
reminded herself that without the Troubles she'd never have come here, and without
them, like Farrell, she would leave' (254). She finds the normalisation of violence quite
shocking: 'In Belfast, murder is within the realm of ordinary revenge' (309). But the
Troubles provoke passionate indignation as well as voyeuristic fascination. To Estrin,
they express a scandalous urge to self-destruction: 'This country is full of people dying
for bullshit. That's not pride. It's low self-esteem' (197). In Estrin's savagely demythologising view, the cultic rites of martyrdom are merely an infantile fetishisation of
death: 'Dying for a united Ireland, what did that mean? It was like dying for
Munchkinland, like dying "because"' (324). She catalogues the evidence for seeing
Northern Irish politics as a series of perverse, self-defeating gestures: Gerry Adams
refusing to take his seat in Westminster; Unionists responding to Enniskillen by
boycotting their own council meetings; Long Kesh prisoners shivering on the floors

of freezing cells in which they have smashed the windows, broken the furniture and smeared the walls with their own faeces; the IRA pursuing the 'juvenile logic' which says '*If you don't let us have this country we're going to blow it up piece by piece*' (214).

Estrin falls in love with Farrell, the unlikely Belfast hotelier who used to be an independent bomb disposal man. Farrell is another displaced person, a renegade from his own people, contemptuous of the monolithic ideologies of Unionism and especially Nationalism. National aspiration, he says in an echo of Estrin, is like professing faith in 'the Easter Bunny or Santa Claus' (38); a sign of 'arrested adolescence', an inability to accept that life is an 'ordinary bollocks' and not necessarily one of Britain's making. People turn to a salvationist Nationalism, he maintains, because they are 'too terrified to live in a world where no one is in control: there is no God' (39), but in reality they are condemning themselves to a culture of victimhood and defeat since Nationalism can only ever be an aspiration, never a reality, just as 'the IRA can only exist as long as it fails' (40). Farrell boasts of having no affiliation of any kind, of contenting himself with performing 'a balancing act of impartial disruption' (85). Recognising the 'essential integrity of nearly every point of view', he refuses to hold any. He operates alone, unwelcome everywhere, alienated from every faction. Like Estrin, he doesn't believe in anyone's capacity to affect anything, but needs the Troubles to convince him of the value of life. Even more nihilistic than Estrin, he 'gladly watched his city self-destruct to reflect his own degradation' (395). Ruthlessly pragmatic and unscrupulously manipulative, he has no compunctions about taking up with another woman, not for love, but to safeguard his political ambitions. Yet, paradoxical character that he is, the anarchically sceptical Farrell is committed to a prototype of the 'Peace Process', and, for all his avowed independence, eventually discovers love with the unconventional Estrin, though too late, for external circumstances, in a final ironic twist, bring their relationship to a premature end.

Farrell's political partner is the libidinal and equally transgressive Angus McBride, whose task it is to persuade Protestant Unionists to agree to the power-sharing executive, as it was Farrell's job to bring Catholic Nationalists along. Farrell's diatribe against Nationalists is mirrored in Angus's disparagement of hard-line Unionists. Angus denies any 'two nations' theory, insisting instead on the basic similarity of the two traditions and their paramilitary representatives: 'The Northern Irish fought this hard from being so hopelessly homogenous they could drown' (336). The liberal humanist ideal, of which the power-sharing executive is the political expression, is in the hands of these two unscrupulous manipulators motivated entirely by pragmatism and not at all by morality. The only way power-sharing can be achieved, Angus believes, is through obfuscation and dirty tricks; and if they don't work he's prepared to reject democracy altogether in an all-out war against extremists and terrorists. Ultimately, neither he nor Farrell is really concerned about what happens to the North. At the end, Angus is more exercised by obtaining revenge against Farrell, who has seduced Angus's girlfriend, Roisin St Clair, a Republican poet from West Belfast. This Angus accomplishes by arranging for an IRA bomb to be concealed in a birthday present for Estrin. Private life is as much a hotbed of treachery and betrayal as the political world.

Sexuality and politics are intimately connected. As Farrell says of Roisin: 'Sure, stuck on the right boyfriend, she'd smuggle bazookas in her boot across the border with the best of them. With Angus I expect she's stitching Union Jacks for the Apprentice Boys' (26). To locate the roots of violence in sexual subjectivity is to de-politicise the Troubles. Understandably, the Provos object to such explanation, as when the Republican hard man, Michael Callaghan, rounds on Farrrell's sexualised disparagement of Nationalist aspiration: 'You might explain to us, then ... why we're such sad wee folk, clinging all confused to some wet dream of a united Ireland' (32). But this doesn't stop Farrell pursuing an exhaustive sexual reading of the conflict. 'The Troubles were a long fuck' (184), he says, and in detailing an elaborate erotics of violence he describes four kinds of orgasm corresponding to four kinds of outcome to the Troubles. Farrell's conclusion is that 'Northern Ireland is a bad fuck. They're still getting off on it, but they can't come. And it took more and more stimulation for either partner to feel anything at all' (187). Later in the novel, the extended description of Estrin's protracted, joyless masturbation – 'Estrin came twenty-five times' (294) – enacts in purely sexual terms the idea of the endless play of unsatisfied desire, which is everywhere written into the novel's political discourse. Estrin recognises that her lifetime of travelling from one country to another typifies this deferral or elusiveness of closure: 'It's a hunger like C.S. Lewis's magic Turkish delight: the more you eat, the more you want, because you didn't taste what you had before ... I have a problem with wanting what I've already got ... I no sooner get my butt to Belfast than I start frantic plans to fly to the Soviet Union' (57). She describes her relationship with Farrell as a constant movement back and forth through space: 'Sometimes she forced herself to pull away from him so she could enjoy going back, each time to visit new tourist attractions – the Pyramids, St Stephen's Green, the Roman Catacombs' (59); and attempts to rationalise this paradoxical sexual jour-neying: '*she would not come*. A traveller may be excited, but never satisfied. Besides, can't you understand that pleasure is grotesque? What can possibly happen next but that someone will take it away?' (63). Violence, sex, travel, eating: these are the inter-related domains in which are focused the novel's meditations on the restless play of desire. Emulating the Hunger Strikers whom she despises, Estrin is similarly impelled towards a self-annihilating transcendence: 'now that she'd found a man (Farrell) more like her and more splendid than any man in any country, she was bound to forswear him more completely than any man before ... She would deny herself so completely after three weeks of tea and eleven years of travel that, sidereal, she would evaporate' (325).

Another way of reading the Troubles suggested by the novel is through the preoccupations of postmodernism. Farrell enunciates his theory of 'bits' (129) in relation to both the city and the psyche of the people who inhabit it: 'As you are in pieces, so shall your cities fragment' (129). In Farrell's view, 'a *united* Ireland, *unionism* aspired to the same paradise, where you thought one clear thought without compulsively thinking the opposite at the same time' (130). The North becomes an exemplary site of struggle for wholeness, unity and totalisation. 'Both nationalists and Loyalists', he says, 'were yearning for the same cohesion' (130). Rather than being shocked by the continual litany of atrocity, Farrell is surprised that there isn't more, that people aren't 'utterly disassembled' (130). Belfast is once again constructed as a place of radical, irreducible postmodern difference and unreality. Reality seems to have been emptied of meaning, displaced by incomprehensible images, copies without originals. Estrin is struck by the falseness of the exotic appeal of the North, whether of the picture postcard Castlecaulfield cottage variety or the macabre images of violence which the young soldier naively thinks are 'the real thing' (250). Violence can only give the illusion of reality:

> [W]e're not sure we exist. It makes us dangerous, because we could end up making trouble, like pinching ourselves to check we're still here. I dislike scapegoating TV, but it is true that my country watches too much. That sensation of looking at a screen, it's easy to keep feeling that way when you look out the window. (206)

Estrin feels she inhabits a 'lifeproof' world where 'triumphs and tragedies happen only to people in books' (206), where real life always seems to be elsewhere, and people can no longer perceive themselves as agents, able to make things happen: 'we hire a handful from Hollywood to live for us, and they're only faking' (206). Farrell voices a similar sense of unreality:

> Now it was clear why the gun had seemed 'unreal'. He'd seen this scene before. Farrell lived in an era when two dimensions had overtaken three. Real life was subordinated to wide screen, the very inventor of 'real life' – for before the talkies, what other kind of life was there? (192)

The Troubles he reads about in the newspapers don't match the Troubles he knows first-hand – 'so where was the real view, or was there any? For Farrell often experienced the conflict as trumped up' (129). A chapter on Estrin's visit to the Linen Hall Library uncovers the processes of history-making and the 'black carnival' (176) of commodifying the Troubles: 'both Sinn Féin and the UDA promptly delivered issues of *Combat, Welcome to Fascist Ulster* pamphlets, and Ard fheis agendas by the box every month, anxious to be recorded, sonorous in their responsibility to History, here a somewhat cheapened Muse who mythologised tragedies overnight: if IRA volunteers were murdered in November, their ballad would be out on cassette to meet the Christmas rush' (174). To the Library come 'academics from Oxford and Harvard', 'foreign hyenas' picking over information for another manuscript; 'novelists, of course, had gotten in on the feed for years' (175).

Shriver's text, in the way it echoes and whispers a multitude of prior texts, deliberately reflects this Baudrillardian notion of the 'pre-cession of simulacra'. Estrin's description of Farrell in bed is reminiscent of the geographical conceit that John Donne employed in describing his mistress going to bed: 'Estrin found the world of Whitewells and this man on its bed the source of infinite, patient fascination. As the universe shrank ever further to two patches of face, Farrell's mouth opened into a cavernous place ... Farrell had swallowed the world, and all that ever was could be found there – the Taj Mahal, the Eiger, the Ganges, Cape Canaveral, the Smithsonian Institute, and Estrin's favorite *U.S. Out of Nicaragua* coffee cup back on Springfield Road' (60–1). The Peace Line intertext is Frost's 'Mending Wall': 'Sure something there was that did love a wall in this town' (208). The description of the Castlecaulfield cottage is indebted to William Carlos Williams, for 'in the late-afternoon sun ... the cottage exuded the radiant clarity of a wheelbarrow, a rooster' (248). After an explosion, the scene in which a van engine flies through a kitchen where the family is having breakfast is 'like a cartoon' (210). Estrin sees her own situation as an absurdist re-writing of an old script: 'Estrin could not remember one time watching a sit-com where a pregnant woman totters back from a clinic after eating nothing for almost three weeks, dreading calling the father, who is off drinking with a load of paramilitaries on the Antrim coast' (357).

Estrin figures the problematic of postmodern identity. Her 'theory of over-adaptation' (309) codifies her awareness of the dangers of fluidity and mobility. 'I can travel because I'll relinquish one reality for another without much of a fight' (309) – like zapping from one TV channel to another in the popular image of postmodern culture. In this respect, the North is again exemplary, for it 'has adapted, beautifully' to the most outrageous happenings and normalised the most atrocious violence. The soul of the place has been lost: 'Now, maybe you have to assume some shape, but I see people as closer to gas or vapor than furniture. Besides, if there is such a thing as identity, then it just is and you don't have to worry it' (311). The paramilitaries are chasing a chimera, the ungraspable phantom of life. Estrin sees that identity is not fixed; it eludes consistency and coherence: 'Everything Estrin was she also was not ... Anything she claimed would also be a lie' (312). She is drawn to divided cities for she herself is a creature of contradictions – 'brave but still essentially safe, loving edges but never quite living on any of them. She wanted a man/she did not. She did not want children/ she should. She would not be a woman/ she was one, and how; she wanted to leave/Christ did she want to stay' (312–3). The result: she feels 'confused, vague, boring' (320) and has 'lost all comprehension of what she was doing on this island' (320). Farrell's love is a possible transformative force, but her relationship with Farrell, which she admits 'started out as parody' (256), emerges too late as 'the real thing'. Rather, her redemption apparently lies within, in her own female body, in a superior femininity which appreciates and harbours the true value of life:

> Because it was true that Farrell was browning inside, but the seeds remained gold in him ... Estrin had panned one from his river of sweat in Whitewells, and she would secrete the nugget home, slipped far up inside, the way wives smuggled messages from Long Kesh. She would sneak the best of the country through customs undeclared. He could not be trusted with his own treasure. He had to be wrested from himself, and she had pickpocketed the shining spiral, the 44-carat corkscrew. For once, like it or not, Farrell O'Phelan had given himself away. (391)

Colin Bateman is another writer whose comic treatment of the Troubles suggests carnivalistic overthrow of dominant Troubles language and discourse. *Divorcing Jack* and *Cycle of Violence* are both comedy thrillers, the Troubles background providing many of the usual ingredients of the popular thriller: rollercoaster action, labyrinthine plotting, car chases, gun battles, throbbing menace, Gothic horror, cliff-hanging – or, rather, balcony-hanging – suspense, bloody murder, abduction, blackmail, even CIA involvement. All of this is presented in terms of farce, and narrated from the point of view of a dishevelled, hard-drinking, wise-cracking young journalist who goes under the name of Dan Starkey in *Divorcing Jack* and Kevin Miller in *Cycle of Violence*. In the first novel, Starkey returns with a pizza to find that while he has been out his girlfriend, Margaret, has been attacked by the paramilitaries. He is just in time to hear her cryptic dying words – 'Divorce Jack'.[98] Starkey faints, is sick in the bathroom, can't stop shaking; then he hears the sound of an intruder: 'I flung the door open and with arms flailing like Chinese table tennis bats plunged into the darkness' (69). Only at the end of the chapter, in Starkey's absurdist mock-musings over the recent turn of events, do we find out the identity of the mysterious visitor: 'I sat and thought of lovely Margaret. I had heard the last words she would ever speak, she had died in my arms. I wondered what she would think of me now, would she still love me now that I had pushed her mother down the stairs and broken her neck?' (70). Later, he and Parker, a black CIA man, are involved in a car chase through Belfast, pursued by four drunken Protestant paramilitary skinheads with FTP etched

---

98 Colin Bateman, *Divorcing Jack* (London: HarperCollins,1995), p. 68. Hereafter, page references will be incorporated into the text.

on their foreheads – 'just written. Like with a felt pen. It stands for Fuck the Pope. It's a dead giveaway. Actually, they're improving. Usually they can't spell FTP' (98–9). The mockery of terrorists continues in *Cycle of Violence*. Miller regains consciousness to find himself strapped to a hairdresser's chair, the captive of Curly Bap, local IRA chieftain by night, hairdresser by day, leader of the Catholic equivalent of the Shankill Butchers – the 'Crossmaheart Hairdressers'.[99] While waiting for Miller to come round, Curly Bap passes the time giving him 'a tight curly perm', then hands him over to an assassination squad consisting of two men in blue overalls. Meanwhile, Curly Bap is himself the target of a UVF bombing mission, carried out by two 'potatoes' (151), one Davie Morrow whose most recent court appearance had been to answer charges of having a pound of stolen mince steak down the front of his trousers, and Tom O'Hanlon, an insurance salesman who hopes his present bombing mission will make him 'a man amongst men, a hero of Ulster, a Red Hand Commando' (153). As it turns out, Tom is more 'Red-Faced Commando':

> Tom, unfamiliar with engines more powerful than a hairdryer, managed to flood the Volvo before he was three hundred yards from base. With the clock ticking, Davie pushed and Tom steered. Two hundred yards further on they were stopped by a police patrol. Their documents were checked and found to be in order, and the police joined in the pushing. The engine finally fired and they took off.
>
> Tom, however, was practically in convulsions by this stage and turned into an unfamiliar corner of the housing estate and immediately lost himself in the labyrinthine complexities of its interior. (CV 151–2)

Taking the familiar thriller genre, Bateman invests it with a cultural mythology very different from that found in the classical British model of crime fiction (Christie, Doyle) or the democratised American version (Hammett, Chandler). *Divorcing Jack* is a futuristic novel set at a time when the Alliance Party are in the ascendant and Brinn is an Alliance Prime Minister in-waiting. In the background are the familiar mythemes of contemporary Ulster: the respectable politician with a terrorist past, the continual feuding between UVF and IRA, actual and reported gun battles, bombings and other outrages. The plot mechanisms of the thriller genre maintain a sequence of events – a cycle of violence – in which terrorism is related to child abuse. The novel is set mostly in Belfast, but moves briefly to Bangor, Co. Down and to the mythical Crossmaheart (a version of the notorious border town of Crossmaglen in Co. Armagh) which becomes the main setting in *Cycle of Violence*. Crossmaheart, with its two pubs – one for the Protestants and one for the Catholics – is a microcosm of a

---

99 Bateman, *Cycle of Violence*, p. 149. Hereafter, page references will be incorporated into the text.

divided and devastated province, a parody of the traditional picture postcard Irish village. Situated in the middle of 'Bandit Country' and referred to by the security forces as 'the Congo' (DJ 205), it is home to an assortment of neanderthal grotesques:

> Crossmaheart people made fun of everyone. Normal or disabled. Crossmaheart still had a Cripples Institute. There were no special people in Crossmaheart. There were no physically or intellectually challenged people. There were mentals and cripples. There were no single-parent families, there were bastards and sluts. There were natural-born mentals and mental cases, nuts who had made themselves crazy through wielding a gun in the name of one military faction or another. (CV 22–3)

Through such descriptions of Crossmaheart and its inhabitants, Bateman emphasises the pervasive brutality of those communities which spawn the paramilitaries.

Bateman's fiction is intertextually very self-aware, its situations and language frequently recalling American westerns or gangster movies. When Starkey arrives for the first time in Crossmaheart, he is like the lone cowboy riding into a ghost-town, and he's greeted by the boy in the post office with a 'Howdy stranger' (206). The IRA man, Cow Pat Coogan, is modelled on stereotypical images of American gangsters and wild west cattle rustlers. The narrator compares his situation to that of Cary Grant in Hitchcock's *North by Northwest*, 'where the guy is chased all over the place by bad guys and the cops alike ... And no one will believe him and everyone keeps betraying him ... but instead of suave, sophisticated Cary Grant you have a fuckin' eejit like me runnin' around'. And towards the end of the novel, he further elaborates on the novel's 'epic quality?': 'It's *The Prisoner of Zenda*. It's *The Thirty-Nine Steps*. It's *The Godfather*. He's creating the Legend of the Paper Cowboy' (DJ 249). Through these allusions, Bateman's fiction constitutes itself as parody, as a comic cannibalization of past narrative and filmic styles.

As a thriller writer Bateman's interest is not simply in terrorist acts in themselves, but in how the Northern situation can be used to arouse the usual thriller pleasures of suspense. Like any thriller writer he knows how to increase or prolong suspense by including narrative elements which do not necessarily contribute much to plot development. While aiming to hold the reader's interest in the central action of his novels – the desperate hunt for a crucial piece of evidence that will solve the mystery and expose the villains (the names of the four men who attacked Marie's sister fifteen years ago in *Cycle of Violence*, the Dvorak tape containing Brinn's taped confession of his terrorist past in *Divorcing Jack*) – Bateman incorporates the incidental pleasures of Romantic comedy (the relationship between Miller and Marie in *Cycle of Violence*, and between Starkey and Patricia in *Divorcing Jack*), and comedy of manners (especially the satirical treatment of terrorists and politicians in both novels). The whole business of investigation, pursuit/evasion and resolution is overwhelmed by an array of heterogeneous material and a disruptively satirical point of view. The particular pleasure of the thriller has often been explained in terms of Freudian psychology.[100] Freud tells the story of watching his grandson playing in his pram, throwing a toy out of the pram and exclaiming 'Fort!' (gone away) and then drawing it back on a string to the cry of 'Da!' (here).[101] Freud interprets the child's play as an attempt to control the loss of a desired presence (the mother) and to discover pleasure in the postponed return of that presence. The game of 'Fort'-'Da' provides a model of narrative as consolation for what has been lost. All narrative originates in some kind of loss or displacement, which arouses tension that is both painful and pleasurable. It is pleasurable because we know that the object which is lost will be returned to us, that the sex attackers will be tracked down and uncovered, and Brinn's tape will be found and his secret revealed. But Bateman's fictions are not simply Barthesian *textes de désir*[102] – formulaic texts which work single-mindedly towards discovery and resolution which is always postponed to the dénouement. His stories contain all kinds of pleasurable creative excess or supplementarity, such as that provided by 'character', descriptions of places, humour and verbal play. They do not even necessarily complete the ritual process that brings about the restitution of the desired presence. The classical Realist thriller is a conservative form which guarantees that 'Da' will follow 'Fort', that absence will be transformed into presence. *Divorcing Jack* more or less follows that pattern, ending on an upbeat note with the reuniting of Starkey and his wife, and a prospect of political stability following the purging of the body politic. But in *Cycle of Violence* 'poetic justice' is more remote, displaced by a stronger intuition of the absurd: unmasking the sex attackers does not lead to Marie's recovery and union with Miller, but to her suicide and Miller's gratuitous death. Eschewing the happy ending, this novel closes on a depressed note of acceptance of the ineluctability of absence, loss and disappointment.

One of the most obvious digressive features provided by Bateman's fiction is 'character'. 'Character' in Bateman is the expression of human vitality and idiosyncrasy, the sign of creativity, a constant source of both humour and pathos. Bateman specialises in a fiction of picturesque extremes which, like fairy-tale and melodrama, simplifies the potential complexity of the world into vivid polarities of good and evil personified by larger-than-life characters. Without psychological depth or complexity, character tends towards caricature. But the plot structure of the interrupted journey or quest – a version of the picaresque form – brings the hero into contact with a wide variety of characters to produce a colourful, kaleidoscopic Ulster version of the *comédie humaine*.

---

100 See Dennis Porter, *The Pursuit of Crime: Art and Ideology in Detective Fiction* (New Haven: Yale University Press, 1981), pp 100–11.   101 See Sigmund Freud, *Beyond the Pleasure Principle*, trans. and ed. James Strachey (London: Hogarth Press, 1961).   102 See Roland Barthes, *The Pleasure of the Text*, trans. Richard Miller (London: Cape, 1976).

Bateman's narrator both contributes to the plot and is an intrinsically entertaining creation. He is the ultimate 'Honest Ulsterman', the embodiment of a self-conscious, ironic, knowing, yet largely optimistic humanism. He is the average, street-wise urbanite with whose speech, attitudes and life-style the reader can easily identify. His counterculturalism is grounded in a hedonistic life-style of drink, parties, sex and pop music. He is the scandal of bourgeois society. No respecter of authority, he takes the law into his own hands. He is motivated as much by selfish or pragmatic impulses (Miller hopes to free Marie from her past so that he can have sex with her; Starkey is driven by an instinct of self-preservation) as by moral principle or social conscience. Miller works for a middle-of-the-road newspaper in a social environment where there is no middle ground. Though emphatically apolitical, he is the scourge of terrorism, bigotry and hypocrisy. Starkey is a self-confessed Unionist, but 'Unionist with a sense of humour' (9). Interviewed for a job as a Government guide to foreign visiting journalists, he makes clear that he could stick to the Government line only 'up to a point' (9). Both narrators embody a populist ideology which continues the myth of heroic individualism opposed to the corrupt institutions of Church, State and corporate business. They are both free-lance operators unburdened by the responsibilities of family or domesticity; deracinated individuals haunting the margins of respectable society like the cowboys of the frontier myths. At the beginning of *Cycle of Violence* Miller is banished to the edge of the civilised order when he is despatched to Crossmaheart, Starkey is continually in transit on the fringes of society after he is ejected from his marital home at the beginning of *Divorcing Jack*. In their dual role as independent urban folk heroes and the voice of social conscience, they display a knowledge of how to survive in a corrupt and dangerous world, and a capacity, despite their cynicism, to hold on to hope. If any political programme is implied in Bateman's fiction, it is one that envisions the inauguration of a new, more rational, tolerant, less atavistic society.

What more than anything defines Bateman's heroes is the flamboyant verbal ingenuity expressed in inventive word-play, jokes, sardonic one-liners, the epigrammatic flourish, a love of puns ('I have no idea what the proper term for a nun's head-dress is. Possibly a Godpiece' (DJ 141)), extravagant similes ('a manic waving of my arms like a mime artist on acid' (DJ 69)), and the re-vamping of proverbial formulae ('I was down shite street without a petrol bomb' (DJ 76), 'Proddies have a habit of fucking up operations like this. They ... couldn't organize a piss-up in a brewery. Correction. They usually do organize a piss-up in a brewery before they try anything and that's why they fuck it up' (DJ 98)). Even the titles of the two novels highlight a typical linguistic self-consciousness. The fiction, generally, with its comic-strip naming ('Giblet O'Gibber', 'Cow Pat Coogan') grotesque caricature and wild-eyed action, its blurring of the boundary lines between the comic and the macabre, its sudden switchings of languages and voices, decentres authoritative systems of thought, and enacts a carnivalistic overthrow of 'respectable' or 'serious' modes of discourse. Starkey is continually weighing his words: 'I leant down and kissed her back. No, not her back, her cheek' (DJ 15) – as is Miller: 'He used words for a living, but for the life of him, for the life of his father, he couldn't decide on the words to describe his complexion – was it pasty-faced or pastry-faced?' (CV 9). From the beginning of *Cycle of Violence* we are made aware of Miller's critical sensitivity to the establishment language:

> [T]he doctor arrived, nodding, perspiring, as if he was about to make a meal of it, but when he had to say it he was admirably abrupt. Miller had expected him to say that his father had been promoted to glory, like it was a good thing. Or that he had lost him, as if his skeletal frame had bounded off and was hiding in the nether regions of the hospital. But as it was it wasn't much beyond, 'I'm sorry, he's dead', and it was a relief. (CV 5–6)

Bourgeois values are already subject to parodic attack here. Comedy undermines authority. The language of politicians, which strives for programmatic unity, is particularly susceptible to the disunifying, decentralising urban folk pressures exerted by Bateman's protagonists. Thus, in *Divorcing Jack* Brinn's words are under constant threat of exposure and erasure from the sceptical Starkey. Through this willingness to indulge the polymorphous diversity of language, Bateman lays claim to the space of linguistic licence and imaginative free play where he can assert the rights of imaginative risking and verbal pleasure against the logocentrism and puritanism of the 'straight' world. As genre fiction and as Troubles fiction, Bateman's novels are disrupted or decentred by their own linguistic playfulness. On this view, Bateman's language exemplifies Julia Kristeva's notion of the 'semiotic' as a libidinal force within language and society which disrupts stable meanings and institutions. A political reading of Bateman's fiction which would take account of the historical conditions in which it was written and in which it is interpreted and used, might thus see in its linguistic playfulness and addiction to burlesque and slapstick an implicit punkish (and puckish) anarchism or libertarianism, a revolutionary potential which questions existing society and prevailing power relations. At the very least, it's a fiction which refutes and re-writes Declan Kiberd's reductive image of Protestantism as 'a curious blend of resolution and hysteria, of barbarous vulgarity and boot-faced sobriety'.[103]

Eureka Street, written in 1996 at the time of the second cease-fires, reflects the new mood of optimism: 'suddenly Belfast seemed again a place to be. Because, sometimes they glittered, my people here. Sometimes they shone'.[104] Like McNamee's

103 Declan Kiberd, *Anglo-Irish Attitudes* (Derry: Field Day Theatre Company, 1984), p. 22. 104 Robert MacLiam Wilson, *Eureka Street* (London: Minerva, 1997), p. 314. First published London: Secker &

Resurrection Man, Eureka Street is set entirely within Belfast, but Wilson's novel has an impressive amplitude, encompassing a wider range of social and political reference, and of individual human life. While including a sensational violence, Wilson refuses to be transfixed by it. Instead, it is figured as an intrusion upon a much larger narrative field. The frame of reference is the totality of human life. Indeed, the novel is written against those reductive versions of identity and history that are easily manipulated by the ideologues in the service of particular social or political interests. Wilson rejects essentialist and absolutist ideas, and sets out to expose the partial, biased readings of history that are used to validate and reinforce wishful self-images, and to justify violence. He proposes instead a version of history, location and identity as a rich fabric of interweaving, overlapping, competing narratives:

> The city is a repository of narratives, of stories. Present tense, past tense or future. The city is a novel ....
>   ... cities are the meeting places of stories. The men and women there are narratives, endlessly complex and intriguing. The most humdrum of them constitutes a narrative that would defeat Tolstoy at his best and most voluminous. The merest hour of the day of the merest of Belfast's citizens would be impossible to render in all its grandeur and all its beauty. In cities the stories are jumbled and jangled. The narratives meet. They clash, they converge or convert. They are a Babel of prose. (215–16)

Wilson's panoptic, panchronic, 'Our Town' perspective emphasises the marvel and the beauty of the ordinary. In the popular mind, Belfast is simply 'bad':

> Belfast shared the status of the battlefield. The place-names of the city and country had taken on the resonance and hard beauty of all history's slaughter venues. The Bogside, Crossmaglen, The Falls, The Shankhill and Anderstown. In the mental maps of those who had never been in Ireland, these places had tiny crossed swords after their names. People thought them deathfields – remote, televised knackers' yards. Belfast was only big because Belfast was bad. (14)

But in Wilson's re-writing of the city, Belfast is transfigured, as even his foregrounded street names – 'Eureka', 'Hope', 'Poetry' – would indicate. Contemplating ordinary lives, his prose moves beyond irony and satire towards a rhapsodic, Whitmanesque celebration, an exquisitely tender evocation of Belfast and its people 'marvellous in their beds. They are epic, these citizens, they are tender, murderable' (217).

   Murder comes in the form of the bomb-blast, which abruptly terminates some of these life-stories. Sharing Patterson's fascination with the endless interaction of human narratives, Wilson indicates how the bomb disrupts a complex, extended network of relationships in which the individual is inscribed:

> And not just the lives of the victims but the lives they touched, the networks of friendship and intimacy and relation that tied them to those they loved and who loved them, those they knew and who knew them. What great complexity. What richness.
>
> What had happened? A simple event. The traffic of history and politics had bottlenecked. An individual or individuals decided that reaction was necessary. Some stories had been shortened. Some stories had been ended. A confident editorial decision had been taken. (231)

The violence of the bombers is figured as a failure of imagination. Earlier, the protagonist, Jake Jackson, another author lookalike, had 'worked out why it was always easy to hit people. It was because I had no imagination' (62). This insight is then expanded into one of Wilson's somewhat puerile moralising spiels:

> The human route to sympathy is a clumsy one but it's all we've got. To understand the consequences of our actions we must exercise our imaginations. We decide that it's a bad idea to hit someone over the head with a bottle because we put ourselves in their position and comprehend that if we were hit over the head with a bottle, then, my goodness, wouldn't that hurt! We swap shoes. (62)

The bombers, through their murderous action, wish to put bounds on future horizons of possibility; to impose their own simple, linear, closed narrative. But the futility of this effort is suggested by the novel's insistence on life's flux and change:

> The way they were doing these things had changed the face of the city in the last ten years. Protestant areas were Protestant no longer. Working-class areas had become bourgeois. The city was moving outwards like a spreading stain. (381)

The bombers are forces of a sterile conservatism which attempt to block the free play of history, geography and identity as open-ended processes of transformation. The novel ends with an image of Belfast as a living organism, a whisper of the divine, which transcends the given categorisations:

> I think of my city's conglomerate of bodies. A Belfastful of spines, kidneys, hearts, livers and lungs. Sometimes, this frail cityful of organs makes me seethe

and boil with tenderness. They seem so unmurderable and, because I think of them, they belong to me.

Belfast – only a jumble of streets and a few big bumps in the ground, only a whisper of God. (396)

The grafitti – IRA, INLA, UVF, UFF – that is inscribed on Belfast's city walls mark out territory, and shorthands the selective histories, bankrupt mythologies and outmoded identities for which people are still prepared to kill:

The tragedy was that Northern Ireland (Scottish) Protestants thought themselves like the British. Northern Ireland (Irish) Catholics thought themselves like Eireans (proper Irish). The comedy was that any once-strong difference had long melted away and they resembled no one as much as they resembled each other. (163)

Wilson satirises these communal entrenchments in describing the fear and bewilderment of Belfast's citizenry when confronted with the mysterious new graffiti, 'OTG', that starts appearing around the city. This shifting signifier is a mischievous intrusion of an unknown new element into the situation. It confounds the existing lines of sectarian demarcation by threatening the binary purity of the established terms of conflict.

Delighting in contradiction, in the carnivalistic overthrow of accepted social, political and literary hierarchies and monolithic ideological programmes, Wilson agitates against the reductive, linear histories and identities which the ideologues would seek to impose:

It wasn't so much that real history was rewritten. Real history was deleted. Its place was taken by wild and improbable fictions. Ireland was the land of story and Just Us campaigners had always been the best storytellers. They edited or failed to mention all the complicated, pluralistic, true details. (326)

His satire is directed with particular venom against a credulous America, entranced by the exoticised Irish, easy prey to wolverine ideologues like Jimmy Eve of the Just Us party (thinly veiled parodies of Gerry Adams and Sinn Féin). The whole cultural apparatus of Romantic Nationalism is ridiculed for propagating illusory representations of historical reality. Jake, Chuckie and some of their friends attend 'An Evening of Irish Poetry' where the star attraction is Seamus Heaney, disguised as 'the great man' Shague Ghintoss:

It went on. It was as bad as could be. The great man, Ghintoss, got up and read. He read about hedges, the lanes and the bogs. He covered rural topography in detail. It felt like a geography field trip. In a startling departure, he read a poem about a vicious Protestant murder of a nice Catholic. There were no spades in this poem, and only one hedge, but by this time the crowd were whipped into such a sectarian passion they would have lauded him if he'd picked his nose ... These people gathered close together, snug in their verse, their culture, they had one question. Why can't Protestants do this? they asked themselves. What's wrong with these funny people? (176)

The passage is typical of Wilson's exuberant facetiousness, though wide of the mark in its assessment of Heaney. The anti-Heaney campaign is in fact transposed from a 1995 *Fortnight* review, which Wilson wrote in the wake of Heaney's winning the Nobel Prize for literature. In this review, Wilson inveighs against what he sees as Heaney's failure to investigate modern Northern Ireland – 'he (Heaney) has left out that unpoetic stuff, that very actual mess'[105] – and ridicules the Laureate's pre-occupation with 'the hedges and the peat' ('Heaney's Ireland is a place I've never been, his Irishness is a thing I've never known').[106] Repudiating the claims made at 'the Nobel prize-fest' that Heaney straddles and speaks to both traditions, Wilson comments: 'Far from saying to each violent extreme: a plague on both your houses, Heaney has said: a plague on neither of your houses, can I have another honorary degree, please?'[107] Wilson's grossly reductive polemic which brands Heaney 'risible', 'bogus', 'dangerous' and 'corrosive'[108] says less about Heaney than it does about the young writer's anxiety to kill off the father, the 'strong precursor', in order to clear a space for his own independent creativity. 'Anything that I and writers like me have ever written', says Wilson, 'has tried to be a rejection of the comfortable amiabilities of Heaney and writers like him.'[109]

Eureka Street's primary satirical target are those who would presume to justify violence. The opening chapters draw the reader into the lives of a range of Belfast characters, who are observed closely and affectionately, the loose, episodic structure reflecting the casual order of real experience. Chapter 11 introduces Rosemary Daye, whose peregrinations through the streets and shops of Belfast are charted closely, much as Joyce details the precise odysseys of his characters through the streets of Dublin. But in contrast to the gloomy paralysis of Dublin, Wilson's Belfast teems with life and expresses itself in a highly colourful, energetic and idiomatic language. Just as we are getting to know Rosemary, suddenly she 'stopped existing' (222). With great skill, Wilson recreates textually the shock and disbelief occasioned by the bomb blast, then moves to describe the effects of the blast with forensic calm, at first eschewing emotion and authorial comment. Focusing on the individual human suffering, he records the

Warburg, 1996. Hereafter, page references will be incorporated into the text.   105 Robert MacLiam Wilson, 'The Glittering Prize', *Fortnight*, November 1995, 5–7, p. 6.   106 Ibid., p. 7.   107 Ibid., p. 6.   108 Ibid., p. 7.   109 Ibid.

scene with memorable vividness, and a shocking and unflinching objectivity. Gradually, moral outrage comes to the surface, through irony, satire and outright polemic:

> It was notable, nevertheless, how many people still refused to understand what had happened. Several of the shocked onlookers sat staring dumbly at the excrement and tissue and blood, incapable of comprehending how political this was. One naive fireman, upon retrieving what seemed to be a portion of a severed head, naively believed this to have been a sadistic act. A woman with a bloody face who comforted her young son near the bookshop had no real conception of the historical imperatives leading to such an event'. (227)

Wilson insists on de-politicising the event and seeing it only in terms of concrete, immediate experience. He is determined to re-inscribe 'all the complicated, pluralistic, true details' which the ideologues have written out of their narratives of history and identity. By placing the arguments of the Sinn Féin apologists alongside the realities of human suffering, he mocks the abstract political rationalising with a Swiftian *saeva indignatio.*

For Wilson, the supreme value is the individual, not abstract causes, and through a range of representative episodes, he emphasises how the personal life has a habit of overflowing or defying the constraints of communal orthodoxy. The lesbian relationship between two very ordinary, middle-aged, working-class Belfast women, Peggy and Caroline, is doubly transgressive: first, in its affirmation of life and love in the midst of atrocity and, second, in scandalising the strict Protestant morality of Eureka Street and Sandy Row, where several husbands 'gave their wives preventative beatings just in case they might have considered stepping out of line in this most unprotestant fashion' (341). The only politics that are understandable are those which centre the individual's pragmatic concerns and engage a reality of concrete particulars:

> The majority politics in Northern Ireland were not political. The citizens were too shy to give the grand name of principle to any of the things that they believed. And that peaceful majority spent its life keeping down jobs, buying washing-machines and houses and vacuum-cleaners and holidays and carry-cots.

This is the kind of politics that Jake's best friend, Chuckie, understands. Chuckie is Wilson's burly and burlesque personification of extraordinary ordinariness, the representative of an irrepressible human energy that is unclassifiable, unpredictable and knows no boundaries. Defying all the existing structures of logic, common sense and communal expectation, he is living embodiment of the 'contradictions' (164) Jake longs for. A Protestant from the Shankill, his best friends are Catholics, his proudest possession a photograph of himself and the Pope. With no education or special skills, he becomes a multi-millionaire through the power of 'his own absurd and mega-lomaniac fantasies'. On both personal and business levels, Chuckie's story is a comic fantasy of success. Underlying his buffoonery lies a vibrant social conscience. Rejecting the rhetoric of imperialism, self-determination and revolutionary socialism pedalled by Jimmy Eve, and even the usefulness of classifications such as Protestant and Catholic, Chuckie stands for a post-Nationalist, post-Unionist, non-ideological pragmatism of job-creation projects and the industrial rebuilding of Belfast: 'There are no nationalities, only rich and poor. Who gives a shit about nationhood if there's no jobs and no money? (331). The narrative tone is as ringingly approving of Jake's and Chuckie's political views as it is critical of the likes of Jimmy Eve and Aoirghe. At the end, Aoirghe and Jake do come together, but only after she has surrendered the public world of politics for the superior world of love and sex.

This is the novel's great discovery, its Eureka cry – to be open to difference, to see that the Other can be enriching, rather than something to be distrusted or abomi-nated or brought under control or colonised. Out of this new, pluralistic, postmodern humanism, a new political agenda suggests itself, for to be able to see the attractions of the Other is to escape the conventional ethnocentric pieties and open up the pos-sibilities of a rejuvenating multiculturalism. Wilson endorses Patterson's emphasis on the need to cross borders and blur identities, for such action is the prerequisite of evolving new cultural formations, new histories, new identities. Jake enunciates the principle of cultural pluralism which informs the whole novel:

> In my early years, I had often hoped that the future would be different. That from out of the dark mists of Ireland's past and present a new breed would arise. The New Irish. When all the old creeds and permutations would be contradicted. (164)

While preserving a superficial commitment to the protocols of Realism, the novel cannot be judged entirely by the criteria of Realism. It is notable for the great variety of its generic provenance, incorporating as it does the dislocating forms and structures of satire, fantasy, burlesque, parody, pastiche, as well as a powerful discourse of lyrical affirmation. Reconfiguring the North within a richly polygeneric, polyvocal narrative structure, Wilson works upon a recognisably familiar world, employing various dislocating or defamiliarising strategies to expose its grotesque absurdities while, at the same time, allowing Utopian, forward-looking images of universal justice and peace to envision the possibility of a positive transformation of the course of history itself. As Jake says: 'It's a big world and there's room for all kinds of endings and any number of commencements' (396).

CHAPTER FIVE

Political fiction: re-writing the colonial narrative

> Many Irish republicans and nationalists hold the view that the conflict in
> the North of Ireland since the late 1960s ... is misrepresented in contem-
> porary prose fiction. The perception of distortion and bias is felt most
> acutely when the novels and short stories in question handle the history
> and development of modern Irish republicanism and the beliefs, values,
> motivations and intentions of Irish republicans.[1]

Thus, Patrick Magee, former IRA man who planted the bomb at the Conservative Party
conference in Brighton in 1984, and who has written extensively on Troubles fiction.
There has been, Magee claims, 'a massive lacuna of representation', a failure to give
expression to the 'collective voice of grievance'[2] of Irish Republicanism and of those
disparaged communities who, far from viewing the IRA as a terror machine, regard it
as a people's army. This 'misrepresentation', Magee believes, is nowhere more evident
than in the stereotypical images of Irish Republicans which populate Troubles fiction –
'Irish republicans and Irish republicanism, with scant exception, have been caricatured,
misunderstood, marginalised, and travestied – in short, woefully misrepresented in
troubles fiction'[3]. 'Misrepresentation', he claims, is not only typical of the British colonial
attitude but illustrates the failure of the liberal pluralist aesthetic to develop an
authentically inclusive agenda. Since the focus of Magee's study is the popular Troubles
novel, it is worth remembering that while stereotyping may indeed be a symptom of
prejudice, it always goes on in the work of popular and minor writers. The 'serious'
writer we expect to be able to complicate the simple stereotype by incorporating into it
some sense of individual character. Magee, it would seem, has little confidence in the
power of the individual imagination to transcend its historical circumstances.

   Magee's analysis is supported by Ronan Bennett, another former IRA activist,
who, in a 1994 article in *The Guardian*, complained about the Northern Irish middle-
class (Catholic as well as Protestant) and their cultural apparatus of theatre, film and
literature for being 'neutral, apolitical, disengaged'. Troubles fiction, Bennett asserted,

> adheres to a set of complacent conventions about the Troubles: that it is an
> irrational and bloody slaughter without solution; that both sides, republican

---

1 Patrick Magee, *Troubles fiction*, p. 1.   2 Ibid., p. 328.   3 Ibid., p. 2.

and loyalist, are as bad as the other; that normal, sensitive people do not get involved, and if they do, it is reluctantly or through intimidation; and as soon as they are in, they want out; that the British presence may at times be heavy-handed and inept but at bottom is well-intentioned and indispensable.[4]

Bennett says he does not believe these conventions to be true, but that that is not the point: the point is that 'art, if it is to be worth anything, should be in tension with norms and given wisdom'. The 'given wisdom' he further expounds:

> In fiction – and the same is true of most film and television drama – the Troubles are thus presented as an appalling human tragedy, devoid of political content. Like any bloody struggle anywhere ... it becomes nothing more than a series of repulsive and meaningless massacres, destructive of communities and the human spirit in equal part.[5]

'Appalling human tragedy' and 'repulsive and meaningless massacres', Bennett believes, may be transformed – made meaningful – if they are re-written within a 'political' narrative. Troubles fiction, in Bennett's opinion, is 'uniform', 'predictable', 'generalised' and 'clichéd' because it has failed to explore 'the political causes of the conflict' and the 'psychological hinterland' of those involved:

> These men are invariably depicted as of low intelligence, often with a severe physical deformity, cowardly, bullying – especially towards their own comrades – and driven by bloodlust. If they have politics, they are the politics of the fanatic or the simple-minded, and easy to ridicule.[6]

Even the younger generation of writers fails Bennett's strict political test: Robert MacLiam Wilson is castigated as 'part of the self-conscious post-modernist generation that finds any strongly-held belief inherently ridiculous', and summarily dismissed for labelling Republicanism 'fascist', treating Irish culture as 'a joke', and depicting the conflict as 'meaningless slaughter'.[7] To reduce 'the conflict's complexities to good versus evil', says Bennett, is propaganda, not art.[8] The poetry of Ciaran Carson and Derek Mahon, along with Wilson's fiction, are Bennett's examples of such bourgeois 'propaganda'. The main object of Bennett's attack is clearly the whole liberal humanist philosophical and moral outlook which, he claims, demonises the enemy in time of war and, rather than provide any intelligent analysis of the conflict, contents itself with affirming an escapist optimism and naive faith in the indestructability and essential goodness of the human spirit. Bennett advocates another more authentic kind of art:

4 Ronan Bennett, 'An Irish answer', *Guardian Weekend*, 16 July, 1994, p. 8.   5 Ibid.   6 Ibid.   7 Ibid.
8 Ibid.

There exists another art of the troubles. It is out of the mainstream and consequently less well known, but it is gaining in confidence and becoming more insistent. It stems from another culture, the one affected most profoundly by the conflict – the culture of working-class nationalism.[9]

Out of the culture of working-class Nationalism came a fiction which challenged what its writers perceived as the distortions and bias of the mainstream Troubles novel. Emerging in the 1980s, in the wake of the 1981 Hunger Strikes and Britain's policy of criminalising Republicanism, Sinn Féin's electoral successes, and revelations of British miscarriages of justice and use of 'dirty tricks', new young writers such as Morrison and Bennett, who were themselves actively involved in the Republican movement, expressed the growing political confidence. On the political front, Sinn Féin's peace initiative, articulated in two documents, *A Scenario for Peace* (1987) and *Towards a Lasting Peace* (1992) recognised the need for Sinn Féin to co-operate strategically with others – constitutional Nationalists in the North, members of the political establishment in the South, and the Irish-American lobby – to create a Nationalist consensus, and secure as broad a hearing as possible for the Republican analysis. Sinn Féin's participation in the 'Peace Process' and the Legislative Assembly was intended to serve as a further challenge to British colonial hegemony by peaceful means. Writers such as Morrison and Bennett, by re-telling what they believed was the colonial narrative of British imperialism, set out to complement, in the realm of art and culture, Sinn Féin's counter-hegemonic thrust at the political level.

Polemical gestures: Danny Morrison's *West Belfast* (1989)

In his book, *Literature and Culture in Northern Ireland Since 1965*, Richard Kirkland refers to the 'extraordinary self-assertion' of the Northern Irish bourgeois literary establishment, 'to which the matter of dealing adequately with the subject of violence is no longer as pressing as the need to be answerable to the community on behalf of its own values'.[10] In *West Belfast*, Morrison attempts to deal with the subject of violence by, first of all, making himself answerable, not to the bourgeois literary community, but to the ordinary working-class, Republican community of West Belfast. And, if the bourgeois literary establishment, as Kirkland suggests, envisions the poet or novelist 'as paradigm of a truly heterogeneous society',[11] Morrison is more concerned to become a voice for the criminalised Irish soul, a publicist for the oppressed minority, a political consciousness-raiser on behalf of the Republican movement. The writer and the political activist become closely identified as the new

9 Ibid.   10 Richard Kirkland, *Literature and Culture*, p. 66.   11. Ibid.

Republican literature establishes direct links with the social and political struggle. For the committed writer, literature and politics, aesthetics and ethics, are inextricably linked.

There is a potential problem here for the political writer who adopts a basically Realistic form. He must find ways of representing the play of relatively abstract social and political forces, and the gradual formation of new forces, new social consciousness, within a form which has been developed primarily to express the individual and individual relationships. Realism evolved to express individual consciousness as it is grounded in a particular, carefully delineated social and moral order, a given network of relations with other people, with the past, with the environment, with God. The writer writes out of a tradition which provides an agreed sense of the nature of reality and social values, and which is suspicious of experiment and the pursuit of novelty. The revolutionary writer, however, feels the need to re-imagine his destiny rather than simply accept an inherited one. He wants to defamiliarise the social and political dominants, to expose the false consciousness of historical reality. He wants to re-make his world, not merely reflect an agreed reality. Revolutionary representation holds out the possibility of transformative re-configuration of current political constructions that exclude or invalidate difference and the plurality of desire. Danny Morrison's *West Belfast*, in exploring the possibilities for what Derrida calls a 'discourse which borrows from a heritage the resources necessary for the deconstruction of that heritage',[12] offers graphic illustration of some of the problems of textual production and articulation for a revolutionary politics defined by and incorporated within the conventions of bourgeois humanist Realism.

The personalised stories of John, Angela, Jimmy, Catherine and Peter are periodically displaced by extended sections of quasi-journalistic reportage of historical data. The lives of individual characters, we are to understand, are intimately bound up with events in the public world. The novel challenges the conventional privileging of the personal over the political such as we find in *Cal*, in order to propose an alternative to MacLaverty's hero-victim. Where Cal's original action against state authority is presented as transgression requiring repentance and contrition, John O'Neill is a figure of heroic revolt. Where Cal conforms to a stereotype of Catholic masochistic victimage, John is determined to resist the role of victim and sees political action as an essential part of this process. Where Cal is defined largely in terms of his psychosexual subjectivity detached from other forms of socio-political identity, John's political relations are more substantially productive of identity than his sexual relations. If, as Cleary says, *Cal* 'must be read as a narrative act of nationalist contrition whereby the Catholic Nationalist guiltily offers himself up as a sacrifice to the proper authority of the Northern Ireland state against which he has offended',[13]

12 Derrida, *Writing and Difference*, trans. A. Bass (Chicago, n.p. 1978), p. 282.

then the narrative drive of *West Belfast* is committed not only to legitimising the desire for Irish unification, but the IRA violence which is used to achieve it.

Cleary sees *Cal* as expressive of a 'paralyzing ambivalence' underlying contemporary Irish Nationalism:

> *Cal*'s complex logic of desire and disavowal draws on the paralysing ambivalence with which certain types of contemporary Irish nationalism are beset. Many nationalists, Northern and Southern, are considerably interested in the ideal of a united Ireland; most of them, however, also find IRA violence in the name of that ideal repugnant. This ambivalence has led many to express a complex sense of guilt about their own continued investment in the goal of reunification, and some to distance themselves from or even to repudiate Irish nationalism altogether.[14]

West Belfast sets out to remove this guilt and ambivalence by providing a moral and political rationale for armed struggle, and a heroic image of the freedom fighter.

In pursuing this objective, the novel is in constant danger of producing polemical gestures, wish-fulfilment fantasies and politically significant rituals rather than genuinely imaginative insights. Thus, in *West Belfast*, the conflict tends to become a simple, melodramatic confrontation between good and evil. The hero, John, is the personification of virtue and nobility, the scourge of bigots like his Protestant workmate, Bronco, and bullies like the second steward, Hutchinson, or the despotic Captain Kellner. He attends Ruskin College where he educates himself in labour law, and becomes the champion of the proletariat and an inspiration to the downtrodden. Finding himself in one of the usual sailors' haunts in a foreign port, 'He thought of what his mother would think of him if she could see him here. His conscience snapped and he got up to leave.'[15] As Angela's lover, he surprises her with his capacity for 'affection, wonder and awe', and writes her embarrassingly clichéd, sentimental love letters. Subjected to brutal interrogation and torture by the security forces, he stalwartly refuses to break under pressure. He is a picture of the revolutionary saint.

John's brother, Jimmy, is likewise fulsomely idealised. At age eleven, Jimmy's 'real qualities were his humour, his generosity and his general demeanour which just about made him loved by everyone' (87). If his parents argue, 'he would mediate with a, "Now, now, you two. Behave yourselves ..." which usually brought them around' (87). So sensitive is he that when news of the Aberfan disaster comes on TV, he 'burst into tears and ran upstairs' (88). He sends his Halloween money off to the appeal fund rather than spend it on himself. As a volunteer, Jimmy 'was good, very courageous'

13 Joe Cleary, '"Fork-tongued on the border bit"', p. 252. 14 Ibid., p. 254. 15 Danny Morrison, *West Belfast* (Cork and Dublin: Mercier Press, 1989, p. 97. Hereafter, page references will be incorporated into the text.

(190), and, hearing of his younger brother's exploits, 'John felt a glow of pride line the edge of his desolation' (191). Jimmy's death is used to emphasise a family's, and even a community's sense of loss, but not to raise any difficult questions about the necessity of armed struggle or about the universal human tragedy that is being played out on the streets of West Belfast.

John's girlfriend, Angela McCann, is less sympathetically presented, though just as much of a stereotype. She is an image of wayward, restless youth. Her story is a morality tale about the dire consequences of departing from traditional Irish values in the London *gehenna* of sex and drugs. Once separated from John's steadying influence and adrift in London, Angela's decline quickly accelerates. Eventually, however, she is reunited with her family and with John, whom she fortuitously meets again when visiting her brother in Long Kesh. In a letter to John, she expresses regret for her failure to appreciate his true worth in the past. Having renounced selfishness and acquired a social conscience, she now qualifies for partnership with John. In the course of the novel, only Angela is allowed to offer any serious criticism of West Belfast ('Parochialism, narrow-mindedness, choked her', 138) and of John ('If only he hadn't been so serious and old fashioned', 90). But while she may voice the reactions of a good many readers, the party faithful can discount the seriousness of her criticisms since she has been shown to be a weak and foolish character.

The novel's central family, the O'Neills, is a model of conservative, Catholic virtue, hard-working, supportive, and harmonious. The larger community of West Belfast is also eulogised for its heroic quality, its resilience, courage, solidarity, and triumphant human spirit:

> John heard a noise in the distance of chanting, of singing, of screaming but not in a frightened sense. It got louder and louder and brought people to their windows, then to their front doors. Thousands of women from Andersonstown, Turf Lodge, Ballymurphy, St James and Rodney and from areas on up the Falls, hearing about the first break of the blockade, marched down to the British army cordons and pulled the barbed wire barricades aside. They were carrying bread, milk, vegetables, meat parcels, biscuits. Some pushed prams, some were old people outraged by the curfew and who had never felt strong enough or motivated enough to act so defiantly before.
>
> 'Come out! Come out!' they screamed. 'The curfew is broken! The curfew is broken!'
>
> John turned around. He was excited. He turned to thank the old man standing behind him but the old man was crying and sobbing from relief, from pride, from a renewed faith in his community at a time when he felt so isolated and devastated. (134)

In passages such as these, Morrison attempts to turn his novel into a celebration of life and the evolution of the collective (Republican) soul, an assertion of the universal will to live and survive. He wants to highlight social injustice and focus upon the plight of the proletariat while persuading us that these are men and women, not simply the raw material of Republican dogma.

The main technique that is used to justify armed revolt is the marshalling of minutely detailed factual evidence of British state oppression, Unionist intransigence, and Loyalist threat and provocation. It is intended that the sheer, cumulative weight of this evidence will put the justification for violent resistance beyond question. The formation of the IRA is explained as a defensive measure against the combined forces of colonial and state oppression: 'Behind the barricades a new IRA was being built to ensure that nationalists were never left defenceless again' (114). Morrison asks us to see the emergence of the IRA as a result, not a cause, of social unrest; as part of a quasi-Darwinian, deterministic process of social evolution whereby new social forms arise in response to new social conditions. Reversing the terminology of the official discourse, the language of criminality, pogrom and demonic possession is applied, not to the IRA, but to the state forces. Terrorism is now portrayed as the work of the British state, not the vulnerable, oppressed Nationalist defenders. The chapter title, 'The Pogroms', relates the treatment of Catholic Nationalist West Belfast by the British forces to the organised persecution and massacre of the Jews in World War II. To Catherine, Jimmy's death at the hands of a British soldier is the work of 'something diabolical'; 'a crime committed by someone against her son and her family' (183). Morrison's inverts the traditional opposition between (English) civilians and (Irish) barbarians. With the account of escalating state terrorism and John's interrogation and torture, the novel moves into a nightmarish realm of excess, infamy and Gothic horror. The language of common sense and self-evident facts gives way to the different appeal of a language of sensation and violated sensibility:

> The Brits were dancing and whooping and a soldier held the captured rifle above his head like a scalp. Then another Brit, a fuckin' black bastard, lifted Jimmy's head by his hair and shook him. He was the one who was clocked. We were still in the area and one of the boys popped up from behind a garden wall and blew him away. (192)

At this point, however, the distinction between civilian and barbarian dissolves.

The main argument for armed struggle is the argument of last resort. Inevitably, political necessity comes into conflict with personal conscience, Catholic morality, and civilised values. This conflict is a potential source of great dramatic power and interest, but it is never fully exploited in Morrison's novel, which exhibits a marked reluctance to put its own ideas under any significant pressure. Its most sustained attempt to do so is in the extended interior monologue which is given to the IRA man, Stevie, just before he shoots a British soldier. In *Ripley Bogle*, Robert MacLiam Wilson throws down the following challenge:

> Think about killing someone. Go on. Some guy. Some poor sorry sod. Anyone. Think about killing him. Take your time. Think about it. Think about his life, his mom and dad. Think about his children ... Think about his industry and his kindness, his clemency and tenderness. Think about him buying his unfashionable shoes and his painfully vulgar jackets. Think about his bad jokes and embarrassments. Think about his baby talk and teeth, his flask and sandwiches, his snapshots, his overdraft, his furniture, his handwriting, his bald patch, his favourite meals, his cigarettes, his football team, his dirty socks, his face and his span of years. Think about him. Think about his life.
>   Bye bye Belfast.[16]

Morrison, speaking through the persona of Stevie, takes up Wilson's challenge, with disastrous results:

> I think of this man. He is somebody's son, perhaps a good man, maybe even a loving husband. We both speak the same language, could have stolen the same bars of chocolate from the corner shop, told the same juvenile jokes to our mates, and sheltered from the same storms as they fell a few hours apart on our lands. I came up on the same music and television as he did, the Beatles and Coronation Street ....
>   Already I can hear the familiar sermon echoing all the comparisons and lecturing me, the killer. I can see those comparisons myself right down to our mutual likes and dislikes in food, Granny Smith's apples, flowing butter on warm white bread, plenty of salt and vinegar on the fish and chips.
>   We may even have supported the same team for the FA Cup.
>   He probably doesn't even want to be here. (173-4)

Having thought about the common humanity shared by victim and executioner, Stevie insists on their irreconcilable difference. Like Wilson's *Ripley Bogle*, he attempts to envision his victim as an individual human being, but ultimately his actions are determined by political, not humanitarian, considerations:

> He has no right to be here and if he doesn't want to be here then he shouldn't be here ... He would just as quickly rob me of breath if ordered or if the fancy took him ... I know the thief below the bow and wrapping paper. (174-5)

16 Robert MacLiam Wilson, *Ripley Bogle* (London: Picador, 1989), p. 162.

Preferring to pursue the quarrel with others rather than the quarrel with self, Morrison shies away from difficult areas of thought and feeling. Doubts are never strong enough to shake resolve:

> My conscience reminded – not beset – by the occasional doubt is also a remarkable process which keeps me right. I entertain doubts precisely because they strengthen my singlemindedness, my convictions. (175)

The ease with which the argument for violence is allowed to outweigh conventional religious and moral considerations diminishes our sense of the tragic waste occasioned by the necessary political action, and makes Stevie's comment, 'I'm not as callous as this and there's always, always, always, a psychological unease, a sense of violation and wrong, about killing this man' (175), sound hollowly rhetorical. At the end of his monologue, when Stevie's thoughts return to the individual human being he is about to kill, the writing once again is unbearably glib and sentimental:

> I hear on the news that the corporal is dead, that he was married with two children, aged four and one. I clench my teeth and swallow hard and I will often think of this man.
>   I curse the life that has brought me to this....
>   I'll live for him and in some sort of communion with him.
>   One thing for sure.
>   I'll think about him more often than his commanding officer.
>   I'll maybe even be still thinking about him when his widow has stopped.
> (177)

The expresssion of humanistic moral concern sounds like a merely dutiful but unconvincing addendum to a ritualised polemic.

Inside the IRA: Ronan Bennett's *The Second Prison* (1991); Danny Morrison's *The Wrong Man* (1996)

Bennett's *The Second Prison* is a rather more sophisticated first novel from a Sinn Féin/IRA perspective than Morrison's, though Bennett's could hardly be said to fulfil the requirements of a socially and politically committed fiction as prescribed in his *Guardian* article. Where Morrison in *West Belfast* focuses on the beginnings of the Troubles and the re-activation of the IRA in 1969 in a spirit of new hope and nationalist self-assertion, *The Second Prison* is set in the '80s, when the revolutionary movement is exhausted, dispersed and corrupted, no longer a life-force but a death-cult, undermined by distrust and betrayal, its violence turned inward against its own.

Idealism has been eroded, the Republican organisation fragmented into a series of competing egos, locked into an endless cycle of violence. Bennett portrays a fallen world where there is no forgiveness or redemption. The traditional humanist faith in human nature comes under severe pressure; the categories of 'good' and 'evil' are blurred. By developing an elaborate correspondence between the terror leader. Augustine Kane, and Henry Tempest, the Special Branch man sent over from England to deal with Kane's terrorist cadre, Bennett implies that there is no real moral difference between the hunted and the hunter: the official representative of the state is a mirror image of the terrorist killers. Authority destroys those who serve it. The novel's moral relativism is further instanced in the role given to the inveterate criminal Englishman Benny. It is Benny, thief, killer and conscienceless liar, who articulates the novel's central truth: 'Getting out of here (prison) is only the first step. It's getting out of the second prison – that's the real challenge',[17] he insists, urging upon Kane the need to break out of the 'second prison' which confines the individual in the past, and in his own (mis)conceptions. But more than truth-teller, Benny is also the novel's primary agent of renewal and hope for the future, a vibrant if deeply tainted personification of unquenchable human spirit.

'Speculation on the political causes of the conflict is territory most novelists resolutely refuse to cross',[18] Bennett complained of Northern Irish novelists in his *Guardian* article. *The Second Prison* shows little interest in crossing that territory either. The novel is a revenger's tragedy rather than historical or political fiction; a psychological rather than a political thriller. The political situation, despite Bennett's close attention to locational and temporal marking, doesn't enter into the story. The characters, whether terrorists or policemen, do not serve a cause or community or institution; they do not represent anything larger than themselves. They are all lone, alienated figures. The motivation is closer to that in McNamee's *Resurrection Man* than that in Morrison's *West Belfast*. Recalling McNamee's Victor Kelly, leader of the loyalist terror gang, Bennett's Provo leader, Augustine Kane, pursues a similar project of self-discovery and self-realisation through violence, which is in fact profoundly self-destructive, alienating him from community and former comrades, and inhibiting him from forming normal social and sexual relations. Indeed, Bennett's remarks on McNamee's treatment of Loyalist terrorism in his *Guardian* article could apply as well to his own treatment of Republican terrorism in *The Second Prison*: 'McNamee is not interested in the ideology of the murder gangs or the political ends they serve: his preoccupation is with the inner life, and his portrait of the interior landscape of Ulster loyalism is unremittingly bleak, psychopathologies shaped by

17 Ronan Bennett, *The Second Prison* (London: Review, 2000), p. 90. First published London: Hamish Hamilton, 1991. Hereafter, page references will be incorporated into the text.   18 Bennett, *Guardian Weekend*, p. 8.

neurosis, inadequacy and sexual fear'.[19] Unlike Morrison in *West Belfast*, Bennett refuses to idealise his IRA men. The Troubles are represented in precisely the way Bennett accused other Northern Irish writers of representing them – as 'irrational and bloody slaughter, without solution', 'a series of repulsive and meaningless massacres, destructive of communities and the human spirit in equal part', 'appalling human tragedy, devoid of political content.'[20] This is also the way his right-thinking characters (Cappy, Roisin, Ralph, Benny, Ruth) perceive terrorist action. The novel's cast of IRA men reflects the range of stereotypes Bennett listed in his article. These include 'the psychopathic republican' (Seanie, and to some extent Dec and Kane); the character of 'low intelligence, often with a severe physical deformity' (the cripple Maxi); those who are 'cowardly, bullying – especially towards their own comrades' (Dec and Seanie who turn informers and then, against the express command of their OC, summarily execute the pathetic Maxi to divert attention from their own guilt). Instead of 'the daughter of the republican who falls in love with the British soldier' we have the even more unlikely situation of the wife of the Branch man falling in love with the Republican terror unit's OC. However, in the creation of his protagonist /narrator, Kane, Bennett manages to penetrate the stereotypical images of the terrorist to produce an interesting, complex and stylish study of corrupted idealism. Whatever may have been his original motives for terror, Kane is now completely absorbed by a personally conceived vendetta against a former comrade and a personal power-struggle with Tempest. His motives for killing are understood in terms of a desire for revenge or control. He admits himself that his major inspiration has been Seanie's capacity for ruthless killing, and that his role as unit OC fulfils a profound need for power and control. More idealistic reasons such as 'loyalty' to community or comrades, or the need to preserve internal discipline, are treated with scepticism. Like Tempest, like Dec, he has 'lost his way' (136, 178). Lost and lonely and disillusioned, Kane is forced to review his past, and reckon the price, in personal terms, that his career in terror has exacted. At the end, he confronts the tragic possibility that a fuller, freer life is forever denied him.

Bennett's central theme is the struggle to break out of the 'second prison'. Kane learns that it is possible to become imprisoned in a system of his own making. Ranged around him are a series of characters who by example or argument attempt to help him escape the 'second prison' and re-invent himself. His old comrade, Dec, and Dec's wife, Cappy, have years ago already made the move, leaving Belfast to settle with their children in London. They recognise the threat that Kane poses when he suddenly reappears after five years to settle old scores. Cappy pleads with him to let them make a new start and get on with their lives. Later, Dec also pleads with Kane: 'I want to get on with my life. There's no point in this craziness' (126), and even attempts to kill Kane

19 Ibid., p. 55.   20 Ibid., p. 6.

to remove the threat he represents. Kane's girlfriend Roisin is another character who has managed to detach herself from her past and begin a new life and career as a solicitor in London. She tries to persuade Kane to come with her: 'You don't belong, you're a prisoner here. Let's leave, let's get free'(42). In prison, Kane's fellow inmates, Ralph and Benny, challenge his fatalism. Ralph longs for freedom from prison and escape with his girlfriend Ruth. He espouses a simple life of hedonistic pleasure which he intends to buy with his ill-gotten gains, and which the ascetic Kane despises him for. Benny warns Kane against self-imprisonment in a destructive mind-set: 'If you want my advice, you concentrate on getting out of this case, forget Maxi, forget Dec and start living a life. You, my friend, have got to bust out of the second prison' (130). Benny says he admires 'people who have an ideal' (151), but doesn't believe that Kane is any longer motivated by idealism. At this stage Kane refuses to listen and reacts angrily to Benny's ridicule. To take Benny's advice, Kane says, would be to 'repudiate everything I was part of ... turning my back on the rules I have lived my life by' (130). Kane still clings to an ideal of loyalty to his own people and to the movement. Angry and disturbed by what Benny has said, he returns to his own prison cell: 'I pulled the door behind me and locked myself in' (131).

On his release from prison, Kane is visited by Roisin, who reinforces Benny's advocacy of the need to escape the 'second prison', and shares Benny's opinion that Kane is now driven simply by 'revenge' and bloodlust. Recalling Cappy's, Benny's and Roisin's arguments, Kane acknowledges what he has missed in life – money, wife, family, security. Bennett forcefully reminds us of the sacrifices demanded of the committed terrorist, even as he uncovers the degradation of an original idealism. The greatest illusion of all has been Kane's idea that terrorism granted him control over his own and others' lives. In reality, his political commitment has been a prison. Terrorism may have placed other people's lives in his hands momentarily, but it has been at the cost of his own emotional development: 'You have such experience', Ruth says to him, 'But emotionally, what do you know? When did part of you stop growing?' (222). Political activism has meant the death of the heart and the denial of love. Kane finally recognises that Tempest has been in control all along: 'I realized that I had never been in control of any sort. I had been pushed and pulled with nothing more than the pathetic illusion of freedom. For the last six years, Tempest had been in control of my life, directing me here and there, to do this and that. He shared my absurd illusion' (226).

Shortly before his release, Kane meets Ruth for the first time. With Ruth, he moves toward the establishment of a private world of love and trust as an alternative to the 'second prison' of revenge killing and control games. 'You sound like a doctor. Is there a cure?' he says to Ruth, and she replies: 'I will cure you, my love' (232). Images of sickness and disease spread through the whole novel: love is proposed as 'cure' in a world sick unto death. The value of individual life is elevated above the claims of community or politics: 'When I kissed her I dreamed of a journey to another place, where our pasts would be wiped out, where our lives would begin again, as happy lovers setting out together have a right to expect' (260-1). But Kane's escape never becomes reality; it's never more than a dream, with Ruth as lyrical accompanist: 'You will love Seville and Andalucia', she tells him, 'the orange trees and the olive groves, the Sierra. There are so many things I want to show you' (266). Bennett sets up the familiar opposition between public and private worlds, but the private world has been deeply contaminated by the treachery and corruption of the public world, and it remains to be seen whether the bonding of this unlikely pair is strong enough to withstand the pressure of the past and the Machiavellian intrigue in the world around them.

The final actions of the novel are, in fact, dictated by Kane's desire for vengeance against Dec and confrontation with Tempest. Driven by a dangerous fatalism, Kane feels the past can be exorcised only by violence. There is, he believes, no escape from the 'second prison'. He takes off with Benny at the end, but shares none of Benny's faith in the possibility of a new and better life. 'I know I can't go on like this, like my life is not my own' (272), he says, and Bennett holds out little hope that he can ever achieve a life of his own. Tempest is Kane's nemesis, returning at the end, a ghostly presence resurrected from the dead, to plague Kane's future.

The evil spectre of colonialism haunts Bennett's Gothic. As a Branch man sent over to Belfast from England to eliminate native dissidence and impose English law, Tempest occupies a 'colonial' position in the narrative, his style of policing presented as a homologue of the oppressive colonialist state. Viewed as a decolonising subject, Kane has been denied his humanity by the colonising power, forced to inhabit a world in which all meaningful moral landmarks have been swept away. At that point, colonialism equates with absurdism and nihilism. Colonial violence breeds an answering subaltern violence: the writing of the narrative of violence, which is now in the hands of the subaltern, strips legitimacy from colonial violence, but so also from subaltern violence. Subaltern violence, attempting its own narrative and excuse, recognises its own mirroring of the violence of colonialism. The discourse of mimicing can speak not only of learnt civility but also of learnt barbarism. As Caliban remarks to Prospero – 'You taught me language, and my profit on't / Is I know how to curse. The red plague rid you / For learning me your language' (*The Tempest*, 1, ii, 365-7). Bennett's study of the relation between colonial spy-master and the brutalised oppressed focuses the ambivalence, the potential violence and regret at the heart of all colonial power struggles.

Bennett's critique of colonial authority and suspicion of bourgeois morality re-writes the conventional conservative thriller, subverting élitist detective fantasies (Poe's Dupin, Gaboriau's M. Lecoq, Conan Doyle's Sherlock Holmes, Christie's Poirot) and the crime thriller's conventionally mainstream values. His radicalism is of a particularly bleak and ironic strain, involving, among other things, an unmasking of 'dirty tricks' and the violence of official society; the perception of crime as a product of specific colonial conditions; a questioning of the concepts of criminality and justice. These elements of social critique are consciously situated and constructed within a formal radicalism. In disrupting the linear flow of the narrative, the novel frustrates conventional expectations concerning coherent, cause-and-effect development of plot. The first person narration is fragmented and elliptical. It leaps about in time, shifts abruptly between locales, producing ironic or ambiguous juxtapositions, and creating tension and suspense. The narrative is full of hidden persuaders, plots, secret organisations, evil systems, all kinds of conspiracies. As in Deane's *Reading in the Dark*, the past is a mosaic to be pieced together. Truth is elusive. We are implicated in the novel's concern with deception and self-deception, forced through a maze of half-truth, partial information, bizarre coincidence, our sense of entrapment in a labyrinthine world heightened by the echo effects in repeated references (such as those relating to sickness or losing one's way); and by the technique of mirror imaging (Tempest and Kane, Tempest and Seanie, Kane's pursuit of Dec and Tempest's pursuit of Kane). The subjectivisation of the narrative destabilises the objective social world, and calls into question moral and 'philosophical' meaning, the naive assumptions of rational humanism. But though meaning may be disrupted and deferred, it is ultimately attainable, in the manner of the classic detective story. The novel's subjective distortions ultimately resolve themselves into a coherent, integrated narrative of past events. A check is placed on the performing self-consciousness and self-reflexiveness of postmodernism. The incipient spirit of cultural subversiveness and anarchy is restrained. For all its disruptiveness, this is not a fiction about itself and its processes, but about objective reality and life in the world. It is only superficially anti-rationalist and anti-Realist.

Like *The Second Prison*, *The Wrong Man* is also set in the '80s – more than a decade later than *West Belfast*, in the years between early 1981 and late 1984, and, like Bennett's novel, reflects on an exhausted and corrupted idealism. Also like Bennett's novel, Morrison's is genre fiction employing the techniques of the thriller. It tells the story of Raymond Massey who has been imprisoned in Long Kesh for seven years, four of them spent 'on the blanket' in protest against the British Government's refusal to grant IRA prisoners political status. When he is released, he meets an old girlfriend, Róisín Reynolds, whom he shortly marries; but he finds difficulty in reconciling his love for Róisín and her son with his continued commitment to the Republican cause. Meanwhile, after rescuing eighteen year old Tod Malone from a gang of neighbourhood youths, Raymond introduces the young man to the IRA. After taking part in a number of IRA missions, Tod becomes disillusioned and turns informer. In the words of the blurb on the back of the book,

This dark and sinister tale infiltrates the activities of the IRA during the Troubles in Northern Ireland, exposing a complex and contradictory world of brutality and bravery, of loyalty and betrayal, a place of hatred and love. Gripping and absorbing, this novel provides an extraordinary insight into paramilitary activities in this war-torn country.

In dealing with the activities of the IRA, the novel has all the usual thriller ingredients – suspense, fear, mystery, exhilaration, excitement, violence. The French film critic, Pascal Bonitzer, in his influential essay, 'Partial vision: film and the labyrinth', provides a model for the way the thriller creates suspense in his concept of 'partial vision',[21] the idea that what is not shown or heard is just as significant as what is heard and seen. The very first image in *The Wrong Man* is of Tod 'drowsily not knowing whether this was his own bed or if it were day or night outside, except that he felt concussed and still drunk'.[22] As Diane Farquharson remarks, 'the condition of "not knowing" suffuses the novel'.[23] It does so by virtue of a narrative style which continually emphasises 'partial vision': 'As he (Tod) looked down, an image appeared – a small patch of floral pattern on a carpet. He realized he was seeing out of one eye, which had a limited scope' (1). Tod has to try and piece together a picture of what's going on around him:

> He tried to listen but could hear nothing except his own breathing and the rumblings of his insides. He imagined that the room was bare and he alone. His sore neck had thawed a little, allowing him to tilt his head back more freely and find the gap in the hood. He moved his eye along the carpet. To his right a newspaper was spread out. On it were a screwdriver, a claw hammer and carpenter nails. (2)

Tod models the reader's activity: we are reading in the dark, wondering if Tod is an informer, if his captors really are the UDA, if they have mistaken him for his brother, if they are taking him off to shoot him. From the outset, the novel destabilises the reader's understanding of events, our narrative expectations are held in suspension, our desire for narrative control denied. Narration is volatile, chracterised by sudden shifts in time, locale and point of view. Chronological narrative is splintered, the reader's attention fractured. We are left to fill in the gaps by making deductions from the clues that are left. There are at least two main stories – Raymond's and Roisin's, or, to put it another way, the public story and the private story – which exist in a tensely contrapuntal relationship throughout the novel.

21 Pascal Bonitzer, 'Partial vision: film and the labyrinth', trans. Fabrice Ziolkowski, *Wide Angle*, 4, 4 (1982), pp 53–63.   22 Danny Morrison, *The Wrong Man* (Cork: Mercier Press, 1996), p. 1. Hereafter, page references will be incorporated into the text.   23 Diane Farquharson, 'Resisting genre and type: narrative strategy and instability in Danny Morrison's *The Wrong Man* and Seamus Deane's *Reading in the Dark*', in Bill Lazenbatt (ed.) *Northern Narratives, Writing Ulster* (Jordanstown: University of Ulster), pp 89–112, p 91.

Bonitzer adduces the metaphor of the labyrinth to explain the way the thriller blocks the reader's or spectator's vision. Morrison's convoluted plot is such a labyrinth, creating uncertainty, laying traps, causing delays, while at the same time drawing us further into the story. We are led through a series of twists and turns which have their spatial equivalent in the maze of side streets, back entries and traffic-crowded throughfares of the city – just as Los Angeles in *The Big Sleep* or New York in *The French Connection* is turned into labyrinthine space. In *The Wrong Man*, an extended episode concerns Raymond drawing a number of undercover SAS men through the Belfast labyrinth before delivering them to their deaths at the hands of the IRA in a car-park ambush. Other theorists have used other models to describe the way thriller suspense is created. Lars Ole Sauerberg's theory of suspense viewed as a product of 'concealment' (hiding information from us) and 'protraction' (delaying telling us the truth),[24] and Noel Carroll's 'interrogatory' model' (the narrative poses questions that we are anxious to have answered),[25] are all relevant to the structural organisation of *The Wrong Man*: the novel begins by raising the question of Tod's culpability as an informer, but conceals the evidence and delays revelation of the truth until near the end of the story. This is effected through the use of flashback which takes us away from the moment of Tod's captivity and back three years to the time when he first met Raymond and first joined the IRA. Structurally, the novel completes the image of a labyrinthine circle.

As well as providing an account of the 'thrills' of Provo derring-do, Morrison is concerned to explore an ideology, a morality and way of life – the world of Republican paramilitarism. And so, while exploiting all the mandatory visceral appeal of the conventional thriller, *The Wrong Man* also deals with troublesome feelings of pathos, guilt and regret, and attempts a more complex characterisation of the IRA man than the stereotype of the revolutionary saint in *West Belfast*, or that of the psychopathic killer of much popular fiction. In a boldly subversive generic transformation, Morrison re-writes the bomber and assassin as the thriller's new hero, and turns the official representatives of law and order – the RUC and the British army – into the villains. For what the thriller genre offers is a melodramatic division of the world between two simplistically warring allegorical factions. Within that basic structure, Morrison undeviatingly reproduces the British state as 'Evil' and examines the IRA's claim to represent the 'Good'.

Jerry Palmer, in his book *Thrillers* (1978), argues that there are only two elements which are 'absolutely indispensable' to the thriller genre – the 'hero' and the 'conspiracy'. 'The excitement that every thriller reader demands', says Palmer, 'is the moral sympathy accorded the hero in his struggle against evil, it is "seeing things through

24 See Lars Ole Sauerberg, *Secret Agents in Fiction* (New York: St. Martin's Press, 1984). 25 See Noel Carroll, 'Toward a theory of film suspense', *Persistence of Vision*, I, 1, (Summer 1984), pp 65–89.

his eyes"'.[26] In the IRA man, Raymond Massey, Morrison creates a hero who is designed to claim our sympathy and allegiance. His courage and commitment are exemplary. Tod 'knew that he wanted to follow Raymond Massey everywhere and anywhere because Raymond Massey was so confident that he made you feel invincible and immortal' (48). The novel develops a contrast between the young 'raker' who joins the IRA for personal (not political) reasons – to acquire a more macho self-image, and the veteran campaigner. Tod is a portrait of hedonistic, irresponsble youth, disloyal to both wife and comrades, incapable and resentful of the commitment he sees in others, and ready to admit that he is 'a manipulative, exploitative, egotistical individual who had squandered nobility' (197). Raymond, on the other hand, is a model of ideologically-founded, self-sacrificing and inspirational commitment. As Tod recognises, 'Raymond towered over him more than ever: his consistency, integrity, resolve, commitment. His sacrifices. I am not fit to tie his laces' (156). But Morrison doesn't present Raymond simply as the indisputable exemplar of 'nobility'. Even Tod questions Raymond's kind of life: 'I am sick of it all. I wasn't cut out for thus type of life, and this war's never going to end. It's never going to end. I've been wasting my time. We've all been wasting our time' (155). The young man who revelled 'euphorically' (35) in Raymond's display of physical strength against the neighbourhood gang at the beginning of the novel is eventually sickened by violence and paranoia: 'He wanted to leave the past behind. He wanted peace. He wanted to look the living in the eye and impart a trust and an assurance: he would never again have hand or part in the taking of human life' (153). The violence of Raymond's actions inhibits the reader's identification with the character. In the description of Raymond's encounter with the gang that had beaten Tod up, the language is alienating as well as heroising. Raymond metamorphoses from animal ('Raymond roared like an animal' (32)), to sea monster, to warrior, to 'freak wave', to sordid street-fighter: 'Raymond rose like some sea monster coming up from air, except his face was that of a warrior and the sewer rod was raised high above his head like a broadsword. With full force he brought it down dead centre across his enemy's head, splitting it open' (34). Later, we see him cold-bloodedly assassinating the UDA man, Joe Powderley, organising bombing runs into the city centre, luring SAS men to their deaths in an IRA ambush, sneaking up to place a bomb under a prison officer's car, staking out a British undercover man's house in preparation for another assassination. The revulsion the reader feels at the hero's acts of violence is offset by recognition of an even greater evil embodied by the agencies of institutionalised law enforcement. Raymond is meant to represent the way the fundamentally moral man, driven by a desire for freedom and justice, is tainted by the evil he confronts and forced to resort to extreme measures in doing battle with the enemy. In Palmer's terms, 'conspiracy' is presented 'as

26 Jerry Palmer, *Thrillers* (London: Edward Arnold, 1978), p. 82.

a heinous criminal act, as something that everyone will find atrocious and unfor-givable',[27] but in the scheme of Morrison's novel the major 'conspiracy' is that of the corrupt state apparatuses – both 'Ideological' (religious, educational, family, legal, political, communicational and cultural) and 'Repressive' (army and police) – rather than that of the so-called terrorists whose 'conspiracy' is construed as merely reactive. As Palmer says, 'the hero is justified in being who he is, and behaving in the way that he does, by the threat of conspiracy .... insofar as something goes wrong with the world in the thriller ... it is always the fault of the others. If it were not for these others, the hero would not have to intervene, for the world is basically, in the version offered by the thriller, a good place'.[28] In Morrison's novel, the hegemonic authority of the British colonial system is viewed as more dangerous to the survival of liberal demo-cracy – the entire western way of life – than the IRA. 'Conspiracy' is the dissemblance of the state: the 'conspirators' are the state authorities which hide behind masks of ideological control. The fictional world of *The Wrong Man*, as the title implies, is one in which things may not be as they seem.

One of the strongest challenges to Raymond's heroic status comes from Róisín. She accuses him of sacrificing the present, and the possibility of love, family and a comfortable, normal domesticity for an impossible ideal. She feels as much a victim of Raymond's Republicanism as of her ex-husband's infidelities. Raymond, she thinks, is 'flawed but faithful' (54). He fails to provide for his family, he doesn't support her by minding her son when she's trying to prepare for her examinations, he inhibits her self-growth and self-realisation, he disappoints her sexually. She comes to regard him as a 'millstone of a husband' (141). Her complaint against him shades into the recognisable humanitarian opposition to atrocity: 'Some IRA attacks had caused furious rows between them. She couldn't understand how he could defend many of the things the IRA did' (60). She strikes not only at his failure as a husband and father, but at the very moral and practical justification for his actions: 'I beg you. Give it up. It's going nowhere, you must know that. Look at that child shot dead last week. A wee baby. What cause can justify that? It's shameful' (126-7). 'Murderer! Murderer! Murderer!', she screams at him as their marriage finally founders.

Nevertheless, Morrison intends the reader to approve of his hero despite the violence of his actions, and to adopt his hero's moral perspective despite the force of Róisín's challenge. Raymond's exploits, as we are constantly reminded, are altruis-tically, not personally, motivated. We are supposed to root for him in all that he sets out to do, and to the extent that Morrison manages to arouse this identification between reader and hero he creates thriller suspense. Raymond exemplifies a kind of personally conceived 'nobility' which links him to the existentialist thriller hero, the alienated individual cut off from the supports of tradition and religion, who confronts

27 Ibid., p. 181. 28 Ibid., pp 86–7.

issues of integrity, identity, death, commitment, in his struggle against the powers of darkness. In an absurd world, the classic thriller's 'poetic justice' is irrelevant. Morrison's novel ends, not with the triumph of 'Good' over 'Evil', but in despair and death – Bobby is killed on a stake-out, Raymond is shot dead by Tod's British handlers, Raymond's last act is to shoot Tod, Tina is in prison, Róisín's is 'the face of decency destroyed' (197), Tod's wife Sal is left with a child and no husband. No significant change in the world has been brought about. The mythic pattern of order and justice restored to a corrupt society remains unfulfilled.

The *Wrong Man* expresses a generalised anxiety realised in abstract and mythic terms similar to that found in a particular sub-species of thriller – 1940s *film noir* – with which Morrison's highly cinematic novel exhibits a strong affinity. Like 1940s *film noir* which, in the words of John Belton, dealt with 'a uniquely American experience of wartime and postwar despair and alienation as a disorientated America readjusts to a new social and political reality',[29] Morrison's *noir* thriller reflects a mood of wartime upheaval as a politicised and aggressive Republican underclass challenges the dominant British social and political order in Northern Ireland. Added to this, both the '40s *film noir* and Morrison's '90's *noir* thriller are conditioned by the threat to masculinity and patriarchal power which was a significant feature of these eras, arising from women attaining increased independence after the second world war and from advances in the women's movement, both inside and outside Irish Republicanism in the '80s and '90s. Formally, stylistically and affectively, the novel has many *noir* characteristics: dark city streets; a mood of gloom, pessimism and anxiety; predictable narrative elements such as murder-plots, stake-outs, surveillance ops., chases; a tough, cynical, proletarian protagonist who inhabits a corrupt society and comes under threat from female influence. Though Róisín does not deliberately use her sexuality to ensnare or emasculate the male, she poses just as serious a threat to male independence and patriarchal power as the traditional *noir femme fatale*. As devoted mother determined to get an education for herself and yearning for domestic normality, Róisín is in fact more like the 'good woman' than the *femme fatale*, but she is still represented as inherently dangerous to the male hero, holding out to him a seductive alternative to the violent *noir* world. As in film *noir*, the men ultimately control the narrative of *The Wrong Man*, but although the novel is dominated by patriarchal discourse the female characters, especially Róisín, are given substantial subjectivity. The female protagonist is not completely textually suppressed and proves a worthy opponent to the male hero, Raymond, in the domestic sphere. Róisín retains control of her own body and fertility, deciding for herself when she will or won't go off the pill; she puts her demands strongly as wife and mother; she refuses to be completely confined by the marital home or the responsibilities of motherhood;

29 John Belton, *American Cinema/American Culture* (New York and London:McGraw-Hill, 1994), p. 184.

her potential sexual power is emphasised by the way Tod's male gaze records her body erotically. Without intending to be a *femme fatale* she is still a 'fatal' woman, refusing to bend to the male, and instead standing up to him with a phallic knife in her hand, denouncing him as 'Murderer!' and 'Wanker!' (150) who has failed to satisfy her as a woman. Reflecting the contemporary discussion around 'woman', Morrison is prepared to fulfil the feminist demand for strong, angry, independent women without in the end overturning patriarchy or the political imperative.

The Derry metanarrative: Seamus Deane's *Reading in the Dark* (1996)

All Deane's writings, says Edna Longley, are a species of autobiography. Even the *Field Day Anthology* is 'most persuasively read as Derry autobiography'.[30] In his 'General introduction', she says, he 'conflates – as Irish autobiographers tend to do – personal history with a narrative of Ireland'.[31] As for *Reading in the Dark*, 'this book powerfully represents the condition – and conditioning – of Catholic Derry during the years that incubated the troubles'.[32] The novel is an Irish Republican *bildungsroman* rehearsing the experiences of a nameless, working-class Catholic boy growing up in Derry in the 1940s and '50s, surrounded by political treachery, sectarian violence, rumours and family secrets. As a version of Irish Gothic, Deane's Derry is a place full of ghosts and shadows, terrible secrets, domestic violence, the return of the repressed. Its darkness, 'emblematic of the political situation',[33] is lit by fires and bonfires, and echoes to the sound of Orange drums and a mother's sobbing. Imagery of fire pervades the novel – the burning distillery; the unsettling Mr Bamboozelem who, in his 'coat of flame', seemed 'suddenly on fire'; the mother's demented guilty cry, 'Burning. It's burning. All out there, burning';[34] the secret past 'burning, burning' (108) up through the concreted patch at the back of the family home where the rose bushes used to be. The 'concrete' world is infused with ghostly sounds and presences, present reality with the poisonous irruptions of the past. The novel, which is set in a border region and crosses between Derry and Donegal, occupies a kind of liminal space where the real world and fairy-land, fact and fable, fiction and autobiography, private and public, meet. Following the model of the 'country boy' (Deane's schoolfriend Seamus Heaney?) whose essay won the teacher's praise – 'I kept remembering that mother and son waiting in the Dutch interior of that essay, with the jug of milk and the butter on the table, while behind and above them were those wispy, shawly figures from the rebellion, sibilant above the great fire and below the

30 Edna Longley, 'Autobiography as history', review of *Reading in the Dark*, *Fortnight*, November 1996, p. 31. 31 Ibid. 32 Ibid. 33 'Reading in the Dark: an interview with Seamus Deane', *English & Media Magazine*, 36 (Summer 1997), pp.17–20, p.19. 34 Seamus Deane, *Reading in the Dark* (London: Cape, 1996), p. 139. Hereafter, page references will be incorporated into the text.

aching, high wind' (21) – Deane writes his own childhood as 'a Dutch interior' haunted by the past, transforming autobiography into history, domestic tragedy into 'allegory of a people's grief'.[35]

Opening with a shadow on the stairs and the boy narrator's statement 'We were haunted' (4), the novel continues by elaborating a powerful sense of instability, insubstantiality and unreality. There are frequent references to disappearing and the disappeared. The second section is entitled 'Disappearances' and alludes to stories of fairies who 'take away' (7) human children, the narrator's idea of Hell – 'where the blackness sucked you into a great whiplash of flames and you disappeared forever' (7), and recollections of a visit to the circus where Mr Bamboozelem 'disappeared in a cloud of smoke', disturbing the child's comfortable sense of reality. In the next section, we hear of the central disappearance in the novel, the time 'when Uncle Eddie disappeared' (8). Eddie's brother, the narrator's father, 'would not speak of it at all' (9). Eddie is the novel's absent centre. The section entitled 'Accident' records the narrator's early experience of the way any account of the past is subject to distortion to suit the teller's own purposes. The narrator, from an elevated vantage point on 'the parapet above Meenan's Park', watches a tragic accident when a lorry ran over a young boy. In a short time, however, in this community where 'everybody hated the police' it is a recklessly driven police car which is blamed for the young boy's death. The next section, entitled 'Feet', moves the narrator from a position of privileged knowledge to a restricted perspective under the kitchen table. From this limited angle of vision he pieces together the scene from the appearance and movements of people's feet. The section enacts in miniature the novel's central concern with the struggle to construct, from a position of partial or limited knowledge, a reading of events of the past. What destabilises the narrative more than anything is its concern with secrets and betrayal. As Deane explains, 'one of the first effects of betrayal is to make you feel, "I never knew that person", "I don't know her", "I don't know him". And that person suddenly loses substance, becomes almost shadowy.'[36] A secret once exposed suddenly defamiliarises what was known: 'The first effect is to make everything phantasmal. Everything you thought was secure and actual has now become almost ghostly and haunting, and yet at the same time, the very moment it becomes that, it becomes super-real: it is the reality that puts the quotidian, one that you thought was secure, out of court'[37]

Two critical paradigms – the postmodernist and the post-colonial – suggest themselves as having particular relevance to Deane's novel, though the limitations of each need to be carefully noted. Like *Ripley Bogle*, *Reading in the Dark* exhibits a postmodern concern with its own linguistic construction and conventionality. The

35 Terry Eagleton, 'The Bogside bard', *New Statesman*, 30 August 1996, p. 46. **36** *English & Media Magazine*, p. 19. 37 Carol Rumens, 'Reading Deane', *Fortnight*, July/August 1997, p. 30.

novel is made up of short, fragmented, disjunct episodes indicative of the struggle for narrative coherence. At the centre of the novel is the figure of the child listening to others' stories, learning from them, so that he can construct more competently the narrative of his own and his family's experience. This is a story about the process of writing a story, about the way a narrative is composed out of diverse materials – folklore, rumour, overheard conversation, a child's partial understanding of the mysterious adult world around him. And it is a story about the suppressions, omissions, withholdings and evasions that are part of the narrative process: the text of this family history is also a 'field of the disappeared'. For most of the time, the boy-narrator is reading in the dark, trying to decipher the meaning of what he sees and hears, until eventually he comes to perceive the pattern in events, the mosaic effect which they produce.

As he grows up, he becomes more adept at manipulating narrative. He learns how to elicit information from others, especially when they may have strong personal reasons for not wishing to disclose what they know. His relationships thus become marked by an increasing self-consciousness, by calculation, deviousness and obtuseness. He also learns to judge the status of the various narratives which he encounters. Early on, when Crazy Joe tells him an ostensibly true story about a local man, Larry McLaughlin, the boy is completely taken in, and is indignant and disappointed when he discovers that the story has no basis in fact but is merely one of Crazy Joe's crazy tales. Later, however, when he is dealing with Grandfather and mother, the narrator shows much more circumspection and discrimination in his assessment of their accounts of the past: 'And even then, when it had all been told, I had the sense of something still held back, something more than she knew, something Grandfather had cut out' (127). He eventually realises that the person with most knowledge is Mother, and he longs to obtain from her the master-narrative of the family history – 'just the one set of facts, the one story that cancelled all the others, the one truth she could tell' (206). Much of the narrative is in the interrogative mode, with the narrator questioning himself about the significance of the information he has obtained: 'And how did I know I had been told the truth? Shouldn't I just ask her? What did you know, Mother, when you married my father? What did he know? When did you tell each other? Why did you silence me, over and over?' (206); or in the speculative mode, with the narrator tentatively constructing ghostly narratives to try and understand the events of the past: 'Then, maybe, Grandfather took out a revolver and handed it to Larry and told him to go in and do it. And Larry crawled along the passageway to the space where Eddie sat on the wishing-chair, and he hunkered before Eddie and he looked at him and, maybe, said something, maybe, told him to say his prayers, and then he shot him, several times or maybe just once, and the fort boomed as though it were hollow' (185). But, gradually, we see a shift in narrative stance from that of passive, bewildered, sometimes victimised or silenced or marginalised child observer to that of increasingly powerful, central controller of the narrative. After he and Liam hear their father's account of Eddie's death, the narrator comments: 'For once, I knew more than he (Liam) did. Than either of them did. It was like being a father to both of them, knowing more' (133).

Eventually, he reaches the point where he must interpret the facts and arrange them into a narrative: 'A choice, an election, was to be made between what actually happened and what I imagined, what I had heard, what I kept hearing' (182). Then comes the stage when, his narrative complete, the narrator decides to convert it from oral to written form: 'I decided to write it all out in an exercise book, partly to get it clear, partly to rehearse it and decide which details to include or leave out' (194). Yet another displacement is signed in his decision to convert his written narrative from English to Irish in order to hide its true significance from his parents. The text, that is, is not only subject to editorial decisions but determined by the social, or, in this case, familial conditions of its production. Factual history, he learns, is discursively constructed and is affected by subjective, textual, institutional and political factors. Not even the narrator's version of the family history is pure. He never finds out the full story. There are things that others know which he doesn't know. He never knows, for example, the extent of his father's knowledge. Commenting on the novel's final words which refer to the father's innocence, Deane emphasised the essential ambiguity of the narrative: 'The father is innocent, in a way, but I'm using that ambiguity: how much does he really know? Is that innocence of someone who preserved it by not asking?' No grand narrative of the past, as Deane went on to say, is available:

> The master-story is his (the boy's) search for one. And I think it's a sad search – not because I'm saying bluntly there is none, but that there was none available to him in those circumstances. Yet at the same time I've sympathy for him, because he could only have done what he did, given his sensibility, given his training, given the way in which he was taught, given his eagerness to know the family history so that he could situate himself and his parents in it.[38]

Along with Brian Friel in *Making History*, Deane questions the possibility of a true narrative. There is no such thing as History, only histories. History, penetrated by myth and fiction, is a kind of insubstantial shadow-play:

> Hauntings are, in their way, very specific. Everything has to be exact, even the vaguenesses. My family's history was like that too. It came to me in bits, from people who rarely recognised all they had told. Some of the things I remember, I don't really remember. I've just been told about them so now I

38 Ibid., p. 30.

feel I remember them, and want to the more because it is so important for others to forget them. (225)

Not only does full truth remain forever elusive, but the disinterested quest for truth only alienates the boy from his parents and his community. The limits of the boy's rational, empirical approach to 'truth' are the limits of the revisionist mode of historiography, which, Deane said in another interview, involves the imposition of alien English values of 'fairness' and 'objectivity': ' It's impossible to be measured about Ireland', he said, 'Perhaps one shouldn't try'.[39] After all his efforts to discover the facts of the past, the boy learns that the 'truth' of a situation can never be simply reduced to the 'facts': 'there are some things he doesn't really know and can't know, because they're not known at the level of fact'.[40] Yet, however difficult it may be to recover the truth of the past, Deane resists any suggestion of postmodern quietism. Reading may take place in the dark, but the effort to understand takes place nonetheless.

Deane's interrogation of the epistemological norms of the historical description of reality is conducted with a view, not to dismantle, but to rescue, the possibility of coherent subjectivity, historical significance and ethical stability. The novel is a re-examination, not a refutation of the Realist premise that the 'real' exists as a primary condition which can be faithfully transcribed through the secondary means of language. Deane plays with fictionality in ways which challenge ontological and epistemological certainty, but he does this in order to demonstrate the difficulty of constructing a workable history, not to invalidate the humanist quest for truth and moral value.

The novel's formal procedures model the possibilities for an imaginative re-combining of elements of the past and the social world to form new and liberatory orders. At the centre of the book is the figure of the questioning narrator, situated at some remove from family, alienated from the psyche of the community, probing the stories the family has constructed to explain itself to itself. In doing so, he becomes increasingly aware of the way narrative works ideologically to mask the truth. The private world, he comes to see, is situated within a political world and conditioned by a communal consciousness. In his 1975 essay, 'Irish poetry and Irish Nationalism', Deane characterised Northern poets as detached from national feeling, more concerned to pursue an ideal of individual and imaginative freedom than to act as spokesmen for their communities, more interested in redrafting 'the emotional geography of the respective areas in terms, not of history and politics, but of the free personality'.[41] The preference for lyric poetry, which lends itself to personal expression of interior freedom, as opposed to epic and narrative, was, he argued, symptomatic

39 Nick Fever, 'A kind of life sentence', *Guardian*, 28 October 1996, p. 9.   40 *English & Media Magazine*, p. 18.   41 Seamus Deane, 'Irish poetry and Irish Nationalism', in Douglas Dunn (ed.), *Two Decades of Irish Writing* (Cheadle: Carcanet, 1975), pp 4–22.

of this turn from politics and community. *Reading in the Dark*, written out of the colonial antagonisms and cultural myths which inform the Catholic Nationalist community in Derry, re-establishes Northern epic. The novel is concerned to penetrate the rational mind and unearth the 'atavistic' layers of Irish experience without which, Deane has claimed, understanding of the Northern conflict remains ineffectual. The child narrator, whose perceptions have been structured within an English, literate, empirical, rationalist educational system undergoes a process of re-education into a deeper understanding of communal values and strategies for survival in the colonial state, even as he interrogates those values and strategies. There is a rupture that has to be healed between the lived and the learned, myth and history, traditionalism and revisionism. The re-mythologisation of the child re-inserts him within the communal codes while his participation in the rationalist drive of modernity gives him critical distance from a mystifying false consciousness.

Deane's insistence on the colonial context of his entire cultural project invokes a colonial critical paradigm. In his essay, 'Heroic styles: the history of an idea', he describes Irish history as 'a long colonial concussion'[42] and one of the aspects of this 'concussion' which Deane emphasises in *Reading in the Dark* is the way colonial pressures and oppressions breed a culture of secrets and lies in both the political and personal spheres. Catholic Nationalist Derry depends on a secret army. Treachery and betrayal always go along with secrecy. The informer is particularly hated. The treachery may be overt, like McIlhenny's, the man who betrayed everyone in the novel – his lover (the narrator's mother), his wife (Katie) and their unborn child (Maeve), his IRA comrades, and Eddy, the narrator's uncle who was mistakenly executed by the IRA as an informer while McIlhenny escaped to America. Or the betrayal may be of a subtler kind, though no less destructive, like the mother's keeping from her husband her love of McIlhenny and the knowledge that Eddy had not brought shame upon the family but had, in fact, been mistakenly executed on the orders of her own father. These unsayable secrets drive the mother to depression, madness and dumbness. In this novel where the personal and the political are so closely intertwined, the mother's grief, says Deane, 'is, in some ways, aligned to Irish history'.[43] Conditioned to let the coloniser speak for her, the mother has no language for her guilt and grief: 'The mother is, in her grief, taking the shock, the trauma of a history into herself, but can find no escape from it.'[44]

The narrator too is caught in the colonial bind. In his essay, 'History lessons: postcolonialism and Seamus Deane's *Reading in the Dark*,' Liam Harte details 'the discursive struggle for the boy's subjectivity'[45] between the state forces (the educational

42 Seamus Deane, 'Heroic styles: the history of an idea', in *Ireland's Field Day* (London: Hutchinson, 1985), pp 45–59.   43 *English & Media Magazine*, p. 18.   44. Ibid., p. 19.   45 Liam Harte, 'History lessons: postcolonialism and Seamus Deane's Reading in the Dark', *Irish University Review*, 30, 1 (Spring/Summer

system and the police force) which seek to construct him as an obedient subject, and the anti-colonialist, Nationalist forces in his community which would produce him as a potential insurgent. The Catholic Church is seen as politically ambivalent. There are representatives such as Brother Regan who colludes with the hegemonic power to urge the boys to trust to God's justice in the next world rather than paramilitary action in this one. Later, the school is visited by 'a priest in British army uniform' whose global perspective reduces the Northern Irish conflict to insignificance: 'We must recognize the irrelevance of our internal difference in face of the demands of world history' (199-200). A different set of signals comes from the history teacher who, after the boys have been to see *Beau Geste*, 'rebuked us for admiring all that English public-schoolboy nonsense in the movie' (157). The young narrator encounters a more direct form of ideological control when the police, acting on the word of an informer, arrest the boy and his father and brutally interrogate them about a gun, 'a gift to my father from a young German sailor'. The next chapter, 'Fire', features the boy in postures of outright defiance during a St Patrick's Day riot.

Situated in the midst of the hegemonic struggle between competing discourses, and surrounded by a culture of lies and treachery in his own community, the boy strives to achieve knowledge and understanding, an independent voice. His bid for selfhood challenges the colonial ethos of secrecy, repression, acquiescence, dumbness – the 'maimed condition'[46] personified by his mother. As Deane explains :

> One way of coming into self-possession, of overcoming any kind of oppression, colonial or otherwise, is to take charge of interpretation yourself, not to allow yourself to be interpreted by others. This novel is a kind of parable of that attempt (and a painfully abortive attempt) on the part of a young kid.[47]

The child at the centre of the novel determined to make sense of the familial past is clearly a figure of the author who in his *magnum opus, The Field Day Anthology*, sought to make sense of the Irish cultural past. As Deane said of his own effort as novelist, poet, critic and scholar: 'It's one of the ways of overcoming the sense of being dispossessed – to come into possession through interpretation, through understanding'.[48] The child's is a limited, 'abortive' effort to achieve selfhood because of his naively iconoclastic thought that he can wrest the secrets of the past from an unnecessarily obtuse older generation. There is a level of communal self-representation, existing as oral, folkloric culture, from which he has become alienated as a result of his acquisition of a rational, educated, literate culture. Deane has spoken of how there were for him two kinds of narrative in the novel. One is associated with folktale, legend and oral tradition, and is

2000), pp 149–62, p. 152.   **46** *English & Media Magazine*, p. 18.   **47** Carol Rumens, 'Reading Deane', p. 30.   **48** Ibid.

expressive of a magical view of the world and a sense of wonder and mystery. This is the narrative of the older, uneducated generation, whose stories 'are very subtly coded ways of dealing with trauma and difficulty'.[49] The other kind of narrative is associated with the more rational form of the novel and the drive for understanding and explanation. It is represented by the young boy's questioning, secular, analytical intelligence which has been shaped by a modern educational system (dating from the Education Act of 1947 which made free secondary education available to all). In pursuit of the 'facts', the boy fails to understand the oral, folkloric modes of language which the older generation use to encode their colonial trauma – the local legends of the disappeared, the supernatural tales of hauntings, metamorphosis and deception, of mysterious sex-change and identity-change, of entombment and entrapment, and all the other tropes of dispossession contained in the stories told by the boy's father, aunt Katie and Crazy Joe. The boy doesn't recognise at first how the stories of his parents' generation 'actually deal with the very thing that he was trying to pursue',[50] nor does he appreciate how, in pursuit of the facts of the past, he 'has done a profound injustice to both his parents',[51] threatening the bond of love between them, and between them and him. Realising this, the boy feels guilty, yet cannot avoid pursuing the truth. Eventually, however, he learns the value of indirection and the silent compromises forced upon a colonial people in the interests of survival. He agrees to become a collaborator in his mother's anxious wish to keep the facts from his father: 'I could tell him nothing, though I hated him not knowing. But only my mother could tell him. No one else. Was it her way of loving him, not telling him? It was my way of loving them both, not telling either. But knowing what I did separated me from them both' (187). He comes to recognise that the shadow which existed externally, separating mother and son, is himself: 'Now the haunting meant something new to me – now I had become the shadow' (217). As Deane remarked in the *Fortnight* interview, the boy 'never earns a name. He never achieves sufficient identity (to use that terrible word!) to deserve the name or the sense of self he's looking for in relation to his parents', but he does come to respect and understand his mother's wish for 'forgetfulness' ('Go away, give me a day of forgetfulness'), her desire to leave the past alone, to keep things secret, which, Deane agreed, is indicative of a 'political way out: forget the past, forget Ireland'.[52]

   The last section of the novel tells of the mother suffering a stroke and losing the power of speech completely, 'just as the Troubles came in October 1968' (230): 'Now, as the war in the neighbourhood intensified, they (the boys' parents) both sat there in their weakness, entrapped in the noise from outside and in the propaganda noise of the television inside' (231). Theirs is a double entrapment, caught as they are in both the colonial predicament and in the alienated postmodern world of the simu-

49 Ibid., p. 29.   50 Ibid., p. 29.   51 *English & Media Magazine*, p.18.   52 Carol Rumens, 'Reading Deane', p. 30.

lacrum. Yet the novel ends on a note of reconciliation and hope. While the war rages, the older generation find a way to renew intimacy through silence: 'All through this, my father remained as silent as my mother. I imagined that, in her silence, in the way she stroked his hand, smiled crookedly at him, let him brush her hair, bowing her head obediently for him, she had told him and won his understanding. I could believe now, as I never had when a child, that they were lovers' (231). Outside, the 'noise' of civil disturbance breaks the old silence of compromise and repression as a new generation makes its revolutionary presence felt. History re-directs myth. With the father's death, in July 1971, the mother sleeps 'the last sleep of the old world' (233). The curfew is about to end, the streets are cleared of barricades, the shadow is no longer on the stairs, innocence is dead. The future belongs to the likes of the narrator. No longer burdened by the pain of guilt and betrayal, and now reconciled to his parents, he combines the modern, educated perspectives of the university graduate with a sensitivity to pre-modern, oral cultural modes symbolised by the gypsy boy on horseback, an ancestral figure of itinerant, rural freedom, a fugitive yet defiant spirit of place: 'As though in a dream, I watched a young gypsy boy jog sedately through the scurf of debris astride a grey-mottled horse. Bareback, he held lightly to the horse's mane and turned out of sight in the direction the army had taken hours before, although it was still curfew' (233). Here, autobiography as history culminates in a transcendent poetic image of the young gypsy boy rising Phoenix-like from 'the scurf of debris' – a Gaelicised version of Edmund Muir's post-nuclear vision of new beginnings in his poem 'Horses'. Often we have the feeling that Deane's novel really wants to be poetry, and nowhere more so than in this closing section where, it would seem, the young gypsy boy has escaped into an alien discursive field from the poetic hippodrome to which he more properly belongs. Deane's fiction expresses the same desire as that which informs his non-fictional writing – a wish to restore to the aesthetic its full capacity for the political. Eagleton, in his enthusiastic review of the novel, mounts a pre-emptive strike against any oppositional critique: '... reading this novel one can already hear the grinding of the literary Unionist knives. Isn't this just the sort of nostalgic, superstitious, violence-ridden stuff one would expect from a Bogside bard?'[53] It is possible, however, to recognise, along with Eagleton, the 'nostalgic', 'superstitious' and violent elements in Deane's (Republican) 'Derry metanarrative', as well as the consignment of Protestant Derry to the dark margins ('foreign territory, the estrangement of Protestants with their bibles', 143) or to a monologically negative discourse of gerrymandering, police harrassment, and savagery ('those savages with their tom-toms', 125), without holding to any Unionist ideological point of view.

53 Terry Eagleton, 'The Bogside bard', p. 46.

CHAPTER SIX

Women's writing

A feminist practice of literary theory not only discovers structural inequalities in society, but embraces a transformative function to indicate possibilities of challenge and change. The feminist model is thus related to psychoanalysis and Marxism, to postcolonial theories and queer theory, which all address different kinds of inequalities hidden within the grand narratives of the established, hegemonic culture. Women's writing can simply encode and reinforce the hegemonic structures of belief and feeling or it can be subversive, challenging dominant modes of understanding and offering alternative ways of thinking and feeling. A feminist theory provides a framework of analysis through which to read and assess this potentially revolutionary literature.

In their 1980 *Crane Bag* essay, 'Images of women in Northern Ireland', Margaret Ward and Marie-Therese McGivern complain of the negative mass media images of women in Northern Ireland's phallocratic culture:

> Passive victims of the troubles, viragos of the barricades, advocates of a messianic peace. Our contention is that none of these stereotypes reveal the true situation of women living in a socially deprived, war-torn, rigidly patriarchal society.[1]

In a review of Troubles fiction between 1969 and 1989 entitled 'Mothers, whores and villains', Bill Rolston concludes that there are 'few positive images'[2] of women to be found in the fiction. This chapter tests that conclusion, investigating the representation of women in the North, but concentrating on exclusively female-authored texts. This focus on the woman as writer is not intended to imply that the only 'authentic' representations of women can come from women themselves: there is a dangerous essentialism, detrimental to feminism, contained in that assumption, and there are examples of sensitive explorations of female identity and subjectivity by male authors (for example, David Park, whose *Stone Kingdoms* is discussed in Chapter 4) which make visible the marginality, vulnerability and eccentricity of women in phallocentric culture. Rather, the 'gynocritical' approach is useful because it allows for consideration of the specific historical and material conditions under which women's writing takes place. Yet another kind of feminist approach concentrates on the textuality of the

1 *Crane Bag*, 4, 1 (1980), pp 66–72.   2 Bill Rolston, 'Mothers, whores and villains: images of women in novels of the Northern Ireland conflict', *Race and Class*, 31, 1 (1989), pp 41–57, p. 41.

text, a concern which is most obviously demonstrated in the fiction of Deirdre Madden and Briege Duffaud. However, these writers' post-structuralist concern with language and subjectivity, while it discovers the gaps and fissures of language into which the displaced subject may insert her/himself, does not identify those spaces (or that subject) as specifically feminine. Since for these writers the gender of the writer or character is not material, their fiction may be more readily unlocked through Macherey, Derrida and Baudrillard than through Cixous, Iragaray and Kristeva, and is therefore considered in the chapter on Northern postmodernism (Chapter 4).

The writing considered in the present chapter is centrally concerned with women's efforts to define themselves against the oppressive economic, psychic, ideological and textual structures of Northern Irish patriarchy. This literature uncovers and challenges patriarchy in the home, the Church, education, politics, paramilitarism, the work-place, in culture at large, and even in women themselves. It addresses themes of the construction of femininity and gender-role stereotyping, setting out to reconstitute femininity in positive, normative terms (emotion, intuition, love, personal relation-ships, co-operation, nurture) while critiquing the traditional masculine attributes of aggression and desire for dominance. Commonly, women's writing enforces a separation between the public political world, understood as a threatening, sectarian 'masculine' domain, and a superior 'feminine' world of personal feeling and relation-ship. In much women's writing, the sacralised feminine sites of domestic, creative or sexual privacy are violated by the brutalising agents of the public world (Johnston's *Shadows on Our Skin*, O'Riordan's *Involved*, Madden's *Hidden Symptoms* and *One by One in the Darkness*), but the female character is much less likely to adopt the traditional postures of passivity and subjection. Female discontent and rebelliousness, as we see from such different fictions as Johnston's *The Illusionist* and Molloy's *No Mate for the Magpie*, is not the neurotic disorder of the perennial 'mad woman', but a response to a social structure which is uncongenial, oppressive and damaging to women. Feminine resistance involves destabilising androcentric constructions of history, questioning the relevance of male 'liberationist' projects to the lives of ordinary women, and reconstituting the division between the private and public realms through a feminist sexual politics which uncovers the political in the personal. Male definitions and control of both public and private space are challenged, and various forms of female self-redefinition and self-assertion are re-centred: concepts of personal creativity and expression (Johnston's *The Railway Station Man* and *The Illusionist*), women-bonding and acts of co-operation (Mary Costello's *Titanic Town*, David Park's *The Stone Kingdoms*), maternal revival in feminism (Kate O'Riordan's *Involved*, Lionel Shriver's *Ordinary Decent Criminals*). Sometimes the intersection of public and private, male and female worlds is the site of a tense but productive, isolation-ending process of mutual self-definition for both male and female characters, as in Edna O'Brien's *The House of Splendid Isolation*. O'Brien's study of the imposition of male definitions, assumptions and power on the intimate life of a vulnerable old woman treats sexual politics in moral, human terms rather than in the explicitly sexual manner of her early equally controversial fiction. Apart from Shriver's uninhibited American probings, women's writing, perhaps because of the tight gag of Ulster puritanism, has generally taken a conservative approach to the presentation of intimate sexual relations as the site of feminist struggle. For most of the writers the significant aspects of sexual politics are located in the family, the world of business, and in politics. Interestingly, the fiction's new feminised politics tends to articulate the particular concerns of women within one or other of the two communities (Beckett's *Give Them Stones*, Costello's *Titanic Town*), rather than demonstrating the transcultural ideal enunciated by Monica McWilliams, leader of the Women's Coalition Party:

> From the civil rights campaigns of the sixties, to the community projects and women's centres in the mid-1970s and 1980s, women in Northern Ireland have played a central role in the development of alternative political structures. Women have created safe, yet subversive, spaces where they can organize together around issues of concern which cross the sectarian divide while 'agreeing to disagree' on the more divisive ones ...
>
> They have been able to overcome the fragmentation of the earlier years by acknowledging their different traditions and by pursuing innovative ways of working across the traditional political boundaries ... by crossing the traditional boundaries and drawing women from different political traditions into their movement. Women from the mainly working-class areas have set the major pre-cedents for the 'politics of transition' now taking place. Learning to listen, to share, and to respect each others' identities have been their guiding principles.[3]

The fiction offers little evidence of this kind of cross-cultural *political* organisation of women. Frances Molloy and Jennifer Johnston present memorable examples of women 'crossing the traditional boundaries', but these characters do so as individuals, and not for any political reasons. While Molloy's narrative alter ego in *No Mate for the Magpie*, following the pattern outlined by McWilliams, participates in the Northern Civil Rights marches and the Anti-Vietnam protests of the late '60s, she resists ideological control and retains a broadly humanist perspective on life. For Johnston, as for many women writers, McWilliams' 'safe, yet subversive space' is the interior, private space of mind and art, not the public space of political activism.

3 Monica McWilliams, 'Struggling for peace and justice: reflections on women's activism in Northern Ireland', in Joan Hoff and Moureen Coulter (eds.), *Irish Women's Voices: Past and Present, Publication of the Journal of Women's History*, Vol. 6 No. 4/Vol. 7 No. 1 (Winter/Spring, 1995), pp 32–4.

Women writers have generally favoured Realist over anti-Realist modes. Postmodern notions of fracture, dissensus and discontinuity, when applied to the surrounding world, may be useful in mobilising deconstructive discourses to oppose hegemonic patriarchy; but when applied to the female self, these same notions undermine the possibility of an integrated identity capable of putting forward a coherent critique or engaging in meaningful politics. Briege Duffaud's *A Wreath upon the Dead* exemplifies the postmodern self-reflexive mode, in which all attempts to reconstruct the past, identity and meaning are collapsed into a process of endless free textual play. But if Northern Irish women's writing, as Eve Patten has shown, falls largely within the conventional categories of Realist fictional autobiography and social criticism, the lineaments of a considerable range of other genres or sub-genres may also be discerned – the romantic thriller in O'Riordan's *Involved*; Irish Gothic in O'Brien's *The House of Splendid Isolation*; a concoction of metafiction, fictionalised memoir and historical fiction in Duffaud's *A Wreath upon the Dead*; the Big House tradition in Johnston's *The Old Jest* and *How Many Miles to Babylon?*; the working-class *bildungsroman* in Beckett's *Give them Stones* and Costello's *Titanic Town*, the *petit récit* in Molloy's *No Mate for the Magpie*, 'war literature' in all the fiction considered here, the ultra-Realism of American 'New Journalism' in Lionel Shriver's *Ordinary Decent Criminals*. There is no single voice or style or point of view, but in all of these ways women attempt to negotiate the North and its Troubles, and, by complicating or interrogating traditional rigid, oppositional divisions of Protestant/Catholic, Unionist/Nationalist, unsettle dominant notions of reality, and contribute to the creation of what Bakhtin calls a 'heteroglossic' reality composed of multiple discourses which allows for possibilities of transformation and social change.

Feminising liberal humanism: Jennifer Johnston's *Shadows on Our Skin* (1977), *The Railway Station Man* (1984), *The Illusionist* (1995), *How Many Miles to Babylon?* (1974), and *The Old Jest* (1979)

Shadows on Our Skin is the first of Johnston's novels to deal directly with the contemporary Northern Irish Troubles. Though more usually associated with the Big House novel, Johnston concentrates on the dynamics of an urban Catholic working-class family in *Shadows on Our Skin*. The novel is more reminiscent of Sean O'Casey than Elizabeth Bowen or Molly Keane. Re-writing O'Cascy, Johnston transfers the action from the Dublin tenements during the Troubles of the 1920s to Derry's backstreet terrace houses during the Troubles of the 1970s. The novel focuses on eleven year old Joe Logan and his relationships with his demanding father, his protective mother, his older brother, Brendan, returned from London to become involved with the Provos, and his new friend, Kathleen, a local Protestant schoolteacher. However, the destructive effect of political violence on personal relationships makes this the most pessimistic of all Johnston's novels. Johnston repeats O'Casey's negative treatment of politics and 'political' men, and presents similarly heroic, non-political women. Mr Logan is a shiftless, drunken, braggart, his speech as full of sentimental abstraction as the paycock's though lacking the latter's humour and flamboyance. Without Boyle's Falstaffian monumentalism, Logan is merely pathetic. As Joe listens to his father's excited stories of shooting British soldiers, he wonders 'How big a sin is it to hate?'[4] But it is Mrs Logan, a Derry Juno, who most thoroughly deflates her husband's pretensions. She is the backbone of the family, the practical provider and carer who recognises the danger of eloquent words and the 'hero stories' which glamourise sordid acts of violence: 'Words. Words. Words. God. If I'd've had the guts I'd've left you. To drown in your words' (67–8). Unlike Juno who had the courage to leave Boyle to support her daughter, Mrs Logan remains trapped. But like Juno, Mrs Logan places more importance on people than on ideas or ideologies, and rejects any form of political agitation. These women can see nothing beyond hard work and conformity. They are interested only in their families. To the end, neither Mrs Logan nor Juno understands anything about political freedom or social justice. 'If you go around creating destruction', Mrs Logan tells her son Brendan, 'you ask for what you get' (66). Brendan's political feeling is denigrated not only by his mother but also by Kathleen: 'He's in a state of great confusion' Kathleen says, 'Tangled up somehow. A lot of the wrong ideas pushing the right ideas rather hard .... He's not very strong ... No strength inside. His mind is too open to suggestion' (176–7). From a female perspective, politics is a distortion of the human. But while both O'Casey and Johnston are suspicious of the political life, they treat the non-political woman's point of view with some degree of self-reflexive irony. Consequently, the opinions of Juno, Nora, Mrs Logan and Kathleen are never allowed unproblematic normative value. These women would like to will politics away, but as both writers show, politics cannot be willed away, they keep breaking into the personal sphere. In this situation, something more meaningful than Mrs Logan's pacific instinct and weary resignation to the sanctity of state law is required. Like O'Casey, Johnston arouses our sympathy for her hard-working, long-suffering women and is mindful of the dangerous vanities and recklessness of men but, also like O'Casey, she does not advance any simple pacifist or feminist message. What we have, rather, is a powerful humanist lament at the tragic effects of political violence, a resigned or fatalistic repudiation of politics in general which never quite escapes irony. Ultimately, the novel's pessimism lies in its failure to imagine any alternative agency of social change to Nationalist paramilitary chaos.

As well as representing something of a departure for Johnston, *Shadows on Our Skin* develops several key themes and narrative procedures that appear repeatedly in

---

4 Jennifer Johnston, *Shadows on Our Skin* (London: Penguin, 1991), p. 64. First published London: Hamish Hamilton, 1977. Hereafter, page references will be incorporated into the text.

Johnston's fiction. First, there are the narrative strategies designed to guarantee the supreme value of the individual. Personal life and personal relationships form the locus of authentic existential fulfilment in Johnston's fictional world. Events are structured according to a moral economy in which private space and personal relationships constitute a superior, 'feminine', civilising domain that is constantly threatened by the dehumanising, 'masculine' forces bearing down on it from the public, political world. Joe finds a new companionship and understanding with Kathleen, but the sectarian imperative destroys the only real source of hope and meaning in the novel. Similarly, external circumstances conspire to collapse the relationship between Captain Charles Prendergast and the young local boy Diarmuid Toorish in *The Captains and the Kings*, Alex and Jerry's friendship in *How Many Miles to Babylon?*, the peculiarly productive relationship between Nancy Gulliver and Major Barry in *The Old Jest*, the love which Helen Cuffe discovers with Roger Hawthorne in *The Railway Station Man*, and the relationship between Miranda and Cathal in *Fool's Sanctuary*. Public and private worlds are, in fact, closely intertwined. The private world, especially marriage, is commonly constructed as a battleground. In *Shadows on Our Skin* the world of family, through father and older son, echoes to the violent rhetoric of the political world, and is as full of 'hate'. In *How Many Miles to Babylon?* the Moores' marriage is a tense and deadly affair: 'Their words rolled past me up and down the polished length of the table. Their conversations were always the same, like some terrible game, except that unlike normal games, the winner was always the same. They never raised their voices, the words dropped malevolent and cool from their well-bred mouths.'[5] A link between the marital, the maternal, and the martial is suggested in the way the domestic war at home drives Alex to war in Europe, thus satisfying his mother's wish for heroic sacrifice. In *The Railway Station Man* and *The Illusionist*, the female characters, Helen Cuffe and Sheila Glover, are the victims of a destructive emotional violence within the context of marriage. The violence of the external world precipitates self-questioning and awareness of the limitations of the familiar ordering of history and experience. It promotes the making of courageous new life choices, the forging of new identities and alliances, often of a socially or politically transgressive nature. This is particularly evident in Nancy's 'awakening' in *The Old Jest*, Alex's liaison with Jerry in *How Many Miles to Babylon?*, and Helen's reinvention of herself after her husband's violent death in *The Railway Station Man*.

Another important element of *Shadows on Our Skin* which reappears in succeeding novels is the central figure of the artist or writer. Joe is an incipient poet, a dreamer longing for escape from the constricted conditions of his life through words:

5 Jennifer Johnston, *How Many Miles to Babylon?* (Glasgow: Fontana, 1981), p. 7. First published London: Hamish Hamilton, 1974. Hereafter, page references will be incorporated into the text.

What is there for me, he wondered, if I can't make words dance, as the birds are dancing? A man with a brush and tubes of colour can put these patterns on a page so that you can recognise them. Say, ah, yes. Can I, with a biro pen and a string of words? Where? How do you start? What are the rules? Do you just find them out as you go along? Trial and error ... There should be someone you can talk to. One day my head will burst and words will spill out and be blown away by the wind and get caught in the branches of the trees. My words. Everybody's words, when you come to think about it. Oh, help. (139–40)

'Words' are continually being foregrounded in the novel. 'Words. Words. Words,' Mrs Logan shouts exasperatedly at her husband. Surrounded by the old-fashioned patriotic rhetoric of his father, his mother's narrow realism, the militant idiom of his older brother, Kathleen's modern, post-Nationalist discourse of liberal pluralism, Joe has choices to make about the way he's going to use words. In the novel's opening sequence he is trying out different poems expressing very different attitudes to his father. The version he likes best is the one that 'had a ring about it' (8), not the one with the most truth in it. Words can betray us into unreality. As another writer, Helen Cuffe, says on the first page of *The Railway Station Man*: 'To be accurate, and it is in the interests of accuracy that I am struggling with these words';[6] while Alex Moore in *How Many Miles to Babylon?* undermines his own narration, and any version of history, by telling us: 'I can juggle with a series of possibly inaccurate memories, my own interpretation, for what it is worth, of events' (1). Joe is progenitor of a series of writers or artists in Johnston's fiction, including not only Helen and Alex but also Nancy Gulliver in *The Old Jest*, Constance Keating in *The Christmas Tree*, and Sheila Glover in *The Illusionist*. In all of these novels, Johnston is interested in the struggle for authentic selfhood in circumstances where the individual feels threatened or distorted by the pressures of family, parenthood, marriage, politics or the past. Through writing, these characters attempt to free themselves from the received patterns of meaning in which they have been inscribed. In telling their own stories they declare their own control over them, their capacity to re-write both personal and national identity and to re-insert personal experience and individual conscience into the grand narratives of war, politics or marriage. *Shadows on Our Skin* is a third person narration, but much of it is focalised through Joe, enabling us to see the challenge which Joe offers to his father's inherited politics. In the later novels we see more developed acts of self-definition through self-expression: Nancy's reassessment of the values of the Big House, Helen's distancing herself from the slogans of militant

---

6 Jennifer Johnston, *The Railway Station Man* (London: Review, 1998), p. 1. First published London: Hamish Hamilton, 1984. Hereafter, page references will be incorporated into the text.

Nationalism, and both her and Sheila's rejection of the social ideology of marriage and the conventional codings of parenthood. The great danger is fossilisation. Johnston's fiction, as much as Friel's drama, emphasises the need to be able to respond productively to changing circumstances, to 'translate' the scripts of the past to ensure their relevance and usefulness to the present and the future.

After *Shadows on Our Skin*, there are only two other Johnston novels (out of a total of twelve) – *The Railway Station Man* (1984) and *The Illusionist* (1995) – which refer explicitly to the recent Troubles. Even these two novels are, first and foremost, expressions of the Romantic desire for individual freedom, their focus of attention the struggle of a central female character to achieve self-definition and self-fulfilment, the dream of an unconditioned life free from the controls of patriarchy, parenthood and politics. *The Railway Station Man* and *The Illusionist* are concerned with individuals struggling to compose (in both the existential and literary senses) their lives in the aftermath of political violence and marital breakdown. In an interview of 1995, Johnston, while declaring herself 'a republican', touched on her fictional concerns and values:

> What is important to me are values. My fixed point is how you react to people you love. I'm a woman and I'm Irish, but above all else I'm a writer and those two other things just happened to be part of my life. I'm trying to confront the agony of individuals getting on with their lives and not going mad in the process. It isn't all about sad, broken Ireland ... I don't care about the big issues. What I care about is how we manage to live with the big issues going on around us and how we manage to face ourselves.[7]

Johnston may be seen here as declaring her own independence as a writer from the pressure of history and the literary expectations deriving from Nationalism or postcolonialism. *The Railway Station Man* and *The Illusionist* would seem to say that for Johnston gender and sexual issues, not colonial oppression, are the most pressing political factors in women's lives. Yet, 'sad, broken Ireland' may be glimpsed in or behind the struggles of the protagonists of these two novels who are, first, writers, then women, and then Irish. Feminism can be importantly supportive of postcolonialism. Both patriarchy and imperialism exert analogous forms of domination, the experiences of women under patriarchy parallelling those of colonised subjects. Both feminism and postcolonialism oppose such domination. From a political perspective, the 'act of union' that is enacted in *The Railway Station Man* between Helen Cuffe and the Englishman in Ireland, Roger Hawthorne, is very much on Helen's terms, while in *The Illusionist* Sheila struggles to preserve her (Irish) name and identity

7 Jennifer Johnston, 'Prodding Republicanism', *Fortnight*, April 1995, pp 36–7.

from her English husband who wants to name and define her: 'He called me Star.'[8] The politics of aestheticism in the two novels is more contentious. To say that the protagonists' efforts to create an authentic identity tends to be conceived in aesthetic, gender and existential terms rather than political and moral terms begs obvious questions: are these simply novels of egotistical sensitivity? To what extent is their commitment to the sanctity of private feeling and an ideal of individual freedom pursued in defiance of history, politics and moral concern? Is is true that the world of Johnston's fiction is 'a small world', like Jane Austen's 'little bit of ivory two inches wide'?[9]

The majority of *The Railway Station Man* is told in the third person, but this third person narration is enveloped by opening and closing sections which are in the first person. The opening section introduces the entire narrative as memoir, the construction of a fifty year old woman, Helen Cuffe: 'At this moment, as I write these words ...' (1). Helen is an artist living in seclusion in Donegal, looking back, in elegiac mood, on the events of three years before when her English lover, the eponymous 'railway station man', Roger Hawthorne, and her son, Jack, were killed in an explosion. Heidi Hansson has described the significance of first person narration:

> To say 'I' is to claim integrity, which literally means wholeness and clearly contradicts the postmodern idea of a fractured self. The circumstance that a first person narrative usually establishes a coherent, speaking self therefore rather suggests a feminist position, since feminism presupposes a subject that can be liberated. At the same time, the use of so-called I-language undercuts the political impact of the texts by making them overtly personal.[10]

As teller of the tale, Helen occupies a position of power. She has the authority to determine the way events are presented. She is figured in the role of subject rather than object. At the same time, as Hansson points out, since first person narration is unavoidably subjective, it may be judged unreliable and therefore dismissable. This is particularly true of women's narratives, especially when they complicate or disturb conventional (male) positions: 'The truth of a first person narrative is thus compromised from the outset, which makes the strategy an instance of the postmodern preoccupation with the nature of truth as well as a liberating speech act.' *The Railway Station Man's* shift from first to third person narration may thus be read as Helen's

8 Jennifer Johnston, *The Illusionist* (London: Minerva, 1996), p. 5. First published London: Sinclair-Stevenson, 1995. Hereafter, page references will be incorporated into the text. 9 Rüdiger Imhof, 'A little bit of ivory two inches wide: the small world of Jennifer Johnston's fiction', *Études Irlandaises*, 10 (December 1985), pp 129–44. 10 Heidi Hansson, 'To say "I": female identity in *The Maid's Tale* and *The Wig My Father Wore*', in Elmer Kennedy-Andrews (ed.), *Irish Fiction since 1969* (Gerards Cross: Colin Smythe, 2002).

attempt to achieve aesthetic distance from her experience so that she can exert objective control over it. Structurally, that is, the novel expresses (female) desire for an omniscient authority.

As a fictional strategy, first person narration has an obvious attraction to the writer concerned with the individual's struggle for self-determination through self-expression. Recognising that existence is an aesthetic act, Helen struggles to become her own supreme fiction. This is a novel about Helen becoming her own author, refusing to let others speak for her, recovering the sense of self which she feels years of marriage and motherhood have threatened to obliterate. She is determined to reclaim freedom and subjectivity by rejecting the conventional female roles and expectations that have governed her life. She won't allow even her love for Roger to threaten her fledgling selfhood: 'I want to own myself' (201), she tells him. 'I don't want you to give me anything. I want my own space' (201), recognising that if freedom is Roger's gift it isn't really freedom. After rejecting his marriage proposal she notices a lark in the sky: ' "Hail to thee, blithe spirit", she shouted at the splintering sky' (202) – 'splintering' because of her tears, but also because feeling and relationship are threatening to disrupt freedom. In her experience, marriage has been a trap. Her husband, Dan, a mathematics teacher, is remembered as an oppressive, controlling influence. A 'neat, well-ordered man' (16), he lived by a rigid adherence to 'the structures' (16), and showed only philistine contempt for his wife's artistic interests. Helen's free spirit inevitably feels unbearably trammelled by marriage to a man who 'likes perspectives, neat lines, colours that matched and stayed inside confining lines' (5). Thinking back to Christmas 1975 and the moment she heard that Dan had been shot by terrorists who had mistaken him for an Inspector in the RUC, she says she cannot forgive his killers but that his death brought 'an amazing feeling of relief, liberation' (12). As so often in Johnston's novels, family inhibits or distorts the process of self-realisation. Helen would like to escape from parenthood as well as marriage: 'God-dammit, the disease of parenthood is terminal', she cries, and feels guilty for making Jack feel like 'an orphan' when he was growing up. As well as rejecting the conventional private world of marriage, family and parenthood, she rejects the public world of political action. Where Jack cynically dismisses individual human suffering as the unavoidable by-product of the necessary political action, Helen can only see the world in terms of individuals. Using Jack and and Helen, Johnston stages the debate between bourgeois liberal humanism and militant Republicanism, between the claims of personal freedom and those of political responsibility. It's a rather one-sided debate. Jack is presented as naively addicted to clichéd abstractions, she is sceptical and independent-minded. He is fixed in his beliefs, she is fluid, 'drifting'. Doubt is cast on the integrity of Jack's political commitment by his own admission that he is motivated by a desire for 'glory' (207) and a need to compensate for his bourgeois, Protestant, West Brit background; she responds imaginatively and courageously to the new possibilities of modernity by breaking from traditional social structures and obligations. Refusing the narratives of others, she accepts the existential challenge of authoring her own authentic narrative of personal identity. To do so she attempts to withdraw into an autonomous realm of the free imagination, and makes no apology for her committed ivory towerism: 'If my ivory tower, as you call it, falls down, I'll build another one' (156). She espouses a Romantic sense of the capacity of the imagination to redefine the oppressive, violent social world to form a new liberatory, individualistic, feminine order, which exists in the privileged realm of art. In this reading, *The Railway Station Man* is a typical modernist text concerned fundamentally with the artistic process itself, the struggle to affirm transcendence through art. Helen's narration, as an act of self-emancipation and self-definition, an assertion of idiosyncratic female identity, expresses itself as aesthetic reality. The coherence, significance and order that are absent in life are found in the aesthetics of composition. Life is redeemed through art. The raw materials of experience are lifted, first, into the subjective flow of Helen's first person, present tense stream of consciousness in the opening and closing sections of the novel, then transposed into her third person ordering of the events of the past (in the fictional present), and then integrated into a higher aesthetic unity or totality through the use of symbol, repetition, analogy and metaphor. The novel's 'meaning' is constructed not only through plot and character, but through a complex web of cross-references, equivalences and echoes which constitute a system of internal linguistic coherence. The references to 'needless deaths' and the larks in the first couple of pages reverberate in organicist fashion throughout the novel, acquiring larger contexts and meanings. Roger's repeated World War II memory of the 'poor mad creatures' wandering distractedly through the woods of Arnhem after the British bombed the asylum is used to generalise the present violence in the North, and is echoed by Helen in her closing image of Manus, a fugitive from his own violence, 'running up over the back hills. Cold hills with little shelter ... alone, frightened, exposed under the bright moon, the flinty stars, running'. However opposed she is to Manus, Helen herself identifies with the fugitive kind and the asylum patients. She is frequently referred to by others and by herself as 'mad': 'I'm not sure where the boundaries are between sanity and madness ... There is such a fine line between people who can accept the formalised madness of the world and those who can't' (112–13). 'Madness', she suggests, is in the world's eyes; it is the mark of individualists like Roger and herself. When Roger asks her if she thinks he's mad, she replies: 'We all have a right to live the way we want' (112), words which Roger later echoes: '"What's fact or fantasy?" he said. "Madness or sanity? We all live our lives in our own way"' (136). The novel, ending with Manus 'Running. Running', returns us to the point from which we started and the opening images of recovered stillness, quietness and rebuilding in the aftermath of the explosion: Damian has built a studio 'out of three tumbledown sheds', Helen 'wanted the sea imprisoned there for me alone' (1), she anticipates imposing some pattern on the traumatic events of her life. This open-ended, cyclical structure locks the characters into an historical, preordained pattern and enforces a fatalistic sense of history as the eternal recurrence of an essential, unchanging human condition. Through these totalising strategies Johnston may be seen to produce an effect of a self-contained, self-referring unified world of art in which the everyday problems of female identity and political struggle are transmuted into aesthetic form.

Yet Johnston may be shown not to really believe the autonomy theory often associated with modernism. A postmodernist or feminist reading will interrogate the possibility of autonomous identity divorced from history, nation and traditional values. Postmodernism questions ideas of unity and totality: feminism invokes notions of subjective transformation. From the postmodern/feminist perspective, Helen's aestheticising impulse towards self-transformation is always being checked and problematised by external conditions. If Johnston recognises the emancipatory potential of self, the possibility of authoring one's own aesthetic identity, she also insists, from the very opening words of her novel, on the inhuman cost, in terms of 'isolation' and 'insulation'. Only by shedding attachments is the imagination free to construct its own reality. As soon as Helen moves into the everyday social world she risks losing identity in someone else's (Roger's) gaze. But even when she remains sequestered in her private space she is not immune from the savagery of the outside world: 'God damn you, Jack, for throwing this rock into the pool of my isolation' (170), she protests, when she learns of her son's terrorist activity. She can only paint by denying relational ties, traditional situatedness as a woman, natural erotic impulses, family obligations, socially imposed roles, Even if such a self could be internally constructed and maintained, without engagement with history it would have no purchase on the world. Significantly, Helen's suite of four paintings to which she gives the title 'Man on a Beach' depicts the progressive elimination of man, much to Damian's chagrin: ' "Where am I?" he asked. "What have you done with me?" His voice sounded slightly panic-stricken, as if she had disposed of his reality in some way' (187–8). Helen's painting bears witness to the stark ideal of a non-human society. Vaguely, she recognises the impossibility of closing out the world of history. 'Three people are happy, she thought, as she pulled the curtains tight almost as if to keep out the world's unhappiness. That's a crazy sentimental thought if ever there was one' (189); while Roger counsels her to accept life by accepting life's imperfection: 'Only in art, Helen, is there any approach to perfection achieved' (175).

Ironically, in Helen's narrative of female self-discovery and self-assertion, it is two *men*, Roger and his helper Damian, who are given the most humane and balanced insights into the relationship between self and society. Roger is the mysterious outsider, generous, charming, curious about life, appreciative of art and crafts-manship, a non-coercive male, the bringer of dance and spontaneity and love to

Helen's insulated existence. Recalling the famous 'Hemingway hero', he's a bearer of scars, a war veteran haunted by a violent past and obsessed by 'all the needless dead', indifferent to conventional values and expectations, suspicious of abstract causes, free from illusions about politics or patriotism. In several ways he resembles Helen: both are impelled by a desire to hide away, both are victims of family pressures, both have experienced the public world as a threat to personal integrity and individuality, both wonder if they are 'mad' in wanting to live outside the usual social boundaries. Both are devoted to a principle of expressive freedom – Helen through her painting, Roger through restoring the railway station. But where she attempts to transcend relationship through art as sacred space, he wants to rescue self from an impossible ideal of autonomy which threatens love and relationship, and from an equally disastrous ideal of social commitment which results in 'needless deaths'. He represents a mode of imaginative realisation and empathy modelled on Christ's and Gandhi's example of 'courage', 'love' and 'commitment to lead the other way' (175), that is, the way of non-violence.

Damian is another artist-figure: 'In other times he would have made a most superior cabinet maker. Marvellous hands … imagination. A craftsman' (32). He is always ready to place his skills at Helen's disposal, even building her an artist's studio. He and Roger are united by their interest in 'craftsmanship' which transcends class, racial or political division. Like Roger, Damian is also an outcast, the topic of malicious rumour and local suspicion about his Provo connections. A contrast is developed between Jack's abstract, doctrinaire political commitment and Damian's more mature, humane view of political violence. Where Jack blithely dismisses the human suffering, Damian has learnt from his grandfather the tragedy and inhumanity of the necessary political action:

> 'You'll have to shoot them out, he used to say. They'll never go any other way. If you want them out you'll have to shoot them out. They simply don't understand the need that people have for freedom. People would rather be poor and suffer and be free. The English … he always talked about the English … don't understand a stupid thing like that. So you'll have to shoot them out lad, and the quicker the better'.
> 'Well? Wasn't he right?'
> 'He didn't think it was right. He thought it was inevitable … like an operation without an anaesthetic, painful and possibly maiming. To be born Irish is a bitter birth, lad'. (58–9)

Ends (a just social order) do not justify means (not even violence as means of last resort). By attributing this insight to members of the historically victimised group, Johnston confers upon it a powerful moral authority. The friendship which develops between Damian and Helen represents a border crossing for both characters, a movement on the part of each beyond inherited values and attitudes: the former Provo and the Protestant woman who has lost husband, lover and son to political violence achieve a durable if unequal friendship denied to Joe and Kathleen in *Shadows on Our Skin* or Alex and Jerry in *How Many Miles to Babylon?* For the first time, Johnston is able to imagine at least a minimally optimistic emblem of social reconciliation, allowing her to contemplate a future beyond simply isolation or flight.

At the other end of the spectrum from Helen's aesthetic, liberal humanist disengagement is the kind of rabid political commitment represented by Jack and Manus. Johnston's strongest criticisms are reserved for these two characters whose involvement in the 'big issues' exacts an even higher price on their humanity than Helen's isolationist aestheticism does on hers. Manus is a dangerous, renegade Provo with strongly fascistic tendencies. Diametrically opposed to all that Helen stands for, he is the philistine proponent of art's subordination to political usefulness. His so-called political commitment is no more honourable than Jack's, and just as self-serving: 'Manus doesn't believe in democracy, Manus likes to run things his own way' (167). Johnston's liberal humanism finds it hard to extend any kind of moral seriousness to political violence, whatever her sympathies with the ends it avowedly serves.

Her central character is the individual trying to get on with life and not going mad in the process, trying to live with the big issues going on around her. Though Helen nominally controls the narrative, she resists the grand narratives of family, nation, justice, reason, and refuses final answers: 'All those questions', she says at the end, 'And no answers' (216). Her narrative resists the rule of logic and rationalism – 'I'll always prefer my mysteries to your conclusions' (156), she tells Jack. In her opening first person narration she speaks out of the flux of consciousness, addressing the reader directly, to remind us of the constructed, provisional nature of her story: 'I had hoped not to explain. Explanations are so tedious for the writer as well as the reader ...' (4); 'I remember so little of those years. It's probably just as well otherwise I might bore you with tedious domestic details' (8). The reality she proceeds to construct is notably attenuated by ghostly presences, the frequent eruptions of the unconscious. By incorporating bits of background film sound-track or snatches of songs playing on the gramophone, or by including intertextual references to poems (especially Yeats's 'Song of Wandering Aengus' and Shelley's 'To a Skylark') she elaborates an ironic counternarrative that amplifies but also destabilises the novel. The view from postmodernism, feminism or postcolonialism highlights the internal contradictions in Johnston's ostensible adherence to modernist notions of autonomy and allows us to recognise the authorial anxiety in Helen's efforts to lay the ghosts of obligation.

The Illusionist is a consistently first person narration, and it bears many similarities to the story of *The Railway Station Man*. Like *The Railway Station Man*, *The*

Illusionist presents the challenge offered by an emergent, self-assertive female voice to a patriarchal 'dominant', represented in the later novel by a charming but oppressively controlling husband, Martyn, the 'illusionist' of the title. Like Helen Cuffe's husband, Dan, Sheila's estranged husband, Martyn, is a victim of terrorist violence: 'Perhaps it was the sort of end he would have wished; here one minute and gone the next. A sleight-of-hand ending to his invented life. An IRA bomb in a London street and Martyn in his station wagon with a hundred and fifty white doves neatly caged in the back' (90). As the note of wry humour here would suggest, the Troubles do not stimulate the usual narrative of liberal humanist protest against man's inhumanity to man. Rather, the novel's central concern is man's inhumanity to woman within the estate of marriage. The Irish theme is remote and marginal. Though Sheila is Irish and returns to live in Dublin after the break-up of her marriage, her narrative refers to that period of her life spent in London and Suffolk and there is little sense of her character as a product of a particular (Irish) place. Martyn's death is not the book's decisive event. His death is important only insofar as it precipitates Sheila's story of her marriage to Martyn which ended fifteen years before. The bomb which kills him is more *deus ex machina*, a fictional device, than a manifestation of the motion of history. Johnston is not interested in the historical and political situation which produced the bombing, nor in consequences beyond the effects which the bombing has on the personal lives of Robin (Martyn and Sheila's daughter) and Sheila. Her main concerns are the intimate details of people's lives, characters and personal relationships, not the 'big issues'. Yet from the perspective of postcolonialism, Sheila's revolt against patriarchy and her struggle for existential and artistic freedom may be read as a potent allegory of decolonisation.

Though Johnston has lived in Northern Ireland throughout most of the period of the Troubles, settling near Derry after her second marriage in 1979, she has written relatively little fiction that is centrally concerned with the current situation in the North – *Shadows on Our Skin* and *The Railway Station Man* are the exceptions. In the rest of her work she seems either to escape into the past, the South or private worlds where the convulsions in the North could, apparently, be repressed if not ignored. I propose to provide a context for a couple of these novels which have no ostensible connection with the Troubles of the '70s by placing them next to the Northern situation within which they were written. In doing so, I hope to draw out an oblique, disrupted fictional perspective on the Northern Troubles, and to indicate the novels' relevance to contemporary social and intellectual debate on the North. Thus, an early novel, *How Many Miles to Babylon?* concentrates on the First World War, but, as Johnston explained in an interview, the First World War had for her important connections with the contemporary Troubles:

The effect that World War I had – the massacre of a whole generation of young men – embittered a large number of people who remained. In Ireland, it was the beginnings of the troubles we are now in. I'm not denigrating what happened in 1916, because I think it was a piece of magnificent nonsense. It should never have happened, but it was magnificent, and it, in fact, probably is the reason why Ireland is in the terrible situation it is in now. I think that, had the uprising not happened, come 1918, we would have had Home Rule. There would have been no problems about the North because the British wouldn't have allowed there to be problems, and we would have moved on from there in some cumbersome but logical way to being a Republic. Once that happened, something cracked in us and we suddenly saw ourselves as people with freedom dangling in front of us, and we couldn't wait any longer. Therefore, that war had had an extraordinary effect on the country ... I think I used it as a metaphor for what is presently happening.[11]

The 'woman's writing' paradigm is also not without relevance in approaching *How Many Miles to Babylon?* Though concentrating on major events in world history and adopting the male point of view of Alex Moore, the novel preserves and exploits the dichotomy between the feminised, sacred space of private feeling and personal relationships, and the threatening, 'masculine' domain of war and politics. In accordance with the standard revisionist, demythologising line which Johnston takes in her interview, she constructs the traditionally antagonistic colonial situation in terms of a homo-erotic relationship between Protestant Anglo-Irish Alex from the Big House and native Catholic peasant Gerry who works on the Big House estate. Their self-sacrificial friendship transcends the barriers of race, creed and class. The union of the two characters functions as a metaphor for an evolved, peaceful political consolidation and social integration at a time of historical crisis. Through Alex and Jerry's relationship, Johnston imagines a 'nationalising embrace', the reconciliation of divided Ireland. Jerry, in espousing the ideas of Patrick Pearse and joining the British army to learn his trade for the Republican cause, represents the Irish will to self-determination. Alex belongs to a progressive socially responsible strand of Anglo-Ireland which is receptive to change. His father, in attempting to dissuade his wife from encouraging Alex to join the British army, tells her: 'I have never aspired to being an Englishman. Nor have I such aspiration for my son' (40). And to Alex he confides: 'Things will change. Here, I mean. I'm not talking about the outside world ... Here, the land must come first. You understand. It is this country's heart. It was taken from the people.

11 'Q and A with Jennifer Johnston', *Irish Literary Supplement*, Fall 1984; in Jurgen Kamm, 'Jennifer Johnston', in Rudiger Imhof (ed.), *Contemporary Irish Novelists* (Tubingen: Gunter narr 1990), pp 125–41, pp 126–7.

We ... I must be clear ... We took it from the people. I would like to feel that it will, when the moment comes, be handed back in good order' (42–3). Later, Alex, in countering Jerry's revolutionary Nationalism, articulates the dream of reconciliation: 'We need each other though. Your kind and mine. You'll see' (111). The novel expresses a preference for a version of the 'national romance' over a revolutionary Romantic Nationalism. But even though Alex and Jerry can both look forward to a new social and state order, the relationship between the two characters ends tragically as a direct result of their entanglements in the British institutional system of military discipline. Read against the contemporary Northern crisis, the novel's dream of reconciliation in an all-Ireland context is further radically problematised. Northern Protestantism constitutes a kind of political unconscious of the novel. In an interview, Johnston complained about the intransigence of Northern Protestants who stand in the way of the attainment of her Republican ideal:

> I am a republican, but I am also concerned with the Protestant faith. I find it hard that, in the north, Protestants are unable to address their heritage and refuse to stand up and say 'We are still here because we want to be here and we are not going to put up with this shit'. We must look to reality and decide that we want to be part of this heritage and stop looking at it as oppression.[12]

Joe Cleary has pointed out how the Northern Irish 'love-across-the-divide' story (epitomised by Joan Lingard's fiction, Bernard MacLaverty's *Cal*, Neil Jordan's *The Crying Game*), 'cannot emerge as a full-fledged "national romance" celebrating the consolidation of the Northern Irish State unless it takes the form of a unionist wish-fantasy and ignores the hostility of Northern nationalists';[13] similarly, the all-Ireland love-across-the-divide story, in aspiring to symbolise the process of state consolidation, can only produce a Nationalist wish-fantasy which ignores the hostility of Northern Unionists. In both cases, the result is 'a despairing flight from politics'[14] and retreat into private worlds.

The Old Jest (1979) is another of Johnston's novels which may be seen to comment indirectly on the contemporary Troubles. Set in 1920 during the Anglo-Irish War, the novel moves back and forth between first and third person narration. Like her Swiftian namesake, Nancy Gulliver is engaged in a journey of self-discovery. Hers is one of the first of Johnston's narratives of female self-determination. The opening diary entry, on the day of her eighteenth birthday, begins, 'Today I want to become a person'.[15] She must do so as the old, traditional Ascendancy world which she has

12 Jennifer Johnston, 'Prodding Republicanism', *Fortnight* 36–7.   13 Joe Cleary, '"Fork-Tongued on the border bit"', p. 241.   14 Ibid., p. 241.   15 Jennifer Johnston, *The Old Jest* (Glasgow: Fontana, 1980), p. 10. First published London: Hamish Hamilton, 1979. Hereafter, page references will be incorporated into the text.

known all her life disintegrates, its collapse not only lamented but understood and accepted. Without mother and father, her home about to be sold, surrounded by death, violence and political disturbance, unsure of her feelings and loyalties, confused by sexual desire, she confronts 'Troubles' of both a personal and political nature. The novel ends with Nancy's words: 'The great thing is you can always chose, and then, as Bridie says, you've no one to blame but yourself' (158). The eight days covered by the novel are the period of Nancy's 'awakening'. During this time she grows up, begins to choose for herself what she will think and feel, and acquires experience of a wider world beyond the carefully guarded limits of her Ascendancy upbringing. She is a model of the existential heroine engaged in the process of discovering the grounds of an authentic existence, one without illusion, but also without despair.

Ranged around Nancy are various influences and pressures with which she must negotiate in order to construct her story and her life. Chief of these is the mysterious figure of Major Angus Barry aka the 'Travelling Man' and 'Cassius' ('the beastly conspirator'[72]), who Nancy momentarily thinks might be her long-lost father. He is, rather, her spiritual father, a postmodernist guru who regales Nancy with the benefit of his experience. Refusing any fixed identity and any encumbrance from the past, Barry continually stresses the uncertainty of life and meaning but, equally, he insists on the need to 'feel you have a reason for being alive' (57). This involves being continually open to change and experience; it involves improvising a life for yourself, avoiding fixity which is a kind of death, being prepared to fight for what you believe:

'By and large man has to pick up the use of his functions as he goes along. It's important to understand that. The young have no patience'.

'When the war is over ... what will happen then?'

He laughed.

'There'll be another one ... I mean the people fighting together now will fight each other. It always happens like that'.

She took another sip from her cup.

'Then the people who win will sit on their thrones and exploit everyone, just the way they've been exploited before. It will be very sad and little progress will have been made. Some people will have too much to eat and others not enough'.

'It all seems very pointless. Why do you do it?'

'Me? I'm not fighting specifically against the British. I hope I'm fighting for the people. I don't want power. I want to see justice for everyone and I'm prepared to kill anyone who seriously threatens ...' (68–9)

Barry, scion of the Anglo-Irish Ascendancy, has turned traitor to his class. Defying all the usual categories, he is the ultimate boundary crosser. The most difficult lesson of all that he passes on to Nancy is that concerning the justification of revolutionary violence;

> 'There are conscienceless men, utterly unscrupulous, who will go to any lengths to make sure that the world remains the way they want it to remain. No possibility of change. They crush and destroy ... aspirations ... hope. People must at least be allowed to hope'.
>
> 'It's the killing ...'
>
> 'After all', he said gently, 'your grandfather was a killer too, no one makes sarcastic remarks at him for that. Not at all. They gave him medals and a pension'. (100)

Also assisting in Nancy's emotional and political development is the young Dublin revolutionary, Joe Mulhare. His vitality, quick wit and lively humour make him a strikingly personable contrast both to the moribund dinosaurs of the Big House, and to the usual demonic representations of the terrorist. The spirit of youth and drive, herald of a new revolutionary consciousness, Joe speaks for political commitment and activism: 'When people ask for rights and don't get them, then they have to fight' (116). In allowing herself to be drawn into the secret world of the urban guerilla, Nancy repudiates the kind of middle-class respectability and conservatism epitomised by Harry, the young man whom she initially idealises. Harry is a Dublin stock-broker who captivates the naive Nancy with his male strength and assurance: 'There is really no need to be frightened if you're with Harry; nothing terrible could ever happen to you when you are with him' (50). Harry is supremely sane, practical, ambitious and rigidly conventional. He marries Maeve, whose father, a Catholic land-developer, is buying the Big House. The future, it would seem, lies with the Harrys and Maeves, the men and women who are 'not amazing in any way' (36), the people with small souls and modest dreams, the conscientious materialists who don't want trouble. Nancy's changed relationship with Harry in the course of the novel marks her own achievement of maturity. Recognising his narrow snobbery, his complacency and lack of insight and feeling, Nancy has no enthusiasm for the kind of brave new world the newly monied middle-class will usher into existence: 'He will keep the place up to the mark and she will play her white piano in the drawing room and they will never notice our bruised ghosts lurking in the corners' (96).

In moving towards a political commitment, Nancy recognises the need to reassess her Ascendancy values and attitudes. The decay of the old order is powerfully suggested by the decrepitude of Grandfather, nominal head of the Big House, the last male in the line, immobilised in a wheelchair, rambling in his senility, lost to the past and no longer able to direct affairs. But even Aunt Mary, echoing Barry's words, recognises the need to confront reality and adapt to changing circumstances:

'Everything's changing. You must realise that. I suppose it's for the best, but I don't imagine I will ever know for sure. Change takes time. You must be part of that. That's important. You must move, re-energise. Don't just drift as I have always done' (94). Accepting that the old, aristocratic way of life has to give way to modern commercial interest, she faces the inevitable with dignity and a humane concern that Grandfather won't be made to suffer too much in the transition. At dinner with Aunt Mary and the Miss Brabazons in the aftermath of the shooting of the twelve British soldiers at the Curragh, Nancy announces her Republican sympathies, to the consternation of all present. Aunt Mary at this point is still 'drifting', even attempting to deny that there is a war. Miss Brabazon disallows such evasiveness: 'Of course it's a war, Mary dear, whether you like it or not, and one day you're going to have to decide which side you're on. Nancy, for what it's worth, seems to have made her decision'. However, by the end of the novel, when interrogated by the British Army captain, Aunt Mary lies to protect Barry, demonstrating that even she has the capacity to cross the conventional boundaries of her class.

The Big House civilisation as it is presented in the novel is not a malicious or satirical portrait. Johnston's Ascendancy is less obdurately set against facing up to reality than Elizabeth Bowen's. Nancy's Republican sympathies are balanced by her affectionate Yeatsian regard for the grace and 'gentleness' of an old order:

> My most beautiful and tender memories will always be of this place, even this simple moment – the drone of bees, the smell through the kitchen door of baking bread, the shadows on the cobblestones, Bridie rattling her sweeping brush out of an upstairs window. I have inside me that gentleness, that calm, from which to begin to explore the real life that waits. I can never be undermined because of that. Maybe that is just hopefulness. Though nothing will ever be the same, I can draw on the strength that this way of living has given me ... (129)

Read against the Northern Irish context in which the novel was written, *The Old Jest* projects a discourse of anti-colonial Nationalism supported by existentialist notions of choice and 'commitment', and the evocation of a civilised, aristocratic ideal derived from colonial influence and symbolised by the disappearing Big House.

Feminising Marxism: Mary Beckett's *Give Them Stones* (1987)

Give Them Stones is the first person narrative of Martha Murtagh and tells the story of the struggle of a strong, independent-minded woman to define and maintain a sense of herself in an oppressively patriarchal society, amidst the pressures not only of marriage and family, but of colonialism and paramilitarism. The novel begins with a description of the knee-capping of a youth by the IRA outside Martha's home bakery on the Falls Road. Her reaction immediately establishes the kind of character she is – principled, courageous, determined to speak out against cruelty and injustice:

> I was telling myself that I couldn't keep quiet about this. I had kept my head down long enough, so careful of myself, frightened of any change, never taking any risks. But I'd have no respect at all for myself if I didn't let them know what I thought. I'd tell them they were getting no more money from me in their weekly collection and I'd tell them why.[16]

The narrative then moves back in time from the 1980s to Martha's childhood in the 1920s, sketching in more of her origins and family background. Martha recalls the poverty of her early life, Protestant intimidation of Catholics in the Belfast shipyards, the internment of her father and uncle in the '20s, her decision to leave school at fourteen to go to work in the local mill. The two main political influences in her childhood are her Uncle Jimmy's traditional Nationalism and, contrarily, her Uncle Joe's espousal of militant socialism. She remembers Uncle Joe's favourite saying that he had learnt from a book and that gives the novel its title: 'When they ask for bread don't give them crackers as does the Church, and don't, like the State, tell them to eat cake. Explain that man cannot live by bread alone and give them stones' (15). Martha springs from a tradition of resistance and revolt. Her own story, as we come to see, is poised between the claims of an insular Nationalism and transnational socialism. As a child she thrills to her father's stories of Wolfe Tone and the United Irishmen, and is filled with a sentimental longing for a recovered national vitality and dignity: 'I'd think wouldn't it be lovely if it were really our own country that we could be proud in, instead of being kept in cramped little streets with no jobs for the men and sneered at by the people who deprived us. it was as if we were all in prison looking out at a beautiful world we'd never walk free in' (18). Later, she expresses her admiration of Bernadette Devlin and Gerry Fitt, 'but would have liked them better if they had said they wanted a united Ireland' (117). At this stage, so entranced is she by the Nationalist dream that she remains oblivious to the materialist basis of Tone's, Devlin's and Fitt's political projects. But from the beginning Martha is also – at least symbolically – closely associated with the labour movement. Her Uncle Joe remembers that 'she was born in the General Strike in January 1926' (15). As an adult, she adopts a materialist, not a nationalist, outlook and identity when she opens a home bakery. Reversing her Uncle Joe's nostrum, she opts to give the people bread, not stones,

---

16 Mary Beckett, *Give Them Stones* (New York: Beech Tree Books, William Morrow, 1987), p. 10. Hereafter, page references will be incorporated into the text.

adapting the traditional female role of nurturer to an economic and business agenda. After spending the war years as an evacuee with elderly aunts in the country, she returns to Belfast in 1946 and, after marrying Dermot, sets up a bakery business in order to be financially independent of her husband, and to raise four sons. She is driven not simply by a profit-making motive, for she gives her bread away free when the local women are unable to pay. Moreover, her business fulfils a social need, for she enjoys the company of the women who are her customers. As the critic Megan Sullivan insists, Beckett, through the characterisation of Martha, defies the Marxist definition of 'labour' and 'value'.

Martha defies other labellings as well, specifically the meanings which the colonial power and the paramilitaries alike would attempt to impose upon her. Not long after the arrival of the British Army in the North, an army officer visits to find out why Martha has refused to serve his soldiers:

> 'Are you a Republican?' he asked and I shrugged. I was going to be a heroine but instead I said, 'I am a home baker.'
> Other women came in and he strode out.
> 'What did he want?' they asked. 'What was all that about?'
> 'I don't want the soldiers in this shop any more,' I said. 'He tried to find out why'. (123)

When her son Danny, an IRA man, is shot, she is visited by another army officer, asking why she had closed her shop. Again, she refuses to be defined by, or to be answerable to, the representative of the colonial power:

> 'You closed in sympathy with an IRA man?' he asked.
> I just shrugged. It was none of his business.
> 'Was it a gesture of defiance?' he demanded.
> 'It's a very wee shop,' I said, 'and your men aren't allowed in here so it couldn't matter to them.'
> 'Were you intimidated?' he asked and I was raging.
> 'Listen, you,' I said, 'it's my shop and my business and I'll open or shut as I please and nobody intimidates me'. (126)

The next day British soldiers descend upon her shop and search it roughly. Acknowledging only the identity of woman worker, Martha must submit to the colonial power which punishes those recalcitrant subjects who refuse to 'work' on its terms. But Martha insists on remaining independent. She refuses to allow herself to be 'commodified' or used by either the British army or the paramilitaries for their own purposes. She is eventually burnt out of her home and shop for not paying protection money to the IRA. At the end, unbowed and unbroken, she looks forward to life in a new house and continuing her business in new premises. She becomes a symbol of the free, indomitable human spirit.

Megan Sullivan emphasises what she sees as Beckett's progressive feminist treatment of women's political and sexual identity in terms of an application of Marxist theory to women in (post)colonial locations:

> In a particularly feminist re-reading of nationalist ideology and materialist politics, Beckett's text demonstrates that Martha the worker and business owner provides bread (the 'stones' of the novel's title) for women and encourages them to brandish this 'useful thing' as sustenance against the nationalist, Republican, and state forces that oppress them.[17]

Sullivan's reading suppresses other lines of development in Beckett's characterisation of Martha. If, through Martha, Beckett crystallises a positive image of female self-definition, there is also recognition of the limits of the philosophy of self-reliance. Martha's development may thus also be seen as a move away from a strict feminist self-sufficiency, which borders on self-absorption, towards both tentative embracement of party politics and a new, albeit qualified, sense of the mutuality of marriage. Martha does not end up as detached from Republican politics as Sullivan suggests, for after Dermot gains compensation for loss of their home with the help of Sinn Féin, Martha realises the material benefits of solidarity with an organised political party. Similarly, she comes to consider the potential of marriage as a business partnership. The novel closes with these words:

> 'Dermot,' I said, shaking his shoulder a bit. 'Will you help me to see about a grant or a loan or something to open a new bread shop?'
> 'I'll do anything at all for you,' he said, only a wee bit awake.
> 'Anything in the world for you, Martha.' It was not true, of course. He wouldn't even give me any money unless I kept on at him. Maybe he thought it was true, though. At any rate, it was nice to listen to. After all, maybe I don't always face the truth about myself either.' (152)

While Martha's may be the strong voice of female independence and determination, as a character she is emotionally repressed, deadly humourless and utterly charmless. Her priggish rectitude and puritan rigidity are not at all attractive. She seems to be drawn into marriage more by the sight of Dermot's mother's gas stove

17 Megan Sullivan, '"Instead I said I am a home baker": nationalist ideology and materialist politics in Mary Beckett's *Give Them Stones*', in Kathryn Kirkpatrick (ed.), *Border Crossings: Irish Women Writers and National Identities* (Dublin: Wolfhound, 2000), pp 227–49, p. 245.

than by Dermot himself. Throughout, she remains coldly detached from both husband and children: 'One morning Dermot came out of the house and stood there beside me. I glanced up at him and found him looking down at me with the same fondness that he used to have for his mother. I couldn't have that at all. I went back into the shop and started brushing everywhere' (137). Dermot's anxiety about her after they are burnt out of home and shop is summarily dismissed, and she refuses to give him the least comfort and support after he has lost what he has always regarded as his family home. Perversely and self-pityingly, she thinks that Dermot 'doesn't care a thing about me' (147) – this of a perennially good-natured man who from the moment Martha decides to start a business has given practical help – looking after the children, building her a shed from which to sell her bread, offering to serve in the shop. When the flood ruins her flour, he buys her another bag, but she is unable to express her gratitude: ' "Thank you," I said, "oh, thank you. I am grateful." I felt that he was good, that I didn't treat him properly, that I should hug him and put my head on his chest but I couldn't do that in front of the children and besides I didn't want to change the way things were. If I got closer to Dermot there would be another boy baby to look after before Christmas' (111). She admits that the only thing which gives her a sense of value is baking bread. Her eldest son, Patrick, shocks her not only by telling her of his rejection of his religion but by his matter-of-fact acceptance that his mother was always too busy to be bothered with her family: ' "You're not pretending to be worried about me?" he said. "That'd be a bit of a change. You never had any time for us all our lives, not one of us. All you cared about was your baking and your shop" ' (139). At the end, Martha momentarily admits self-doubt – 'maybe I don't always face the truth about myself either'. However, the novel, lacking any self-interrogating, self-reflexive dimension, is unable to exploit the narrative potential of Martha's closing acknowledgement.

Where Sullivan applauds the novel for its inauguration of an Ulster feminist icon, Eve Patten, writing from a postmodern, pluralist point of view, objects to the novel's centripetal, mythologising tendencies. While presenting Martha's refusal of stereotypical categorisation, whether that imposed by the agents of colonialism (the British army officers), paramilitarism (the local IRA) or patriarchy (Martha's husband, Irish society at large), Beckett runs the risk, in Patten's view, of freeing her subject from one kind of stereotype only to imprison her in another – that of 'struggling woman'. As a character, Martha is produced and legitimised through an unambitious Realism in which verisimilitude is sought through a combination of 'fictional bio-graphy' and a 'documentating of recent history (or one side of it at least)' which 'is never more than one step from reportage':

> The identity of the stoical female protagonist becomes archetypal via the experience of the individual, and Beckett's book becomes a sociological tract ...

This is not, in itself, a problem, but it points to a dangerous trend; namely, that a fictional biography of a woman, intertwined with the political history by which it is determined, is somehow sacrosanct and above imaginative distortion. Beckett's novel confers authenticity on one kind of woman's experience in the north of Ireland, to the exclusion, we must assume, of other experiences ... One distinct identity is promoted as valid. Others are not.[18]

Patten objects to Beckett's kind of novel for its limited representation of female identity, which is seen as a consequence of the novel's lack of style and imagination, its failure to challenge the conventional relationship between political reality and fictional narrative. Operating within restrictive Realist perspectives, the novel closes itself off from irony and self-consciousness.

The return of the repressed: *House of Splendid Isolation* (1994)

House of Splendid Isolation, though set in the environs of Limerick, presents a terrorised community, like that of the North, where the Garda are on the same side as the British army and the RUC against the threat posed by the IRA. A notorious IRA man, Frank McGreevy, has fled South and seeks sanctuary in the decaying big house of an old woman, Josie O'Meara, whose uncle had been killed in the '20s by the Black and Tans. Despite her Republican attachments, Josie is revolted by the current violence in the North and by the reputation of her unwelcome visitor. However, her feelings of civilised outrage are complicated as she overcomes prejudice against the fugitive, and begins to see him as an individual human being, an activist motivated by a desire for 'Justice. Personal identity. Truth',[19] deeply and sincerely committed to the fight for his country's freedom. Compared to earlier fiction such as Terence de Vere White's *The Distance and the Dark*, Eugene McCabe's *Victims*, Benedict Kiely's *Proxopera* or Brian Moore's *Lies of Silence*, *House of Splendid Isolation* builds up, through the old woman's interactions with McGreevy, an increasingly sympathetic picture of the terrorist.

The novel reflects O'Brien's own strong Republican sympathies. Patrick Magee tells us that 'McGreevy is a composite created from O'Brien's meetings with several republicans she visited in Portlaoise prison, although the main influence for the character is widely held to be Dominic McGlinchey'.[20] McGlinchey became leader of the Irish National Liberation Army (INLA) in 1982 and, as the historian Tim Pat Coogan explains, was 'for a time the best-known Republican leader in Ireland. Some

18 Eve Patten, 'Women & Fiction 1985–1990', *Krino*, pp 2–3.   19 Edna O'Brien, *The House of Splendid Isolation* (London: Phoenix, 1997), p. 98. First published London: Weidenfeld & Nicolson, 1994. Hereafter, page references will be incorporated into the text.   20 P.J. Magee, *Troubles Fiction*, Appendix, p. 47.

of the worst atrocities of the entire Troubles took place under him'.[21] McGlinchey's terrorist career began when, at the age of seventeen, he joined the Provisionals after his release from Long Kesh, following the internment swoops of 1971. He became, says Coogan, 'a legendary figure in his native South Derry',[22] even incorporating 'something of a Robin Hood element into his image'.[23] In 1977 he was captured by the Gardai and began a five-year prison sentence in Portlaoise. During this time he seems to have fallen out with the Provos and joined the INLA. According to Coogan, McGlinchey was responsible for 'scores of deaths ... many of these by his own hand',[24] including the deaths of eleven soldiers and six civilians in the Droppin' Well Inn bombing at Ballykelly in 1982, and of three members of the congregation in the 'Darkley massacre' in South Armagh in 1983 when terrorists sprayed a gospel service with bullets. A dictatorial and ruthless leader, McGlinchey is reported to have conducted interrogations 'with the aid of instruments such as a red-hot poker'.[25] In her reference to McGreevy's wife's murder in the novel, O'Brien reflects something of the circumstances of McGlinchey's wife's violent death in 1987, when two terrorists burst into her Dundalk home and shot her while she was bathing their two young children. McGlinchey himself was murdered in front of his son in a Drogheda street in 1994, apparently by revenge-seeking ex-colleagues. Coogan, who also visited McGlinchey in Portlaoise, was – like O'Brien – evidently attracted by the ordinary humanity of the man: 'Short, slight, balding, he seemed tired, reduced by his past and by prison, and in no way threatening or a "mad dog"' – he appeared to be chiefly concerned with making good his promise to devote time and care to his children.'[26]

During the early '90s O'Brien was also closely associated with Gerry Adams, the Sinn Féin leader, whom she admiringly described in an American paper as 'thoughtful and reserved, a lithe, handsome man ... Given a different incarnation in a different century, one could imagine him as one of those monks transcribing the gospel into Gaelic.'[27] More than twenty years earlier she had made clear where her political loyalties lay:

> When I was in Derry recently I had a strong wish to be shot by the British
> Army, and that for two reasons – to bring to the attention of the world – however
> fleetingly – a world apparently inured to everything but a splashy death;
> that the British Army have been shooting and continuing to shoot on Irish
> soil ... Ireland is the world's problem as much as Czechoslovakia was in 1969 ...
> The second reason for the momentary death wish was paradoxical. My own
> people, that is to say the Catholics, regarded me as another kind of traitor; the
> inference being 'you from the South, you forgot us, let us down' ... I did not

21 Tim Pat Coogan, *The Troubles*, p.329.   22 Ibid., p. 329.   23 Ibid., p. 330.   24 Ibid.   25 Ibid., p. 331.
26 Ibid., p. 330–1.   27 Reported by James Adams in the *Sunday Times*, 6 February. 1994, pp 10–11, under the caption 'Kneecapped! How Gerry Adams' US visit crippled the special relationship'.

even have the self sop of being a sympathetic journalist. Easy therefore the death wish when one wanted to say 'I feel for you, I am with you, I don't know how else to express it'.[28]

This longing to say something on the subject of the Troubles may have been partly fulfilled by *House of Splendid Isolation*, the only one of her novels to engage with the Northern conflict. Noting that the novel was written before the cease-fires in 1994, Sandra Pearce asked O'Brien in an interview two years later if the novelist saw 'a possibility for peace' in 1996. O'Brien's reply reiterated the official Republican line:

> The reins of peace are in England's hands, but John Major (at the time of the interview, John Major was Prime Minister) depends on Unionist votes to carry certain bills through Parliament, in fact, not to bring the government down. It's as simple as that. So, since the cease-fire, there's been a lot of talk about the peace 'process', but there hasn't been anything that I could say to you, or that any reasonable person could say to you, that England had done to move it on. They haven't. Now the intermediate reasoning of John Major or indeed Tony Blair is – we support the Union so we can't rock the boat. But behind it is something much deeper and more bitter which is that Ireland is the last wound of British imperialism. There is no doubt about that. Everybody talks about the violence of the IRA and the IRA have been very violent, but let us also talk about the violence of the SAS, of the Ulster paramilitaries. As many Catholics as Protestants were killed in the last twenty-five years. That's not mentioned. That's not given the headlines. We have to be very, very candid. We have to put all the deaths on the table. The second difficulty, and England knows it, is to shift the intransigent stance of Unionists. Their mantra is 'No Surrender!' But that means stasis. Constitutional change, cross-border liaison with the South and above all the police to become a mixed force of Catholics and Protestants – these are the first steps toward change. And Unionists will oppose them to the bitter end.[29]

House of Splendid Isolation offers a more interesting, complex and imaginatively involved picture of the situation, in line with the artistic credo which O'Brien also articulates in her interview with Pearce – 'The text is all that matters – over political correctness or any other dogmatism'.[30] The novel is no straightforward polemic of solidarity with 'my people', no simple romanticisation of the gunman. It is candid

---

28 Edna O'Brien, 'A reason of one's own', *Times Saturday Review*, September 30, 1972. Quoted by Raymonde Popot, 'Edna O'Brien's Paradise Lost', in Patrick Rafroidi (ed.), *The Irish Novel in Our Time* (Publications de L'Université de Lille), p. 285. 29 Edna O'Brien in Interview with Sandra Pearce, *Canadian Journal of Irish Studies*, 22, 2 (December 1996), pp 5–8, p.6. 30 Ibid., p. 8.

enough to talk in detail about 'the violence of the IRA', and reveals a view from the South that is deeply ambivalent. McGreevy's invasion of Josie's house initiates the tragic encounter of two 'Irelands': the old, ailing, traditionally victimised female Ireland, and the new, self-assertive, masculine Ireland. In her 1976 semi-auto-biographical commentary on Ireland, *Mother Ireland*, O'Brien follows standard Nationalist practice in feminising Ireland:

> Countries are either mothers or fathers, and engender the emotional bristle secretly reserved for either sire. Ireland has always been a woman, a womb, a cave, a cow, a Rosaleen, a sow, a bride, a harlot, and, of course, the gaunt Hag of Beare.[31]

Josie is an ironic composite of Irish female experience – emigrant, serving girl, abused wife, abandoned lover, and now the exploited 'woman of the house' (76) of Irish tradition. But unlike the Shan Van Vocht, Cathleen Ni Houlihan, the 'poor old woman' who demands the blood-sacrifice of her sons in order to rejuvenate the nation, Josie is repelled by McGreevy's militarism, claiming a gendered superiority over a destructive masculinity: 'If women ran your organisation there would be no shooting ... no bombs' (77). To the extent that Josie's story is one of determined, anti-patriarchal personal struggle for her woman's rights and place in marriage, she is a figure of reconstructed Irish womanhood. But though she has attained certain freedoms in the personal sphere, she has done so at a terrible price, including the life of her unborn child. Politics represent another kind of male threat, which she reveals herself tragically unable to deal with. She attempts to deny politics: 'Politics were one thing when brave men were shot long ago for their beliefs, or brave women hid volunteers in settle beds or churns, but politics had become a racket, hijacking, robberies, mindless assassinations' (53–4). However, she discovers that she cannot claim political innocence: 'The dark threads of history looping back and forth and catching her and people like her in their grip, like snares' (54). Unwittingly, her interventions in the political world lead to the deaths, first of her husband James, and then, twenty years later, of McGreevy. Torn between a humane impulse to avert further killing and loyalty to the killer whom she has come to love, Josie's ambivalence proves fatal to both McGreevy and herself. Her loyalty to McGreevy stems from personal feeling rather than ideological solidarity. She never accepts the moral legitimacy of the IRA man's actions but learns respect for his commitment to an ideal and is attracted to him as a man.

The views of others in the novel are used to amplify the sense of ambivalence in the Southern attitude to IRA violence. Rory the Guard exhibits a professional interest

---

31 Edna O'Brien, *Mother Ireland* (Weidenfeld and Nicolson, 1976), p. 11.

in seeing McGreevy caught, but evinces a secret admiration of the excitement of the fugitive's life, and of his courage and skill in evading capture: 'Even in his outrage he gave the fella credit and said, "That's my boy, McGreevy, that's my baby"' (11). Rory's wife expresses more conventional sentiments of 'dread of these faceless men with their guns and their hoods' (9). While hiding on a farm, McGreevy assists in the birth of a calf, and the grateful farmer, who recognizes the fugitive, treats him hospitably and admiringly. The farmer's wife reacts differently. To her, McGreevy is simply 'a murderer' (16), an embodiment of 'the killing instinct of man as opposed to the child-bearing instinct of womankind' (17). McGreevy's notoriety seems to precede him everywhere he goes. To ordinary Irish people – Teresa the fast food vendor whose van he commandeers, Colette the hairdresser who recognises the wig he has been using as a disguise, Martin the Snooper – McGreevy is a mythical figure, 'a psychopath' (195), 'a savage' (151), 'a pervert'(151), a threat to lonely women in their beds, rumoured even to be the spreader of foot and mouth disease. Josie imagines the reaction of her doctor: 'For her visitor he would have no time. Like most people he called them thugs, sickos, and said if the country were to be united in the morning he and his kind would be criminals out of a job' (96). To others, such as Creena and her mother, McGreevy is a hero, and the Guards who are chasing him are traitors to their country. The same troubling thought occurs even to the Guards themselves. After shooting one of McGreevy's comrades, Tommy 'says in a broken voice – "Half of you hopes you got him and the other half hopes you didn't"', to which his fellow Guard, Ned, adds: 'I know ... I'd be the same ... We're all Irish under the skin' (177). The spirit of the land rises up before them with a darkly ironical message:

> It was as they went down the road towards their car that he (Tommy) gripped Ned. A figure started out of the bushes, then walked slowly towards him and for a moment he thought he was one of them (the IRA), come for revenge. Before he could even think, the figure gripped his arm, mashed it and said: 'I'm proud of what you did for Ireland this night,' and then he disappeared into the pockets of darkness and for all they knew the man was a ghost or a phantom come to give them heart.
> 'Who do you think he was?' Tommy said.
> 'A shepherd ... Weird.'
> 'I always heard that this part of the country held the powers of darkness in it.' (178–9)

The Guards are the ones who feel like transgressors, desecrators of the spirit of place, offenders against the territorial numen. Only by demonising McGreevy can they repress atavistic identification with the IRA and toe the official government line. Repeatedly, a distinction is drawn between the heroic and now sacrosanct violence of 1916–22 which brought about the establishment of the independent Southern state, and the venality of the current IRA. Cormac the Guard raises with his colleague, Matt, the troubling thought: 'But if you'd been in 1916 you'd be on their side', which Matt quickly – but unconvincingly – attempts to counter by saying: 'That's different ... That's a totally different ball game ... These guys are without conscience, without ideals and with only one proclamation, money and guns, guns and money' (187). Matt's opinion is precisely that which the novel as a whole, through the characterisation of McGreevy, forcefully refutes. In the end it is Cormac who fires the shot that kills McGreevy, an action which leaves the young policeman wracked by guilt, a pathetic spectacle with his 'hung head and the pink hands pawing the atmosphere for mercy' (210). There are clearly disruptive undercurrents in the Southern political mind which threaten the orderly surfaces of the official body politic. Even Josie senses that the spirit of 1916 may not be all that remote from the present struggle, but was 'still there like spores, lurking' (85). McGreevy's appearance signals the return of the repressed. His presence activates violent memory, stirs the political unconscious of the nation. He comes as a reminder to the South of unfinished business: '"The South forgot us", he said. Forlorn. Aggrieved. A likeness to those children in fable banished, exiled in lakes for hundreds of years, cut off from the homeland' (99). His presence in her house forces Josie to excavate her past, to question her own attitudes to politics, the IRA, the past. She turns up her uncle's old diary – 'A Volunteer's Diary' (82) – in which she reads about the hardships of the life of a flying columnist in 1921. By including the two epigraphs, the first a statement of Sir John Davies, Attorney General in Ireland in 1606 ('*For St Patrick did only banish the poisonous worms, but suffered the men full of poison to inhabit the land still; but his Majesty's blessed genius will banish all those generations of vipers out of it, and make it, ere it be long, a right fortunate island*'); the second, a statement of Lloyd George after dispatching the Black and Tans to Ireland in 1920 ('*We have murder by the throat*'), O'Brien suggests a continuum of anti-colonial struggle in Ireland stretching from the seventeenth century to the present day. The 'generations of vipers' have not been exterminated but Hydra-like have survived into the present and leave the narrator at the end of the novel wondering if they will ever be 'sated' (212). The novel further ironises Sir John Davies' dismissal of 'the men full of poison' by humanising the terrorist and recognising the idealism that motivates him. The imagery of vipers and animals that is used to describe McGreevy is counterbalanced by an alternative mythology in which he appears as 'Cuchullain' (188), 'Mad Sweeney' (207), a 'sungod' (210), a Christian martyr with 'the blobs of half-melted frost, dripping from the trees, like tears or holy water being sprinkled on him' (207).

History is an apparently timeless continuum. The novel questions the possibility of change or progress: 'In thirty years what will he be. Who will he be. Will the land be sated. Will his heart be heavy. Or will everything continue just as it is.' (212).

O'Brien writes the Troubles as Gothic. *House of Splendid Isolation* is a haunted fiction in which McGreevy is a ghost of the past, a violent revenant committed to fulfilling the dream of Irish independence. Josie's unborn child haunts her mother's narrative, and it is the child's ghostly voice which, in two sections entitled 'The Child', frames the entire novel. The child speaks of 'the murmurs that come out of the earth' (3) and places the action in a 'wild' (3) folkloric, magical landscape beyond the pale of time and history: 'It weeps, the land does, and small wonder. But the land cannot be taken. History has proved that. The land will never be taken. It is there' (215). The novel moves toward a simple universalist message, with the child accepting her killer mother, as an increasingly 'feminised' McGreevy (who in prison 'did the sewing for the others, sewed on buttons and patched their jeans' (184), who cleans Josie's house, whose capacity for tenderness, family devotion, and communicativeness are emphasised) and a re-politicised Josie come to accept and respect each other. The novel has been constructed as a 'going in', a 'journey' to 'get to know' (216), a crossing borders to enter terrain that is alien or taboo, in order to discover a common humanity:

> 'As the killer is close to him whom he kills'. That's in a book. But to be close in body or bayonet is not enough. To go in, within, is the bloodiest journey of all. Inside you get to know. That the same blood and the same tears drop from the enemy as from the self, though not always in the same proportion. To go right into the heart of the hate and the wrong and to sup from it and to be supped. It does not say that in the books. That is the future knowledge. The knowledge that is to be. (215–16)

The narrative presumes to transcend division, to move from the historical and the political into the Romantic, symbolic, archetypal and mythical realm through a celebratory lyricism that owes a good deal to William Faulkner. O'Brien identifies with Faulkner, she says, because of 'his obsession with the blood boiling within the land, his courage and his convoluted visceral style. Then the madness. The underlying desperation which tips over into madness. Making a poem through the medium of prose. All prose should be poetry'.[32] In comparison with some of O'Brien's other writings, *House of Splendid Isolation* benefits from a greater restraint and control over style and structure so that she manages (for the most part) to avoid the worst excesses of her Faulknerian and Joycean poeticising. But there is another journey which *House of Splendid Isolation* leaves us still to take, one which would take us into the heart of the hate and the wrong felt by the Northern Protestant 'Other' of McGreavy's militant Republicanism.

32 Edna O'Brien in interview with Pearce, p. 6.

Feminising the thriller: Kate O'Riordan's *Involved* (1995)

Involved is a version of the romance *cum* thriller novel. At the centre of the story is the romantic involvement of Catholic, working-class Belfast boy, Danny O'Neill, with Southern Irish Big House girl, Kitty Fitzgerald, a love affair which is threatened and finally destroyed by Danny's other involvements in politics and family. Like *Cal*, *Involved* enforces a separation between the private and public worlds, and emphasises the superiority of the private, apolitical world of self-realisation, self-expression and individual relationships over the public world of social commitment and political action. But *Involved* is a more explicitly and thoroughly gendered narrative than *Cal*, constructing the inferior public world as essentially 'masculine' and the superior world of sexuality, domesticity and personal realisation as an essentially 'feminine' realm. In flight from the world of politics and violence, Cal discovers love and withdraws into his forest retreat: Danny, on the other hand, resists Kitty's attempts to claim him from family and politics, and refuses to escape with her into an apolitical privacy in London. Having postulated an intractible and uncompromising maleness, O'Riordan is left to discover some other kind of value beyond that of the traditional romance. She finds it in the resources of a heroic femininity.

Involved is not told in the first person, but the narrative is largely focused through Kitty, as when it dilates upon the sexual romance:

> She put her arms around him and gently drew his head down to kiss his lips. He withdrew from her embrace slowly. His fists clenched involuntarily as his feet scuffed the grass. He smiled sheepishly at her and she wanted to tell him then, how strong and intense was this love she felt for him, how it sometimes felt like a paliptating, ever-present ache, deep within the pit of her stomach. But he was moving away from her, pointing to the rectangular slab of rock. She understood what was required, and posed as he took his picture. She was glad in a way that she had elected to be silent. He would have felt diminished by his inability to match her pretty speech.[33]

Even here, there are ominous recognitions of male restiveness within 'her embrace'. As Danny moves outside Kitty's sphere of influence his actions suggest a desire to reclaim or reassert his masculinity ('His fists clenched involuntarily'): she, in turn, submits to his directives, positioning herself where Danny indicates, and, in deference to his feelings, is 'glad' to suppress her own. By shifting the focus from the sensuous inwardness of Kitty's 'palpitating, ever-present ache' to Danny's photography, the perspective is externalised, and the photograph becomes symbolic of the novel's

33 Kate O'Riordan, *Involved* (London: Flamingo, 1995), p. 102. Hereafter, page references will be incorporated into the text.

repeated emphasis on a distinctively male framing of experience, particularly of the female image. The critic Laura Mulvey writes: 'In a world ordered by sexual imbalance, pleasure in looking has been split between active/male and passive/female. The determining male gaze projects its fantasy onto the female figure, which is styled accordingly ... she holds the look, and plays to and signifies male desire'.[34] At this stage of the novel, Kitty is willing to collude in the masculine desire to fix the woman in a stable and stabilising identity, to allow her femininity to function as masquerade, that is, as a representation of male desire, but the text's reflexivity, its foregrounding of Danny's spectatorial complacency, suggests that O'Riordan is not at all unselfconscious about the gap between an empowered subject and a disempowered object. Later, Kitty finds herself once more self-consciously, but much more uncomfortably, caught in the determining male gaze, this time that of Danny's older brother, Eamon. Eamon and Kitty accidentally meet in the kitchen the morning after he has discovered her and Danny making love there:

> He shifted his position against the dresser. She could see that he was beginning to enjoy himself and she had the impression that Eamon might enjoy himself greatly at another's expense, once he had gained the upper hand. Furthermore, she could now admit to herself, in a sweat of self-recrimination, that she had enjoyed to an extent and yes, even encouraged, by means of a bending from the waist here – a leisurely stretch there, his stealthy, scorch-eyed admiration .... Then, as easily as he had entrapped her, with a last sideways glance, he released her ... (161–2)

Through repeated use of specular imagery, O'Riordan emphasises the role of the voyeuristic, fetishising male gaze in female sexual objectification. The male gaze divests women of their subjectivity, reducing them to sexual objects (the way Kitty is seen in the above examples, but also, even more offensively, the way the prostitute Maureen is seen by Eamon) in an attempt to subdue feminine power and independence. In the novel's gendered economy of spectatorship, as both of the above passages illustrate, authority is denied female spectatorship even as the female protagonist's point of view serves to qualify and revise the male gaze.

The novel opens up the gap between male and female perspectives. Kitty is consistently presented in attitudes of self-questioning, inner directed contemplation, while Danny is antithetically presented (usually from Kitty's point of view) as an emotional illiterate with a simple, practical view of life:

---

34 Laura Mulvey, 'Visual pleasure and narrative cinema', in Antony Easthope and Kate McGowan (eds), *A Critical and Cultural Theory Reader* (Buckingham: Open University Press, 1992), pp. 158–66, p. 162.

She thought about that for a while. In some respects, it was easy for Danny, things either were or they were not, you loved or you hated, the lights were green or they were red, he did not acknowledge amber ...

Remarkably, Kitty's recognitions of male/female difference are nearly always expressed with understanding, even compassion, rather than resentfully or with a sense of female superiority. When, in a state of severe distress Kitty tells Danny that she knows her mother hates her, the writing gently mocks the inadequacy of Danny's emotional response, but also acknowledges the practical advantages of his obtuseness:

'It's alright Kit, shh, it's alright. Don't worry about it. She hates you, you hate her, so what? What of it?' Danny crooned in her ear, misconstruing her distress. She opened her mouth to try to explain to him, then closed it again. He would never understand – it was not the revelation of her mother's hate which disturbed so greatly, it was the extent of her own impotent, superfluous love and the knowledge that much of what she had considered written on stone now proved far from runic. She was the one who was floundering, Danny was safe in his harbour of absolutes. She turned to him. (109)

Or, again, when she sees his difficulty handling her feelings of grief over her father's death, any criticism of Danny is matched by self-criticism and tempered by recognition of the kind of upbringing that has made Danny what he is:

[W]hen she tried to articulate to him how she was feeling, she could see him physically back away from the pain in her eyes.

She tried to put it into concrete terms so that he might comprehend a little better. Dealing in the abstract, the purely emotive was never Danny's strong suit ... he was, after all, from a household which subjugated emotion ...

Furthermore, she saw to her sadness that her every effort to explain this hollow emptiness inside her, instead of drawing Danny closer, pushed him further away. He could not compete with such feelings and therefore felt threatened ... (141)

It is a distinctively female perspective, even when Kitty is not narratively present, that is brought to bear on the public, political world. This is the case in the novel's powerfully written opening account of Eamon's visit to the home of the informer, Martin Fogarty, to issue Fogarty with a final warning. Through her unflinchingly objective narration, O'Riordan elicits our sympathies for the terrorised informer and his family, and our antipathy against the sinister enforcer who, before he leaves, offers a sickening demonstration of his capacity for casual sadism by holding up the family's puppy and calmly eviscerating it before their eyes. O'Riordan proceeds to suggest that Eamon's politics are no more than a psychotic displacement of a frustrated sexual drive. The sadistic cruelty of his supposedly political actions, as Eamon himself is made uncomfortably aware, produces a perverted sexual thrill: 'And the erections. They had begun to bother him. They smacked of perversity' (5). The evident pleasure he takes in intimidation and torture undermines his political arguments. For O'Riordan, the psycho-sexual is anterior to, and more important than, other forms of subjectivity such as the social and political.

Eamon is a stereotypical godfather, produced from the same mould as Mac-Laverty's Skeffington. Both Eamon and Skeffington are schoolteachers with local hardmen ready to do their bidding; both wear a mask of respectability, civilisation and religious piety behind which lies a chilling propensity for sadistic cruelty; both are presented as complacent fanatics, glib rationalisers of violence, ruthless controllers; both are viewed as cases of arrested emotional development, unmarried and still living with their mothers; both are sexually frustrated and able to relate to women only as mother or whore. On leaving the Fogartys' home, Eamon's thoughts turn to Maureen, a local prostitute. As soon as he enters her sexual domain, the masterful controller and community protector suddenly metamorphoses into a pathetic child. He wants Maureen to treat him like a child, and after the sexual act, sobs like a child. Briefly, the narrative perspective shifts to Maureen, whose view of Eamon registers contempt of his sexuality and masculinity: 'He was so damn heavy. Slabbering and grunting like a pig. So strange, a man like him to be such a wain' (23). The animal imagery that Eamon had used to denounce the hapless Fogarty ('You should die like a whimpering dog' 13) is now turned against Eamon himself. When he approaches Maureen 'she exuded a musky, high, perspiratory odour, redolent of greasy mutton' (21), and after the sexual act is over, he wonders 'how he could possibly have entered her. Right now, a jar of pig's liver seemed an eminently more attractive proposition' (24). To Maureen, he is typical of many men, 'weeping like babies in her arms, recoiling their flaccid worms to creep home, frightened as rabbits' (22). She thinks of his performance as being like 'the startled thrusts of a bullish teenager' (23). In her presentation of Eamon, O'Riordan exposes the contradictions contained within the patriarchal order. Eamon is the representative of male power within his community, yet he needs the presence of the mother to give order and meaning to his world, and the whore to provide the illusion of his male power.

From Danny's point of view, of course, Eamon is a hero, not an animal nor a sobbing child. Soon after the description of Eamon's killing of the Fogartys' pup, we find Danny angrily ridiculing what he takes to be Kitty's ignorance of Belfast: 'To the likes of you and bloody "Daddy" we're all not much better than some strain of fucking – I don't know what – mongrel, yes, that's it. Fucking mongrels. Not part of that lot and not part of your lot. With our funny accents and lust for killing' (43). This is all very ironic for we have already seen that 'lust for killing' is – quite literally – what motivates Eamon, and that to him people like Fogarty and Maureen are no more than 'fucking mongrels'. Danny's perspective is never allowed much narrative space or status. The suggestion of infantilism, which is laid against Eamon, is later also applied to Danny. Kitty, we are told, 'determined that in time she would help Danny to sever the umbilical cord that bound him to Belfast – and to Eamon' (135). From the novel's feminised narrative perspective, Danny, like his brother, hasn't properly grown up yet because of his inability to free himself from old attachments. He will never really be a man until he breaks from his Belfast friends (a sniggering bunch of feckless youths who haunt the local snooker hall), the dangerous influence of his brother (a repellingly sinister impresario of murder and mutilation), and from Ma (the stereotypical Irish mother). Only when he has freed himself from these baleful influences can the passional female hope to lead him into a private Utopia of love and domesticity.

The feminised critique of Belfast's terror politics is most strongly registered in the episode when young Liam Fogarty reappears towards the end of the story to tell Kitty of his horrific punishment shooting and the murder of his father, both actions carried out on Eamon's orders. Eamon and Danny's attempts to offer rational political explanation of the savagery are swallowed up by the force of Kitty's revulsion. Kitty 'could not shake the boy's face from her mind. The memory made her want to retch' (174). She reaches the point where her loyalty to Danny is brought into question. Ultimately, she acts according to conscience, risking her relationship with Danny in order to speak up for the victims of terror such as Liam Fogarty and his father, and against the cruelty of self-appointed executioners such as Eamon O'Neill. But even this action of Kitty's is ambiguous. However 'ashamed' (178) she may feel at allowing her love for Danny to occlude moral conscience, she continues living with him for three months after she learns from Liam Fogarty the full extent of Eamon's barbarity, and her decision to contact the authorities to inform on Eamon is finally precipitated by personal pique at Danny's failure to ring her over the Easter holidays. Kitty is denied any unequivocally idealistic motive in turning Eamon in: her action, it is suggested, is both self-serving and public-spirited – but arguably all the more realistically believeable.

Kitty is depicted as a tolerant, reflective, liberal-minded young woman, and she is aware that these qualities continually threaten to betray her into the stereotypical role of the passive, compliant, possessive female: 'Without meaning to, she had become the very thing, the type of emotionally dependent, obsessive woman she had once despised' (149). But there is another side to her character which is much more self-assertive, and which shows itself in her determination to fight for what she wants. This is the Kitty who refuses to be intimidated by either Eamon or her own mother. She pushes Danny into leaving Belfast to go and live in London, and puts up a spirited resistance against his family's efforts to seduce him back to Belfast with the possibility of a job. She bravely confronts Eamon to tell him to back off and let her and Danny get on with their lives together. She has the courage to make the momentous decision to inform on Eamon, and the personal resources to build a new life for herself and her young son in Canada. At the end, it is this image of the strong, independent, self-sufficient 'new woman', whose fulfilment now lies in maternity rather than sexuality, which is stressed.

In contrast, Ma and Maureen are characters derived from traditional male representations of the female. The presentation of old Ma O'Neill, the doyenne of domesticity, presiding over her warm kitchen-world, owes as much to the mother stereotype of Nationalist ideology as to realistic portraiture. Ma is the Shan Van Vocht, the poor old woman, the figure of Mother Ireland who, according to tradition, demands blood-sacrifice of her sons in order to ensure the fertility of the land. In the figure of Maureen, derived from another mythic male construction of femininity, the *magna mater* mutates into the whore-mother, the devouring female or lethal succubus, of whom Eamon demands: 'Get – off – my – shoulders. Now' (22). This figure is created out of masculine fear and desire, and represents the need to control and subordinate the whole female sex. It reveals an intense alienation from the female, a profound misogyny. In Maureen's company, Eamon regresses to sobbing child requiring his mother's comfort, but he also finds her physically repulsive and even terrifying, and she awakens in him murderous hatred of the female: 'He did not like her to see him naked but she crept around his shoulder. The urge to reach up his hand behind him and snap her stupid neck was almost overwhelming' (22).

Ma's daughter and Eamon and Danny's sister, Monica, represents the female who has detached herself from the decolonising discourses in which women have been constructed in subordinate roles, but who still feels trapped and powerless in patriarchy. A native of Belfast, Monica encourages the tourist, Kitty, to see Republican violence simply as 'crime' (90) rather than legitimate political action: 'Hoods are the problem. The real problem in Belfast' (89), she insists. But although she has distanced herself from Republican ideology, she feels entrapped by marriage and a victim of the sexist prejudices of her parents who gave educational opportunities to their sons which were denied to her: 'And how did I get like this? Hmm? Because I did what was expected of me ... Eamon and Danny were expected to go to college, expected to have careers while I ... who have twice the brains of the two of them put together, was expected to get married. It's an ancient story, isn't it?' (120). Monica is thus made to play a part in a strategic narrative displacement of the politics of the Troubles, and the centering of a new sexual politics, of which the protagonist, Kitty, is the main exemplar.

In the presentation of Kitty, we see the female self in process, battling to deliver herself from inherited, alienating (male) mythic appropriation, so that the female is no longer merely the object on which the male subject is constructed, but actively engaged in creating her own subjectivity. The transfiguration of Kathleen Ni Houlihan into Kitty Con is accomplished through O'Riordan's determined extrication of the image of the female self from the patriarchal iconology and ideology of Irish Republicanism, and from the barbarism which is associated with the Republican ethos. 'Hero-worship of the male Gael is part of the Nationalist pitch to women',[35] writes Edna Longley, referring to a propaganda image of Irish women which Kitty vividly contradicts. O'Riordan would seem to share Longley's view that 'as a general rule: the more Republican, the less feminist',[36] and manages to provide a particularly ironic gloss on Bernadette (Devlin) McAliskey's assertion in *Mother Ireland* that 'the best young feminist women today are those who have come through the experience of the republican movement'.[37] In *Involved*, feminism and militarism is a contradiction in terms. A product of post-Nationalist Southern Ireland, Kitty shows little interest in the continuing colonial struggle in the North, a place where she feels quite alien, and which she views with both distaste and horror. Recognising that life lived through received ideology lacks authenticity, she connects with a primal female self through child-rearing. Maternity is indispensible to her discovery of the plenitude of female experience: 'Now that she had Kevin, she didn't need anyone else. She was not unaware that it had been that way with Danny too, but now it did not seem to matter how much love she poured into one person. Kevin was a bottomless vessel' (197). Maternity, which has so often been negatively valued in feminist discourse, becomes for Kitty the essential female experience. In this respect, O'Riordan differs markedly from Jennifer Johnston. Johnston's matraphobia sees motherhood as a site of oppression, equated with society's need to appropriate female identity to a traditional, fixed role which compromises the female's opportunity to develop and change. Johnston's women in *The Railway Station Man* and *The Illusionist* resist society's and children's predilection for accessible, static, immutable mothers, and refuse to perpetuate the myth of fixed identity from which they have struggled to extricate themselves. Toril Moi's deconstructive feminist criticism warns against the assumption of a monolithic female identity, specifically the essentialist notion that motherhood is true fulfilment:

> Gratifying though it is to be told that women are really strong, integrated, peace-loving, nurturing and creative beings, this plethora of new virtues is no less essentialist than the old ones, and no less oppressive to all those women who do not want to play the role of Earth Mother. It is after all patriarchy, not feminism, which has always believed in a true female/feminine nature;

---

35 Edna Longley, 'From Cathleen to Anorexia', p.190.   36 Ibid., p. 191.   37 Ibid.

the biologism and essentialism which lurk behind the desire to bestow female virtues on all female bodies necessarily plays into the hands of the patriarchy.[38]

In Moi's terms, O'Riordan recycles the patriarchal construction of women by emphasising her protagonist's quintessential link with nature through maternity. However, O'Riordan significantly revises the patriarchal construction by emphasising maternity outside marriage and without reference to any form of paternal authority. She poses a disruptive threat to the phallocratic social order and its values by reinterpreting ideas of motherhood and mothering along lines proposed by the feminist critic Adrienne Rich who, in her study, *Of Women Born: Motherhood as Experience and Institution*, distinguishes between the experience of motherhood and patriarchy's attempts to control that experience through the institution of motherhood.[39] Kitty turns motherhood into a site of feminist struggle, claiming the potential for pleasure and self-fulfilment through rearing her child on her own terms. Yet even if we set aside the arguments for seeing O'Riordan's revival of the cult of motherhood as a reaffirmation of stereotypical, essentialist views of women as nurturers and peace-makers, we are left with a picture of motherhood as compensation for failure in other areas of a woman's life. Refusing to remain fixed by and in the oppressive male gaze, Kitty opts for an autonomous self, taking her own personal route to freedom – from family, boyfriend, community, nation: yet if Kitty's emigration functions as metaphor for an evolving radical self-transformation, the difficulty of flying the nets of the past are fully acknowledged. Kitty's re-location is not wholly of her own choice or making, but arranged by her (male, colonial) British handlers; and, as the closing lines of the novel indicate, she is unaware that even in Saskatchewan she has not managed to escape Eamon's gaze.

Fictionalising the Women's Peace Movement: Mary Costello's *Titanic Town* (1992)

Titanic Town is a first novel, reflective of the author's experiences as a teenager growing up in a Catholic, working-class family in Anderstown in West Belfast. Like Beckett's *Give Them Stones*, it is a semi-autobiographical fictional memoir, exemplifying the Northern Irish (woman) writer's addiction to a sociological, journalistic, confessional mode which Eve Patten finds intellectually and imaginatively limited. The book in its published form differs from the manuscript version which was written in Melbourne, where Costello has lived since 1981. Originally, she tells us in an interview,

---

38 Toril Moi, 'Feminist, female, feminine', in Catherine Belsey and Jane Moore (eds.), *The Feminist Reader* (Basingstoke: Macmillan, 1997), p. 109. 39 See Adrienne Rich, *Of Woman Born: Motherhood as Experience and Institution* (London: Virago, 1977).

the story 'had an Australian framework with Annie McPhelimy (the fictional me) in exile in Australia and recalling her past'.[40] Having had the manuscript rejected by Australian publishers and eventually accepted by a London house, Costello agreed to delete the Australian references while retaining the retrospective first person narration. Belfast is 'Titanic Town': 'It struck me', she says in her interview, 'that "The Titanic" was a symbol of Belfast, seductive yet doomed.'[41] Only by distancing herself from that doom and despair, she remarks, could she write the book: 'When you're there, you get caught up in what's going on. You're so absorbed in it and appalled by it. It fills you with such despair when you see the brutality and the killing that nothing is worth doing, certainly not writing a crappy book about it.'[42] While admitting the difficulty of severing her ties with Ireland, she nevertheless emphasises her appreciation, on a personal level, of the new freedoms which life in Australia affords: 'I also thoroughly enjoy multiculturalism. My husband is from Mauritius and I think attitudes are healthier here towards mixed marriages than they are in Ireland.'[43]

The novel exudes historical authenticity and *verisimilitude*. Covering the period of the late '60s and into the '70s, the narrative unfolds against the Civil Rights marches, the outbreak of the Troubles, the arrival of the British army in Northern Ireland, the emergence of the Provisional IRA, Operation Motorman, the introduction of internment, and the rise and fall of the Women's Peace Movement. The novel also closely follows events in the West Belfast community and, more particularly still, in the McPhelimy family. The situation of Republican West Belfast, and the individuals involved, are presented with a notable insight, humour and sympathetic understanding. The narrative point of view is that of a schoolgirl. The focus of attention is not events in the public, political world but the concerns of a teenage girl having to deal with a mother who has taken to both politics and valium, a father with a stomach ulcer, neighbours who intimidate the family out of their home, a shortage of discos and boyfriends, not to mention the terrors of 'O' and 'A' levels. The novel avoids sentimentality, for however redolent of vitality, courage and resilience the portrait of community and family life may be, it is not the kind envisioned in the traditional mythologies of Catholic Nationalism. In *Titanic Town*, the brutality on the streets permeates the domestic front, affecting community and family relationships.

Costello exemplifies the idea of the artist as spokesperson for her people. Indeed, the book's central action is the emergence of a community spokesperson, Annie's mother, Bernie, whose role is thus analogous to that of the author who is similarly concerned with articulating a community, its desires, beliefs and internal tensions. Thus, the political thrust of the novel lies not so much in any direct political inter-

---

40 'Swimming from *The Titanic*: Mary Costello talks to Simon Caterson', *Irish Studies Review*, 8 (Autumn 1994) , pp 6–8, 6.   41 Ibid., p. 6.   42 Ibid.   43 Ibid., p. 7.

vention but in its capacity to speak for the tribe. In demonstrating continuity with the *mythos* of community, *Titanic Town* displays the kind of congruence which Heaney claimed existed between his work and his community:

> Poetry is born out of the watermarks and colourings of the self. But that self in some ways takes its spiritual pulse from the inward spiritual structure of the community to which it belongs; and the community to which I belong is Catholic and nationalist ... I think that poetry and politics are, in different ways, an articulation, an ordering, a giving of form ...to inchoate pieties, prejudices, world-views, or whatever. And I think that my own poetry is a kind of slow obstinate papish burn, emanating from the ground I was brought up on.[44]

In the novel, the private world is contextualised by being set against public pressures, and Costello continually emphasises, formally as well as thematically, the inextricable connections between the private and public spheres. While tapping into the community's ideological view of the world, she manages, through a substantially constituted female standpoint (Bernie's even more than Annie's, since the mother's dominant presence tends to overshadow her daughter's in both family and narrative terms) to develop a space for protest against individually damaging aspects of community on one hand, and against the forces of an invasive colonialism and terrorist Loyalism on the other hand. As well as this, the novel self-reflexively critiques this critique by incorporating a range of alienating devices – farcical humour, satire and irony – to subvert the moral idiom mobilised by Bernie and the Peace Women to oppose political violence.

In his Field Day essay, 'Civilians and barbarians', Deane expresses his concern over the complications that arise

> when modes of discourse other than the political become involved. The moral code, much favoured of course by the Churches, although not ignored in the least by either governments, armies or the media, has a distorting effect on the political realities involved. For it is based (however hypocritically) on the notion of an immutable Natural Law, or Moral Code, the peremptory force of which applies more directly to the terrorists than to the soldier of the State.[45]

Deane's point is that the moral argument, in claiming to be grounded in the universal condition of mankind, construes the conflict in broad abstract, allegorical terms: peace versus war, good versus evil, civilians versus barbarians. But while claiming to

---

44 Seamus Heaney, in interview with Seamus Deane, 'Unhappy and at Home', in *Crane Bag*, 1 (1977), p. 67.
45 Seamus Deane, 'Civilians and barbarians', in *Ireland's Field Day* (London: Hutchinson, 1986), p. 41.

transcend politics, the moral idiom is actually deeply embedded in politics and is constantly subject to political manipulation. Consequently, the distinction between the moral and the political is 'suspect':

> Nothing demonstrated this more than the Peace Movement, one of the most successful of all political exploitations of a moral code which was in fact a political code. Hardly anyone remembers that the incident which sparked the movement off began with the killing of an IRA man, who was driving a car, by a British soldier – who was himself in no danger. The charismatic movement in Catholicism and the evangelical movement in Protestantism combined to display, in front of the cameras, the longing for peace by a population disturbed by the guerillas within their ranks – not by the army, or the police, or the unemployment, housing conditions and so forth. As farces go, it was one of the most successful of modern times.
>
> But it was an important success. For it changed nothing. Therefore it was a success for the State. It merely confirmed and spread the demonising ideology.[46]

While there were many local peace initiatives during the '70s on both sides of the sectarian divide, most of them with a majority female membership, many of them formed in immediate spontaneous response to some particularly tragic event, the most celebrated was the Women's Peace Movement to which Deane alludes, which was formed in 1976 by Mairéad Corrigan (Catholic) and Betty Williams (Protestant), whose efforts won them the 1976 Nobel Peace Prize. In Costello's version of the Women's Movement, Bernie's activism is sparked off by the random killing of a local resident, Mrs Dillon, who was killed by a sniper's bullet on her way home from the shops. But Bernie's movement is an exclusively Catholic West Belfast initiative which resists any ecumenical tendency or any agenda for cross-community reconciliation. The Protestant Peace Women, led by Mrs Lockhart, are presented as middle-class caricatures and Bernie is anxious to make clear that there is no connection between her movement and the Protestant Assembly of Women. Despite the usual liberal lamentation over the death and destruction on the streets, Bernie's is, initially at least, a modest programme with the specific goal of securing a change to the IRA's sniping timetable so that the lives of local residents and children will not be put at risk. As the narrator comments: 'It seemed a harmless enough initiative – a group of local women getting together to improve living conditions ... A little deft negotiation should do it nicely. The adjustment of a few timetables and everybody would be happy. The IRA could keep shooting and the women could keep shopping.'[47] In

---

46 Ibid., p. 41.   **47** Mary Costello, *Titanic Town* (London: Methuen, 1992), p. 162. Hereafter, page references will be incorporated into the text.

contrast to the real-life Women's Peace Movement, as described by Deane, Costello's Peace Women remain grounded in a paramilitary pragmatics which they want to see modified, not removed. Bernie explains their position in a television interview with Mr Hill:

> 'I believe that I am speaking for a large section of the people of Anderstown when I say that we want peace and the chance to lead normal lives. However, we are not turning our backs on the IRA, because we do need the IRA for a number of reasons. Firstly we need them to defend us in case of a Protestant backlash' – Mr Hill's Protestant nostrils flared noticeably – 'and secondly we need them to maintain law and order within Anderstown, as we cannot rely on the RUC'. (176)

The aspect of the real-life movement which Costello does faithfully reflect is its political naivety, which makes it so vulnerable to political exploitation, not only by the State authorities and the paramilitaries but also by the media. The central events in the book, Bernie's meetings with the IRA leadership and the representatives of the British government, are used to highlight the powerlessness of the moral argument when it comes up against politics. The IRA leader, Finbar, a sympathetically drawn figure, understands the moral force of Bernie's case, but re-asserts the political reality that however regrettable the violence may be, it will continue as long as the British presence threatens the community. Bernie and her friend Deirdre innocently carry the IRA's four demands – united Ireland, troops out, no more house raids, prisoner release – to Mr Brandywell, the British representative at Stormont:

> 'All we want is peace,' Deirdre added quickly.
> 'But not peace at any price?' inquired Brandywell wryly. (213)

Where for Bernie and Deirdre 'peace' is an absolute right, Brandywell's reply immediately re-situates the absolute category of 'peace' in the idiom of political economy. The Peace Women constitute an emblem of female energy, determination and commitment, but they are shown to be pathetically inadequate to deal with the establishment and counter-hegemonic power structures, both exclusively male, which would thwart, marginalise and take over those who seek to work through new channels. Brandywell and Finbar are mirror images of courtesy and sympathetic understanding, but their relationship with the Peace Women is paternalistic and exploitative. It is only when Bernie watches herself and Deirdre on television handing over the 60,000 signatures which they have collected in petition against 'all use of force and violence at the present time' (220) that she realises how they have been used by the system:

'You've done very well indeed.' Mr Brandywell's nicely modulated English voice sounded in every ear and heart. The Peace Women had done very well for Mr Brandywell, for the British Government, very well indeed ... 'Are you pleased with us, Mr Brandywell?' It would echo forever: *Very, very pleased. You've done well indeed.* Bernie's heart stopped with a thump, her legs weakened, bowels churned. She suddenly understood what they had done, how it would be seen, how useless it all was. At that second her intuition told her that this would be the end, not the start of it. There would be no peace. There could be none. (241)

Like the real-life Peace Movement, Bernie's movement was not organised to eliminate the causes of violence, only to propose an end to it. Costello shows how it could only display an aspiration, demonstrate an enthusiasm, but was fatally disabled in lacking any political analysis and any clear programme for social change. It lacked reality. Unlike the Civil Rights radicals of 1968–9 who mobilised minority opinion around a pragmatic programme of provocative marches to put pressure on Westminster to ameliorate specific grievances, the Peace Movement, while successful in arousing intense emotion in opposition to violence, could not translate this rather amorphous response into sustained political action. As the American historian of the Troubles, Bowyer Bell, remarks,

> Unlike the Provos, for example, the Peace People could not agree on what was the matter with Ireland – except the present, the violence, the poverty, the misery – and these were effect, not cause. Nor could they agree on what was to be done, except love thy neighbour and follow the precepts of the Gospels. They had no vision of an ultimate Ireland except an improved model of the present.[48]

Titanic Town reflects the sense of failure and hopelessness that characterised the '70s. Towards the end of the novel, a local Catholic boy, Jimmy Carson, is shot dead in cold blood by a Loyalist paramilitary. This is immediately followed by two BBC news reports, years later, the first about the deaths of two British soldiers who mistakenly drove into a funeral cortège on its way to Milltown cemetery, the second about the extradition of a leading Republican, Francis Fallon, from the South to the North. The narrator then describes seeing the photograph of one of the dead soldiers in the newspaper: 'One dead soldier and Father Regan. They are flanked on the page by El General Pinochet, and Fergie in a pink ski-suit' (338). The world is no longer

---

48 Bowyer Bell, *The Irish Troubles: A Generation of Violence 1967–1992* (Dublin: Gill and Macmillan 1993), p.523.

constructed within a unitary frame of reference, the tightly-knit community of West Belfast. News items zap from one cultural context to another; perspectives are fragmented, pluralised and continually changing. Chronological narrative is replaced by collage. Meaning is mediated by television news reports, the radio, newspaper photographs, rather than produced from direct experience: 'And now here's that grim patch of ground starring in award-winning photographs of dead bodies and ministering priests' (339). In the photograph of the dead soldier, the imperialist imperative is swallowed up in an image of universal suffering: 'He's lying sprawled and bloody like a crucifixion, his chest red with blood, and more blood pouring from the head wound, running into surrounding puddles. A bit of Anderstown that will be forever England' (338). The priest in the photograph is 'Father Regan, who didn't mind my marrying a heathen, didn't insist that the children be brought up Catholics' (339), a detail which indicates the distance that has opened up between the narrator and traditional Catholic family values. In her mind, the death of the soldier merges with that of Jimmy Carson, and these tragedies are in turn linked with thoughts of 'eyeless Mrs Nolan' who earlier in the book and years ago was blinded by a plastic bullet, and the young cockney soldier, Lionel Thurston, who was shot by a sniper outside the McPhelimys' house. The collage form which is used to construct this closing composite image of human suffering enacts at the level of structure a powerful sense of powerless, non-linear stasis. The final chapter, significantly entitled 'Bogged', re-states the problem, rantingly, exasperatedly, without answer or progression, a climactic outburst of indignation at the fossilised postures and intransigent attitudes in which both communities in the North seem endlessly trapped:

> Her rambling, and the rest of us egging them on. For the cause, for queen and country, for peace, with justice or at any price. For there will be no surrender, fuck pope and queen both the same. Sons, sisters, fathers, daughters, husbands and brothers will not be grudged, though they go out to break their strength and die. We will not give an inch and shall not be moved, till the last drops of blood, orange and green, run down the street, through our four green fields, one of them in bondage, to mingle with the rivers of ceaseless rain, seep into the brown sucking bog, and piss, peacefully at last, out into Belfast Lough, in the wake of the Titanic. (340)

Conclusion

The majority of the fiction that has been reviewed in this study is marked by a concern to challenge old constructions of the Northern Irish Troubles, old 'Truths' of the past (Nationalism, Unionism, Christian humanism, patriarchy) and to (re-)centre or (re-)activate some of the *petits récits* which the master discourses attempted to suppress in order to validate their own hegemonic positions. These micronarratives are extremely varied and include Morrison's West Belfast, Bennett's IRA, Deane's 'dark' family archive, Costello's Peace Women, Park's anthropologism and feminist-lesbianism, Beckett's feminised Marxism, Johnston's feminised individualism, O'Riordan's maternity, and Wilson's, Patterson's and Bateman's pluralist *jouissance*. In this sense, the majority of the fiction on the North and its Troubles since the late '60s is written to an identifiably postmodern agenda, as the relative greater length of Chapter 4 of this book would imply. The fiction included in the other chapters is clearly also more or less shaped by postmodern concerns and styles but, since it declares itself primarily in other terms, is considered under other headings. The prevalence of the postmodern is no surprise since the years covered by this study correspond to the period which is usually regarded as the era of the postmodern. More importantly, the North is itself an exemplary site of postmodern heterogeneity, breakdown, hybridity, dual inheritance, exile and cultural pluralism. Yet, despite the North's historical affinity to the postmodern condition, most of the fiction considered in this study is written and read within a dominant liberal humanist/Realist framework. Such a conventional format, it has been suggested, represents a compensating effort to affirm a reassuring stability, if only at the aesthetic level, in the midst of social and political breakdown. One of the aims of this study has been to examine how much of that traditional liberal humanist/Realist agenda has to be compromised or revised to survive in a violently heterogeneous society; how far a re-invigorated pluralist, postmodern humanism, transcending religious division, constructs an insurgent counter-hegemony.

In the radical shift from the modern centring on time to the postmodern emphasis on space, the physical and cultural city becomes the paradigmatic site of the postmodern. Most of the fiction considered in this study is city-based: *Cal, Silver's City, Lies of Silence, A Hole in the Head, Burning Your Own, Fat Lad, The International, Eureka Street, Resurrection Man, Ordinary Decent Criminals, Hidden Symptoms, The Healing, Stone Kingdoms, Divorcing Jack, Titanic Town, Give Them Bread, Involved, West Belfast, The Wrong Man* are entirely or substantially set in Belfast, while *Shadows on our Skin* and *Reading in the Dark* are set in Derry, and *Ripley Bogle* and *The Second Prison* shift between Belfast and London. In those novels adopting a thriller format, the presiding metaphor of the city is the labyrinth. More generally, the fiction writes the city as a place of danger, whether from war-time German bombs (as in *Give Them Bread*) or, more commonly, from sectarian violence. Some novels set up a contrast between the public world of politics, ideology and violence centred in the city, and a superior private, domestic realm of personal and sexual fulfilment associated with escape from the city. The traditional idea persists that, while the city may be the place of deracinated, decadent (post)modernity, the rural world implies stability, inheritance, rootedness and piety. Novels such as *Proxopera, Nothing Happens in Carmincross, One by One in the Darkness* and *Cal* focus a sense of nostalgia for a lost past, for a kind of paradise that, according to Lyotard, defines modernity. On the other hand, the city, read as cultural metaphor, is a palimpsest of interconnected histories, communities, cultures and languages. Iain Chambers, in an essay entitled 'Cities without Maps', discusses the way maps of cities, like any form of representation, simplify, elide and occlude aspects of the real life of cities:

> Beyond the edge of the map, we enter the localities of the vibrant, everyday world and the disturbance of complexity. Here we find ourselves in the gendered city, the city of ethnicities, the territories of different social groups, shifting centres and peripheries – the city that is a fixed object of design (architecture, commerce, urban planning, state administration) and yet simultaneously plastic and mutable: the site of transitory events, movements, memories.[1]

Living in the fluid environment of the city, we are forced to cross boundaries, enter unfamiliar zones, embrace heterogeneity, diversity and otherness. Wilson's and Patterson's protagonists are exemplary metropolitan adventurers in their aptitude for such transcultural excursion. McNamee's 'Resurrection Man' and Leitch's Silver, however, are characters who are unable to live in cities without maps and are disoriented and overwhelmed by the modern city's infinitely complex and continually shifting signs and signifiers.

If this fiction registers the impact of universal civilisation (modernisation, internationalism, technologism and relativism), it may also be seen to demonstrate a resistance to any trend towards cultural conformity by integrating local or indigenous resources (sense of place, historical or journalistic reportage, Ulster style and idiom, folkloric and legendary material) with cosmopolitan styles and foreign narratives. Fidelity to local origins co-exists with responsiveness to the otherness of the universal postmodern condition – the loss of the grand narratives of the past, the experience

1 Iain Chambers, 'Cities without maps', in Julian Wolfreys (ed.), *Literary Theories: A Reader and Guide* (Edinburgh University Press, 1999), pp 611–25, p. 612.

of dissensus, heterogeneity and fragmentation. The result is a multiple, open fiction combining global concerns with a critical regionalism. As Seamus Heaney says in his essay 'The Sense of Place':

> We are no longer innocent, we are no longer just parishioners of the local. We go to Paris at Easter instead of rolling eggs on the hill at the gable. 'Chicken Marengo! It's a far cry from the Moy', Paul Muldoon says in a line depth-charged with architectural history. Yet those primary laws of our nature are still operative. We are dwellers, we are namers, we are lovers, we make homes and search for our histories.[2]

And in Heaney's poem, 'Alphabets' (from his 1987 collection *The Haw Lantern*), we may discern the evolution of contemporary Northern writing in the poet's tracing of a trajectory from the death of a naturalist to the birth of a postmodernist. The child, embedded in a natural, rural, residually pagan first world, is displaced and reconstructed in a symbolic, technological, globalised world of unity-in-diversity:

> As from his small window
> The astronaut sees all he has sprung from,
> The risen, aqueous, singular, lucent O
> Like a magnified and buoyant ovum –
>
> Or like my own wide pre-reflective stare
> All agog at the plasterer on his ladder
> Skimming our gable and writing our name there
> With his trowel point, letter by strange letter.[3]

This linking of local identity with a cosmopolitan identity not only produces a distinctive aesthetics but suggests a possible politics capable of transcending the British/Irish, Unionist/Nationalist conflict in the North. As Richard Kearney explains:

> It is becoming evident that the best prospect of overcoming the sovereignty dispute in Northern Ireland is in the context of a European federation of regions. And what the continuing debate on European regionalism brings home, again and again, is that if regional power without European integration runs the risk of neo-tribalism, an integrated Europe without devolution to the regions runs the risk of neo-imperialism. Both extremes are equally

2 Seamus Heaney, *Preoccupations: Selected Prose 1968–1978* (London: Faber, 1980), pp 147–8.   3 Seamus Heaney, 'Alphabets', *Opened Ground: Poems 1966–1996* (London: Faber, 1998), pp 292–4.

undesirable and equally avoidable, if the proper balance between international and subnational association is to be struck.[4]

Though Kearney may look to Europe for a solution to Ireland's political problems, the major cultural influences, as the work considered in this study would suggest, are transatlantic rather than European: not so much a cry of 'Chicken Marengo!' as 'Chicken McDonald's!' It may also be said that internationalism of any kind does not have strong cultural roots in the parochial Ulster soil. A conservative Ulster society has had about as much time for the foreign and exotic as for the ideal of ecumenism between Nationalist and Unionist ideology. Nevertheless, multi-culturalism is the principle on which Ireland, North and South, has staked its political future. In the Preface to the little book, *Multi-Culturalism: The View from the Two Irelands* (2001), multi-culturalism comes with the imprimatur of Mary McAleese, President of Ireland, who hails it as the basis of the Good Friday Agreement:

> It (the Agreement) seeks to create an institutional and constitutional frame-work within which people from both main communities and both main traditions can come together to work for their mutual benefit, without abandoning their basic identities or beliefs. Inspired by universal concepts of reconciliation, equality and parity of esteem, it specifically recognises the 'full and equal legitimacy and worth of the identities, senses of allegiance, and ethos of all sections of the community in Northern Ireland'. It has led to the strengthening of human rights and equality provisions. The importance of respect, understanding and tolerance in relation to linguistic diversity is enriched in the Agreement.[5]

In general, the fiction considered in this study is 'inspired by universal concepts of reconciliation, equality and parity of esteem'. It is aware of the problems and dangers of crossing borders and confronting the challenge of new ideas and experiences – and of the even greater dangers and problems of our not doing so and remaining isolated in 'our own little enclaves'. Historically, cultural hybridity between English colonisers and native Gael was regarded with hostility, but, as Declan Kiberd suggests, 'somehow quite a lot of writers managed the trick'[6] of cultural fusion. The multi-cultural 'trick' involves not just acknowledging eclecticism and dispersal as inevitable consequences of consumer society, but drawing on the transformative potential of these trends to make differences fruitful. As Edna Longley comments,

---

4 Richard Kearney, *Postnationalist Ireland: Politics, Culture, Philosophy* (London and New York: Routledge, 1997), p. 104.   5 Mary McAleese, 'Foreword', *Multi-Culturalism: The View from the Two Irelands* (Cork: Cork University Press in association with the Centre for Cross Border Studies, Armagh, 2001), p. vii. 6 Ibid., p, 45.

multi-culturalism – or 'inter-culturalism' as she prefers to call it – must signify 'cultural exchange' not merely 'cultural co-existence'.[7] The Northern Irish problem, she says, challenges some deep-seated assumptions in both the UK and the Republic:

> Some sovereignty, as well as traditional self-understanding may have to be sacrificed to a more Scandinavian concept of the archipelago: to the indivisible 'weave of diversity', to inter-culturalism in every direction.[8]

Similarly, Kiberd, writing from the South, rejects essentialist notions of identity to recommend a Joycean eclecticism, openness and assimilitativeness:

> That state in which everyone is open to his or her own strangeness seems a good basis on which to build a cultural democracy, which calls for respect for its own products even as it offers a similar tenderness to newcomers.[9]

The challenge, as outlined by Kearney, is 'to turn "weak eclecticism" into "radical eclecticism" – to transform the existing jumble of cultural fragments into carnivalesque collage ... draw from old and new in "recreative", non-dogmatic ways'.[10]

Kearney's construction of a positive postmodernism is exemplified by most of the 'postmodern' writers considered in this book, writers who not only recognise the loss of the grand narratives but who, in the words of François Lyotard, are past the 'period of mourning' for them. If these writers do not go as far as Wilson or Bateman in the direction of carnivalesque collage, they all illustrate, to a greater or lesser extent, the potential of combining 'old' and 'new' in recreative, non-dogmatic ways. In doing so, they transform the feelings of impotence and defeat of an older liberal humanism (represented by White, McCabe, Kiely, Moore, Leitch and MacLaverty) into a new postmodern humanist recognition of the positive potential of difference, diversity and multiplicity. Thus, we have Wilson's and Patterson's liberating narratives of hybridity, inclusiveness and interconnectedness; Bateman's anarchic 'Protestant' carnivalesque; Park's deconstruction of the old myths of home, family and identity, and reconstitution of the self through narratives of 'healing' grounded in concepts of self-authorship, feminism and heroic individualism; and women writers such as Johnston, Beckett, Costello, O'Riordan and Molloy discovering a politics of the personal capable of unmasking the structures of male privilege and domination concealed in an apparently universalist liberal humanism.

However, eclecticism and diversity, instead of offering opportunities to demonstrate powers of imaginative recreation, can simply overwhelm. Rigorous respect for difference can lead to paralysis, panic or disorientation. The dangers attending

7 Ibid., p. 5.　8 Ibid., p. 44.　9 Ibid., p. 73.　10 Richard Kearney, *Postnationalist Ireland*, p. 65.

heterogeneous language games are highlighted in Briege Duffaud's novel, *A Wreath upon the Dead*. The search for truth amongst the multiple versions of it that are on offer may not lead out of the labyrinth. Critical judgment may find itself impotent before an undifferentiated pluralism, the endless free play of the signifier. In Eoin McNamee's ironically titled *Resurrection Man*, it is the protagonist's inability to inhabit a shifting, unpredictable, unreliable postmodern world which breeds an intolerable and ultimately murderous frustration. Victor Kelly is happiest when he is withdrawn from the outside world and confined within the known world of the prison. Similarly, in Ronan Bennett's novel, there is no end to nightmare, no escape from the 'second prison' of the fixed thinking of the past into a more relaxed, multiple, open society.

Moreover, if postmodern multi-culturalism is the dominant literary and cultural model of the period, it is not, as Longley reminds us, a self-evident good. The desire to accommodate difference may seem to involve a denial or distortion of one's own identity and traditions in order to make room for others. Multi-culturalism stands accused of dissolving society into competing tribes and creating 'a moral and cultural wasteland'; of being 'a menace to life and liberty' by nurturing 'an army within waiting for an opportunity to destroy the society that sustains them'.[11] The 'open society' is always open to political and conceptual manipulation. Multi-culturalism means different things to different people. The Unionist view is not the same as the Nationalist. Thus, Longley criticises the Republic for its reluctance to acknowledge its 'Britishness', and Ulster Unionists for their historical failure to acknowledge their 'Irishness'. Deane and Eagleton dissociate themselves from a multi-culturalism that remains politically quietist thereby silently underwriting neo-colonial authority. Morrison and Bennett repudiate its bourgeois, 'liberal' ethic as irrelevant to working-class Irish Republicans.

But to refuse to engage with difference, to reject the notion of a wider or dominant culture, is to court fantasy and fascism. Morrison's emphasis on notions of continuity and community, and re-activation of tribal mythologies – particularly the cult of blood-sacrifice – clearly runs counter to the ideal of postmodern multi-culturalism, the valuation of hybridisation over purity, polyphony over monologue, openness over insularity. *West Belfast* challenges the grand narratives of British imperialism and Unionist hegemony, but the simple inversion of official stereotypes and slogans, while it may help to create a more positive, unified self-image to confront and undo the wrongs of history, merely re-cycles old modes of thinking and confirms the dependence of oppositional politics on the established hegemony. When history indicates division and dispossession, myth provides an answering narrative of unity and reinstatement. The problem is that myth can become fossilised into reactionary

11 Melanie Phillips, 'Britain is in denial about the angry Muslims within', *Sunday Times*, 4 November 2001, p. 17.

social orthodoxy, and pluralism and permissiveness come to represent the intolerable. The myths of Irish Republicanism, like the Loyalist myths of triumphant struggle for religious freedom and civil liberty, can be used to integrate and justify a community or to incarcerate that community in tribal bigotry.

What most of the new, postmodern fiction considered in this study illustrates is that demystification of outmoded, alienating myths can lead to positive new reimaginings, the opening up of new horizons of possibility in a project of universal liberation. While acknowledging their cultural situatedness, these writers maintain a critical distance from the formative myths and traditions of their respective traditions, going beyond 'ideological' fiction to what Kearney calls 'Utopian' fiction, a kind of exploratory fiction characterised by a 'universalist potential', a 'forward look ... which critically reinterprets its ideological backward look in such a way that our understanding of history is positively transformed'.[12] Without rejecting their past, the writers nevertheless strain against its sectarian, insularist and monologic claims, migrating beyond local and national boundaries, negotiating between the old and the new, tradition and modernity, the local and the international. This fiction doesn't cohere into a 'school' or 'movement' or regional tradition, and indeed, as Eve Patten has remarked, to attempt to codify it too strictly would be to deny it its variety and effectiveness as a challenge to the hegemonic structures. The fiction itself, we might say, exhibits a postmodern multiplicity and heterogeneity, a plurality of viewpoints, a resistance to closure and totalisation Moreover, it demonstrates that multiculturalism need not imply a relativist refusal to judge, or woolly liberal belief that any judgment is as good as any other judgment. It shows, rather, that issues of identity, justice, freedom, and so forth are constantly subject to imaginative interrogation and reconstruction, constantly to be debated, revised and determined. It suggests, finally, that there can be no End of History, that we can never be done with doing justice, or reconfiguring identity, or re-mapping the past.

---

12 Richard Kearney, *Transitions*, p. 277.

Bibliography

NOVELS

Bateman, Colin, *Divorcing Jack* (London: HarperCollins, 1995).

——, *Cycle of Violence* (London: HarperCollins, 1995).

Beckett, Mary, *Give Them Stones* (New York: Beech Tree Books, William Morrow, 1987).

Bennett, Ronan, *The Second Prison* (London: Review, 2000), p. 90. First published London: Hamish Hamilton, 1991.

Clancy, Tom, *Patriot Games* (London: Collins, 1987).

Costello, Mary, *Titanic Town* (London: Methuen, 1992),

Deane, Seamus, *Reading in the Dark* (London: Cape, 1996)

Duffaud, Briege, *A Wreath upon the Dead* (Dublin: Poolbeg, 1994. First published Dublin: Poolbeg, 1993

Healy, Dermot, *A Goat's Song* (London: Harvill, 1997). First published London: HarperCollins, 1994

Higgins, Jack *The Savage Day* (London: Collins, 1972).

Johnston, Jennifer, *How Many Miles to Babylon?* (Glasgow: Fontana, 1981). First published London: Hamish Hamilton,

——, *The Illusionist* (London: Minerva, 1996). First published London: Sinclair-Stevenson, 1995.

——, *The Old Jest* (Glascow: Fontana, 1980). First published London: Hamish Hamilton, 1979.

——, *The Railway Station Man* (London: Review, 1998). First published London: Hamish Hamilton, 1984.

——, *Shadows on Our Skin* (London: Penguin, 1991). First published London: Hamish Hamilton, 1977.

Kiely, Benedict, *Nothing Happens in Carmincross* (London: Methuen, 1986), First published London: Gollancz, 1985.

——, *Proxopera* (London: Methuen, 1988). First published London: Gollancz, 1977.

Leitch, Maurice, *Silver's City* (London: Abacus, 1983). First published London: Secker & Warburg, 1981.

McCabe, Eugene, *Victims: A Tale from Fermanagh* (London: Gollancz, 1976).

McLaverty, Bernard, *Cal* (London: Penguin, 1984). First published London: Cape, 1983.

McNamee, Eoin, *Resurrection Man* (London: Picador, 1994).

Madden, Deirdre, *Hidden Symptoms* (London: Faber, 1988). First published Boston and New York: Atlantic Monthly Press, 1986.

——, *One by One in the Darkness* (London: Faber, 1997). First published London: Faber, 1996

Molloy, Frances, *No Mate for the Magpie* (London: Virago, 1983).

Moore, Brian, *Lies of Silence* (London: Vintage, 1992). First published London: Bloomsbury, 1990.

Morrison, Danny, *West Belfast* (Cork and Dublin: Mercier Press, 1989).

——, *The Wrong Man* (Cork: Mercier Press, 1996).

O'Brien, Edna, *The House of Splendid Isolation* (London: Phoenix, 1997. First published London: Weidenfeld & Nicolson, 1994.

O'Riordan, Kate, *Involved* (London: Flamingo, 1995).

Park, David, *The Healing* (London: Cape, 1992).

——, *Stone Kingdoms* (London: Phoenix, 1997). First published London: Phoenix, 1996.

Patterson, Glenn, *Burning Your Own* (London: Minerva, 1993). First published London: Chatto & Windus, 1988.

——, *Fat Lad* (London: Minerva,1993). First published London: Chatto & Windus, 1992.

——, *The International* (London: Anchor, 1999).

Seymour, Gerald, *Harry's Game* (London: Collins, 1975).

Shriver, Lionel, *Ordinary Decent Criminals* (London: Flamingo, 1993). First published New York: Farrar, Straus & Giroux, 1990 under the title *The Bleeding Heart*. Hereafter, page references will be incorporated into the text.

Stuart, Francis, *A Hole in the Head* (London: Martin Brian & O'Keefe, 1977).

White, Terence de Vere, *The Distance and the Dark* (London: Gollancz, 1973).

Wilson, Robert MacLiam, *Eureka Street* (London: Minerva, 1997). First published London: Secker & Warburg, 1996.

——, *Ripley Bogle* (London: Picador, 1989).

BOOKS

Anderson, Benedict, *Imagined Communities* (New York: Verso, 1991).

Anderson, Walter Truett (ed.), *The Fontana Post-modernism Reader* (London: Fontana, 1996).

Barthes, Roland *The Pleasure of the Text*, trans. Richard Miller (London: Cape, 1976).

Bell, Bowyer, *The Irish Troubles: A Generation of Violence 1967–1992* (Dublin, Gill and Macmilalan 1993).

Belton, John, *American Cinema/American Culture* (New York and London: McGraw-Hill, Inc., 1994).

Bhabha, Homi, *The Location of Culture* (London: Routledge, 1993).

Bradbury, Malcolm (ed.), *The Novel Today* (London: Fontana, 1975).

Camus, Albert, *Carnets 1942–1951*, trans. Philip Thody (London: Hamish Hamilton, 1966).

Caruth, Cathy, *Unclaimed Experience: Trauma, Narrative, and History* (Baltimore: Johns Hopkins University Press, 1995).

Cawelti, John, *Adventure, Mystery, and Romance* (Chicago: University of Chicago Press,1976)

Coogan, Tim Pat, *The Troubles: Ireland's Ordeal: 1966–1996 and the Search for Peace* (London: Arrow, 1996)

Corcoran, Neil, *After Yeats and Joyce: Reading Modern Irish Literature* (Oxford: Oxford University Press, 1997).

——, *The Chosen Ground: Essays on the Contemporary Poetry of Northern Ireland* (Bridgend: Seren Books, 1992).

Deane, Seamus,' *Celtic Revivals* (London: Faber, 1985).

—— (ed.), *The Field Day Anthology of Irish Writing* (Derry: Field Day Theatre Company, 1991.

—— (ed.), *Nationalism, Colonialism and Literature* (Minneapolis: University of Minnesota Press, 1990), pp 18–19.

Derrida, Jacques, *Writing and Difference*, trans. A. Bass (Chicago, n.p. 1978).

Eagleton, Terry, *Crazy Jane and the Bishop:: and other Essays on Irish Culture* (Cork: Cork University Press in association with Field Day, 1998)

——, *Nationalism: Irony and Commitment* (Derry: Field Day pamphlet, 1988).

Fennell, Desmond, *Heresy: The Battle of Ideas in Modern Ireland* (Belfast: Blackstaff, 1993).

Freud, Sigmund, *Beyond the Pleasure Principle*, trans. and ed. James Strachey (London: Hogarth Press, 1961).

Gibbons, Luke, *Transformations in Irish Culture* (Cork: Cork University Press, 1996).

Harvey, W.J., *Character and the Novel* (London: Chatto and Windus, 1965).

Heaney, Seamus, *Opened Ground: Poems 1966–1996* (London: Faber, 1998).

——, *Preoccupations: Selected Prose 1968–1978* (London: Faber, 1980).

Hemingway, Ernest, *The Essential Ernest Hemingway* (London: Triad Grafton, 1988).

Hutcheon, Linda, *A Poetics of Postmodernism: History, Theory, Fiction* (London and New York: Routledge, 1988)

Imhof, Rudiger (ed.), *Contemporary Irish Novelists* (Tubingen: Gunter Narr 1990).

Jameson, Frederic, *Postmodernism, or The Cultural Logic of Late Capitalism* (London: Verso, 1991).

Jencks, Charles (ed.), *The Post-Modern Reader* (London: Academy, 1992).

Kearney, Richard, *Across the Frontiers: Ireland in the 1990s: Cultural, Political, Economic* (Dublin: Wolfhound, 1988).

——, *Transitions: Narratives in Modern Irish Culture* (Dublin: Wolfhound, 1988)

Kiberd, Declan, *Anglo-Irish Attitudes* (Derry: Field Day Theatre Company, 1984).

——, *Inventing Ireland: The Literature of the Modern Nation* (London: Vintage, 1996).

Kinsella, Thomas, and W.B. Yeats, *Davis, Mangan, Ferguson?: Tradition and the Irish Writer* (Dublin: Dolmen, 1970).

Kirkland, Richard, *Language and Culture in Northern Ireland since 1965: Moments of Danger* (London: Longman, 1996).

Knight, Stephen *Form and Ideology in Crime Fiction* (London: Macmillan, 1980).

Lloyd, David, *Anomalous States: Irish Writing and the Post-Colonial Moment* (Dublin: Lilliput, 1993).

Longley, Edna, *The Living Stream: Literature and Revisionism in Ireland* (Newcastle-upon-Tyne: Bloodaxe Books, 1994),

Lodge, David (ed.), *Modern Criticism and Theory* (Harlow: Longman Pearson, 2000).

Longley, Michael, *Poems 1963–1983* (London: Penguin, 1985)

McDonald, Peter, *Mistaken Identities: Poetry and Northern Ireland* (Oxford: Clarendon Press, 1997).

Magee, P. J., *Troubles Fiction: A critical history of prose fiction dealing with the conflict in the North of Ireland since the late 1960s*, unpublished DPhil. thesis (Coleraine: University of Ulster, 1999).

Miles, Rosalind, *The Fiction of Sex: Themes and Functions of Sex Difference in the Modern Novel* (London: Vision Press, 1994).

O'Brien, Edna, *Mother Ireland* (London: Weidenfeld and Nicolson, 1976).

Palmer, Jerry, *Thrillers* (London: Edward Arnold, 1978).

Palmer, Paulina, *Contemporary Women's Fiction: Narrative Practice and Feminist Theory* (Hemel Hempstead: Harvester Wheatsheaf, 1989).

Radzinowicz, Leo, *Crime and Ideology* (New York: Columbia University Press, 1966).

Ratfroidi, Patrick, and Maurice Harmon (eds.), *The Irish Novel in Our Time* (Publications de l'Université de Lille, 1976).

Rice, Philip, and Patricia Waugh (eds.), *Modern Literary Theory* (London: Arnold, 1999).

Rich, Adrienne, *Of Woman Born: Motherhood as Experience and Institution* (London: Virago, 1977).

St Peter, Catherine, *Changing Ireland: Strategies in Contemporary Women's Fiction* (Basingstoke: Macmillan, 2000).

Sampson, Denis, *Brian Moore: The Chameleon Novelist* (Dublin: Marino Books, 1998).

Sauerberg, Lars Ole, *Secret Agents in Fiction* (New York: St. Martin's Press, 1984).

Smyth, Gerry, *The Novel and the Nation* (London: Pluto Press, 1997).

Stevens, Wallace, *The Necessary Angel: Essays on Reality and Imagination* (London: Faber, 1951)

Trilling, Lionel, *The Liberal Imagination* (London: Penguin, 1970).

Waugh, Patricia, *Practising Postmodernism Reading Modernism* (London: Edward Arnold, 1992)

White, Terence de Vere, *The Anglo-Irish* (London: Gollancz, 1972).

Wills, Clair, *Improprieties: Politics and Sexuality in Northern Irish Poetry* (Oxford: Clarendon Press, 1993).

ARTICLES AND INTERVIEWS

Bakhtin, Mikhail, excerpt from *The Dialogic Imagination* (1934) in Philip Rice and Patricia Waugh (eds.), Modern Literary Theory (London: Arnold, 1999), pp 256–64.

Barth, John, 'The literature of replenishment: postmodern fiction', in Charles Jencks (ed.), *The Post-Modern Reader* (London: Academy, 1992), pp 172–180.

Baudrillard, Jean, 'The evil demon of images and the precession of simulacra', in Thomas Docherty (ed.), *Postmodernism: A Reader* (Hemel Hempstead: Harvester Wheatsheaf, 1993), pp 194–9.

——, extract from *Simulations*, in Patricia Waugh (ed.), *Postmodernism: A Reader* (London: Edward Arnold, 1992), pp 186–9.

Bell, J. Bowyer, 'The Troubles as trash', *Hibernia*, 20 January 1978, pp 21–2.

Bennett, Ronan, 'An Irish answer', *Guardian Weekend*, 16 July 1994.

Bennett, Tony, 'Marxism and popular fiction', in Peter Humm, Paul Stigant and Peter Widdowson (eds.), *Popular Fictions: Essays in Literature and History* (London: Methuen, 1986), pp 237–65.

Bonitzer, Pascal, 'Partial vision: film and the labyrinth', trans. Fabrice Ziolkowski, *Wide Angle*, 4, 4 (1982), pp 53–63.

Carroll, Noel, 'Toward a theory of film suspense', *Persistence of Vision*, I, 1, Summer 1984, pp 65–89.

Caterson, Simon, 'Swimming from *The Titanic*: Mary Costello talks to Simon Caterson', *Irish Studies Review*, 8, Autumn 1994, pp 6–8.

Clancy, Tom, '"My views on unity', *Irish America* (January 1988), pp 15–17.

Cleary, Joe, '"Fork-tongued on the border bit": Partition and the politics of form in contemporary narratives of the Northern Irish conflict' in *South Atlantic Quarterly*, 95, 1, Winter 1996, pp 227–276.

Carson, Ciaran, '"Escaped from the massacre"?', review of Seamus Heaney's *North*, in *Honest Ulsterman*, 50, Winter 1975, pp 183–6.

Craig, Patricia, 'A Cabinet in Co. Clare', review of *One by One in the Darkness*, *Times Literary Supplement*, 24 May 1996, p. 26.

Deane, Seamus, 'Canon fodder: literary mythologies in Ireland', in Jean Lundy and Aodán MacPóilin (eds.), *Styles of Belonging: The Cultural Identities of Ulster* (Belfast, Lagan Press, 1992)

——, 'Civilians and barbarians', in *Ireland's Field Day* (London: Hutchinson, 1985).

——, 'Heroic styles: the tradition of an idea', in *Ireland's Field Day* (London: Hutchinson, 1985), pp 45–59.

——, 'In the firing line', review of *Lies of Silence* in the *Times Literary Supplement*, 20–26 April 1990, pp 430.

——, 'Irish poetry and Irish Nationalism', in Douglas Dunn (ed.), *Two Decades of Irish Writing* (Cheadle: Carcanet, 1975), pp 4–22.

——, 'Reading in the dark: an interview with Seamus Deane', *English & Media Magazine*, 36, Summer 1997, pp 17–20.

——, 'Remembering the Irish future', *Crane Bag*, 8, 1 (1984), pp 81–92.

——, 'Unhappy and at Home', interview with Seamus Heaney, in *Crane Bag*, 1 (1977), pp 61–7.

Deutsch, Richard, '"Within two shadows": the Troubles in Northern Ireland', in Patrick Rafroidi and Maurice Harmon (eds.), *The Irish Novel in Our Time* (Publications de l'Université de Lille, 1976), pp 131–56.

Eagleton, Terry, 'The Bogside bard', *New Statesman*, 30 August 1996, p. 46.

Eco, Umberto, '"I love you madly," he said self-consciously', in *The Fontana Post-modernism Reader*, pp 31–3.

Farquharson, Diane, 'Resisting genre and type: narrative strategy and instability in Danny Morrison's *The Wrong Man* and Seamus Deane's *Reading in the Dark*', in Bill Lazenbatt (ed.) *Northern Narratives, Writing Ulster* (Jordanstown: University of Ulster) 89–112.

Fever, Nick 'A kind of life sentence', *Guardian*, 28 October 1996, p. 9.

Gebler, Carlo, 'Specifically Personal', review of *One by One in the Darkness*, in *Fortnight*, May 1996, p. 36.

Gergen, Kenneth, 'The healthy, happy human being wears many masks', in Walter Truett Anderson (ed.), *The Fontana Post-Modernism Reader* (London: Fontana, 1996), pp 132–40.

Hansson, Heidi, 'To say 'I': female identity in *The Maid's Tale* and *The Wig My Father Wore*', in Elmer Kennedy-Andrews (ed.), *Irish Fiction Since 1969* (Gerards Cross: Colin Smythe, 2002).

Harte, Liam, 'History lessons: postcolonialism and Seamus Deane's *Reading in the Dark*', *Irish University Review*, 30, 1 (Spring/Summer 2000), pp 149–62.

Hurtley, Jacqueline, Rosa González, Inés Praga and Esther Aliaga (eds.), *Ireland in Writing: Interviews with Writers and Academics* (Amsterdam: Podopi, 1998). Includes interview with Glenn Patterson.

Huyssen, Andreas, 'Mapping the postmodern', in Charles Jencks (ed.) *The Post-Modern Reader* (London: Academy, 1992), pp 40–72.

Imhof, Rudiger, 'A little bit of ivory two inches wide: the small world of Jennifer Johnston's fiction', *Études Irlandaises*, 10 December 1985, pp 129–44.

Kamm, Jurgen, 'Jennifer Johnston', in Rudiger Imhof (ed.), *Contemporary Irish Novelists* (Tubingen: Gunter narr 1990), pp 125–41.

Johnston, Jennifer, 'Prodding republicanism', *Fortnight*, April 1995, pp 36–7.

Jones, Maxine, review of *One by One in the Darkness* in *Tribune Magazine*, 26 May 1996, p. 20.

Knight, Stephen, 'Radical thrillers', in Ian A. Bell and Graham Daldry (eds.), *Watching the Detectives* (Basingstoke: Macmillan, 1990), pp 172–87.

Lazenbatt, Bill, 'A conversation with Francis Stuart', in *Writing Ulster: Francis Stuart Special Issue*, 4, 1996, pp 1–17

Lifton, Robert Jay , 'Protean man', *Partisan Review* (Winter 1968), pp 13–27.

Longley, Edna, 'Autobiography as history', review of *Reading in the Dark*, *Fortnight*, Nov. 1996, p. 31.

——, 'Northern Ireland: poetry and peace', in Karl-Heinz Westarp and Michael Boss (eds.), *Ireland: Towards New Identities* (Aarhus U.P., 1998), pp 103–15.

——, 'Writing, revisionism & grass-seed: literary mythologies in Ireland' in Jean Lundy and Aodán MacPóilin (eds.), *Styles of Belonging: The Cultural Identities of Ulster* (Belfast, Lagan Press, 1991), pp 11–22.

Macherey, Pierre, 'from *A Theory of Literary Production* (1978)' in Antony Easthope and Kate McGowan (eds.), *A Critical and Cultural Theory Reader* (Buckingham: Open University Press, 1997), pp 21–30.

McMinn, Joseph, 'Contemporary novels on the "Troubles"', *Études Irlandaises*, 5, December 1980, pp 113–21.

McWilliams, Monica, 'Struggling for peace and justice: reflections on women's activism in Northern Ireland', in Joan Hoff and Moureen Coulter (eds.), *Irish Women's Voices: Past and Present, Publication of the Journal of Women's History*, 6, 4 / 7, 1, Winter/Spring 1995, p. 32–4.

Moi, Toril, 'Feminist, female, feminine', in Catherine Belsey and Jane Moore (eds.), *The Feminist Reader* (Basingstoke: Macmillan, 1997).

Mulvey, Laura, 'Visual pleasure and narrative cinema', in Antony Easthope and Kate McGowan (eds.), *A Critical and Cultural Theory Reader* (Buckingham: Open University Press, 1992), pp 158–66.

O'Brien, Conor Cruise, 'An unhealthy intersection', *New Review*, 2, 16, July 1975, p. 7.

Parker, Michael, 'Shadows on a glass: self-reflexivity in the fiction of Deirdre Madden', in *Irish University Review*, Spring/Summer 2000, pp 82–102.

Patterson, Glenn, 'I am a Northern Irish novelist', in Ian A. Bell (ed.), *Images of Nationhood in Contemporary British Fiction* (Cardiff: University of Wales Press, 1995), p. 150–4.

Patton, Eve, 'Fiction in conflict: Northern Ireland's prodigal novelists' in I.A. Bell (ed.), *Peripheral Visions: Images of Nationhood in Contemporary British Fiction* (Cardiff: University of Wales Press, 1995), pp 128–48

——, 'Women & fiction 1985–1990', *Krino*, 8–9, 1990, pp 1–7.

Pearce, Sandra, Interview with Edna O'Brien, *Canadian Journal of Irish Studies*, 22, 2, Dec. 1996, pp 5–8.

Randolph, Jody Allen, 'An interview with Eavan Boland', *Irish University Review*, 23; 1, Spring-Summer 1993, p. 130.

Rolston, Bill, 'Mothers, whores and villains: images of women in novels of the Northern Ireland Conflict', *Race and Class*, 31, 1, 1989, pp 41–57.

Rorty, Richard, 'Ironists and metaphysicians', in *The Fontana Post-modernist Reader*, pp 96–102.

Rumens, Carol, 'Reading Deane', *Fortnight*, July/August 1997, p. 29–30.

Sheehan, Ronan, 'Novelists on the novel', interview with Francis Stuart and John Banville, in *Crane Bag*, 3, 1 (1979), p. 76.

Smith, Stan, 'The twilight of the cities: Derek Mahon's dark cinema' in Elmer Kennedy-Andrews (ed.), *The Poetry of Derek Mahon* (Gerards Cross: Colin Smythe, 2002), pp 219–41.

Smyth, Ailbhe, 'The Floozie in the Jacuzzi', *The Irish Review* 6, Spring 1989, pp 7–24,

Sullivan, Megan, '"Instead I said I am a home baker": Nationalist ideology and materialist politics in Mary Beckett's *Give Them Stones*, in Kathryn Kirkpatrick (ed.), *Border Crossings: Irish Women Writers and National Identities* (Dublin: Wolfhound, 2000), pp 227–49.

Titley, Alan, 'Rough rug-headed kerns: the Irish gunman in the popular novel', *Eire-Ireland*, 15, 4, Winter 1980, pp 15–38.

Walters, Suzanne, 'From here to queer: radical feminism, postmodernism, and the lesbian menace (or, Why can't a woman be more like a fag?)', *Signs: Journal of Women, Culture and Society*, 21, 4, 1996.

Ward, Margaret, and Marie-Therese McGivern, 'Images of women in Northern Ireland', in *Crane Bag*, 4, 1, 1980, pp 66–72.

Wilson, Robert MacLiam 'The glittering prize', *Fortnight*, November 1995, pp 5–7.

Biographical notes on the novelists

COLIN BATEMAN was born in Bangor, Northern Ireland, in 1962, the son of a local civil servant. The family was Protestant and Unionist. At the age of seventeen he began work with the local newspaper, the *County Down Spectator*, where he stayed for sixteen years ending up deputy editor. A fan of punk, his first piece was a review of the Sex Pistols. His weekly satirical column in the newspaper won him a Northern Ireland Press Award and a Journalist's Fellow-ship to Oxford University to research an academic paper on Uganda. As a frustrated musician, he developed for a brief time a sideline promoting concerts. *Divorcing Jack* (1995) was his first novel, for which he received the Betty Trask Prize in 1994. Both *Divorcing Jack* and his next novel *Cycle of Violence* (1995) have been turned into films, the latter under the title *Crossmaheart* (which was also used as title for the re-issue of the book). Other novels include *Of Wee Sweetie Mice and Men* (1996), which deals with the career of a hopeless heavyweight boxer in New York; *Empire State* (1997), in which an Irish emigrant obtains employment as a keeper at the building, kidnaps the President, combats racism, and ends up a hero; *Turbulent Priests* (1999); *Wild Harry* (2001); *Shooting Sean* (2001); and *Mohammed Maguire* (2001), another satire on the Troubles in which Mo, son of top Irish Provo Olivia Maguire and Mohammed Salameh, a leading figure in the militant Egyptian fundamentalist group Al-Gamaat Al-Islamia, leaves a Libyan terrorist training camps for Northern Ireland and, through an unlikely series of events, finds himself in the Maze, and responsible for both the 'dirty protest' and the 'blanket protest'.

MARY BECKETT was born in Belfast in 1926 into a family of teachers. After completing her education at St Mary's Training College in Belfast, she herself became a primary teacher in Holy Cross in Ardoyne, Belfast. In 1956 she married and moved to Dublin, where she began writing short stories, first for BBC radio and then for literary magazines in Dublin, Cork and Belfast. She stopped writing for twenty years to raise five children. A collection of short stories, *A Belfast Woman* (1980), was followed by the novel *Give Them Stones* (1987), and a further collection of stories *A Literary Woman* (1990).

RONAN BENNETT was born in 1956 in Belfast. He holds a BA in History and a PhD in Legal History from London University. He was imprisoned in Long Kesh and Brixton Prison for Republican activities in the 1970s, successfully defending himself in a three-month trial at the Old Bailey. He was involved in the campaign to free the 'Guildford Four', co-writing with Paul Hill *The Stolen Years: Before and after Guildford* (1990). As well as *The Second Prison* (1991), he has written two other novels, *Overthrown by Strangers* (1992), and *The Catastrophist* (1998), both studies of the nature of commitment in an international context. He has also written the TV drama on the Troubles, *Love Lies Bleeding* (1993) and another TV drama, *Rebel Hearts* (2001), set during the 1916 Rising.

TOM CLANCY, born in 1947 in Baltimore, is a prolific American thriller writer. He received a Jesuit education at Loyola High School, Towson, Maryland, and graduated from Loyola College, Baltimore, in 1969. He owned and operated an independent insurance business before starting his writing career. He never served in any branch of the US military. *Patriot Games* (1987) was a bestseller and a box-office success when it was transferred to the screen by Paramount Pictures in 1992, with Harrison Ford as Jack Ryan.

MARY COSTELLO was born in 1955 in West Belfast. After graduating in Modern Languages from Queen's University Belfast, she trained as an actress. She set up the children's Albatross Company, and worked with TEAM. She wrote *Titanic Town* (1992) in Melbourne, where she has lived since 1981. The novel has been made into a film with Julie Walters as Annie McPhelimy.

SEAMUS DEANE was born in 1940 in Derry and educated at St Columb's College, then Queen's University Belfast and Cambridge. He taught at University College Dublin, where he was Professor of Modern English and American Literature, before moving to the University of Notre Dame in 1993. His first two collections of poetry were *Gradual Wars* (1972) and *History Lessons* (1983). He was a founding director of the Field Day Theatre Company and wrote two of its early pamphlets, *Civilians and Barbarians* (1983) and *Heroic Styles: The Tradition of an Idea* (1984) which examined the influence of colonialism on Irish culture. *Celtic Revivals: Essays in Modern Irish Literature* (1984) and *A Short History of Irish Literature* (1986) viewed Irish literature in a colonial context, while his monumental *Field Day Anthology of Irish Literature* (1991) set out to reflect in its selections and prefatory essays the multiple, intertwining strands in Irish literary culture. He is also the author of *The French Enlightenment and Revolution in England 1789–1832* (1988), and the autobiographical novel *Reading in the Dark* (1996).

BRIEGE DUFFAUD was born in Antrim. After marriage, she moved to Brittany, where she is currently living. As well as *A Wreath upon the Dead* (1993), she has published a collection of stories of exile and return, *Nothing like Beirut* (1994), and *A Long Stem Rose* (1995), a novel concerning an Irish woman who manages a château/hotel in France and who leaves husband and children to return to Belfast in search of a woman who is a 'lost love'.

DERMOT HEALY was born 1947 in Finea, Co. Westmeath. He has been director of a theatre group and editor of two journals, *The Drumlin* and *Force 10*. His books include a collection of stories, *Banished Misfortune* (1982), which won two Hennessy Awards and the Tom Gallan Award; *Fighting with Shadows* (1984), a novel set on the Fermanagh border; *A Goat's Song* (1994) which won the 1994 Encore Award for best second novel; an autobiography, *The Bend in the Road* (1996) and two books of poems, *The Ballyconnell Colours* (1992) and *What the Hammer* (1998). He wrote the screenplay for *Our Boys* (1980), a film about the Christian Brothers, and for *The Next Bed* (1987). He is a member of Aosdána and lives near Sligo.

JACK HIGGINS, Martin Fallon, James Graham and Hugh Marlowe are all *noms de plume* of Harry Patterson, the most prolific thriller writer to use the Northern Irish Troubles as background. Born in 1929 in Newcastle-upon-Tyne of a Belfast mother, he was raised in Protestant Belfast between the ages of two and twelve, when he returned to England. He studied Sociology at LSE.

JENNIFER JOHNSTON was born in 1930 in Dublin, the daughter of playwright Denis Johnston and actress Sheelagh Richards. She was educated at Park House School and Trinity College Dublin. She married solicitor Ian Smyth in 1951 and began writing fiction. After her second marriage to David Gilliland, she settled near Derry in 1979. *Shadows on our Skin* (1977) was shortlisted for the Booker Prize; *The Old Jest* (1979) won the Whitbread Prize and was filmed as *The Dawning*; *The Invisible Worm* (1991) won *Daily Express* best book, 1992. In 1993 she worked with prisoners in the H-Block, Long Kesh. Johnston has also written drama, including *Desert Lullaby*, premiered at Belfast Lyric Theatre in October 1996.

BENEDICT KIELY was born in 1919 in Dromore, Co. Tyrone, and educated at the Christian Brothers in Omagh, the Jesuits in Co. Laois, and University College Dublin. He worked as a journalist in Dublin (1945–64), taught creative writing at various American universities (1964–8), has lectured at UCD, and contributed to radio and television broadcasts. His first book, *Counties of Contention* (1945) was an historical study attacking the partition of Ireland, while *Poor Scholar* (1947) examined the work and times of the Co. Tyrone fiction writer William Carleton. His *Modern Irish Fiction: A Critique* (1950) was a seminal study of post-independence Irish fiction. He is a prolific short story writer as well as novelist.

MAURICE LEITCH was born in 1933 in Muckamore, Co. Antrim, educated in Belfast and worked as a schoolteacher for six years before joining the BBC as a radio features producer in Belfast, becoming head of BBC radio drama features in London. His first two novels, *The Liberty Lad* (1965) and *Poor Lazarus* (1969), which won the Guardian Fiction Prize, 1969, were banned in the Republic of Ireland. His other novels include *Stamping Ground* (1975), the Whitbread Prize-winning *Silver's City* (1981), *Chinese Whispers* (1987), *Burning Bridges* (1989), *Gilchrist* (1994), *The Smoke King* (1998) and *The Eggman's Apprentice* (2001). A collection of stories, *The Hands of Cheryl Boyd and Other Stories* was published in 1987. Leitch left Northern Ireland in 1970 and lives in London. He worked for the BBC until 1988.

EUGENE MCCABE was born in 1930 in Glasgow, where his family lived until he was nine. He was educated at Castleknock College, Co. Dublin, and University College Cork. In 1964 he took over the family farm (originally purchased by his grandfather), Drumard House, in Co. Monaghan, 400 yards from the Fermanagh border. As well as farming, he started writing in 1962, producing stage-plays and plays for television. His first novel was *Victims: A Tale from Fermanagh* (1976), a version of the third of a trilogy of plays entitled *Victims*. His other fiction includes *Heritage and Other Stories* (1978), and *Death and Nightingales* (1992), a tragic pastoral novella set in the time of Parnell and dealing with political and domestic violence in Fermanagh.

BERNARD MACLAVERTY was born 1942 in Belfast. He worked for ten years as a medical laboratory technician before taking a degree at Queen's University Belfast in 1974 and moving to the Isle of Islay off the west coast of Scotland. In the early 1980s he gave up schoolteaching to devote himself to writing full-time. As well as *Cal* (1983), which was filmed by Pat O'Connor in 1984, he has written three other novels, *Lamb* (1980), *Grace Notes* (1999) and *The Anatomy Lesson* (2001), and four collections of stories: *Secrets and Other Stories* (1977), *A Time to Dance* (1982), *The Great Profundo* (1987) and *Walking the Dog* (1994) which contains some modernist prose fragments. He has also written children's books.

EOIN McNAMEE was born in 1961 in Kilkeel, Co. Down, and educated at St Patrick's College, Armagh, and at Trinity College Dublin, where he studied law. He spent a year as a waiter in New York before returning to Dublin to devote himself to writing. As well as *Resurrection Man* (1989), he has written two novellas, *The Last of Deeds* (1989) and *Love in History* (1992), and a novel *The Blue Tango* (2000) based on an actual murder of the daughter of the prominent Unionist Judge Lancelot Curran in Newtownabbey, Co. Antrim, in the 1950s.

DEIRDRE MADDEN was born in 1960 in Belfast and educated at St Mary's Grammar School, Magherafelt, Co. Derry, Trinity College Dublin, and the University of East Anglia, where she attended Malcolm Bradbury's writing school. She married the poet Harry Clifton and spent three years in Italy. *Hidden Symptoms* (1988) brought her immediate international attention and won the Rooney Prize for Irish Literature in 1987. *The Birds of the Innocent Wood* (1988) won the Somerset Maugham Award, 1989, and *One by One in the Darkness* (1996), the Kerry Ingredients Book of the Year Award. She lives in Toomebridge, Co. Antrim.

FRANCES MOLLOY was born in 1947 in Derry. After what she calls a 'patchy education' she left school at fifteen and went to work in a pyjama factory. In 1965 she spent a short time as a nun. In 1970 she emigrated to England, and lived in Lancaster with her husband and two children. She returned to Ireland in 1988, and lived with Dermot Healy. As well as the auto-biographical novel *No Mate for the Magpie* (1985), she has written short stories, and a play with Ruth Hooley and Nell McCafferty. She died of a stroke in 1999.

BRIAN MOORE was born 1921 into a middle-class, Catholic family, son of a surgeon, and educated at St Malachy's College Belfast. In 1940 he joined the Air Raid Precautions Unit. In 1943 he enlisted with the British Ministry of War Transport and was posted to North Africa, Naples and Marseilles. At the end of the war he worked with the UN in Warsaw. In 1948 he emigrated to Canada, married in 1951, and became a Canadian citizen in 1953. He worked as a journalist on the *Montreal Gazette* until his move to the USA in 1959, first to New York, then Malibu, California, where he lived with his second wife. In addition to novels, he has written short stories and screenplays. His first novels, *The Lonely Passion of Judith Hearne* (1956), *The Feast of Lupercal* (1957) and *The Emperor of Ice-Cream* (1965) are all set in Belfast and deal with the struggle of the individual in a narrowly religious and oppressive society. An *Answer from Limbo* (1962), *I Am Mary Dunne* (1968) and *Fergus* (1970) investigate issues of personal responsibility in the more liberal environment of North America. Though he abandoned his religious faith in his early years, it remained a major theme in many of his novels, including

Catholics (1972), *Cold Heaven* (19830, *The Colour of Blood* (1987), *Black Robe* (1985), *No Other Life* (1993), and *The Magician's Wife* (1997). Some of these later novels, like the very first books he wrote under the pen-name of Michael Bryan, are thrillers. He died in Malibu in 1999.

DANNY MORRISON, born in Belfast in 1953, is a former publicity officer for Sinn Féin, renowned for his slogan 'an Armalite in one hand and the ballot box in the other'. He was convicted of false imprisonment of an RUC informer and sentenced to eight years imprison-ment in Long Kesh. He studied with the Open University during his period of imprisonment. As well as *West Belfast* (1989), and *The Wrong Man* (1996), he has written one other novel, *On the Back of the Swallow* (1994), which deals with the theme of homosexuality. He has also published *Then the Walls Came Down* (1999), letters home from jail, 1990-2.

EDNA O'BRIEN was born in 1930 in Tuamgraney, Co. Clare, and educated at Loughrea Convent of Mercy, Co. Galway, and at Dublin Pharmaceutical College. She worked briefly as a pharmicist, married Ernest Gebler in 1951 and settled in London in 1959. She had two children, Carlo and Sasha, but the marriage ended in acrimonious divorce in 1964. Her first three novels, *The Country Girls* (1960), *The Lonely Girl* (1963), and *Girls in their Married Bliss* (1963) are realistic portrayals of young women's lives in a puritanical and oppressive Ireland, and won their author both acclaim and notoriety, all three novels having fallen foul of the Irish Board of Censors. Later novels such as *August Is a Wicked Month* (1964), *A Pagan Place* (1971), *Night* (1972), *The High Road* (1988), *Time and Tide* (1992), and *Down by the River* (1996) continue her investigation into the place of women in contemporary society. She has also written several volumes of short stories, a commentary on Ireland entitled *Mother Ireland* (1976), plays and screenplays, and a critical study, *James Joyce* (1999). She lives in London.

KATE O'RIORDAN was brought up in the west of Ireland but now lives in London. She is an award-winning novelist, playwright and television screenwriter, and has been the recipient of the *Sunday Tribune*/Hennessy Prize for 'Best Emerging Writer'. *Involved* was shortlisted for the Dillon's First Fiction Prize.

DAVID PARK was born in Belfast in 1955. He is a teacher in Downpatrick, Co. Down, where he lives with his wife, a ceramic artist, and their son. He published a collection of short stories, *Oranges from Spain* in 1990, which offers a series of reflections on growing up in Belfast.

GLENN PATERSON was born in 1961, son of a sheetmetal worker, and brought up in Finaghy, Belfast. He attended Methodist College, Belfast, worked in Crane's bookshop in Belfast for a year and a half, and then went to the University of East Anglia where he gained an MA in Creative Writing. He lived in Manchester after university, returning to Northern Ireland when he was appointed community writer for Lisburn and Craigavon, 1989–91. He is married to an arts administrator and has one daughter. He finds the North a creative, stimulating place to be and says he 'decided against identity being taken from a limited choice of two, identity was multiple. So first of all I think of myself as a Belfast person, I'm Irish, I'm British, I'm European. I hold all those identities simultaneously and they're not exclusive.'

GERALD SEYMOUR was born in 1941 in England. He worked as a ITN reporter in Northern Ireland, and lived in the Irish Republic for some years before returning to England. *Harry's Game* (1975), his first novel, was adapted for TV in 1982 and won the Pye Television Award for best screenplay. Other thrillers involving the Northern Irish Troubles include *The Glory Boys* (1976), and *Field of Blood* (1985).

LIONEL SHRIVER was born in North Carolina, and educated at Columbia University, New York. She took up temporary residence in Belfast in 1987. As well as *Ordinary Decent Criminals* (1992), which was originally published in the United States in 1990 under the title *Bleeding Heart*, she has written four other novels: *The Female of the Species* (1987), *Checker and the Deraileurs* (1988), *Game Control* (1994) and *Double Fault* (1997).

FRANCIS STUART was born in 1902 in Queensland, Australia, the son of Co. Antrim parents. Four months after the birth his father committed suicide in a mental asylum, after which mother and son returned to Ireland, settling with relatives near Drogheda. He was educated at various boarding schools in England, including Rugby. In 1920 he married Iseult Gonne, daughter of Maud Gonne, converted to Catholicism, and took part in the Civil War on the Republican side until captured in 1922. His early novels record his dissatisfaction with the materialism and commercialism of post-revolutionary Ireland and reflect his interest in the mystics. Marital and financial problems contributed to his controversial decision to take up a lecturing appointment in the University of Berlin in 1939. During the war he undertook anti-British broadcasts to Ireland from Germany. At the end of the war he was imprisoned by the French, along with his companion, Gertrud ('Madeleine') Meissner, whom he later married in 1954. He and Madeleine stayed on in Germany after the war, then moved to Paris, then London, eventually returning to Ireland in 1958, shortly after which Madeleine died. Stuart's novels *The Pillar of Cloud* (1948) and *Redemption* (1949), based on his wartime and post-war experiences, are generally regarded as among his best. He received major critical acclaim for *Black List Section H* (1971), another autobiographical fiction, in which he explores the redemptive potential of suffering. Further success accompanied his later, more experimental novels, among them *Memorial* (1973), *A Hole in the Head* (1977), *The High Consistory* (1981), *Finlandia* (1985) and *A Compendium of Lovers* (1990). He married the artist Finola Graham in 1987. He died in 2000.

TERENCE DE VERE WHITE was born in 1912 in Dublin, of a Protestant father and a Catholic mother. The family kept at a distance from the political upheavals of White's childhood and found it difficult to identify with the new social order of post-Independence Ireland. White was given a Catholic schooling and, after completing his education at Trinity College Dublin, entered the legal profession. He married in 1941 and had three children. He took an active part in the cultural life of Dublin, serving on the boards of the Gate Theatre and the National Gallery. He was literary editor of the *Irish Times*, 1961–77. He has written some dozen novels; histories of Ireland, Leinster and the Anglo-Irish; biographies of Isaac Butt, who was the first leader of the Irish Home Rule party at Westminster, and of Tom Moore, the Irish poet. He died in 1994.

ROBERT McLIAM WILSON was born in 1964 in West Belfast, the son of a worker in a bread factory. He was educated locally and at St Catherine's College, Cambridge. *Ripley Bogle* (1992) won the Hughes, Rooney and Betty Trask Prizes for literature, and the Irish Book Award. He married Melanie Hammond, daughter of David Hammond. *Manfred's Pain* (1992) was the study of a man who compulsively abused his concentration-camp survivor wife. *The Dispossessed* (1992), with photographs by Donovan Wylie, investigated poverty in Thatcherite Britain. From 1992–1994 Wilson was Writer-in-Residence at the University of Ulster at Coleraine. He lives in Paris.

Chronology of important events

29 Jan. 1967   Foundation of Northern Ireland Civil Rights Association (NICRA) demanding 'one man one vote'; an end to discrimination and gerrymandering; machinery to deal with complaints against public authorities; disbandment of B- Specials; fair public housing allocation; an end to Special Powers Act.

5 Oct. 1968   RUC baton-charge of Civil Rights marchers in Derry leads to first riots in Catholic Bogside

1-5 Jan. 1969   Queen's University students' People's Democracy march from Belfast to Derry attacked by Loyalists, most notably at Burntollet Bridge on 4 January. Following RUC provocation, barricades are erected in the Bogside.

22 Apr. 1969   Bernadette Devlin, Independent Unity MP for Mid-Ulster, delivers her maiden speech in the House of Commons.

28 Apr. 1969   Resignation of Captain Terence O'Neill as premier of Northern Ireland, following Loyalist bombings of an electricity substation outside Belfast and the Silent Valley reservoir in the Mournes.

Aug. 1969   Fierce rioting in Derry (Battle of the Bogside) and in Belfast's Falls Road leads to British army deployment in Northern Ireland on 14 August. First Republican martyr, fifteen-year-old Gerard McAuley, shot by Protestant sniper on that day. Fear of further attacks on Catholic areas leads to revival of the IRA.

11 Oct. 1969   Publication of the Hunt Report recommending disbandment of the B-Specials and disarming of the RUC leads to Loyalist rioting on Shankill Road, Belfast. First RUC man to die in the Troubles, Constable Arbuckle, shot by a Protestant sniper.

11 Jan. 1970   Sinn Féin (SF) splits into 'Provisional' and 'Official' wings. Foundation of Provisional IRA.

21 Aug. 1970   Foundation of Social Democratic and Labour Party (SDLP) under Gerry Fitt.

9 Aug. 1971   Introduction of internment.

Sept. 1971   Emergence of the Ulster Defence Association (UDA).

30 Oct. 1971   Formation of Democratic Unionist Party (DUP) under Reverend Ian Paisley.

30 Jan. 1972   'Bloody Sunday': after an anti-internment demonstration in Derry the British army shoots dead 13 civilians.

24 Mar. 1972   Stormont Government falls and is replaced by direct rule from Westminster.

21 Jul. 1972   'Bloody Friday': 22 IRA bombs explode in Belfast within 75 minutes, causing nine deaths. Francis Arthur is first victim of the 'Shankill Butchers', a notorious Loyalist murder gang led by Lenny Murphy which was responsible for the deaths of 30 Catholics during the '70s.

31 Jul. 1972	'Operation Motorman': British army cracks down on IRA 'no-go' areas in Derry and Belfast. IRA responds with car bombs on Co. Derry village of Claudy which killed eight people; 1972 was worst year of the troubles with 467 deaths, 10,628 shootings and almost 2,000 bombs.
9 Dec. 1973	Sunningdale Agreement provides for a Power Sharing Executive (which took office on 1 Jan. 1994) and a Council of Ireland.
28 May 1974	Loyalist Ulster Workers Strike brings down the power-sharing Executive. The strike had been accompanied by some of the worst violence of the Troubles, including no-warning car bombs in Dublin and Monaghan on 17 May which killed 33 people.
5 Oct. 1974	Provisionals bomb a Guildford pub killing 5 and injuring 54 people. The 'Guildford Four', after serving 15 years in prison, are released in October 1989, all convictions against them quashed.
21 Nov. 1974	Provisionals bomb a Birmingham pub killing 19 and injuring 182. The 'Birmingham Six', after serving 17 years in prison, are released in 1991, all convictions against them quashed.
31 Jul. 1975	Ulster Volunteer Force attacks the Miami Showband, killing 3 of its members and injuring a fourth.
4 Jan. 1976	Republican massacre of Protestant workers at Kingsmill, South Armagh.
12 Aug. 1976	Foundation of Women's Peace Movement by Mairead Corrigan and Betty Williams.
1 Aug. 1978	Cardinal Ó Fiaich draws public attention to the conditions of the 'blanket men' in Long Kesh engaged in a 'Dirty Protest' against the removal of Special Category status for political prisoners.
3 Mar 1979	Margaret Thatcher becomes Conservative Prime Minister.
27 Nov. 1979	Provisional IRA bomb at Warrenpoint, Co. Down kills 18 soldiers; Provisional IRA bomb at Mullaghmore, Co. Sligo kills 4, including Lord Mountbatten.
28 Nov 1979	John Hume elected leader of the SDLP.
1 Mar. 1981	Bobby Sands goes on hunger strike; 9 Mar. Sands is elected MP for Fermanagh/South Tyrone; 5 May 1981 Sands dies on hunger strike.
3 Oct. 1981	Republican prisoners end the hunger strike following the death of 10 prisoners.
11 Nov. 1982	Northern Ireland Assembly opens at Stormont and is boycotted by the SDLP and SF.
6 Dec. 1982	Worst single atrocity of 1992: an Irish National Liberation Army bomb in the Dropping Well pub in Ballykelly, Co. Derry, kills 11 soldiers and 6 civilians.
30 May 1983	New Ireland Forum comprising Fianna Fáil, Fine Gael, Labour and the SDLP opens in Dublin. It outlines three possible solutions to the Northern crisis: a unitary state, a federal Ireland and joint sovereignty.
9 Jun. 1983	Gerry Adams (SF) and John Hume (SDLP) are the only 2 Nationalists to win seats in the Westminster election.
12 Sept. 1983	Northerners take over leadership of SF, with Gerry Adams elected President.
12 Oct. 1984	IRA attempt to kill Margaret Thatcher and members of her cabinet by planting a bomb in the Grand Hotel, Brighton where the Conservative Party Conference was being held.

19 Nov. 1984	Margaret Thatcher rejects all three New Ireland Forum options ('Out, Out, Out').
15 Nov. 1985	Hillsborough Agreement signed by Garret FitzGerald and Margaret Thatcher.
3 Mar. 1996	Unionist 'Day of Action' in protest against the Anglo-Irish Agreement.
Mar. 1987	3 IRA members are shot dead by the SAS in Gibraltar without being given the chance to surrender.
11 Nov. 1987	IRA bomb kills 11 people at the Enniskillen Remembrance Day ceremony.
9 Nov 1990	The new Northern Ireland Secretary, Peter Brooke, declares that the UK had 'no selfish, economic ot strategic interest in Northern Ireland and was prepared to accept … unification by consent'.
27 Nov. 1990	John Major, elected Conservative party leader, becomes Prime Minister.
17 Apr. 1991	Inter-party talks involving Ulster Unionist Party (UUP), SDLP and the Alliance Party begin at Stormont and continue until 3 July. Loyalist para-militaries declare ceasefire for duration of the talks.
4 Jan. 1992	Provisional IRA bomb devastates Belfast city centre.
17 Jan. 1992	Worst atrocity of 1992: IRA blows up a bus carrying Protrestant workmen at Teebane Crossroads, Co. Tyrone, killing eight workers engaged in construction work for the security forces.
7 Jan. 1993	Albert Reynolds becomes Taoiseach and Dick Spring Deputy Prime Minister in coalition government of Fianna Fáil and Labour.
25 Sept. 1993	John Hume and Gerry Adams publish their joint peace proposals which rejected any internal solution, and accepted that the Irish people as a whole have the right to national self-determination, adding that 'We both recognise that such a new agreement is only achievable and viable if it can earn and enjoy the allegiance of the different traditions on this island, by accommodating diversity and providing for national reconciliation'.
23 Oct. 1993	An IRA bomb on the Shankill Road, Belfast kills 11 people. Gerry Adams is criticised for acting as pall-bearer at the funeral of Thomas Begley, the IRA member killed in the explosion.
30 Oct. 1993	Ulster Freedom Fighters (UFF) retaliate with a gun attack on a pub in Greysteel, Co. Derry, which leaves 7 dead.
15 Dec. 1993	Albert Reynolds and John Major publish the Downing Street Declaration, which pledged the British and Irish governments to the principle of consent and agreement embracing the 'totality of relationships'. It also declared that the role of the British Government was 'to encourage, facilitate and enable the achievement of such agreement'.
19 Jan. 1994	Broadcasting ban on SF is lifted in the Republic.
31 Jan. 1994	Gerry Adams is granted a three-day visa to travel to New York.
24 Jul. 1994	After receiving 'clarification' on the Downing Street Declaration, SF gives the document a guarded welcome.
31 Aug. 1994	IRA calls a 'complete cessation of military operations'.
16 Sept. 1994	John Major lifts broadcasting ban on SF.
4 Oct. 1994	Gerry Adams meets White House officials in Washington.

13 Oct. 1994   The combined Loyalist Military Command (UDA, UVF and the Red Hand Commandos) announce a ceasefire dependent on 'the continued cessation of all nationalist/republican violence'.

1 Nov. 1994   Bill Clinton announces an aid package for Northern Ireland.

10 Nov. 1994   Newry post office worker Frank Kerr killed by IRA during an armed raid.

17 Nov. 1994   Albert Reynolds resigns and Bertie Ahern is elected new leader of Fiana Fáil.

2 Dec. 1994   President Clinton appoints Senator George Mitchell as special American envoy to Ireland.

7 Dec. 1994   Martin McGuiness leads Sinn Féin delegation in exploratory talks at Stormont with Northern Ireland officials.

15 Dec.1994   Fine Gael leader John Bruton elected Taoiseach in a coalition government.

22 Feb.1995   Framework Document is released by British and Irish governments to provide a framework within which all-party negotiations would take place to create a new Ireland. The Joint Declaration affirmed the principle of self-determination; pursuit of exclusively democratic, peaceful means; parity of esteem for both traditions. It also envisaged new North-South institutions and East-West structures.

24 May 1995   President Clinton opens Washington Conference on Investment in Ireland at which Sir Patrick Mayhew meets Gerry Adams.

3 Jul. 1995   Release of Private Lee Clegg after serving two years of a murder sentence.

9-11 Jul.1995   'Drumcree One': after three days of stand-off between Orangemen and RUC, Orangemen are allowed to walk Garvaghy Road in Portadown; Orange march routed along Ormeau Road in Belfast against Nationalist residents' wishes.

Aug. 1995   James Molyneux resigns as leader of the Ulster Unionist party; he is succeeded by David Trimble.

22 Jan. 1996   Mitchell Report recommends that decommissioning and talks should proceed in parallel. John Major effectively rejects the Report.

9 Feb. 1996   IRA ceasefire ends after 18 months with the bombing of London's Canary Wharf, killing two men.

30 May 1996   Forum elections are held. Although SF increased its share of the vote from 10% in both the General Election of 1992 and Euro election of 1994 to 15.47% of the total poll, it remained excluded from all-party talks.

12 Jun.1996   Peace talks get under way at Stormont, chaired by George Mitchell, but excluding SF.

15 Jun.1996   IRA bomb the centre of Manchester.

7-11 Jul. 1996   'Drumcree Two': following widespread Loyalist rioting, the Government reverses its initial decision and allows Orangemen down Garvaghy Road; Orangemen allowed along Ormeau Road and given police protection.

7 Oct. 1996   IRA bomb Thiepval Barracks, Lisburn, injuring 31 people, one of whom later died.

12 Feb. 1997   IRA shoot dead Bombardier Stephen Restorick in Newry, Co. Down, the last British soldier to be killed in the Troubles.

1 May 1997   Labour wins the general election and Tony Blair becomes Prime Minister. He appoints Mo Mowlam Secretary of State for Northern Ireland.

2 Jun. 1997	Alban Maginness (SDLP) is elected first Nationalist Lord Mayor of Belfast.
3 Jun. 1997	Inter-party talks resume at Stormont with SF still excluded.
6 Jun. 1997	General election in the Republic. Bertie Ahern is the new Taoiseach in a coalition government of Fine Fáil, Progressive Democrats and a number of independents.
6 Jul. 1997	'Drumcree Three': Orangemen allowed down Garvaghey Road, causing widespread Nationalist unrest and violence.
20 Jul. 1997	IRA announce a new ceasefire.
12 Aug. 1997	Ken Maginnis (UUP) joins Martin McGuinness (SF) in a TV debate, the first time for a UUP representative and a SF representative to appear together on TV.
26 Aug. 1997	British and Irish Governments set up an Independent Commission on Decommissioning, headed by Canadian General John de Chastelain.
9 Sept. 1997	SF signs up to the Mitchell Principles of non-violence and enters all-party talks.
15 Sept. 1997	Multi-party talks resume at Stormont.
24 Sept. 1997	After 16 months, procedures are agreed at multi-party talks. Independent Commission on Decommissioning formally launched.
7 Oct. 1997	Substantive talks begin at Stormont.
17 Oct. 1997	Mo Mowlam announces setting up of Parades Commission.
11 Dec. 1997	Gerry Adams leads SF delegation to Downing Street, the first meeting between a British Prime Minister and SF for 76 years.
27 Dec. 1997	Irish National Liberation Army (INLA) shoots dead Billy Wright ('King Rat'), leader of the Loyalist Volunteer Force (LVF) in Maze Prison.
20 Feb.1998	SF is expelled from the peace talks because of allegations of IRA involvement in two killings.
23 Mar. 1998	SF rejoins talks.
25 Mar. 1998	Mitchell sets deadline of 9 April for agreement.
31 Mar. 1998	United Nations report on Human Rights is critical of RUC.
10 Apr. 1998	Good Friday Agreement marks the culmination of the peace process. The Agreement provided for: a Northern Ireland Assembly; a North-South Ministerial Council; amendments to Articles 2 and 3 of the Irish Constitution; repeal of the British Government of Ireland Act; a Council of the Isles.
7 May 1998	Emergence of the 'real' IRA is confirmed.
10 May 1998	A special SF conference votes overwhelmingly to support the Agreement and allow members to take seats in the new Assembly.
22 May 1998	Referendums express strong suppor for the Agreement on both sides of the border (71% in the North, 94% in the Republic).
25 Jun.1998	Northern Ireland Assembly elections return 80 pro-Agreement members and 28 anti-Agreement members.
1 Jul. 1998	At the first meeting of the Assembly David Trimble is elected First Minister and Seamus Mallon (SDLP) Deputy First Minister designate.
5 Jul. 1998	'Drumcree Four': during a stand-off between Orangemen and RUC, violence spreads throughout the province, with three boys killed in Ballymoney, Co. Antrim, as a result of a Loyalist attack on their home.

15 Aug. 1998   Real IRA car bomb in Omagh kills 29.

11 Sept. 1998   The first of the paramilitary prisoners are released under the terms of the Agreement.

10 Dec. 1998   John Hume and David Trimble are jointly awarded the Nobel Peace Prize.

18 Dec. 1998   Agreement reached on government departments and cross-border bodies.

15 Jul. 1999   Assembly meeting to nominate Executive ministers collapses over lack of progress on decommissioning. Seamus Mallon resigns as Deputy First Minister.

20 Jul. 1999   Tony Blair and Bertie Ahern initiate a review of the peace process to be chaired by George Mitchell.

17 Nov. 1999   IRA declares readiness to discuss decommissioning and appoint a representative to the decommissioning body.

29 Nov. 1999   Power-sharing executive set up including SF ministers Martin McGuinness and Bairbre de Brun.

1 Dec. 1999   Power is devolved from London.

2 Dec. 1999   Irish government removes its territorial claim over the Six Counties and the IRA appoints a representative to the decommissioning body.

11 Feb. 2000   Secretary of State Peter Mandelson announces suspension of devolution because of lack of progress on decommissioning.

6 May 2000   IRA issues a statement saying that if the Good Friday Agreement was fully implemented it would 'completely and verifiably put IRA weapons beyond use'. It also agrees to engage with de Chastelain.

29 May 2000   UUP approves the party rejoining the Executive and devolution is restored.

6 Jun. 2000   Two international arms inspectors, former Finnish President Marti Ahtisaari and ex-ANC secretary-general Cyril Ramaphosa report that they have secretly inspected IRA arms dumps.

28 Oct. 2000   David Trimble again wins UUC support after announcing ban on SF minisers attending North-South meetings, despite failure of IRA to decommission.

24 Jan. 2001   Peter Mandelson resigns over scandal allegations and is replaced by John Reid.

8 May 2001   David Trimble announces resignation as First Minister effective on 1 July unless IRA starts decommissioning.

7 Jun. 2001   In the general election and local elections SF and anti-Agreement DUP make significant gains at the expense of the UUP and the SDLP.

1 Jul. 2001   David Trimble resigns.

22 Oct. 2001   Gerry Adams tells party activists in West Belfast: 'Martin McGuinness and I have held discussions with the IRA and we have put to the IRA the view that if it could make a groundbreaking move on the arms issue that this could save the peace process from collapse and transform the situation.'

23 Oct. 2001   The international decommissioning body admits it witnessed a 'significant' decommissioning event. Trimble agrees to return to government.

Index